THE SANDBURG TREASURY

THE SANDBURG TREASURY

Prose and Poetry for Young People

Including "Rootabaga Stories," "Early Moon," "Wind Song,"
"Abe Lincoln Grows Up," "Prairie-Town Boy"

CARL SANDBURG

Introduction by Paula Sandburg

Illustrated by Paul Bacon

HARCOURT BRACE JOVANOVICH, INC., NEW YORK

Contents

Introduction

by Paula Sandburg

WHEN I LOOK back now it seems to me that Carl and I were always surrounded by children, books, and animals. The children had everything that the two of us had to give—love, attention, and, in Carl's case, the gift of imagination and humor.

Carl was a wonderful storyteller, and he was never lacking in inspiration. In the early days when the *Rootabaga Stories* were written, there were few stories for children that were not about kings and queens and princes and princesses in castles, or peasants in huts. This was the folklore and literature of Europe. But Carl thought that American children should have something different, more suited to their ideals and surroundings. So his stories did not concern knights on white chargers, but simple people, such as the Potato Face Blind Man who played the accordion, the White Horse Girl and the Blue Wind Boy, or commonplace objects, a rag doll and a broom handle, a knife and fork.

At first Carl read the stories to the girls at the midday meal, partly to find out whether they would enjoy this kind of tale. He found out soon enough, for they were absorbed, delighted with the names, often chuckling over the way he played with words. They had their favorites, I remember. Janet would call for "The Wedding Procession of the Rag Doll and the Broom Handle" or for "Shush Shush," while Margaret liked best "Bimbo the Snip" or "Jason Squiff" with his popcorn hat and popcorn mittens.

Every child, I think, can sympathize with the desire of Gimme the Ax to get away from the house where "everything was the same as it always was" to the Rootabaga Country where things were so different, so impossible.

The prairie town where Carl was born and reared was in the land of Lincoln. It held memories of Lincoln, of the Lincoln-Douglas debates at Knox College, of the underground railway there that operated before

7

and during the Civil War. It had honored the Civil War nurse, Mother Bickerstaff, with a statue. So it was natural that Carl should become interested in writing a biography of Lincoln. He knew that there was no good biography of him available that would appeal to children and this was what he intended to write. But he became so immersed in the book that it developed into a two-volume biography for adults, *The Prairie Years*. With the four succeeding volumes, *The War Years*, it eventually won the Pulitzer Prize for history. After its publication the publishers edited the special version of *The Prairie Years* for younger readers which appears in this volume. By an odd quirk of circumstance a book intended for children became a book for adults and then in turn became a book for children, *Abe Lincoln Grows Up*.

Later, when he wrote his autobiography, *Always the Young Strangers*, he thought that children would be interested in what boyhood was like in the Middle West at the close of the nineteenth century. *Prairie-Town Boy*, which appears in this volume, is Carl's own story, edited for young readers.

Carl loved children, and they in turn were charmed by him. He enjoyed writing for them because he felt that their response to poetry and ideas was honest and direct. He wanted to open their minds to the possibilities that existed beyond their experience.

The wonder and enchantment that Carl created for our children with his stories and poems enriched their lives and the lives of our grandchildren. I hope that all of the children who read these stories and poems will experience some of that pleasure and I hope that some of them will be lucky enough to find an older person who will share it with them as we did.

❀ ROOTABAGA STORIES

To Spink and Skabootch

❀ ❀ ❀

Three Stories About the Finding of the Zigzag Railroad, the Pigs with Bibs On, the Circus Clown Ovens, the Village of Liver-and-Onions, the Village of Cream Puffs

HOW THEY BROKE AWAY TO GO TO
THE ROOTABAGA COUNTRY

GIMME THE AX lived in a house where everything is the same as it always was.

"The chimney sits on top of the house and lets the smoke out," said Gimme the Ax. "The doorknobs open the doors. The windows are always either open or shut. We are always either upstairs or downstairs in this house. Everything is the same as it always was."

So he decided to let his children name themselves.

"The first words they speak as soon as they learn to make words shall be their names," he said. "They shall name themselves."

When the first boy came to the house of Gimme the Ax, he was named Please Gimme. When the first girl came, she was named Ax Me No Questions.

And both of the children had the shadows of valleys by night in their eyes and the lights of early morning, when the sun is coming up, on their foreheads.

And the hair on top of their heads was a dark wild grass. And they loved to turn the doorknobs, open the doors, and run out to have the wind comb their hair and touch their eyes and put its six soft fingers on their foreheads.

And then because no more boys came and no more girls came, Gimme the Ax said to himself, "My first boy is my last and my last girl is my first, and they picked their names themselves."

Please Gimme grew up, and his ears got longer. Ax Me No Questions grew up, and her ears got longer. And they kept on living in the house where everything is the same as it always was. They learned to say just as their father said, "The chimney sits on top of the house and lets the smoke out; the doorknobs open the doors; the windows are always either open or shut; we are always either upstairs or downstairs—everything is the same as it always was."

After a while they began asking each other in the cool of the evening after they had eggs for breakfast in the morning, "Who's who? How much? And what's the answer?"

"It is too much to be too long anywhere," said the tough old man, Gimme the Ax.

And Please Gimme and Ax Me No Questions, the tough son and the tough daughter of Gimme the Ax, answered their father, "It *is* too much to be too long anywhere."

So they sold everything they had, pigs, pastures, pepper pickers, pitchforks, everything except their ragbags and a few extras.

When their neighbors saw them selling everything they had, the different neighbors said, "They are going to Kansas, to Kokomo, to Canada, to Kankakee, to Kalamazoo, to Kamchatka, to the Chattahoochee."

One little sniffer with his eyes half shut and a mitten on his nose laughed in his hat five ways and said, "They are going to the moon, and when they get there, they will find everything is the same as it always was."

All the spot cash money he got for selling everything, pigs, pastures, pepper pickers, pitchforks, Gimme the Ax put in a ragbag and slung on his back like a ragpicker going home.

Then he took Please Gimme, his oldest and youngest and only son, and Ax Me No Questions, his oldest and youngest and only daughter, and went to the railroad station.

The ticket agent was sitting at the window selling railroad tickets the same as always.

"Do you wish a ticket to go away and come back, or do you wish a ticket to go away and *never* come back?" the ticket agent asked, wiping sleep out of his eyes.

"We wish a ticket to ride where the railroad tracks run off into the sky and never come back—send us far as the railroad rails go and then forty ways farther yet," was the reply of Gimme the Ax.

"So far? So early? So soon?" asked the ticket agent, wiping more sleep out his eyes. "Then I will give you a new ticket. It blew in. It is a long slick yellow leather slab ticket with a blue spanch across it."

Gimme the Ax thanked the ticket agent once, thanked the ticket agent twice, and then instead of thanking the ticket agent three times, he opened the ragbag and took out all the spot cash money he got for selling everything, pigs, pastures, pepper pickers, pitchforks, and paid the spot cash money to the ticket agent.

Before he put it in his pocket, he looked once, twice, three times at the long yellow leather slab ticket with a blue spanch across it.

Then with Please Gimme and Ax Me No Questions he got on the railroad train, showed the conductor his ticket, and they started to ride to where the railroad tracks run off into the blue sky and then forty ways farther yet.

The train ran on and on. It came to the place where the railroad tracks run off into the blue sky. And it ran on and on chick chick-a-chick chick-a-chick chick-a-chick.

Sometimes the engineer hooted and tooted the whistle. Sometimes the fireman rang the bell. Sometimes the open-and-shut of the steam hog's nose choked and spit pfisty-pfoost, pfisty-pfoost, pfisty-pfoost. But no matter what happened to the whistle and the bell and the steam hog, the train ran on and on to where the railroad tracks ran off into the blue sky. And then it ran on and on more and more.

Sometimes Gimme the Ax looked in his pocket, put his fingers in, and took out the long slick yellow leather slab ticket with a blue spanch across it.

"Not even the kings of Egypt with all their climbing camels, and all their speedy, spotted, lucky lizards, ever had a ride like this," he said to his children.

Then something happened. They met another train running on the same track. One train was going one way. The other was going the other way. They met. They passed each other.

"What was it—what happened?" the children asked their father.

"One train went over, the other train went under," he answered. "This is the Over and Under Country. Nobody gets out of the way of anybody else. They either go over or under."

Next they came to the country of the balloon pickers. Hanging down from the sky, strung on strings so fine the eye could not see them at first, was the balloon crop of that summer. The sky was thick with balloons. Red, blue, yellow balloons, white, purple, and orange balloons—peach, watermelon, and potato balloons—rye loaf and wheat loaf balloons—link sausage and pork chop balloons—they floated and filled the sky.

The balloon pickers were walking on high stilts picking balloons. Each picker had his own stilts, long or short. For picking balloons near the ground he had short stilts. If he wanted to pick far and high, he walked on a far and high pair of stilts.

Baby pickers on baby stilts were picking baby balloons. When they fell off the stilts, the handful of balloons they were holding kept them in the air till they got their feet into the stilts again.

"Who is that away up there in the sky climbing like a bird in the morning?" Ax Me No Questions asked her father.

"He was singing too happy," replied the father. "The songs came out of his neck and made him so light the balloons pulled him off his stilts."

"Will he ever come down again back to his own people?"

"Yes, his heart will get heavy when his songs are all gone. Then he will drop down to his stilts again."

The train was running on and on. The engineer hooted and tooted the whistle when he felt like it. The fireman rang the bell when he felt that way. And sometimes the open-and-shut of the steam hog had to go pfisty-pfoost, pfisty-pfoost.

"Next is the country where the circus clowns come from," said Gimme the Ax to his son and daughter. "Keep your eyes open."

They did keep their eyes open. They saw cities with ovens, long and short ovens, fat, stubby ovens, lean, lank ovens, all for baking either long or short clowns, or fat and stubby or lean and lank clowns.

After each clown was baked in the oven, it was taken out into the sunshine and put up to stand like a big white doll with a red mouth leaning against the fence.

Two men came along to each baked clown standing still like a doll. One man threw a bucket of white fire over it. The second man pumped a wind pump with a living red wind through the red mouth.

The clown rubbed his eyes, opened his mouth, twisted his neck, wiggled his ears, wriggled his toes, jumped away from the fence, and began turning handsprings, cartwheels, somersaults, and flipflops in the sawdust ring near the fence.

"The next we come to is the Rootabaga Country where the big city is the Village of Liver-and-Onions," said Gimme the Ax, looking again in his pocket to be sure he had the long slick yellow leather slab ticket with a blue spanch across it.

The train ran on and on till it stopped running straight and began running in zigzags like one letter Z put next to another Z and the next and the next.

The tracks and the rails and the ties and the spikes under the train all stopped being straight and changed to zigzags like one letter Z and another letter Z put next after the other.

"It seems like we go halfway and then back up," said Ax Me No Questions.

"Look out of the window and see if the pigs have bibs on," said Gimme the Ax. "If the pigs are wearing bibs, then this is the Rootabaga Country."

And they looked out of the zigzagging windows of the zigzagging cars, and the first pigs they saw had bibs on. And the next pigs and the next pigs they saw all had bibs on.

The checker pigs had checker bibs on; the striped pigs had striped bibs on. And the polka-dot pigs had polka-dot bibs on.

"Who fixes it for the pigs to have bibs on?" Please Gimme asked his father.

"The fathers and mothers fix it," answered Gimme the Ax. "The checker pigs have checker fathers and mothers. The striped pigs have striped fathers and mothers. And the polka-dot pigs have polka-dot fathers and mothers."

And the train went zigzagging on and on, running on the tracks and the rails and the spikes and the ties which were all zigzag like the letter Z and the letter Z.

And after a while the train zigzagged on into the Village of Liver-and-Onions, known as the biggest city in the big, big Rootabaga Country.

And so if you are going to the Rootabaga Country, you will know when you get there because the railroad tracks change from straight to zigzag, the pigs have bibs on, and it is the fathers and mothers who fix it.

And if you start to go to that country, remember first you must sell everything you have, pigs, pastures, pepper pickers, pitchforks, put the spot cash money in a ragbag, and go to the railroad station and ask the ticket agent for a long slick yellow leather slab ticket with a blue spanch across it.

And you mustn't be surprised if the ticket agent wipes sleep from his eyes and asks, "So far? So early? So soon?"

HOW THEY BRING BACK THE VILLAGE OF
CREAM PUFFS WHEN THE WIND
BLOWS IT AWAY

A GIRL NAMED Wing Tip the Spick came to the Village of Liver-and-
Onions to visit her uncle and her uncle's uncle on her mother's side
and her uncle and her uncle's uncle on her father's side.

It was the first time the four uncles had a chance to see their little
relation, their niece. Each one of the four uncles was proud of the
blue eyes of Wing Tip the Spick.

The two uncles on her mother's side took a long deep look into her
blue eyes and said, "Her eyes are so blue, such a clear light blue, they
are the same as cornflowers with blue raindrops shining and dancing
on silver leaves after a sun shower in any of the summer months."

And the two uncles on her father's side, after taking a long deep
look into the eyes of Wing Tip the Spick, said, "Her eyes are so blue,
such a clear, light shining blue, they are the same as cornflowers with
blue raindrops shining and dancing on the silver leaves after a sun
shower in any of the summer months."

And though Wing Tip the Spick didn't listen and didn't hear what
the uncles said about her blue eyes, she did say to herself when they
were not listening, "I know these are sweet uncles, and I am going to
have a sweet time visiting my relations."

The four uncles said to her, "Will you let us ask you two questions,
first the first question and second the second question?"

"I will let you ask me fifty questions this morning, fifty questions
tomorrow morning, and fifty questions any morning. I like to listen to
questions. They slip in one ear and slip out of the other."

Then the uncles asked her the first question first, "Where do you
come from?" and the second question second, "Why do you have two
freckles on your chin?"

"Answering your first question first," said Wing Tip the Spick, "I
come from the Village of Cream Puffs, a little light village on the upland corn prairie. From a long ways off it looks like a little hat you

could wear on the end of your thumb to keep the rain off your thumb."

"Tell us more," said one uncle. "Tell us much," said another uncle. "Tell it without stopping," added another uncle. "Interruptions nix nix," murmured the last of the uncles.

"It is a light little village on the upland corn prairie many miles past the sunset in the west," went on Wing Tip the Spick. "It is light the same as a cream puff is light. It sits all by itself on the big long prairie when the prairie goes up in a slope. There on the slope the winds play around the village. They sing it wind songs, summer wind songs in summer, winter wind songs in winter."

"And sometimes like an accident, the wind gets rough. And when the wind gets rough, it picks up the little Village of Cream Puffs and blows it away off in the sky—all by itself."

"O-o-h-h," said one uncle. "Um-m-m-m," said the other three uncles.

"Now the people in the village all understand the winds with their wind songs in summer and winter. And they understand the rough wind who comes sometimes and picks up the village and blows it away off high in the sky all by itself.

"If you go to the public square in the middle of the village, you will see a big roundhouse. If you take the top off the roundhouse, you will see a big spool with a long string winding up around the spool.

"Now whenever the rough wind comes and picks up the village and blows it away off high in the sky all by itself, then the string winds loose off the spool, because the village is fastened to the string. So the rough wind blows and blows, and the string on the spool winds looser and looser the farther the village goes blowing away off into the sky all by itself.

"Then at last when the rough wind, so forgetful, so careless, has had all the fun it wants, then the people of the village all come together and begin to wind up the spool and bring back the village where it was before."

"O-o-h-h," said one uncle. "Um-m-m-m," said the other three uncles.

"And sometimes when you come to the village to see your little relation, your niece who has four such sweet uncles, maybe she will lead you through the middle of the city to the public square and show you the roundhouse. They call it the Roundhouse of the Big Spool. And they are proud because it was thought up and is there to show when visitors come."

"And now will you answer the second question second—why do you have two freckles on your chin?" interrupted the uncle who had said before, "Interruptions nix nix."

"The freckles are put on," answered Wing Tip the Spick. "When a girl goes away from the Village of Cream Puffs, her mother puts on two freckles, on the chin. Each freckle must be the same as a little burnt cream puff kept in the oven too long. After the two freckles looking like two little burnt cream puffs are put on her chin, they remind the girl every morning when she combs her hair and looks in the looking glass. They remind her where she came from and she mustn't stay away too long."

"O-h-h-h," said one uncle. "Um-m-m-m," said the other three uncles. And they talked among each other afterward, the four uncles by themselves, saying:

"She has a gift. It is her eyes. They are so blue, such a clear light blue, the same as cornflowers with blue raindrops shining and dancing on silver leaves after a sun shower in any of the summer months."

At the same time Wing Tip the Spick was saying to herself, "I know for sure now these are sweet uncles, and I am going to have a sweet time visiting my relations."

HOW THE FIVE RUSTY RATS HELPED FIND
A NEW VILLAGE

ONE DAY WHILE Wing Tip the Spick was visiting her four uncles in the Village of Liver-and-Onions, a blizzard came up. Snow filled the sky, and the wind blew and made a noise like heavy wagon axles grinding and crying.

And on this day a gray rat came to the house of the four uncles, a rat with gray skin and gray hair, gray as the gray gravy on a beefsteak. The rat had a basket. In the basket was a catfish. And the rat said, "Please let me have a little fire and a little salt as I wish to make a little bowl of hot catfish soup to keep me warm through the blizzard."

And the four uncles all said together, "This is no time for rats to be around—and we would like to ask you where you got the catfish in the basket."

"Oh, oh, oh, please—in the name of the five rusty rats, the five lucky rats of the Village of Cream Puffs, please don't," was the exclamation of Wing Tip the Spick.

The uncles stopped. They looked long and deep into the eyes of Wing Tip the Spick and thought, as they had thought before, how her eyes were clear light blue the same as cornflowers with blue raindrops shining on the silver leaves in a summer sun shower.

And the four uncles opened the door and let the gray rat come in with the basket and the catfish. They showed the gray rat the way to the kitchen and the fire and the salt. And they watched the rat and kept him company while he fixed himself a catfish soup to keep him warm traveling through the blizzard with the sky full of snow.

After they opened the front door and let the rat out and said goodby, they turned to Wing Tip the Spick and asked her to tell them about the five rusty, lucky rats of the Village of Cream Puffs where she lived with her father and her mother and her folks.

"When I was a little girl growing up, before I learned all I learned since I got older, my grandfather gave me a birthday present because I was nine years old. I remember how he said to me, 'You will never be nine years old again after this birthday, so I give you this box for a birthday present.'

"In the box was a pair of red slippers with a gold clock on each slipper. One of the clocks ran fast. The other clock ran slow. And he told me if I wished to be early anywhere, I should go by the clock that ran fast. And if I wished to be late anywhere, I should go by the clock that ran slow.

"And that same birthday he took me down through the middle of the Village of Cream Puffs to the public square near the Roundhouse of the Big Spool. There he pointed his finger at the statue of the five rusty rats, the five lucky rats. And as near as I can remember his words, he said:

" 'Many years ago, long before the snow birds began to wear funny little slip-on hats and funny little slip-on shoes, and away back long before the snow birds learned how to slip off their slip-on hats and how to slip off their slip-on shoes, long ago in the faraway Village of Liver-and-Onions, the people who ate cream puffs came together and met in the streets and picked up their baggage and put their belongings on their shoulders and marched out of the Village of Liver-and-

Onions saying, "We shall find a new place for a village, and the name of it shall be the Village of Cream Puffs."

" 'They marched out on the prairie with their baggage and belongings in sacks on their shoulders. And a blizzard came up. Snow filled the sky. The wind blew and blew and made a noise like heavy wagon axles grinding and crying.

" 'The snow came on. The wind twisted all day and all night and all the next day. The wind changed black and twisted and spit icicles in their faces. They got lost in the blizzard. They expected to die and be buried in the snow for the wolves to come and eat them.

" 'Then the five lucky rats came, the five rusty rats, rust on their skin and hair, rust on their feet and noses, rust all over, and especially, most especially of all, rust on their long curved tails. They dug their noses down into the snow, and their long curved tails stuck up far above the snow where the people who were lost in the blizzard could take hold of the tails like handles.

" 'And so, while the wind and the snow blew and the blizzard beat its icicles in their faces, they held on to the long curved tails of the rusty rats till they came to the place where the Village of Cream Puffs now stands. It was the rusty rats who saved their lives and showed them where to put their new village. That is why this statue now stands in the public square, this statue of the shapes of the five rusty rats, the five lucky rats with their noses down in the snow and their long curved tails lifted high out of the snow.'

"That is the story as my grandfather told it to me. And he said it happened long ago, long before the snow birds began to wear slip-on hats and slip-on shoes, long before they learned how to slip off the slip-on hats and to slip off the slip-on shoes."

"O-h-h-h," said one of the uncles. "Um-m-m-m," said the other three uncles.

"And sometime," added Wing Tip the Spick, "when you go away from the Village of Liver-and-Onions and cross the Shampoo River and ride many miles across the upland prairie till you come to the Village of Cream Puffs, you will find a girl there who loves four uncles very much.

"And if you ask her politely, she will show you the red slippers with gold clocks on them, one clock to be early by, the other to be late by. And if you are still more polite, she will take you through the middle of the town to the public square and show you the statue of the five rusty, lucky rats with their long curved tails sticking up in the

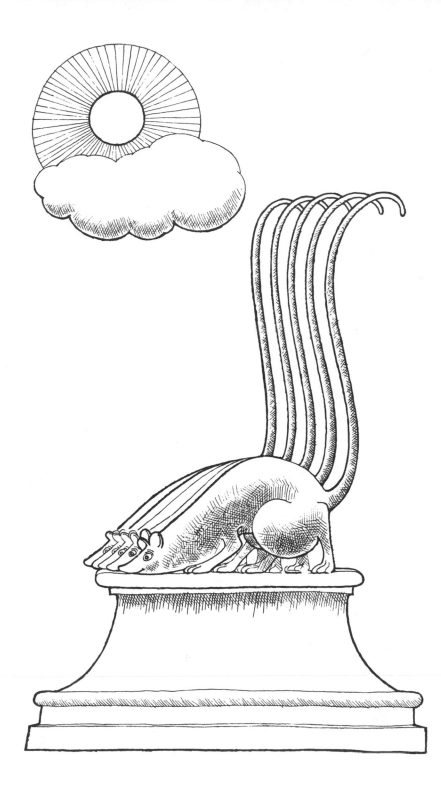

air like handles. And the tails are curved so long and so nice you will feel like going up and taking hold of them to see what will happen to you."

❀ ❀ ❀

Five Stories About the Potato Face Blind Man

PEOPLE: *The Potato Face Blind Man*
Any Ice Today
Pick Ups
Lizzie Lazarus
Poker Face the Baboon
Hot Dog the Tiger
Whitson Whimble
A man shoveling money
A Watermelon Moon
White Gold Boys
Blue Silver Girls
Big white moon spiders
Zizzies
Gimme the Ax again

THE POTATO FACE BLIND MAN WHO LOST THE DIAMOND RABBIT ON HIS GOLD ACCORDION

THERE WAS A Potato Face Blind Man used to play an accordion on the Main Street corner nearest the post office in the Village of Liver-and-Onions.

Any Ice Today came along and said, "It looks like it used to be an 18-carat-gold accordion with rich pawnshop diamonds in it; it looks like it used to be a grand accordion once and not so grand now."

"Oh, yes, oh, yes, it was gold all over on the outside," said the Potato Face Blind Man, "and there was a diamond rabbit next to the handles on each side, two diamond rabbits."

"How do you mean diamond rabbits?" Any Ice Today asked.

"Ears, legs, head, feet, ribs, tail, all fixed out in diamonds to make a nice rabbit with his diamond chin on his diamond toenails. When I play good pieces so people cry hearing my accordion music, then I put my fingers over and feel of the rabbit's diamond chin on his diamond toenails, 'Attaboy, li'l bunny, attaboy, li'l bunny.' "

"Yes, I hear you talking, but it is like dream talking. I wonder why your accordion looks like somebody stole it and took it to a pawnshop and took it out and somebody stole it again and took it to a pawnshop and took it out and somebody stole it again. And they kept on stealing it and taking it out of the pawnshop and stealing it again till the gold wore off so it looks like a used-to-be-yesterday."

"Oh, yes, o-h, y-e-s, you are right. It is not like the accordion it used to be. It knows more knowledge than it used to know just the same as this Potato Face Blind Man knows more knowledge than he used to know."

"Tell me about it," said Any Ice Today.

"It is simple. If a blind man plays an accordion on the street to make people cry, it makes them sad, and when they are sad, the gold goes away off the accordion. And if a blind man goes to sleep because his music is full of sleepy songs like the long wind in a sleepy valley, then while the blind man is sleeping, the diamonds in the diamond rabbit all go away. I play a sleepy song and go to sleep, and I wake up and the diamond ear of the diamond rabbit is gone. I play another sleepy song and go to sleep and wake up, and the diamond tail of the diamond rabbit is gone. After a while all the diamond rabbits are gone, even the diamond chin sitting on the diamond toenails of the rabbits next to the handles of the accordion, even those are gone."

"Is there anything I can do?" asked Any Ice Today.

"I do it myself," said the Potato Face Blind Man. "If I am too sorry, I just play the sleepy song of the long wind going up the sleepy valleys. And that carries me away where I have time and money to dream about the new wonderful accordions and post offices where everybody that gets a letter and everybody that don't get a letter stops and remembers the Potato Face Blind Man."

HOW THE POTATO FACE BLIND MAN
ENJOYED HIMSELF
ON A FINE SPRING MORNING

ON A FRIDAY morning when the flummywisters were yodeling yisters high in the elm trees, the Potato Face Blind Man came down to his work sitting at the corner nearest the post office in the Village of Liver-and-Onions and playing his gold-that-used-to-be accordion for the pleasure of the ears of the people going into the post office to see if they got any letters for themselves or their families.

"It is a good day, a lucky day," said the Potato Face Blind Man, "because for a beginning I have heard high in the elm trees the flummywisters yodeling their yisters in the long branches of the lingering leaves. So—so—I am going to listen to myself playing on my accordion the same yisters, the same yodels, drawing them like long glad breathings out of my glad accordion, long breathings of the branches of the lingering leaves."

And he sat down in his chair. On the sleeve of his coat he tied a sign, "I Am Blind *Too*." On the top button of his coat he hung a little thimble. On the bottom button of his coat he hung a tin copper cup. On the middle button he hung a wooden mug. By the side of him, on the left side on the sidewalk, he put a galvanized iron washtub and, on the right side, an aluminum dishpan.

"It is a good day, a lucky day, and I am sure many people will stop and remember the Potato Face Blind Man," he sang to himself like a little song as he began running his fingers up and down the keys of the accordion like the yisters of the lingering leaves in the elm trees.

Then came Pick Ups. Always it happened Pick Ups asked questions and wished to know. And so this is how the questions and answers ran when the Potato Face filled the ears of Pick Ups with explanations.

"What is the piece you are playing on the keys of your accordion so fast sometimes, so slow sometimes, so sad some of the moments, so glad some of the moments?"

"It is the song the mama flummywisters sing when they button loose the winter underwear of the baby flummywisters and sing:

> "Fly, you little flummies,
> Sing, you little wisters."

"And why do you have a little thimble on the top button of your coat?"

"That is for the dimes to be put in. Some people see it and say, 'Oh, I must put in a whole thimbleful of dimes.' "

"And the tin copper cup?"

"That is for the baseball players to stand off ten feet and throw in nickels and pennies. The one who throws the most into the cup will be the most lucky."

"And the wooden mug?"

"There is a hole in the bottom of it. The hole is as big as the bottom. The nickel goes in and comes out again. It is for the very poor people who wish to give me a nickel and yet get the nickel back."

"The aluminum dishpan and the galvanized iron washtub—what are they doing by the side of you on both sides on the sidewalk?"

"Sometime maybe it will happen everybody who goes into the post office and comes out will stop and pour out all their money, because they might get afraid their money is no good any more. If such a happening ever happens, then it will be nice for the people to have some place to pour their money. Such is the explanation why you see the aluminum dishpan and galvanized iron tub."

"Explain your sign—why is it, 'I Am Blind *Too.*' "

"Oh, I am sorry to explain to you, Pick Ups, why this is so which. Some of the people who pass by here going into the post office and coming out, they have eyes—but they see nothing with their eyes. They look where they are going, and they get where they wish to get, but they forget why they came, and they do not know how to come away. They are my blind brothers. It is for them I have the sign that reads, 'I Am Blind *Too.*' "

"I have my ears full of explanations, and I thank you," said Pick Ups.

"Good-by," said the Potato Face Blind Man as he began drawing long breathings like lingering leaves out of the accordion—along with the song the mama flummywisters sing when they button loose the winter underwear of the baby flummywisters.

POKER FACE THE BABOON
AND HOT DOG THE TIGER

WHEN THE MOON has a green rim with red meat inside and black seeds on the red meat, then in the Rootabaga Country they call it a Watermelon Moon and look for anything to happen.

It was a night when a Watermelon Moon was shining. Lizzie Lazarus came to the upstairs room of the Potato Face Blind Man. Poker Face the Baboon and Hot Dog the Tiger were with her. She was leading them with a pink string.

"You see they are wearing pajamas," she said. "They sleep with you tonight, and tomorrow they go to work with you like mascots."

"How like mascots?" asked the Potato Face Blind Man.

"They are luck bringers. They keep your good luck if it is good. They change your bad luck if it is bad."

"I hear you, and my ears get your explanations."

So the next morning when the Potato Face Blind Man sat down to play his accordion on the corner nearest the post office in the Village of Liver-and-Onions, next to him on the right-hand side sitting on the sidewalk was Poker Face the Baboon and on the left-hand side sitting next to him was Hot Dog the Tiger.

They looked like dummies—they were so quiet. They looked as if they were made of wood and paper and then painted. In the eyes of Poker Face was something faraway. In the eyes of Hot Dog was something hungry. Whitson Whimble, the patent clothes wringer manufacturer, came by in his big limousine automobile car without horses to pull it. He was sitting back on the leather-upholstered seat cushions.

"Stop here," he commanded the chauffeur driving the car.

Then Whitson Whimble sat looking. First he looked into the eyes of Poker Face the Baboon and saw something faraway. Then he looked into the eyes of Hot Dog the Tiger and saw something hungry. Then he read the sign painted by the Potato Face Blind Man saying, "You look at 'em and see 'em; I look at 'em and I don't. You watch what their eyes say; I can only feel their hair." Then Whitson Whimble commanded the chauffeur driving the car, "Go on."

Fifteen minutes later a man in overalls came down Main Street with a wheelbarrow. He stopped in front of the Potato Face Blind Man, Poker Face the Baboon, and Hot Dog the Tiger.

"Where is the aluminum dishpan?" he asked.

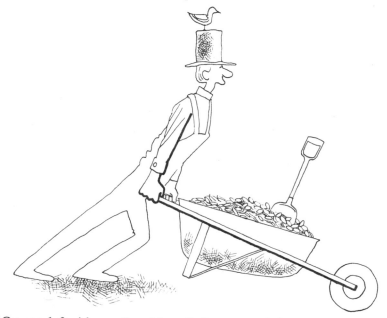

"On my left side on the sidewalk," answered the Potato Face Blind Man.

"Where is the galvanized iron washtub?"

"On my right side on the sidewalk."

Then the man in overalls took a shovel and began shoveling silver dollars out of the wheelbarrow into the aluminum dishpan and the galvanized iron washtub. He shoveled out of the wheelbarrow till the dishpan was full, till the washtub was full. Then he put the shovel into the wheelbarrow and went up Main Street.

Six o'clock that night Pick Ups came along. The Potato Face Blind Man said to him, "I have to carry home a heavy load of money tonight, an aluminum dishpan full of silver dollars and a galvanized iron washtub full of silver dollars. So I ask you, will you take care of Poker Face the Baboon and Hot Dog the Tiger?"

"Yes," said Pick Ups, "I will." And he did. He tied a pink string to their legs and took them home and put them in the woodshed.

Poker Face the Baboon went to sleep on the soft coal at the north end of the woodshed, and when he was asleep, his face had something faraway in it, and he was so quiet he looked like a dummy with brown hair of the jungle painted on his black skin and a black nose painted on his brown face. Hot Dog the Tiger went to sleep on the hard coal at the south end of the woodshed, and when he was asleep, his eyelashes had something hungry in them, and he looked like a painted dummy with black stripes painted over his yellow belly and a black spot painted away at the end of his long yellow tail.

In the morning the woodshed was empty. Pick Ups told the Potato Face Blind Man, "They left a note in their own handwriting on perfumed pink paper. It said, *'Mascots never stay long.'* "

And that is why for many years the Potato Face Blind Man had silver dollars to spend—and that is why many people in the Rootabaga Country keep their eyes open for a Watermelon Moon in the sky with a green rim and red meat inside and black seeds making spots on the red meat.

THE TOBOGGAN-TO-THE-MOON DREAM
OF THE POTATO FACE BLIND MAN

ONE MORNING IN October the Potato Face Blind Man sat on the corner nearest the post office.

Any Ice Today came along and said, "This is the sad time of the year."

"Sad?" asked the Potato Face Blind Man, changing his accordion from his right knee to his left knee and singing softly to the tune he was fumbling on the accordion keys, "Be Happy in the Morning When the Birds Bring the Beans."

"Yes," said Any Ice Today, "is it not sad every year when the leaves change from green to yellow, when the leaves dry on the branches and fall into the air, and the wind blows them and they make a song saying, 'Hush baby, hush baby,' and the wind fills the sky with them and they are like a sky full of birds who forget they know any songs."

"It is sad and not sad," was the blind man's word.

"Listen," said the Potato Face. "For me this is the time of the year when the dream of the white moon toboggan comes back. Five weeks before the first snow flurry this dream always comes back to me. It says, 'The black leaves are falling now and they fill the sky, but five weeks go by, and then for every black leaf there will be a thousand snow crystals shining white.' "

"What was your dream of the white moon toboggan?" asked Any Ice Today.

"It came to me first when I was a boy, when I had my eyes, before my luck changed. I saw the big white spiders of the moon working, rushing around climbing up, climbing down, snizzling and sniffering. I looked a long while before I saw what the big white spiders on the moon were doing. I saw after a while they were weaving a long toboggan, a white toboggan, white and soft as snow. And after a long while of snizzling and sniffering, climbing up and climbing down, at last the toboggan was done, a snow-white toboggan running from the moon down to the Rootabaga Country.

"And sliding, sliding down from the moon on this toboggan were the White Gold Boys and the Blue Silver Girls. They tumbled down at my feet because, you see, the toboggan ended right at my feet. I could lean over and pick up the White Gold Boys and the Blue Silver Girls as they slid out of the toboggan at my feet. I could pick up a whole handful of them and hold them in my hand and talk with them. Yet, you understand, whenever I tried to shut my hand and keep any of them, they would snizzle and sniffer and jump out of the cracks between my fingers. Once there was a little gold and silver dust on my left hand thumb, dust they snizzled out while slipping away from me.

"Once I heard a White Gold Boy and a Blue Silver Girl whispering. They were standing on the tip of my right-hand little finger, whispering. One said, 'I got pumpkins—what did you get?' The other said, 'I got hazel nuts.' I listened more, and I found out there are millions of pumpkins and millions of hazel nuts so small you and I cannot see them. These children from the moon, however, they can see them, and whenever they slide down on the moon toboggan, they take back their pockets full of things so little we have never seen them."

"They are wonderful children," said Any Ice Today. "And will you tell me how they get back to the moon after they slide down the toboggan?"

"Oh, that is easy," said Potato Face. "It is just as easy for them to slide *up* to the moon as to slide down. Sliding up and sliding down is the same for them. The big white spiders fixed it that way when they snizzled and sniffered and made the toboggan."

HOW GIMME THE AX FOUND OUT
ABOUT THE ZIGZAG RAILROAD AND
WHO MADE IT ZIGZAG

ONE DAY GIMME the Ax said to himself, "Today I go to the post office and around, looking around. Maybe I will hear about something happening last night when I was sleeping. Maybe a policeman began laughing and fell in a cistern and came out with a wheelbarrow full of goldfish wearing new jewelry. How do I know? Maybe the man in the moon going down a cellar stairs to get a pitcher of buttermilk for the woman in the moon to drink and stop crying, maybe he fell down the stairs and broke the pitcher and laughed and picked up the broken pieces and said to himself, 'One, two, three, four, accidents happen in the best-regulated families.' How do I know?"

So with his mind full of simple and refreshing thoughts, Gimme the Ax went out into the backyard garden and looked at the different necktie poppies growing early in the summer. Then he picked one of the necktie poppies to wear for a necktie scarf going downtown to the post office and around looking around.

"It is a good speculation to look nice around looking around in a necktie scarf," said Gimme the Ax. "It is a necktie with a picture like whiteface pony spots on a green frog swimming in the moonshine."

So he went downtown. For the first time he saw the Potato Face Blind Man playing an accordion on the corner next nearest the post office. He asked the Potato Face to tell him why the railroad tracks run zigzag in the Rootabaga Country.

"Long ago," said the Potato Face Blind Man, "long before the necktie poppies began growing in the backyard, long before there was a necktie scarf like yours with whiteface pony spots on a green frog swimming in the moonshine, back in the old days when they laid the rails for the railroad, they laid the rails straight."

"Then the zizzies came. The zizzy is a bug. He runs zigzag on zigzag legs, eats zigzag with zigzag teeth, and spits zigzag with a zigzag tongue.

"Millions of zizzies came hizzing with little hizzers on their heads and under their legs. They jumped on the rails with their zigzag legs and spit and twisted with their zigzag teeth and tongues till they twisted the whole railroad and all the rails and tracks into a zigzag railroad with zigzag rails for the trains, the passenger trains and the freight trains, all to run zigzag on.

"Then the zizzies crept away into the fields where they sleep and cover themselves with zigzag blankets on special zigzag beds.

"Next day came shovelmen with their shovels, smooth engineers with smooth blueprints, and water boys with water pails and water dippers for the shovelmen to drink after shoveling the railroad straight. And I nearly forgot to say the steam and hoist operating engineers came and began their steam hoist and operating to make the railroad straight.

"They worked hard. They made the railroad straight again. They looked at the job and said to themselves and to each other, 'This is it —we done it.'

"Next morning the zizzies opened their zigzag eyes and looked over to the railroad and the rails. When they saw the railroad all straight again, and the rails and the ties and the spikes all straight again, the zizzies didn't even eat breakfast that morning.

"They jumped out of their zigzag beds, jumped onto the rails with their zigzag legs, and spit and twisted till they spit and twisted all the rails and the ties and the spikes back into a zigzag like the letter Z and the letter Z at the end of the alphabet.

"After that the zizzies went to breakfast. And they said to themselves and to each other, the same as the shovelmen, the smooth engineers, and the steam hoist and operating engineers, 'This is it—we done it.' "

"So that is the how of the which—it was the zizzies," said Gimme the Ax.

"Yes, it was the zizzies," said the Potato Face Blind Man. "That is the story told to me."

"Who told it to you?"

"*Two little zizzies*. They came to me one cold winter night and slept in my accordion where the music keeps it warm in winter. In the morning I said, 'Good morning, zizzies. Did you have a good sleep last night and pleasant dreams?' And after they had breakfast, they told me the story. Both told it zigzag, but it was the same kind of zigzag each had together."

❀ ❀ ❀

Three Stories About the Gold Buckskin Whincher

PEOPLE: *Blixie Bimber*
Peter Potato Blossom Wishes
Jimmy the Flea
Silas Baxby
Fritz Axenbax
James Sixbixdix
Jason Squiff, the cistern cleaner
Rags Habakuk, the ragman
Two daughters of the ragman
Two blue rats
A circus man with spot cash
A moving-picture actor
A taxicab driver

THE STORY OF BLIXIE BIMBER AND THE POWER OF THE GOLD BUCKSKIN WHINCHER

BLIXIE BIMBER GREW up looking for luck. If she found a horseshoe, she took it home and put it on the wall of her room with a ribbon tied to it. She would look at the moon through her fingers, under her arms, over her right shoulder but never—never over her *left* shoulder. She listened and picked up everything anybody said about the ground-hog and whether the groundhog saw his shadow when he came out the second of February.

If she dreamed of onions, she knew the next day she would find a silver spoon. If she dreamed of fishes, she knew the next day she would meet a strange man who would call her by her first name. She grew up looking for luck.

She was sixteen years old and quite a girl, with her skirts down to her shoe tops, when something happened. She was going to the post office to see if there was a letter for her from Peter Potato Blossom Wishes, her best chum, or a letter from Jimmy the Flea, her best friend she kept steady company with.

Jimmy the Flea was a climber. He climbed skyscrapers and flag-poles and smokestacks and was a famous steeplejack. Blixie Bimber liked him because he was a steeplejack, a little, but more because he was a whistler.

Every time Blixie said to Jimmy, "I got the blues—whistle the blues out of me," Jimmy would just naturally whistle till the blues just naturally went away from Blixie.

On the way to the post office, Blixie found a gold buckskin *whincher*. There it lay in the middle of the sidewalk. How and why it came to be there, she never knew and nobody ever told her. "It's luck," she said to herself as she picked it up quick.

And so—she took it home and fixed it on a little chain and wore it around her neck.

She did not know and nobody ever told her a gold buckskin whincher is different from just a plain common whincher. It has a *power*. And if a thing has a power over you, then you just naturally can't help yourself.

So—around her neck fixed on a little chain Blixie Bimber wore the gold buckskin whincher and never knew it had a power and all the time the power was working.

"The first man you meet with an X in his name you must fall head over heels in love with him," said the silent power in the gold buckskin whincher.

And that was why Blixie Bimber stopped at the post office and went back again asking the clerk at the post office window if he was sure there wasn't a letter for her. The name of the clerk was Silas Baxby. For six weeks he kept steady company with Blixie Bimber. They went to dances, hayrack rides, picnics, and high jinks together.

All the time the power in the gold buckskin whincher was working. It was hanging by a little chain around her neck and always working. It was saying, "The next man you meet with two X's in his name you must leave all and fall head over heels in love with him."

She met the high school principal. His name was Fritz Axenbax. Blixie dropped her eyes before him and threw smiles at him. And for six weeks he kept steady company with Blixie Bimber. They went to dances, hayrack rides, picnics, and high jinks together.

"Why do you go with him for steady company?" her relatives asked.

"It's a power he's got," Blixie answered. "I just can't help it—it's a power."

"One of his feet is bigger than the other—how can you keep steady company with him?" they asked again.

All she would answer was, "It's a power."

All the time, of course, the gold buckskin whincher on the little chain around her neck was working. It was saying, "If she meets a man with three X's in his name, she must fall head over heels in love with him."

At a band concert in the public square one night she met James Sixbixdix. There was no helping it. She dropped her eyes and threw her smiles at him. And for six weeks they kept steady company going to band concerts, dances, hayrack rides, picnics, and high jinks together.

"Why do you keep steady company with him? He's a musical soup eater," her relatives said to her.

And she answered, "It's a power—I can't help myself."

Leaning down with her head in a rainwater cistern one day, listening to the echoes against the strange wooden walls of the cistern, the gold buckskin whincher on the little chain around her neck slipped off and fell down into the rainwater.

"My luck is gone," said Blixie. Then she went into the house and made two telephone calls. One was to James Sixbixdix, telling him she couldn't keep the date with him that night. The other was to Jimmy the Flea, the climber, the steeplejack.

"Come on over—I got the blues, and I want you to whistle 'em away," was what she telephoned Jimmy the Flea.

And so—if you ever come across a gold buckskin whincher, be careful. It's got a power. It'll make you fall head over heels in love with the next man you meet with an X in his name. Or it will do other strange things because different whinchers have different powers.

THE STORY OF JASON SQUIFF AND WHY HE HAD A POPCORN HAT, POPCORN MITTENS, AND POPCORN SHOES

JASON SQUIFF WAS a cistern cleaner. He had greenish yellowish hair. If you looked down into a cistern when he was lifting buckets of slush and mud, you could tell where he was; you could pick him out down in the dark cistern by the lights of his greenish yellowish hair.

Sometimes the buckets of slush and mud tipped over and ran down on the top of his head. This covered his greenish yellowish hair. And then it was hard to tell where he was, and it was not easy to pick him out down in the dark where he was cleaning the cistern.

One day Jason Squiff came to the Bimber house and knocked on the door.

"Did I understand," he said, speaking to Mrs. Bimber, Blixie Bimber's mother, "do I understand you sent for me to clean the cistern in your backyard?"

"You understand exactly such," said Mrs. Bimber, "and you are welcome as the flowers that bloom in the spring, tra-la-la."

"Then I will go to work and clean the cistern, tra-la-la," he answered, speaking to Mrs. Bimber. "I'm the guy, tra-la-la," he said further, running his excellent fingers through his greenish yellowish hair, which was shining brightly.

He began cleaning the cistern. Blixie Bimber came out in the backyard. She looked down in the cistern. It was all dark. It looked like nothing but all dark down there. By and by she saw something greenish yellowish. She watched it. Soon she saw it was Jason Squiff's head and hair. And then she knew the cistern was being cleaned and Jason Squiff was on the job. So she sang tra-la-la and went back into the house and told her mother Jason Squiff was on the job.

The last bucketful of slush and mud came at last for Jason Squiff. He squinted at the bottom. Something was shining. He reached his fingers down through the slush and mud and took out what was shining.

It was the gold buckskin whincher Blixie Bimber lost from the gold chain around her neck the week before when she was looking down into the cistern to see what she could see. It was exactly the same gold buckskin whincher shining and glittering like a sign of happiness.

"It's luck," said Jason Squiff, wiping his fingers on his greenish yellowish hair. Then he put the gold buckskin whincher in his vest pocket and spoke to himself again. "It's luck."

A little after six o'clock that night Jason Squiff stepped into his house and home and said hello to his wife and daughters. They all began to laugh. Their laughter was a ticklish laughter.

"Something funny is happening," he said.

"And you are it." They all laughed at him again with ticklish laugher.

Then they showed him. His hat was popcorn, his mittens popcorn, and his shoes popcorn. He didn't know the gold buckskin whincher had a power and was working all the time. He didn't know the whincher in his vest pocket was saying, "You have a letter Q in your name, and because you have the pleasure and happiness of having a Q in your name, you must have a popcorn hat, popcorn mittens, and popcorn shoes."

The next morning he put on another hat, another pair of mittens, and another pair of shoes. And the minute he put them on, they changed to popcorn.

So he tried on all his hats, mittens, and shoes. Always they changed to popcorn the minute he had them on.

He went downtown to the stores. He bought a new hat, mittens, and shoes. And the minute he had them on, they changed to popcorn.

So he decided he would go to work and clean cisterns with his popcorn hat, popcorn mittens, and popcorn shoes on.

The people of the Village of Cream Puffs enjoyed watching him walk up the street, going to clean cisterns. People five and six blocks away could see him coming and going with his popcorn hat, popcorn mittens, and popcorn shoes.

When he was down in a cistern, the children enjoyed looking down into the cistern to see him work. When none of the slush and mud fell on his hat and mittens, he was easy to find. The light of the shining popcorn lit up the whole inside of the cistern.

Sometimes, of course, the white popcorn got full of black slush and black mud. And then when Jason Squiff came up and walked home, he was not quite so dazzling to look at.

It was a funny winter for Jason Squiff.

"It's a crime, a dirty crime," he said to himself. "Now I can never be alone with my thoughts. Everybody looks at me when I go up the street.

"If I meet a funeral, even the pall bearers begin to laugh at my popcorn hat. If I meet people going to a wedding, they throw all the rice at me as if I am a bride and a groom all together.

"The horses try to eat my hat wherever I go. Three hats I have fed to horses this winter.

"And if I accidentally drop one of my mittens, the chickens eat it."

Then Jason Squiff began to change. He became proud.

"I always wanted a white beautiful hat like this white popcorn hat," he said to himself. "And I always wanted white beautiful mittens and white beautiful shoes like these white popcorn mittens and shoes."

When the boys yelled, "Snowman! Yah-de-dah-de-dah, snowman!" he just waved his hand to them with an upward gesture of his arm to show he was proud of how he looked.

"They all watch for me," he said to himself. "I am distinguished— am I not?" he asked himself.

And he put his right hand into his left hand and shook hands with himself and said, "You certainly look fixed up."

One day he decided to throw away his vest. In the vest pocket was the gold buckskin whincher, with the power working, the power saying, "You have a letter Q in your name, and because you have the pleasure and happiness of having a Q in your name, you must have a popcorn hat, popcorn mittens, and popcorn shoes."

Yes, he threw away the vest. He forgot all about the gold buckskin whincher being in the vest.

He just handed the vest to a ragman. And the ragman put the vest with the gold buckskin whincher in a bag on his back and walked away.

After that Jason Squiff was like other people. His hats would never change to popcorn nor his mittens to popcorn nor his shoes to popcorn.

And when anybody looked at him down in a cistern cleaning the cistern or when anybody saw him walking along the street, they knew him by his greenish yellowish hair, which was always full of bright lights.

And so—if you have a Q in your name, be careful if you ever come across a gold buckskin whincher. Remember different whinchers have different powers.

THE STORY OF RAGS HABAKUK, THE TWO BLUE RATS, AND THE CIRCUS MAN WHO CAME WITH SPOT CASH MONEY

RAGS HABAKUK WAS going home. His day's work was done. The sun was down. Street lamps began shining. Burglars were starting on their night's work. It was no time for an honest ragman to be knocking on people's back doors, saying, "Any rags?" or else saying, "Any rags? any bottles? any bones?" or else saying, "Any rags? any bottles? any bones? any old iron? any copper, brass, old shoes all run down and no good to anybody today? any old clothes, old coats, pants, vests? I take any old clothes you got."

Yes, Rags Habakuk was going home. In the gunnysack bag on his back, humped up on top of the rag humps in the bag, was an old vest. It was the same old vest Jason Squiff threw out of a door at Rags Habakuk. In the pocket of the vest was the gold buckskin whincher with a power in it.

Well, Rags Habakuk got home just like always, sat down to supper, and smacked his mouth and had a big supper of fish, just like always. Then he went out to a shanty in the backyard and opened up the gunnysack ragbag and fixed things out classified just like every day when he came home, he opened the gunnysack bag and fixed things out classified.

The last thing of all he fixed out classified was the vest with the gold buckskin whincher in the pocket. "Put it on—it's a glad rag," he said, looking at the vest. "It's a lucky vest." So he put his right arm in the right armhole and his left arm in the left armhole. And there he was with his arms in the armholes of the old vest all fixed out classified new.

Next morning Rags Habakuk kissed his wife g'by and his eighteen-year-old girl g'by and his nineteen-year-old girl g'by. He kissed them just like he always kissed them—in a hurry—and as he kissed each one, he said, "I will be back soon if not sooner, and when I come back, I will return."

Yes, up the street went Rags Habakuk. And soon as he left home, something happened. Standing on his right shoulder was a blue rat, and standing on his left shoulder was a blue rat. The only way he knew they were there was by looking at them.

There they were, close to his ears. He could feel the far edge of their whiskers against his ears.

"This never happened to me before all the time I been picking rags," he said. "Two blue rats stand by my ears and never say anything even if they know I am listening to anything they tell me."

So Rags Habakuk walked on two blocks, three blocks, four blocks, squinting with his right eye slanting at the blue rat on his right shoul-

der and squinting with his left eye slanting at the blue rat on his left shoulder.

"If I stood on somebody's shoulder with my whiskers right up in somebody's ear, I would say something for somebody to listen to," he muttered.

Of course, he did not understand it was the gold buckskin whincher and the power working. Down in the pocket of the vest he had on, the gold buckskin whincher power was saying, "Because you have two K's in your name, you must have two blue rats on your shoulders, one blue rat for your right ear, one blue rat for your left ear."

It was good business. Never before did Rags Habakuk get so much old rags.

"Come again—you and your lucky blue rats," people said to him. They dug into their cellars and garrets and brought him bottles and bones and copper and brass and old shoes and old clothes, coats, pants, vests.

Every morning when he went up the street with the two blue rats on his shoulders, blinking their eyes straight ahead and chewing their whiskers so they sometimes tickled the ears of old Rags Habakuk, sometimes women came running out on the front porch to look at him and say, "Well, if he isn't a queer old mysterious ragman and if those ain't queer old mysterious blue rats!"

All the time the gold buckskin whincher and the power was working. It was saying, "So long as old Rags Habakuk keeps the two blue rats, he shall have good luck—but if he ever sells one of the blue rats, then one of his daughters shall marry a taxicab driver—and if he ever sells the other blue rat, then his other daughter shall marry a moving-picture hero actor."

Then terrible things happened. A circus man came. "I give you one thousand dollars spot cash money for one of the blue rats," he expostulated with his mouth. "And I give you two thousand dollars spot cash money for the two of the blue rats, both of them together."

"Show me how much spot cash money two thousand dollars is all counted out in one pile for one man to carry away home in his gunnysack ragbag," was the answer of Rags Habakuk.

The circus man went to the bank and came back with spot cash greenbacks money.

"This spot cash greenbacks money is made from the finest silk rags printed by the national government for the national republic to make business rich and prosperous," said the circus man, expostulating with his mouth.

"T-h-e f-i-n-e-s-t s-i-l-k r-a-g-s," he expostulated again, holding two fingers under the nose of Rags Habakuk.

"I take it," said Rags Habakuk, "I take it. It is a whole gunnysack bag full of spot cash greenbacks money. I tell my wife it is printed by the national government for the national republic to make business rich and prosperous."

Then he kissed the blue rats, one on the right ear, the other on the left ear, and handed them over to the circus man.

And that was why the next month his eighteen-year-old daughter married a taxicab driver who was so polite all the time to his customers that he never had time to be polite to his wife.

And that was why his nineteen-year-old daughter married a moving-picture hero actor who worked so hard being nice and kind in the moving pictures that he never had enough left over for his wife when he got home after the day's work.

And the lucky vest with the gold buckskin whincher was stolen from Rags Habakuk by the taxicab driver.

❀ ❀ ❀

Four Stories About the Deep Doom of Dark Doorways

PEOPLE: *The Rag Doll*
The Broom Handle
Spoon Lickers
Chocolate Chins
Dirty Bibs
Tin Pan Bangers
Clean Ears
Easy Ticklers
Musical Soup Eaters
Chubby Chubbs
Sleepyheads

Snoo Foo
Blink, Swink, and Jink

Blunk, Swunk, and Junk
Missus Sniggers

Eeta Peeca Pie
Meeny Miney
Miney Mo
A Potato Bug millionaire

Bimbo the Snip
Bevo the Hike
A ward alderman
A barn boss
A weatherman
A traffic policeman
A monkey
A widow woman
An umbrella handle maker

THE WEDDING PROCESSION OF
THE RAG DOLL AND THE BROOM HANDLE
AND WHO WAS IN IT

THE RAG DOLL had many friends. The Whisk Broom, the Furnace Shovel, the Coffee Pot, they all liked the Rag Doll very much.

But when the Rag Doll married, it was the Broom Handle she picked because the Broom Handle fixed her eyes.

A proud child, proud but careless, banged the head of the Rag Doll against a door one day and knocked off both the glass eyes sewed on long ago. It was then the Broom Handle found two black California prunes and fastened the two California prunes just where the eyes belonged. So then the Rag Doll had two fine black eyes brand new. She was even nicknamed Black Eyes by some people.

There was a wedding when the Rag Doll married the Broom Handle. It was a grand wedding with one of the grandest processions ever seen at a rag doll wedding. And we are sure no broom handle ever had a grander wedding procession when he got married.

Who marched in the procession? Well, first came the Spoon Lickers. Every one of them had a teaspoon, or a soupspoon, though most of them had a big tablespoon. On the spoons, what did they have? Oh, some had butterscotch, some had gravy, some had marshmallow fudge. Everyone had something slickery sweet or fat to eat on the spoon. And as they marched in the wedding procession of the Rag Doll and the Broom Handle, they licked their spoons and looked around and licked their spoons again.

Next came the Tin Pan Bangers. Some had dishpans, some had frying pans, some had potato peeling pans. All the pans were tin with tight tin bottoms. And the Tin Pan Bangers banged with knives and forks and iron and wooden bangers on the bottoms of the tin pans. And as they marched in the wedding procession of the Rag Doll and the Broom Handle, they banged their pans and looked around and banged again.

Then came the Chocolate Chins. They were all eating chocolates. And the chocolate was slippery and slickered all over their chins. Some of them spattered the ends of their noses with black chocolate. Some of them spread the brown chocolate nearly up to their ears. And then as they marched in the wedding procession of the Rag Doll and the Broom Handle, they stuck their chins in the air and looked around and stuck their chins in the air again.

Then came the Dirty Bibs. They wore plain white bibs, checker bibs, stripe bibs, blue bibs, and bibs with butterflies. But all the bibs were dirty. The plain white bibs were dirty, the checker bibs were dirty, the stripe bibs, the blue bibs, and the bibs with butterflies on them, they were all dirty. And so in the wedding procession of the Rag Doll and the Broom Handle, the Dirty Bibs marched with their dirty fingers on the bibs, and they looked around and laughed and looked around and laughed again.

Next came the Clean Ears. They were proud. How they got into the procession nobody knows. Their ears were all clean. They were clean not only on the outside, but they were clean on the inside. There was not a speck of dirt or dust or muss or mess on the inside nor the outside of their ears. And so in the wedding procession of the Rag Doll and the Broom Handle, they wiggled their ears and looked around and wiggled their ears again.

The Easy Ticklers were next in the procession. Their faces were shining. Their cheeks were like bars of new soap. Their ribs were strong, and the meat and the fat was thick on their ribs. It was plain to see they were saying, "Don't tickle me because I tickle so easy." And as they marched in the wedding procession of the Rag Doll and the Broom Handle, they tickled themselves and laughed and looked around and tickled themselves again.

The music was furnished mostly by the Musical Soup Eaters. They marched with big bowls of soup in front of them and big spoons for eating the soup. They whistled and chuzzled and snozzled the soup, and the noise they made could be heard far up at the head of the procession where the Spoon Lickers were marching. So they dipped their soup and looked around and dipped their soup again.

The Chubby Chubbs were next. They were roly-poly, round-faced smackers and snoozers. They were not fat babies—oh no, oh no— not fat but just chubby and easy to squeeze. They marched on their chubby legs and chubby feet and chubbed their chubbs and looked around and chubbed their chubbs again.

The last of all in the wedding procession of the Rag Doll and the Broom Handle were the Sleepyheads. They were smiling and glad to be marching, but their heads were slimpsing down and their smiles were half fading away and their eyes were half shut or a little more than half shut. They staggered just a little, as though their feet were not sure where they were going. They were the Sleepyheads, the last of all in the wedding procession of the Rag Doll and the Broom Handle, and the Sleepyheads, they never looked around at all.

It *was* a grand procession—don't you think so?

HOW THE HAT ASHES SHOVEL
HELPED SNOO FOO

IF YOU WANT to remember the names of all six of the Sniggers children, remember that the three biggest were named Blink, Swink, and Jink, but the three littlest ones were named Blunk, Swunk, and Junk. One day last January the three biggest had a fuss with the three littlest. The fuss was about a new hat for Snoo Foo, the snowman, about what kind of hat he should wear and how he should wear it. Blink, Swink, and Jink said, "He wants a crooked hat put on straight." Blunk, Swunk, and Junk said, "He wants a straight hat put on crooked." They fussed and fussed. Blink fussed with Blunk, Swink fussed with Swunk, and Jink fussed with Junk. The first ones to make up after the fuss were Jink and Junk. They decided the best way to settle the fuss. "Let's put a crooked hat on crooked," said Jink. "No, let's put a straight hat on straight," said Junk. Then they stood looking and looking into each other's shiny, laughing eyes, and then both of them exploded to each other at the same time, "Let's put on two hats, a crooked hat crooked and a straight hat straight."

Well, they looked around for hats. But there were not any hats anywhere, that is, no hats big enough for a snowman with a big head like Snoo Foo. So they went in the house and asked their mother for *the hat ashes shovel*. Of course, in most any other house, the mother would be all worried if six children came tramping and clomping in, banging the door, and all six ejaculating to their mother at once, "Where is the hat ashes shovel?" But Missus Sniggers wasn't worried at all. She rubbed her chin with her finger and said softly, "Oh lah de dah, oh lah de dah, where is that hat ashes shovel. Last week I had it when I was making a hat for Mister Sniggers; I remember I had that hat ashes shovel right up here over the clock, oh lah de dah, oh lah de dah. Go out and ring the front doorbell," she said to Jink Sniggers. Jink ran away to the front door. And Missus Sniggers and the five children waited. Bling-bling the bell began ringing and—listen—the door of the clock opened, and the hat ashes shovel fell out. "Oh lah de dah, get out of here in a hurry," said Missus Sniggers.

Well, the children ran out and dug a big pail of hat ashes with the hat ashes shovel. And they made two hats for Snoo Foo. One was a crooked hat. The other was a straight hat. And they put the crooked hat on crooked and the straight hat on straight. And there stood Snoo Foo in the front yard, and everybody who came by on the street, he would take off his hat to them, the crooked hat with his arm crooked and the straight hat with his arm straight. That was the end of the fuss between the Sniggers children, and it was Jink, the littlest one of the biggest, and Junk, the littlest one of the littlest, who settled the fuss by looking clean into each other's eyes and laughing. If you ever get into a fuss, try this way of settling it.

THREE BOYS WITH JUGS OF MOLASSES
AND SECRET AMBITIONS

IN THE VILLAGE of Liver-and-Onions, if *one* boy goes to the grocery for a jug of molasses, it is just like always. And if *two* boys go to the grocery for a jug of molasses together, it is just like always. But if *three* boys go to the grocery for a jug of molasses each and all together, then it is not like always at all, at all.

Eeta Peeca Pie grew up with wishes and wishes working inside him. And for every wish inside him, he had a freckle outside on his face. Whenever he smiled, the smile ran way back into the far side of his face and got lost in the wishing freckles.

Meeny Miney grew up with suspicions and suspicions working inside him. And after a while some of the suspicions got fastened on his eyes, and some of the suspicions got fastened on his mouth. So when he looked at other people straight in the face, they used to say, "Meeny Miney looks so sad-like, I wonder if he'll get by."

Miney Mo was different. He wasn't sad-like and suspicious like Meeny Miney. Nor was he full of wishes inside and freckles outside like Eeta Peeca Pie. He was all mixed up inside with wishes and suspicions. So he had a few freckles and a few suspicions on his face. When he looked other people straight in the face, they used to say, "I don't know whether to laugh or cry."

So here we have 'em, three boys growing up with wishes, suspicions, and mixed-up wishes and suspicions. They all looked different from each other. Each one, however, had a secret ambition. And all three had the same secret ambition.

An ambition is a little creeper that creeps and creeps in your heart night and day, singing a little song, "Come and find me, come and find me."

The secret ambition in the heart of Eeta Peeca Pie, Meeny Miney, and Miney Mo was an ambition to go railroading, to ride on railroad cars night and day, year after year. The whistles and the wheels of railroad trains were music to them.

Whenever the secret ambition crept in their hearts and made them too sad, so sad it was hard to live and stand for it, they would all three put their hands on each other's shoulders and sing the song of Joe. The chorus was like this:

Joe, Joe, broke his toe,
On the way to Mexico.
Came back, broke his back,
Sliding on the railroad track.

One fine summer morning all three mothers of all three boys gave each one a jug and said, "Go to the grocery and get a jug of molasses." All three got to the grocery at the same time. And all three went out of the door of the grocery together, each with a jug of molasses together and each with his secret ambition creeping around in his heart, all three together.

Two blocks from the grocery they stopped under a slippery elm tree. Eeta Peeca Pie was stretching his neck, looking straight up into the slippery elm tree. He said it was always good for his freckles, and it helped his wishes to stand under a slippery elm and look up.

While he was looking up, his left hand let go the jug handle of the jug of molasses. And the jug went ka-flump, ka-flumpety-flump down on the stone sidewalk, cracked to pieces, and let the molasses go running out over the sidewalk.

If you have never seen it, let me tell you molasses running out of a broken jug, over a stone sidewalk under a slippery elm tree, looks peculiar and mysterious.

Eeta Peeca Pie stepped into the molasses with his bare feet. "It's a lotta fun," he said. "It tickles all over." So Meeny Miney and Miney Mo both stepped into the molasses with their bare feet.

Then what happened just happened. One got littler. Another got littler. All three got littler.

"You look to me only big as a potato bug," said Eeta Peeca Pie to Meeny Miney and Miney Mo. "It's the same like you look to us," said Meeny Miney and Miney Mo to Eeta Peeca Pie. And then because their secret ambition began to hurt them, they all stood with hands on each other's shoulders and sang the Mexico Joe song.

Off the sidewalk they strolled, across a field of grass. They passed many houses of spiders and ants. In front of one house they saw Mrs. Spider over a tub washing clothes for Mr. Spider.

"Why do you wear that frying pan on your head?" they asked her.

"In this country all ladies wear the frying pan on their head when they want a hat."

"But what if you want a hat when you are frying with the frying pan?" asked Eeta Peeca Pie.

"That never happens to any respectable lady in this country."

"Don't you never have no new style hats?" asked Meeny Miney.

"No, but we always have new style frying pans every spring and fall."

Hidden in the roots of a pink grass clump, they came to a city of twisted-nose spiders. On the main street was a store with a show window full of pink parasols. They walked in and said to the clerk, "We want to buy parasols."

"We don't sell parasols here," said the spider clerk.

"Well, lend us a parasol apiece," said all three.

"Gladly, most gladly," said the clerk.

"How do you do it?" asked Eeta.

"I don't have to," answered the spider clerk.

"How did it begin?"

"It never was otherwise."

"Don't you never get tired?"

"Every parasol is a joy."

"What do you do when the parasols are gone?"

"They always come back. These are the famous twisted-nose parasols made from the famous pink grass. You will lose them all, all three. Then they will all walk back to me here in this store on main street. I cannot sell you something I know you will surely lose. Neither can I ask you to pay for something you will forget, somewhere, sometime, and when you forget it, it will walk back here to me again. Look—look!"

As he said "Look," the door opened, and five pink parasols came waltzing in and waltzed up into the show window.

"They always come back. Everybody forgets. Take your parasols and go. You will forget them, and they will come back to me."

"He looks like he had wishes inside him," said Eeta Peeca Pie.

"He looks like he had suspicions," said Meeny Miney.

"He looks like he was all mixed up, wishes and suspicions," said Miney Mo.

And once more because they all felt lonesome and their secret ambitions were creeping and eating, they put their hands on their shoulders and sang the Mexico Joe song.

Then came happiness. They entered the Potato Bug Country. And they had luck first of all the first hour they were in the Potato Bug Country. They met a Potato Bug millionaire.

"How are you a millionaire?" they asked him.

"Because I got a million," he answered.

"A million what?"

"A million *fleems.*"

"Who wants fleems?"

"You want fleems if you're going to live here."

"Why so?"

"Because fleems is our money. In the Potato Bug Country, if you got no fleems, you can't buy nothing nor anything. But if you got a million fleems, you're a Potato Bug millionaire."

Then he surprised them.

"I like you because you got wishes and freckles," he said to Eeta Peeca Pie, filling the pockets of Eeta with fleems.

"And I like you because you got suspicions and you're sad-like," he said to Meeny Miney, filling Meeny Miney's pockets full of fleems.

"And I like you because you got some wishes and some suspicions and you look mixed up," he said to Miney Mo, sticking handfuls and handfuls of fleems into the pockets of Miney Mo.

Wishes do come true. And suspicions do come true. Here they had been wishing all their lives, and had suspicions of what was going to happen, and now it all came true.

With their pockets filled with fleems they rode on all the railroad trains of the Potato Bug Country. They went to the railroad stations and bought tickets for the fast trains and the slow trains and even the trains that back up and run backward instead of where they start to go.

On the dining cars of the railroads of the Potato Bug Country they ate wonder ham from the famous Potato Bug pigs, eggs from the Potato Bug hens, et cetera.

It seemed to them they stayed a long while in the Potato Bug Country, years and years. Yes, the time came when all their fleems were gone. Then whenever they wanted a railroad ride or something to eat or a place to sleep, they put their hands on each other's shoulders and sang the Mexico Joe song. In the Potato Bug Country they all said the Mexico Joe song was wonderful.

One morning while they were waiting to take an express train on the Early Ohio & Southwestern, they sat near the roots of a big potato plant under the big green leaves. And far above them they saw a dim black cloud, and they heard a shaking and a rustling and a spattering. They did not know it was a man of the Village of Liver-and-Onions. They did not know it was Mr. Sniggers putting paris green on the potato plants.

A big drop of paris green spattered down and fell onto the heads and shoulders of all three, Eeta Peeca Pie, Meeny Miney, and Miney Mo.

Then what happened just happened. They got bigger and bigger—one, two, three. And when they jumped up and ran out of the potato rows, Mr. Sniggers thought they were boys playing tricks.

When they got home to their mothers and told all about the jug of molasses breaking on the stone sidewalk under the slippery elm tree, their mothers said it was careless. The boys said it was lucky because it helped them get their secret ambitions.

And a secret ambition is a little creeper that creeps and creeps in your heart night and day, singing a little song, "Come and find me, come and find me."

HOW BIMBO THE SNIP'S THUMB STUCK TO HIS NOSE WHEN THE WIND CHANGED

ONCE THERE WAS a boy in the Village of Liver-and-Onions whose name was Bimbo the Snip. He forgot nearly everything his father and mother told him to do and told him not to do.

One day his father, Bevo the Hike, came home and found Bimbo the Snip sitting on the front steps with his thumb fastened to his nose and the fingers wiggling.

"I can't take my thumb away," said Bimbo the Snip, "because when I put my thumb to my nose and wiggled my fingers at the iceman, the wind changed. And just like Mother always said, if the wind changed, the thumb would stay fastened to my nose and not come off."

Bevo the Hike took hold of the thumb and pulled. He tied a clothesline rope around it and pulled. He pushed with his foot and heel against it. And all the time the thumb stuck fast, and the fingers wiggled from the end of the nose of Bimbo the Snip.

Bevo the Hike sent for the ward alderman. The ward alderman sent for the barn boss of the street-cleaning department. The barn boss of the street-cleaning department sent for the head vaccinator of the vaccination bureau of the health department. The head vaccinator of the vaccination bureau of the health department sent for the big main fixer of the weather bureau, where they understand the tricks of the wind and the wind changing.

And the big main fixer of the weather bureau said, "If you hit the thumb six times with the end of a traffic policeman's club, the thumb will come loose."

So Bevo the Hike went to a traffic policeman standing on a street corner with a whistle telling the wagons and cars which way to go.

He told the traffic policeman, "The wind changed, and Bimbo the Snip's thumb is fastened to his nose and will not come loose till it is hit six times with the end of a traffic policeman's club."

"I can't help you unless you find a monkey to take my place standing on the corner telling the wagons and cars which way to go," answered the traffic policeman.

So Bevo the Hike went to the zoo and said to a monkey, "The wind changed, and Bimbo the Snip's thumb is fastened to his nose and will not come loose till it is hit with the end of a traffic policeman's club six times, and the traffic policeman cannot leave his place on the street corner telling the traffic which way to go unless a monkey comes and takes his place."

The monkey answered, "Get me a ladder with a whistle so I can climb up and whistle and tell the traffic which way to go."

So Bevo the Hike hunted and hunted over the city and looked and looked and asked and asked till his feet and his eyes and his head and his heart were tired from top to bottom.

Then he met an old widow woman whose husband had been killed in a sewer explosion when he was digging sewer ditches. And the old woman was carrying a bundle of picked-up kindling wood in a bag on her back because she did not have money enough to buy coal.

Bevo the Hike told her, "You have troubles. So have I. You are carrying a load on your back people can see. I am carrying a load and nobody sees it."

"Tell me your troubles," said the old widow woman. He told her. And she said, "In the next block is an old umbrella handle maker. He has a ladder with a whistle. He climbs on the ladder when he makes long, long umbrella handles. And he has the whistle on the ladder to be whistling."

Bevo the Hike went to the next block, found the house of the umbrella handle maker, and said to him, "The wind changed, and Bimbo the Snip's thumb is fastened to his nose and will not come loose till it is hit with the end of a traffic policeman's club six times, and the traffic policeman cannot leave the corner where he is telling the traffic which way to go unless a monkey takes his place, and the monkey cannot take his place unless he has a ladder with a whistle to stand on and whistle the wagons and cars which way to go."

Then the umbrella handle maker said, "Tonight I have a special job because I must work on a long, long umbrella handle, and I will need the ladder to climb up and the whistle to be whistling. But if you promise to have the ladder back by tonight, you can take it."

Bevo the Hike promised. Then he took the ladder with a whistle to the monkey, the monkey took the place of the traffic policeman while the traffic policeman went to the home of Bevo the Hike, where

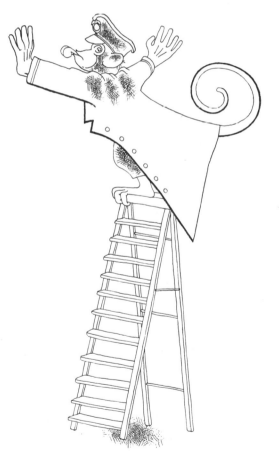

Bimbo the Snip was sitting on the front steps with his thumb fastened to his nose wiggling his fingers at everybody passing by on the street.

The traffic policeman hit Bimbo the Snip's thumb five times with the club. And the thumb stuck fast. But the sixth time it was hit with the end of the traffic policeman's thumb club, it came loose.

Then Bevo thanked the policeman, thanked the monkey, and took the ladder with the whistle back to the umbrella handle maker's house and thanked him.

When Bevo the Hike got home that night, Bimbo the Snip was in bed and all tickled. He said to his father, "I will be careful how I stick my thumb to my nose and wiggle my fingers the next time the wind changes."

❁ ❁ ❁

Three Stories About Three Ways the Wind Went Winding

PEOPLE: *Two skyscrapers*
The Northwest Wind
The Golden Spike Limited train
A tin brass goat
A tin brass goose
Newsies

Young Leather
Red Slippers
A man to be hanged
Five jackrabbits

The Wooden Indian
The Shaghorn Buffalo
The night policeman

THE TWO SKYSCRAPERS WHO DECIDED
TO HAVE A CHILD

TWO SKYSCRAPERS STOOD across the street from each other in the Village of Liver-and-Onions. In the daylight when the streets poured full of people buying and selling, these two skyscrapers talked with each other the same as mountains talk.

In the nighttime when all the people buying and selling were gone home and there were only policemen and taxicab drivers on the streets, in the night when a mist crept up the streets and threw a purple and gray wrapper over everything, in the night when the stars and the sky shook out sheets of purple and gray mist down over the town, then the two skyscrapers leaned toward each other and whispered.

Whether they whispered secrets to each other or whether they whispered simple things that you and I know and everybody knows, that is their secret. One thing is sure: they often were seen leaning toward each other and whispering in the night the same as mountains lean and whisper in the night.

High on the roof of one of the skyscrapers was a tin brass goat looking out across prairies and silver blue lakes shining like blue porcelain breakfast plates, and out across silver snakes of winding rivers in the morning sun. And high on the roof of the other skyscraper was a tin brass goose looking out across prairies and silver blue lakes shining like blue porcelain breakfast plates, and out across silver snakes of winding rivers in the morning sun.

Now the Northwest Wind was a friend of the two skyscrapers. Coming so far, coming five hundred miles in a few hours, coming so fast always while the skyscrapers were standing still, standing always on the same old street corners always, the Northwest Wind was a bringer of news.

"Well, I see the city is here yet," the Northwest Wind would whistle to the skyscrapers.

And they would answer, "Yes, and are the mountains standing yet way out yonder where you come from, Wind?"

"Yes, the mountains are there yonder, and farther yonder is the sea, and the railroads are still going, still running across the prairie to the mountains, to the sea," the Northwest Wind would answer.

And now there was a pledge made by the Northwest Wind to the two skyscrapers. Often the Northwest Wind shook the tin brass goat and shook the tin brass goose on top of the skyscrapers.

"Are you going to blow loose the tin brass goat on my roof?" one asked.

"Are you going to blow loose the tin brass goose on my roof?" the other asked.

"Oh, no." The Northwest Wind laughed, first to one and then to the other. "If I ever blow loose your tin brass goat and if I ever blow loose your tin brass goose, it will be when I am sorry for you because you are up against hard luck and there is somebody's funeral."

So time passed on, and the two skyscrapers stood with their feet among the policemen and the taxicabs, the people buying and selling, —the customers with parcels, packages, and bundles—while away high on their roofs stood the goat and the goose looking out on silver blue lakes like blue porcelain breakfast plates and silver snakes of rivers winding in the morning sun.

So time passed on, and the Northwest Wind kept coming, telling the news and making promises.

So time passed on. And the two skyscrapers decided to have a child.

And they decided when their child came, it should be a *free* child.

"It must be a free child," they said to each other. "It must not be a child standing still all its life on a street corner. Yes, if we have a child, she must be free to run across the prairie, to the mountains, to the sea. Yes, it must be a free child."

So time passed on. Their child came. It was a railroad train, the Golden Spike Limited, the fastest long distance train in the Rootabaga Country. It ran across the prairie, to the mountains, to the sea.

They were glad, the two skyscrapers were, glad to have a free child running away from the big city, far away to the mountains, far away to the sea, running as far as the farthest mountains and seacoasts touched by the Northwest Wind.

They were glad their child was useful, the two skyscrapers were, glad their child was carrying a thousand people a thousand miles a day, so when people spoke of the Golden Spike Limited, they spoke of it as a strong, lovely child.

Then time passed on. There came a day when the newsies yelled as though they were crazy. "Yah yah, blah blah, yoh yoh," was what it sounded like to the two skyscrapers who never bothered much about what the newsies were yelling.

"Yah yah, blah blah, yoh yoh," was the cry of the newsies that came up again to the tops of the skyscrapers.

At last the yelling of the newsies came so strong the skyscrapers listened and heard the newsies yammering, "All about the great train wreck! All about the Golden Spike disaster! Many lives lost! Many lives lost!"

And the Northwest Wind came howling a slow, sad song. And late that afternoon a crowd of policemen, taxicab drivers, newsies, and customers with bundles, all stood around talking and wondering about two things next to each other on the streetcar track in the middle of the street. One was a tin brass goat. The other was a tin brass goose. And they lay next to each other.

THE DOLLAR WATCH AND
THE FIVE JACKRABBITS

LONG AGO, LONG before the waylacks lost the wonderful stripes of oat straw gold and the spots of timothy hay green in their marvelous curving tail feathers, long before the doo-doo-jangers whistled among the honeysuckle blossoms and the bitter-basters cried their last and dying wrangling cries, long before the sad happenings that came later, it was then, some years earlier than the year Fifty Fifty, that Young Leather and Red Slippers crossed the Rootabaga Country.

To begin with, they were walking across the Rootabaga Country. And they were walking because it made their feet glad to feel the dirt of the earth under their shoes, and they were close to the smells of the earth. They learned the ways of birds and bugs, why birds have wings, why bugs have legs, why the gladdy-whingers have spotted eggs in a basket nest in a booblow tree, and why the chizzywhizzies scrape off little fiddle songs all summer long while the summer nights last.

Early one morning they were walking across the corn belt of the Rootabaga Country singing, "Deep Down Among the Dagger Dancers." They had just had a breakfast of coffee and hot hankypank cakes covered with cow's butter. Young Leather said to Red Slippers, "What is the best secret we have come across this summer?"

"That is easy to answer," Red Slippers said with a long flish of her long black eyelashes. "The best secret we have come across is a rope of gold hanging from every star in the sky, and when we want to go up, we go up."

Walking on, they came to a town where they met a man with a sorry face. "Why?" they asked him.

And he answered, "My brother is in jail."

"What for?" they asked him again.

And he answered again, "My brother put on a straw hat in the middle of the winter and went out on the streets laughing; my brother had his hair cut pompompadour and went out on the streets bare-headed in the summertime laughing; and these things were against the law. Worst of all, he sneezed at the wrong time, and he sneezed before the wrong persons; he sneezed when it was not wise to sneeze. So he will be hanged tomorrow morning. The gallows made of lumber and the rope made of hemp—they are waiting for him tomorrow morning. They will tie around his neck the hangman's necktie and hoist him high."

The man with a sorry face looked more sorry than ever. It made Young Leather feel reckless, and it made Red Slippers feel reckless. They whispered to each other. Then Young Leather said, "Take this dollar watch. Give it to your brother. Tell him when they are leading him to the gallows, he must take this dollar watch in his hand, wind it up, and push on the stem winder. The rest will be easy."

So the next morning when they were leading the man to be hanged to the gallows made of lumber and the rope made of hemp, where they were going to hoist him high because he sneezed in the wrong place before the wrong people, he used his fingers winding up the watch and pushing on the stem winder. There was a snapping and a slatching like a gas engine slipping into a big pair of dragonfly wings. The dollar watch changed into a dragonfly ship. The man who was going to be hanged jumped into the dragonfly ship and flew whonging away before anybody could stop him.

Young Leather and Red Slippers were walking out of the town laughing and singing again, "Deep Down Among the Dagger Dancers." The man with a sorry face, not so sorry now any more, came running after them. Behind the man and running after him were five long-legged spider jackrabbits.

"These are for you," was his exclamation. And they all sat down on the stump of a booblow tree. He opened his sorry face and told the secrets of the five long-legged spider jackrabbits to Young Leather and Red Slippers. They waved good-by and went on up the road leading the five new jackrabbits.

In the next town they came to was a skyscraper higher than all the other skyscrapers. A rich man dying wanted to be remembered and left in his last will and testament a command they should build a building so high it would scrape the thunderclouds and stand higher than all other skyscrapers, with his name carved in stone letters on the top of it, and an electric sign at night with his name on it, and a clock on the tower with his name on it.

"I am hungry to be remembered and have my name spoken by many people after I am dead," the rich man told his friends. "I command you, therefore, to throw the building high in the air because the higher it goes, the longer I will be remembered and the longer the years men will mention my name after I am dead."

So there it was. Young Leather and Red Slippers laughed when they first saw the skyscraper, when they were far off along a country road singing their old song, "Deep Down Among the Dagger Dancers."

"We got a show, and we give a performance, and we want the whole town to see it," was what Young Leather and Red Slippers said to the mayor of the town when they called on him at the city hall. "We want a license and a permit to give this free show in the public square."

"What do you do?" asked the mayor.

"We jump five jackrabbits, five long-legged spider jackrabbits over the highest skyscraper you got in your city," they answered him.

"If it's free and you don't sell anything nor take any money away from us while it is daylight and you are giving your performance, then here is your license permit," said the mayor, speaking in the manner of a politician who has studied politics.

Thousands of people came to see the show on the public square. They wished to know how it would look to see five long-legged spider jackrabbits jump over the highest skyscraper in the city.

Four of the jackrabbits had stripes. The fifth had stripes—and spots. Before they started the show, Young Leather and Red Slippers held the jackrabbits one by one in their arms and petted them, rubbed the feet and rubbed the long ears, and ran their fingers along the long legs of the jumpers.

"Zingo," they yelled to the first jackrabbit. He got all ready. "And now zingo!" they yelled again. And the jackrabbit took a run, lifted off his feet, and went on and on and up and up till he went over the roof of the skyscraper and then went down and down till he lit on his feet and came running on his long legs back to the public square where he started from, back where Young Leather and Red Slippers petted him and rubbed his long ears and said, "That's the boy."

Then three jackrabbits made the jump over the skyscraper. "Zingo," they heard and got ready. "And now zingo," they heard, and all three together in a row, their long ears touching each other, they lifted off their feet and went on and on and up and up till they cleared the roof of the skyscraper. Then they came down and down till they lit on their feet and came running to the hands of Young Leather and Red Slippers to have their long legs and their long ears rubbed and petted.

Then came the turn of the fifth jackrabbit, the beautiful one with stripes and spots. "Ah, we're sorry to see you go, ah-h, we're sorry," they said, rubbing his long ears and feeling of his long legs.

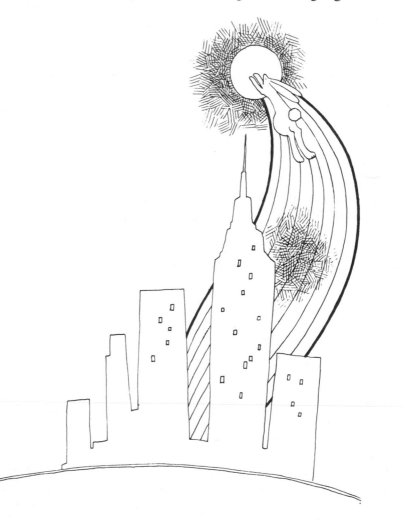

Then Young Leather and Red Slippers kissed him on the nose, kissed the last and fifth of the five long-legged spider jackrabbits.

"Good-by, old bunny, good-by. You're the dandiest bunny there ever was," they whispered in his long ears. And he, because he knew what they were saying and why they were saying it, he wiggled his long ears and looked long and steady at them from his deep eyes.

"Zango," they yelled. He got ready. "And now zango!" they yelled again. And the fifth jackrabbit with his stripes and spots lifted off his feet and went on and on and on and up and up and when he came to the roof of the skyscraper he kept on going on and on and up and up till after a while he was gone all the way out of sight.

They waited and watched, they watched and waited. He never came back. He never was heard of again. He was gone. With the stripes on his back and the spots on his hair, he was gone. And Young Leather and Red Slippers said they were glad they had kissed him on the nose before he went away on a long trip far off, so far off he never came back.

THE WOODEN INDIAN AND THE SHAGHORN BUFFALO

ONE NIGHT A milk-white moon was shining down on Main Street. The sidewalks and the stones, the walls and the windows, all stood out milk white. And there was a thin blue mist drifted and shifted like a woman's veil up and down Main Street, up to the moon and back again. Yes, all Main Street was a mist blue and a milk white, mixed up and soft all over and all through.

It was past midnight. The Wooden Indian in front of the cigar store stepped down off his stand. The Shaghorn Buffalo in front of the haberdasher shop lifted his head and shook his whiskers, raised his hoofs out of his hoof tracks.

Then—this is what happened. They moved straight toward each other. In the middle of Main Street they met. The Wooden Indian jumped straddle of the Shaghorn Buffalo. And the Shaghorn Buffalo put his head down and ran like a prairie wind straight west on Main Street.

At the high hill over the big bend of the Clear Green River they stopped. They stood looking. Drifting and shifting like a woman's blue veil, the blue mist filled the valley, and the milk-white moon filled the valley. And the mist and the moon touched with a lingering, wistful kiss the clear green water of the Clear Green River.

So they stood looking, the Wooden Indian with his copper face and wooden feathers and the Shaghorn Buffalo with his big head and heavy shoulders slumping down close to the ground.

And after they had looked a long while and each of them got an eyeful of the high hill, the big bend, and the moon mist on the river all blue and white and soft, after they had looked a long while, they turned around, and the Shaghorn Buffalo put his head down and ran like a prairie wind down Main Street till he was exactly in front of the cigar store and the haberdasher shop. Then whisk! both of them were right back like they were before, standing still, taking whatever comes.

This is the story as it came from the night policeman of the Village of Cream Puffs. He told the people the next day, "I was sitting on the steps of the cigar store last night watching for burglars. And when I saw the Wooden Indian step down and the Shaghorn Buffalo step out, and the two of them go down Main Street like the wind, I says to myself, 'Marvelish, 'tis marvelish, 'tis marvelish.' "

❀ ❀ ❀

Four Stories About Dear, Dear Eyes

PEOPLE: *The White Horse Girl*
The Blue Wind Boy
The Gray Man on Horseback

Six girls with balloons

Henry Hagglyhoagly
Susan Slackentwist
Two wool yarn mittens

Peter Potato Blossom Wishes
Her father
Many shoes
Slippers
A Dancing Slipper Moon

THE WHITE HORSE GIRL AND
THE BLUE WIND BOY

WHEN THE DISHES are washed at nighttime and the cool of the evening has come in summer or the lamps and fires are lit for the night in winter, then the fathers and mothers in the Rootabaga Country sometimes tell the young people the story of the White Horse Girl and the Blue Wind Boy.

The White Horse Girl grew up far in the west of the Rootabaga Country. All the years she grew up as a girl she liked to ride horses. Best of all things for her was to be straddle of a white horse loping with a loose bridle among the hills and along the rivers of the west Rootabaga Country.

She rode one horse white as snow, another horse white as new-washed sheep wool, and another white as silver. And she could not tell because she did not know which of these three white horses she liked best.

"Snow is beautiful enough for me any time," she said, "new-washed sheep wool or silver out of a ribbon of the new moon, any or either is white enough for me. I like the white manes, the white flanks, the white noses, the white feet of all my ponies. I like the forelocks hanging down between the white ears of all three—my ponies."

And living neighbor to the White Horse Girl in the same prairie country, with the same black crows flying over their places, was the Blue Wind Boy. All the years he grew up as a boy he liked to walk with his feet in the dirt and the grass listening to the winds. Best of all things for him was to put on strong shoes and go hiking among the hills and along the rivers of the west Rootabaga Country, listening to the winds.

There was a blue wind of daytime, starting sometimes six o'clock on a summer morning or eight o'clock on a winter morning. And there was a night wind with blue of summer stars in summer and blue of winter stars in winter. And there was yet another, a blue wind of the times between night and day, a blue dawn and evening wind. All three of these winds he liked so well he could not say which he liked best.

"The early morning wind is strong as the prairie, and whatever I tell it I know it believes and remembers," he said, "and the night wind with the big dark curves of the night sky in it, the night wind gets inside of me and understands all my secrets. And the blue wind of the times between, in the dusk when it is neither night nor day, this is the wind that asks me questions and tells me to wait and it will bring me whatever I want."

Of course, it happened as it had to happen, the White Horse Girl and the Blue Wind Boy met, she straddling one of her white horses, and he wearing his strong hiking shoes in the dirt and the grass. It had to happen they should meet among the hills and along the rivers of the west Rootabaga Country where they lived neighbors.

And of course, she told him all about the snow-white horse and the horse white as new-washed sheep wool and the horse white as a silver ribbon of the new moon. And he told her all about the blue winds he liked listening to, the early morning wind, the night sky wind, and the wind of the dusk between, the wind that asked him questions and told him to wait.

One day the two of them were gone. On the same day of the week the White Horse Girl and the Blue Wind Boy went away. And their fathers and mothers and sisters and brothers and uncles and aunts wondered about them and talked about them because they didn't tell anybody beforehand they were going. Nobody at all knew beforehand or afterward why they were going away, the real honest why of it.

They left a short letter. It read:

To All Our Sweethearts, Old Folks and Young Folks:
We have started to go where the white horses come from and where the blue winds begin. Keep a corner in your hearts for us while we are gone.
The White Horse Girl.
The Blue Wind Boy.

That was all they had to guess by in the west Rootabaga Country, to guess and guess where two darlings had gone.

Many years passed. One day there came riding across the Rootabaga Country a Gray Man on Horseback. He looked like he had come a long ways. So they asked him the question they always asked of any rider who looked like he had come a long ways, "Did you ever see the White Horse Girl and the Blue Wind Boy?"

"Yes," he answered, "I saw them.

"It was a long, long ways from here I saw them," he went on. "It would take years and years to ride to where they are. They were sitting together and talking to each other, sometimes singing, in a place where the land runs high and tough rocks reach up. And they were looking out across water, blue water as far as the eye could see. And away far off the blue waters met the blue sky.

" 'Look!' said the Boy. 'That's where the blue winds begin.'

"And far out on the blue waters, just a little this side of where the blue winds begin, there were white manes, white flanks, white noses, white galloping feet.

" 'Look!' said the Girl. 'That's where the white horses come from.'

"And then nearer to the land came thousands in an hour, millions in a day, white horses, some white as snow, some like new-washed sheep wool, some white as silver ribbons of the new moon.

"I asked them, 'Whose place is this?' They answered, 'It belongs to us; this is what we started for; this is where the white horses come from; this is where the blue winds begin.' "

And that was all the Gray Man on Horseback would tell the people of the west Rootabaga Country. That was all he knew, he said, and if there was any more, he would tell it.

And the fathers and mothers and sisters and brothers and uncles and aunts of the White Horse Girl and the Blue Wind Boy wondered and talked often about whether the Gray Man on Horseback made up the story out of his head or whether it happened just like he told it.

Anyhow this is the story they tell sometimes to the young people of the west Rootabaga Country when the dishes are washed at night and the cool of the evening has come in summer or the lamps and fires are lit for the night in winter.

WHAT SIX GIRLS WITH BALLOONS TOLD THE GRAY MAN ON HORSEBACK

ONCE THERE CAME riding across the Rootabaga Country a Gray Man on Horseback. He looked as if he had come a long ways. He looked like a brother to the same Gray Man on Horseback who said he had seen the White Horse Girl and the Blue Wind Boy.

He stopped in the Village of Cream Puffs. His gray face was sad, and his eyes were gray deep and sad. He spoke short and seemed strong. Sometimes his eyes looked as if they were going to flash, but instead of fire they filled with shadows.

Yet—he did laugh once. It did happen once he lifted his head and face to the sky and let loose a long ripple of laughs.

On Main Street near the Roundhouse of the Big Spool, where they wind up the string that pulls the light little town back when the wind blows it away, there he was riding slow on his gray horse when he met six girls with six fine braids of yellow hair and six balloons apiece. That is, each and every one of the six girls had six fine long braids of yellow hair, and each braid of hair had a balloon tied on the end. A little blue wind was blowing, and the many balloons tied to the braids of the six girls swung up and down and slow and fast whenever the blue wind went up and down and slow and fast.

For the first time since he had been in the village, the eyes of the Gray Man filled with lights, and his face began to look hopeful. He stopped his horse when he came even with the six girls and the balloons floating from the braids of yellow hair.

"Where you going?" he asked.

"Who—hoo-hoo? Who—who—who?" the six girls cheeped out.

"All six of you and your balloons, where you going?"

"Oh, hoo-hoo-hoo, back where we came from," and they all turned their heads back and forth and sideways, which of course turned all the balloons back and forth and sideways because the balloons were fastened to the fine braids of hair which were fastened to their heads.

"And where do you go when you get back where you came from?" he asked just to be asking.

"Oh, hoo-hoo-hoo, then we start out and go straight ahead and see what we can see," they all answered just to be answering, and they dipped their heads and swung them up, which of course dipped all the balloons and swung them up.

So they talked, he asking just to be asking and the six balloon girls answering just to be answering.

At last his sad mouth broke into a smile, and his eyes were lit like a morning sun coming up over harvest fields. And he said to them, "Tell me why are balloons—that is what I want you to tell me—why are balloons?"

The first little girl put her thumb under her chin, looked up at her six balloons floating in the little blue wind over her head, and said:

"Balloons are wishes. The wind made them. The west wind makes the red balloons. The south wind makes the blue. The yellow and green balloons come from the east wind and the north wind."

The second little girl put her first finger next to her nose, looked up at her six balloons dipping up and down like hill flowers in a small wind, and said:

"A balloon used to be a flower. It got tired. Then it changed itself to a balloon. I listened one time to a yellow balloon. It was talking to itself like people talk. It said, 'I used to be a yellow pumpkin flower stuck down close to the ground; now I am a yellow balloon high up in the air where nobody can walk on me and I can see everything.'"

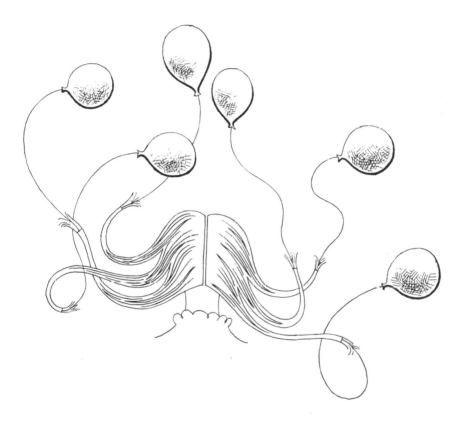

The third little girl held both of her ears like she was afraid they would wiggle, while she slid with a skip, turned quick, and looking up at her balloons, spoke these words:

"A balloon is foam. It comes the same as soap bubbles come. A long time ago it used to be sliding along on water, river water, ocean water, waterfall water, falling and falling over a rocky waterfall, any water you want. The wind saw the bubble and picked it up and carried it away, telling it, 'Now you're a balloon—come along and see the world.'"

The fourth little girl jumped straight into the air so all six of her balloons made a jump like they were going to get loose and go to the sky—and when the little girl came down from her jump and was standing on her two feet with her head turned looking up at the six balloons, she spoke the shortest answer of all, saying:

"Balloons are to make us look up. They help our necks."

The fifth little girl stood first on one foot, then another, bent her head down to her knees and looked at her toes, then swinging straight up and looking at the flying spotted yellow and red and green balloons, she said:

"Balloons come from orchards. Look for trees where half is oranges and half is orange balloons. Look for apple trees where half is red pippins and half is red pippin balloons. Look for watermelons too. A long green balloon with white and yellow belly stripes is a ghost. It came from a watermelon said good-by."

The sixth girl, the last one, kicked the heel of her left foot with the toe of her right foot, put her thumbs under her ears and wiggled all her fingers, then stopped all her kicking and wiggling, and stood looking up at her balloons all quiet because the wind had gone down—and she murmured like she was thinking to herself:

"Balloons come from fire chasers. Every balloon has a fire chaser chasing it. All the fire chasers are made terrible quick, and when they come, they burn quick, so the balloon is made light so it can run away terrible quick. Balloons slip away from fire. If they don't, they can't be balloons. Running away from fire keeps them light."

All the time he listened to the six girls the face of the Gray Man kept getting more hopeful. His eyes lit up. Twice he smiled. And after he said good-by and rode up the street, he lifted his head and face to the sky and let loose a long ripple of laughs.

He kept looking back when he left the village, and the last thing he saw was the six girls each with six balloons fastened to the six braids of yellow hair hanging down their backs.

The sixth little girl kicked the heel of her left foot with the toe of her right foot and said, "He is a nice man. I think he must be our uncle. If he comes again, we shall all ask him to tell us where he thinks balloons come from."

And the other five girls all answered, "Yes," or "Yes, yes," or, "Yes, yes, yes," real fast like a balloon with a fire chaser after it.

HOW HENRY HAGGLYHOAGLY PLAYED
THE GUITAR WITH HIS MITTENS ON

SOMETIMES IN JANUARY the sky comes down close if we walk on a country road and turn our faces up to look at the sky.

Sometimes on that kind of January night the stars look like numbers, look like the arithmetic writing of a girl going to school and just beginning arithmetic.

It was this kind of night Henry Hagglyhoagly was walking down a country road on his way to the home of Susan Slackentwist, the daughter of the rutabaga king near the Village of Liver-and-Onions. When Henry Hagglyhoagly turned his face up to look at the sky, it seemed to him as though the sky came down close to his nose, and there was a writing in stars as though some girl had been doing arithmetic examples, writing number 4 and number 7 and 4 and 7 over and over again across the sky.

"Why is it so bitter cold weather?" Henry Hagglyhoagly asked himself. "If I say many bitter bitters, it is not so bitter as the cold wind and the cold weather."

"You are good, mittens, keeping my fingers warm," he said every once in a while to the wool yarn mittens on his hands.

The wind came tearing along and put its chilly, icy, clammy clamps on the nose of Henry Hagglyhoagly, fastening the clamps like a nipping, gripping clothespin on his nose. He put his wool yarn mittens up on his nose and rubbed till the wind took off the chilly, icy, clammy clamps. His nose was warm again; he said, "Thank you, mittens, for keeping my nose warm."

He spoke to his wool yarn mittens as though they were two kittens or pups, or two little cub bears, or two little Idaho ponies. "You're my chums keeping me company," he said to the mittens.

"Do you know what we got here under our left elbow?" he said to the mittens. "I shall mention to you what is here under my left elbow.

"It ain't a mandolin, it ain't a mouth organ nor an accordion nor a concertina nor a fiddle. It is a guitar, a Spanish Spinnish Splishy guitar made special.

"Yes, mittens, they said a strong young man like me ought to have a piano because a piano is handy to play for everybody in the house and a piano is handy to put a hat and overcoat on or books or flowers.

"I snizzled at 'em, mittens. I told 'em I seen a Spanish Spinnish Splishy guitar made special in a hardware store window for eight dollars and a half.

"And so, mittens—are you listening, mittens?—after cornhusking was all husked and the oats thrashing all thrashed and the rutabaga digging all dug, I took eight dollars and a half in my inside vest pocket and I went to the hardware store.

"I put my thumbs in my vest pocket, and I wiggled my fingers like a man when he is proud of what he is going to have if he gets it. And I said to the head clerk in the hardware store, 'Sir, the article I desire to purchase this evening as one of your high-class customers, the article I desire to have after I buy it for myself, is the article there in the window, sir, the Spanish Spinnish Splishy guitar.'

"And, mittens, if you are listening, I am taking this Spanish Spinnish Splishy guitar to go to the home of Susan Slackentwist, the daughter of the rutabaga king near the Village of Liver-and-Onions, to sing a serenade song."

The cold wind of the bitter-cold weather blew and blew, trying to blow the guitar out from under the left elbow of Henry Hagglyhoagly. And the worse the wind blew, the tighter he held his elbow holding the guitar where he wanted it.

He walked on and on with his long legs stepping long steps till at last he stopped, held his nose in the air, and sniffed.

"Do I sniff something or do I not?" he asked, lifting his wool yarn mittens to his nose and rubbing his nose till it was warm. Again he sniffed.

"Ah hah, yeah, yeah, this is the big rutabaga field near the home of the rutabaga king and the home of his daughter, Susan Slackentwist."

At last he came to the house, stood under the window, and slung the guitar around in front of him to play the music to go with the song.

"And now," he asked his mittens, "shall I take you off or keep you on? If I take you off, the cold wind of the bitter cold weather will freeze my hands so stiff and bitter cold, my fingers will be too stiff to play the guitar. *I will play with mittens on.*"

Which he did. He stood under the window of Susan Slackentwist and played the guitar with his mittens on, the warm wool yarn mittens he called his chums. It was the first time any strong young man going to see his sweetheart ever played the guitar with his mittens on when it was a bitter night with a cold wind and cold weather.

Susan Slackentwist opened her window and threw him a snowbird feather to keep for a keepsake to remember her by. And for years afterward many a sweetheart in the Rootabaga Country told her lover, "If you wish to marry me, let me hear you under my window on a winter night playing the guitar with wool yarn mittens on."

And when Henry Hagglyhoagly walked home on his long legs, stepping long steps, he said to his mittens, "This Spanish Spinnish Splishy guitar made special will bring us luck." And when he turned his face up, the sky came down close, and he could see stars fixed like numbers and the arithmetic writing of a girl going to school learning to write number 4 and number 7 and 4 and 7 over and over.

NEVER KICK A SLIPPER AT THE MOON

WHEN A GIRL is growing up in the Rootabaga Country, she learns some things to do, some things *not* to do.

"Never kick a slipper at the moon if it is the time for the Dancing Slipper Moon when the slim early moon looks like the toe and the heel of a dancer's foot," was the advice Mr. Wishes, the father of Peter Potato Blossom Wishes, gave to his daughter.

"Why?" she asked him.

"Because your slipper will go straight up, on and on to the moon, and fasten itself on the moon as if the moon is a foot ready for dancing," said Mr. Wishes.

"A long time ago there was one night when a secret word was passed around to all the shoes standing in the bedrooms and closets.

"The whisper of the secret was: 'Tonight all the shoes and the slippers and the boots of the world are going walking without any feet in them. Tonight when those who put us on their feet in the daytime are sleeping in their beds, we all get up and walk and go walking where we walk in the daytime.'

"And in the middle of the night, when the people in the beds were sleeping, the shoes and the slippers and the boots everywhere walked out of the bedrooms and the closets. Along the sidewalks on the streets, up and down stairways, along hallways, the shoes and slippers and the boots tramped and marched and stumbled.

"Some walked pussyfoot, sliding easy and soft just like people in the daytime. Some walked clumping and clumping, coming down heavy on the heels and slow on the toes, just like people in the daytime.

"Some turned their toes in and walked pigeon-toe; some spread their toes out and held their heels in, just like people in the daytime. Some ran glad and fast; some lagged slow and sorry.

"Now there was a little girl in the Village of Cream Puffs who came home from a dance that night. And she was tired from dancing round dances and square dances, one steps and two steps, toe dances and toe and heel dances, dances close up and dances far apart, she was so tired she took off only one slipper, tumbled onto her bed, and went to sleep with one slipper on.

"She woke up in the morning when it was yet dark. And she went to the window and looked up in the sky and saw a Dancing Slipper Moon dancing far and high in the deep blue sea of the moon sky.

" 'Oh—what a moon—what a dancing slipper of a moon!' she cried with a little song to herself.

"She opened the window, saying again, 'Oh, what a moon!'—and kicked her foot with the slipper on it straight toward the moon.

"The slipper flew off and flew up and went on and on and up and up in the moonshine.

"It never came back, that slipper. It was never seen again. When they asked the girl about it, she said, 'It slipped off my foot and went up and up, and the last I saw of it the slipper was going on straight to the moon.' "

And these are the explanations why fathers and mothers in the Rootabaga Country say to their girls growing up, "Never kick a slipper at the moon if it is the time of the Dancing Slipper Moon when the ends of the moon look like the toe and the heel of a dancer's foot."

❁ ❁ ❁

One Story—"Only the Fire-Born Understand Blue"

PEOPLE: *Fire the Goat*
Flim the Goose
Shadows

SAND FLAT SHADOWS

FIRE THE GOAT and Flim the Goose slept out. Stub pines stood over them. And away up next over the stub pines were stars.

It was a white sand flat they slept on. The floor of the sand flat ran straight to the Big Lake of the Booming Rollers.

And just over the sand flat and just over the booming rollers was a high room where the mist people were making pictures. Gray pictures, blue, and sometimes a little gold, and often silver, were the pictures.

And next just over the high room where the mist people were making pictures, next just over were the stars.

Over everything, and always last and highest of all, were the stars.

Fire the Goat took off his horns. Flim the Goose took off his wings. "This is where we sleep," they said to each other, "here in the stub pines on the sand flats next to the booming rollers and high over everything and always last and highest of all, the stars."

Fire the Goat laid his horns under his head. Flim the Goose laid his wings under his head. "This is the best place for what you want to keep," they said to each other. Then they crossed their fingers for luck and lay down and went to sleep and slept. And while they slept, the mist people went on making pictures. Gray pictures, blue, and sometimes a little gold but more often silver, such were the pictures the mist people went on making while Fire the Goat and Flim the Goose went on sleeping. And over everything, and always last and highest of all, were the stars.

They woke up. Fire the Goat took his horns out and put them on. "It's morning now," he said.

Flim the Goose took his wings out and put them on. "It's another day now," he said.

Then they sat looking. Away off where the sun was coming up, inching and pushing up far across the rim curve of the Big Lake of the Booming Rollers, along the whole line of the east sky, there were people and animals, all black or all so gray they were near black.

There was a big horse with his mouth open, ears laid back, front legs thrown in two curves like harvest sickles.

There was a camel with two humps, moving slow and grand like he had all the time of all the years of all the world to go in.

There was an elephant without any head, with six short legs. There were many cows. There was a man with a club over his shoulder and a woman with a bundle on the back of her neck.

And they marched on. They were going nowhere, it seemed. And they were going slow. They had plenty of time. There was nothing else to do. It was fixed for them to do it, long ago it was fixed. And so they were marching.

Sometimes the big horse's head sagged and dropped off and came back again. Sometimes the humps of the camel sagged and dropped off and came back again. And sometimes the club on the man's shoulder got bigger and heavier and the man staggered under it, and then his legs got bigger and stronger and he steadied himself and went on. And again sometimes the bundle on the back of the neck of the woman got bigger and heavier and the bundle sagged, and the woman staggered and her legs got bigger and stronger and she steadied herself and went on.

This was the show, the hippodrome, the spectacular circus that passed on the east sky before the eyes of Fire the Goat and Flim the Goose.

"Which is this, who are they, and why do they come?" Flim the Goose asked Fire the Goat.

"Do you ask me because you wish me to tell you?" asked Fire the Goat.

"Indeed it is a question to which I want an honest answer."

"Has never the father or mother nor the uncle or aunt nor the kith and kin of Flim the Goose told him the what and the which of this?"

"Never has the such of this which been put here this way to me by anybody."

Flim the Goose held up his fingers and said, "I don't talk to you with my fingers crossed."

And so Fire the Goat began to explain to Flim the Goose all about the show, the hippodrome, the mastodonic cyclopean spectacle which was passing on the east sky in front of the sun coming up.

"People say they are shadows," began Fire the Goat. "That is a name, a word, a little cough, and a couple of syllables.

"For some people shadows are comic and only to laugh at. For some other people shadows are like a mouth and its breath. The breath comes out, and it is nothing. It is like air, and nobody can make it into a package and carry it away. It will not melt like gold, nor can you shovel it like cinders. So to these people it means nothing.

"And then there are other people," Fire the Goat went on. "There are other people who understand shadows. The fire-born understand. The fire-born know where shadows come from and why they are.

"Long ago, when the Makers of the World were done making the round earth, the time came when they were ready to make the animals to put on the earth. They were not sure how to make the animals. They did not know what shape animals they wanted.

"And so they practiced. They did not make real animals at first. They made only shapes of animals. And these shapes were shadows, shadows like these you and I, Fire the Goat and Flim the Goose, are looking at this morning across the booming rollers on the east sky where the sun is coming up.

"The shadow horse over there on the east sky with his mouth open, his ears laid back, and his front legs thrown in a curve like harvest sickles, that shadow horse was one they made long ago when they were practicing to make a real horse. That shadow horse was a mistake, and they threw him away. Never will you see two shadow horses alike. All shadow horses on the sky are different. Each one is a mistake, a shadow horse thrown away because he was not good enough to be a real horse.

"That elephant with no head on his neck, stumbling so grand on six legs—and that grand camel with two humps, one bigger than the other—and those cows with horns in front and behind—they are all mistakes. They were all thrown away because they were not made good enough to be real elephants, real cows, real camels. They were made just for practice, away back early in the world before any real animals came on their legs to eat and live and be here like the rest of us.

"That man—see him now staggering along with the club over his shoulder—see how his long arms come to his knees and sometimes his hands drag below his feet. See how heavy the club on his shoulders loads him down and drags him on. He is one of the oldest shadow men. He was a mistake, and they threw him away. He was made just for practice.

"And that woman. See her now at the end of that procession across the booming rollers on the east sky. See her the last of all, the end of the procession. On the back of her neck a bundle. Sometimes the bundle gets bigger. The woman staggers. Her legs get bigger and stronger. She picks herself up and goes along shaking her head. She is the same as the others. She is a shadow, and she was made as a mistake. Early, early in the beginnings of the world she was made for practice.

"Listen, Flim the Goose. What I am telling you is a secret of the fire-born. I do not know whether you understand. We have slept together a night on the sand flats next to the booming rollers, under the stub pines with the stars high over—and so I tell what the fathers of the fire-born tell their sons."

And that day Fire the Goat and Flim the Goose moved along the sand flat shore of the Big Lake of the Booming Rollers. It was a blue day, with a fire-blue of the sun mixing itself in the air and the water. Off to the north the booming rollers were blue sea-green. To the east they were sometimes streak purple, sometimes changing bluebell stripes. And to the south they were silver blue, sheet blue.

Where the shadow hippodrome marched on the east sky that morning was a long line of bluebird spots.

"Only the fire-born understand blue," said Fire the Goat to Flim the Goose. And that night as the night before, they slept on a sand flat. And again Fire the Goat took off his horns and laid them under his head while he slept, and Flim the Goose took off his wings and laid them under his head while he slept.

And twice in the night, Fire the Goat whispered in his sleep, whispered to the stars, "Only the fire-born understand blue."

❁ ❁ ❁

Two Stories About Corn Fairies, Blue Foxes, Flongboos, and Happenings That Happened in the United States and Canada

PEOPLE: *Spink*
Skabootch
A man
Corn fairies

Blue foxes
Flongboos
A Philadelphia policeman
Passenger conductor
Chicago newspapers
The Head Spotter of the Weather Makers at Medicine Hat

HOW TO TELL CORN FAIRIES
IF YOU SEE 'EM

IF YOU HAVE ever watched the little corn begin to march across the black lands and then slowly change to big corn and go marching on from the little corn moon of summer to the big corn harvest moon of autumn, then you must have guessed who it is that helps the corn come along. It is the corn fairies. Leave out the corn fairies, and there wouldn't be any corn.

All children know this. All boys and girls know that corn is no good unless there are corn fairies.

Have you ever stood in Illinois or Iowa and watched the late summer wind or the early fall wind running across a big cornfield? It looks as if a big, long blanket were being spread out for dancers to come and dance on. If you look close and if you listen close, you can see the corn fairies come dancing and singing—sometimes. If it is a wild day and a hot sun is pouring down while a cool north wind blows—and this happens sometimes—then you will be sure to see thousands of corn fairies marching and countermarching in mocking grand marches over the big, long blanket of green and silver. Then too they sing, only you must listen with your littlest and newest ears if you wish to hear their singing. They sing soft songs that go pla-sizzy pla-sizzy-sizzy, and each song is softer than an eye wink, softer than a Nebraska baby's thumb.

And Spink, who is a little girl living in the same house with the man writing this story, and Skabootch, who is another little girl in the same house—both Spink and Skabootch are asking the question, "How can we tell corn fairies if we see 'em? If we meet a corn fairy, how will we know it?" And this is the explanation the man gave to Spink who is older than Skabootch, and to Skabootch who is younger than Spink:

All corn fairies wear overalls. They work hard, the corn fairies, and they are proud. The reason they are proud is because they work so hard. And the reason they work so hard is because they have overalls.

But understand this. The overalls are corn gold cloth, woven from leaves of ripe corn mixed with ripe October corn silk. In the first week of the harvest moon, coming up red and changing to yellow and silver, the corn fairies sit by thousands between the corn rows weaving and stitching the clothes they have to wear next winter, next spring, next summer.

They sit cross-legged when they sew. And it is a law among them each one must point the big toe at the moon while sewing the harvest moon clothes. When the moon comes up red as blood early in the evening, they point their big toes slanting toward the east. Then toward midnight when the moon is yellow and halfway up the sky, their big toes are only half slanted as they sit cross-legged sewing. And after midnight when the moon sails its silver disk high overhead and toward the west, then the corn fairies sit sewing with their big toes pointed nearly straight up.

If it is a cool night and looks like frost, then the laughter of the corn fairies is something worth seeing. All the time they sit sewing their next year clothes, they are laughing. It is not a law they have to laugh. They laugh because they are half tickled and glad because it is a good corn year.

And whenever the corn fairies laugh, then the laugh comes out of the mouth like a thin gold frost. If you should be lucky enough to see a thousand corn fairies sitting between the corn rows and all of them laughing, you would laugh with wonder yourself to see the gold frost coming from their mouths while they laughed.

Travelers who have traveled far and seen many things say that if you know the corn fairies with a real knowledge, you can always tell by the stitches in their clothes what state they are from.

In Illinois the corn fairies stitch fifteen stitches of ripe corn silk across the woven corn leaf cloth. In Iowa they stitch sixteen stitches, in Nebraska seventeen, and the farther west you go, the more corn silk stitches the corn fairies have in the corn cloth clothes they wear.

In Minnesota one year there were fairies with a blue sash of corn-flowers across the breast. In the Dakotas the same year all the fairies wore pumpkin-flower neckties, yellow four-in-hands, and yellow ascots. And in one strange year it happened in both the states of Ohio and Texas the corn fairies wore little wristlets of white morning glories.

The traveler who heard about this asked many questions and found out the reason why that year the corn fairies wore little wristlets of white morning glories. He said, "Whenever fairies are sad, they wear white. And this year, which was long ago, was the year men were tearing down all the old zigzag rail fences. Now those old zigzag rail fences were beautiful for the fairies because a hundred fairies could sit on one rail and thousands and thousands of them could sit on the zig-zags and sing pla-sizzy pla-sizzy, softer than an eye wink, softer than a baby's thumb, all on a moonlight summer night. And they found out that year was going to be the last year of the zigzag rail fences. It made them sorry and sad, and when they are sorry and sad, they wear white. So they picked the wonderful white morning glories running along the zigzag rail fences and made them into little wristlets and wore those wristlets the next year to show they were sorry and sad."

Of course, all this helps you to know how the corn fairies look in the evening, the nighttime, and the moonlight. Now we shall see how they look in the daytime.

In the daytime the corn fairies have their overalls of corn gold cloth on. And they walk among the corn rows and climb the corn stalks and fix things in the leaves and stalks and ears of the corn. They help it to grow.

Each one carries on the left shoulder a mouse brush to brush away the field mice. And over the right shoulder each one has a cricket broom to sweep away the crickets. The brush is a whisk brush to brush away mice that get foolish. And the broom is to sweep away crickets that get foolish.

Around the middle of each corn fairy is a yellow-belly belt. And stuck in this belt is a purple moon-shaft hammer. Whenever the wind blows strong and nearly blows the corn down, then the fairies run out and take their purple moon-shaft hammers out of their yellow-belly belts and nail down nails to keep the corn from blowing down. When a rain storm is blowing up terrible and driving all kinds of terribles across the cornfield, then you can be sure of one thing. Running like the wind among the corn rows are the fairies, jerking their purple moon-shaft hammers out of their belts and nailing nails down to keep the corn standing up so it will grow and be ripe and beautiful when the harvest moon comes again in the fall.

Spink and Skabootch ask where the corn fairies get the nails. The answer to Spink and Skabootch is, "Next week you will learn all about where the corn fairies get the nails to nail down the corn if you will keep your faces washed and your ears washed till next week."

And the next time you stand watching a big cornfield in late summer or early fall, when the wind is running across the green and silver, listen with your littlest and newest ears. Maybe you will hear the corn fairies going pla-sizzy pla-sizzy-sizzy, softer than an eye wink, softer than a Nebraska baby's thumb.

HOW THE ANIMALS LOST THEIR TAILS AND GOT THEM BACK TRAVELING FROM PHILADELPHIA TO MEDICINE HAT

FAR UP IN North America, near the Saskatchewan River, in the Winnipeg wheat country, not so far from the town of Moose Jaw, named for the jaw of a moose shot by a hunter there, up where the blizzards and the chinooks begin, where nobody works unless they have to and they nearly all have to, there stands the place known as Medicine Hat.

And there on a high stool in a high tower on a high hill sits the Head Spotter of the Weather Makers.

When the animals lost their tails, it was because the Head Spotter of the Weather Makers at Medicine Hat was careless.

The tails of the animals were stiff and dry because for a long while there was dusty, dry weather. Then at last came rain. And the water from the sky poured on the tails of the animals and softened them.

Then the chilly chills came whistling with icy mittens, and they froze all the tails stiff. A big wind blew up and blew and blew till all the tails of the animals blew off.

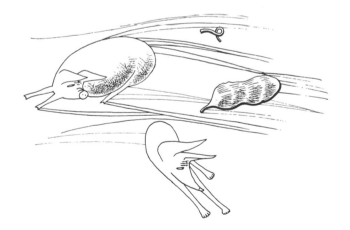

It was easy for the fat stub hogs with their fat stub tails. But it was not so easy for the blue fox who uses his tail to help him when he runs, when he eats, when he walks or talks, when he makes pictures or writes letters in the snow, or when he puts a snack of bacon meat with stripes of fat and lean to hide till he wants it under a big rock by a river.

It was easy enough for the rabbit who has long ears and no tail at all except a white thumb of cotton. But it was hard for the yellow flongboo who at night lights up his house in a hollow tree with his fire yellow torch of a tail. It is hard for the yellow flongboo to lose his tail because it lights up his way when he sneaks at night on the prairie, sneaking up on the flangwayers, the hippers and hangjasts, so good to eat.

The animals picked a committee of representatives to represent them in a parleyhoo to see what steps could be taken by talking to do something. There were sixty-six representatives on the committee, and they decided to call it the Committee of Sixty-Six. It was a distinguished committee, and when they all sat together holding their mouths under their noses (just like a distinguished committee) and blinking their eyes up over their noses and cleaning their ears and scratching themselves under the chin looking thoughtful (just like a distinguished committee), then anybody would say just to look at them, "This must be quite a distinguished committee."

Of course, they would all have looked more distinguished if they had had their tails on. If the big wavy streak of a blue tail blows off behind a blue fox, he doesn't look near so distinguished. Or, if the long yellow torch of a tail blows off behind a yellow flongboo, he doesn't look so distinguished as he did before the wind blew.

So the Committee of Sixty-Six had a meeting and a parleyhoo to decide what steps could be taken by talking to do something. For chairman they picked an old flongboo who was an umpire and used to umpire many mix-ups. Among the flongboos he was called "the umpire of umpires," "the king of umpires," "the prince of umpires," "the peer of umpires." When there was a fight and a snag and a wrangle between two families living next-door neighbors to each other and this old flongboo was called in to umpire and to say which family was right and which family was wrong, which family started it and which family ought to stop it, he used to say, "The best umpire is the one who knows just how far to go and how far not to go." He was from Massachusetts, born near Chappaquiddick, this old flongboo, and he lived there in a horse chestnut tree six feet thick halfway between South Hadley and Northampton. And at night, before he lost his tail, he lighted up the big hollow cave inside the horse chestnut tree with his yellow torch of a tail.

After he was nominated with speeches and elected with votes to be the chairman, he stood up on the platform and took a gavel and banged with the gavel and made the Committee of Sixty-Six come to order.

"It is no picnic to lose your tail, and we are here for business," he said, banging his gavel again.

A blue fox from Waco, Texas, with his ears full of dry bluebonnet leaves from a hole where he lived near the Brazos River, stood up and said, "Mr. Chairman, do I have the floor?"

"You have whatever you get away with—I get your number," said the chairman.

"I make a motion," said the blue fox from Waco, "and I move you, sir, that this committee get on a train at Philadelphia and ride on the train till it stops and then take another train and take more trains and keep on riding till we get to Medicine Hat, near the Saskatchewan River, in the Winnipeg wheat country where the Head Spotter of the Weather Makers sits on a high stool in a high tower on a high hill spotting the weather. There we will ask him if he will respectfully let us beseech him to bring back weather that will bring back our tails. It was the weather took away our tails; it is the weather can bring back our tails."

"All in favor of the motion," said the chairman, "will clean their right ears with their right paws."

And all the blue foxes and all the yellow flongboos began cleaning their right ears with their right paws.

"All who are against the motion will clean their left ears with their left paws," said the chairman.

And all the blue foxes and all the yellow flongboos began cleaning their left ears with their left paws.

"The motion is carried both ways—it is a razmataz," said the chairman. "Once again, all in favor of the motion will stand up on the toes of their hind legs and stick their noses straight up in the air."

And all the blue foxes and all the yellow flongboos stood up on the toes of their hind legs and stuck their noses straight up in the air.

"And now," said the chairman, "all who are against the motion will stand on the top and the apex of their heads, stick their hind legs straight up in the air, and make a noise like a woof woof."

And then not one of the blue foxes and not one of the yellow flongboos stood on the top and the apex of his head, nor stuck his hind legs up in the air, nor made a noise like a woof woof.

"The motion is carried, and this is no picnic," said the chairman.

So the committee went to Philadelphia to get on a train to ride on.

"Would you be so kind as to tell us the way to the union depot?" the chairman asked a policeman. It was the first time a flongboo ever spoke to a policeman on the streets of Philadelphia.

"It pays to be polite," said the policeman.

"May I ask you again if you would kindly direct us to the union depot? We wish to ride on a train," said the flongboo.

"Polite persons and angry persons are different kinds," said the policeman.

The flongboo's eyes changed their lights, and a slow torch of fire sprang out behind where his tail used to be. And speaking to the policeman, he said, "Sir, I must inform you, publicly and respectfully, that we are the Committee of Sixty-Six. We are honorable and distinguished representatives from places your honest and ignorant geography never told you about. This committee is going to ride on the cars to Medicine Hat near the Saskatchewan River in the Winnipeg wheat country where the blizzards and chinooks begin. We have a special message and a secret errand for the Head Spotter of the Weather Makers."

"I am a polite friend of all respectable people—that is why I wear this star to arrest people who are not respectable," said the policeman, touching with his pointing finger the silver and nickel star fastened with a safety pin on his blue uniform coat.

"This is the first time ever in the history of the United States that a committee of sixty-six blue foxes and flongboos has ever visited a city in the United States," insinuated the flongboo.

"I beg to be mistaken," finished the policeman. "The union depot is under that clock." And he pointed to a clock nearby.

"I thank you for myself, I thank you for the Committee of Sixty-Six, I thank you for the sake of all the animals in the United States who have lost their tails," finished the chairman.

Over to the Philadelphia union depot they went, all sixty-six, half blue foxes, half flongboos. As they pattered pitty-pat, pitty-pat, each with feet and toenails, ears and hair, everything but tails, into the Philadelphia union depot, they had nothing to say. And yet though they had nothing to say, the passengers in the union depot waiting for trains thought they had something to say and were saying it. So the passengers in the union depot waiting for trains listened. But with all their listening the passengers never heard the blue foxes and yellow flongboos say anything.

"They are saying it to each other in some strange language from where they belong," said one passenger, waiting for a train.

"They have secrets to keep among each other and never tell us," said another passenger.

"We will find out all about it reading the newspapers upside down tomorrow morning," said a third passenger.

Then the blue foxes and the yellow flongboos pattered pitty-pat, pitty-pat, each with feet and toenails, ears and hair, everything except tails, pattered scritch scratch over the stone floors out into the train shed. They climbed into a special smoking car hooked on ahead of the engine.

"This car hooked on ahead of the engine was put on special for us so we will always be ahead, and we will get there before the train does," said the chairman to the committee.

The train ran out of the train shed. It kept on the tracks and never left the rails. It came to the Horseshoe Curve near Altoona where the tracks bend like a big horseshoe. Instead of going around the long winding bend of the horseshoe tracks up and around the mountains, the train acted different. The train jumped off the tracks down into the valley and cut across in a straight line on a cutoff, jumped on the tracks again, and went on toward Ohio.

The conductor said, "If you are going to jump the train off the tracks, tell us about it beforehand."

"When we lost our tails, nobody told us about it beforehand," said the old flongboo umpire.

Two baby blue foxes, the youngest on the committee, sat on the front platform. Mile after mile of chimneys went by. Four hundred smokestacks stood in a row, and tubs on tubs of sooty black soot marched out.

"This is the place where the black cats come to be washed," said the first baby blue fox.

"I believe your affidavit," said the second blue fox.

Crossing Ohio and Indiana at night, the flongboos took off the roof of the car. The conductor told them, "I must have an explanation."

"It was between us and the stars," they told him.

The train ran into Chicago. That afternoon there were pictures upside down in the newspapers showing the blue foxes and the yellow flongboos climbing telephone poles standing on their heads eating pink ice cream with iron axes.

Each blue fox and yellow flongboo got a newspaper for himself, and each one looked long and careful upside down to see how he looked in the picture in the newspaper climbing a telephone pole standing on his head eating pink ice cream with an iron ax.

Crossing Minnesota, the sky began to fill with the snow ghosts of Minnesota snow weather. Again the foxes and flongboos lifted the roof off the car, telling the conductor they would rather wreck the train than miss the big show of the snow ghosts of the first Minnesota snow weather of the winter.

Some went to sleep, but the two baby blue foxes stayed up all night watching the snow ghosts and telling snow ghost stories to each other.

Early in the night the first baby blue fox said to the second, "Who are the snow ghosts the ghosts of?"

The second baby blue fox answered, "Everybody who makes a snowball, a snowman, a snow fox or a snow fish or a snow pattycake, everybody has a snow ghost."

And that was only the beginning of their talk. It would take a big book to tell all that the two baby foxes told each other that night about the Minnesota snow ghosts, because they sat up all night telling old stories their fathers and mothers and grandfathers and grandmothers told them, and making up new stories never heard before about where the snow ghosts go on Christmas morning and how the snow ghosts watch the New Year in.

Somewhere between Winnipeg and Moose Jaw, somewhere it was they stopped the train, and all ran out in the snow where the white moon was shining down a valley of birch trees. It was the Snowbird Valley where all the snowbirds of Canada come early in the winter and make their snowshoes.

At last they came to Medicine Hat, near the Saskatchewan River, where the blizzards and the chinooks begin, where nobody works unless they have to, and they nearly all have to. There they ran in the snow till they came to the place where the Head Spotter of the Weather Makers sits on a high stool in a high tower on a high hill watching the weather.

"Let loose another big wind to blow back our tails to us, let loose a big freeze to freeze our tails onto us again, and so let us get back our lost tails," they said to the Head Spotter of the Weather Makers.

Which was just what he did, giving them exactly what they wanted, so they all went back home satisfied, the blue foxes each with a big wavy brush of a tail to help him when he runs, when he eats, when he walks or talks, when he makes pictures or writes letters in the snow, or when he puts a snack of bacon meat with stripes of fat and lean to hide till he wants it under a big rock by the river—and the yellow flongboos each with a long yellow torch of a tail to light up his home in a hollow tree or to light up his way when he sneaks at night on the prairie, sneaking up on the flangwayer, the hipper, or the hangjast.

❀ ROOTABAGA PIGEONS

To Three Illinois Pigeons

✿ ✿ ✿

Two Stories Told by the Potato Face Blind Man

PEOPLE: *Blixie Bimber*
Blixie Bimber's mother
The Potato Face Blind Man
A green rat with the rheumatism
Bricklayers
Mortar men
Riveters
A skyscraper

Slipfoot
A stairway to the moon
A trapeze

THE SKYSCRAPER TO THE MOON AND HOW THE GREEN RAT WITH THE RHEUMATISM RAN A THOUSAND MILES TWICE

BLIXIE BIMBER'S MOTHER was chopping hash. And the hatchet broke. So Blixie started downtown with fifteen cents to buy a new hash hatchet for chopping hash.

Downtown she peeped around the corner next nearest the post office where the Potato Face Blind Man sat with his accordion. And the old man had his legs crossed, one foot on the sidewalk, the other foot up in the air.

The foot up in the air had a green rat sitting on it, tying the old man's shoestrings in knots and double knots. Whenever the old man's foot wiggled and wriggled, the green rat wiggled and wriggled.

The tail of the rat wrapped five wraps around the shoe and then fastened and tied like a package.

On the back of the green rat was a long white swipe from the end of the nose to the end of the tail. Two little white swipes stuck up over the eyelashes. And five short, thick swipes of white played pussy-wants-a-corner back of the ears and along the ribs of the green rat.

They were talking, the old man and the green rat, talking about alligators and why the alligators keep their baby shoes locked up in trunks over the wintertime—and why the rats in the moon lock their mittens in iceboxes.

"I had the rheumatism last summer a year ago," said the rat. "I had the rheumatism so bad I ran a thousand miles south and west till I came to the Egg Towns and stopped in the Village of Eggs Up."

"So?" quizzed the Potato Face.

"There in the Village of Eggs Up, they asked me, 'Do you know how to stop the moon moving?' I answered them, 'Yes, I know how —a baby alligator told me—but I told the baby alligator I wouldn't tell.' "

"Many years ago there in that Village of Eggs Up they started making a skyscraper to go up till it reached the moon. They said, 'We will step in the elevator and go up to the roof and sit on the roof and eat supper on the moon.'

"The bricklayers and the mortar men and the iron riveters and the wheelbarrowers and the plasterers went higher and higher making that skyscraper, till at last they were halfway up to the moon, saying to each other while they worked, 'We will step in the elevator and go up to the roof and sit on the roof and eat supper on the moon.'

"Yes, they were halfway up to the moon. And that night looking at the moon, they saw it move, and they said to each other, 'We must stop the moon moving,' and they said later, 'We don't know how to stop the moon moving.'

"And the bricklayers and the mortar men and the iron riveters and the wheelbarrowers and the plasterers said to each other, 'If we go on now and make this skyscraper, it will miss the moon, and we will never go up in the elevator and sit on the roof and eat supper on the moon.'

"So they took the skyscraper down and started making it over again, aiming it straight at the moon again. And one night standing looking at the moon, they saw it move, and they said to each other,

'We must stop the moon moving,' saying later to each other, 'We don't know how to stop the moon moving.'

"And now they stand in the streets at night there in the Village of Eggs Up, stretching their necks looking at the moon and asking each other, 'Why does the moon move, and how can we stop the moon moving?'

"Whenever I saw them standing there stretching their necks looking at the moon, I had a zigzag ache in my left hind foot, and I wanted to tell them what the baby alligator told me, the secret of how to stop the moon moving. One night that ache zigzagged me so—way inside my left hind foot—it zigzagged so I ran home here a thousand miles."

The Potato Face Blind Man wriggled his shoe—and the green rat wriggled—and the long white swipe from the end of the nose to the end of the tail of the green rat wriggled.

"Is your rheumatism better?" the old man asked.

The rat answered, "Any rheumatism is better if you run a thousand miles twice."

And Blixie Bimber going home with the fifteen-cent hash hatchet for her mother to chop hash, Blixie said to herself, "It is a large morning to be thoughtful about."

SLIPFOOT AND HOW HE NEARLY ALWAYS NEVER GETS WHAT HE GOES AFTER

BLIXIE BIMBER FLIPPED out of the kitchen one morning, first saying good-by to the dishpan, good-by to the dishrag, good-by to the dish towel for wiping dishes.

Under one arm she put a basket of peonies she picked; under the other arm she put a basket of jonquils she picked.

Then she flipped away up the street and downtown, where she put the baskets of peonies and jonquils one on each side of the Potato Face Blind Man.

"I picked the pink and lavender peonies and I picked the yellow jonquils for you to be smelling one on each side of you this fine early summer morning," she said to the Potato Face. "Have you seen anybody good to see lately?"

"Slipfoot was here this morning," said the old man.

"And who is Slipfoot?" asked Blixie.

"I don't know. He says to me, 'I got a foot always slips. I used to wash windows—and my foot slips. I used to be king of the collar buttons, king of a million dollars—and my foot slips. I used to be king of the peanuts, king of a million dollars again. I used to be king of the oyster cans, selling a million cans a day. I used to be king of the peanut sacks, selling ten million sacks a day. And every time I was a king, my foot slips. Every time I had a million dollars, my foot slips. Every time I went high and put my foot higher, my foot slips. Somebody gave me a slipfoot. I always slip.' "

"So you call him Slipfoot?" asked Blixie.

"Yes," said the old man.

"Has he been here before?"

"Yes, he was here a year ago, saying, 'I marry a woman, and she runs away. I run after her—and my foot slips. I always get what I want—and then my foot slips.

" 'I ran up a stairway to the moon one night. I shoveled a big sackful of little gold beans, little gold bricks, little gold bugs, on the moon, and I ran down the stairway from the moon. On the last step of the stairway, my foot slips—and all the little gold beans, all the little gold bricks, all the little gold bugs, spill out and spill away. When I get down the stairway, I am holding the sack, and the sack holds nothing. I am all right always till my foot slips.

" 'I jump on a trapeze, and I go swinging, swinging, swinging out where I am going to take hold of the rainbow and bring it down where we can look at it close. And I hang by my feet on the trapeze, and I am swinging out where I am just ready to take hold of the rainbow and bring it down. Then my foot slips.' "

"What is the matter with Slipfoot?" asks Blixie.

"He asks me that same question," answered the Potato Face Blind Man. "He asks me that every time he comes here. I tell him all he needs is to get his slipfoot fixed so it won't slip. Then he'll be all right."

"I understand you," said Blixie. "You make it easy. You always make it easy. And before I run away, will you promise me to smell of the pink and lavender peonies and the yellow jonquils all day today?"

"I promise," said the Potato Face. "Promises are easy. I like promises."

"So do I," said the little girl. "It's promises pushing me back home to the dishpan, the dishrag, and the dish towel for wiping dishes."

"Look out you don't get a slipfoot," warned the old man as the girl flipped up the street going home.

❁ ❁ ❁

Two Stories About Bugs and Eggs

PEOPLE: *Little bugs*
Big bugs
The Rag Doll
The Broom Handle
Hammer and Nails
The Hot Cookie Pan
The Ice Tongs
The Coal Bucket
The Potato Sack
The Bushel Basket
Jack Knife
Kindling Wood
Splinters

Shush Shush
The postmaster
The hardware man
The policeman
The postmaster's hat
A buff banty egg

MANY, MANY WEDDINGS IN ONE CORNER HOUSE

THERE WAS A corner house with corners every way it looked. And up in the corners were bugs with little bug houses, bug doors to open, bug windows to look out of.

In the summertime if the evening was cool or in the wintertime if the evening was warm, they played games—bugs-up, bugs-down, run-bugs-run, beans-bugs-beans.

This corner house was the place the Rag Doll and the Broom Handle came to after their wedding. This was the same time those old people, Hammer and Nails, moved into the corner house with all the little Hammers and all the little Nails.

So there they were, the young couple, the Rag Doll and the Broom Handle, and that old family, Hammer and Nails, and up in the corners among the eave troughs and the roof shingles, the bugs with little bug houses, bug doors to open, bug windows to look out of, and bug games—bugs-up, bugs-down, run-bugs-run, or beans-bugs-beans.

Around the corner of the house every Saturday morning came the Hot Cookie Pan with a pan of hot cookies for Sunday, Monday, Tuesday, Wednesday, and the rest of the week.

The Ice Tongs came with ice, the Coal Bucket came with coal, the Potato Sack came with potatoes. And the Bushel Basket was always going or coming and saying under his breath, *"Bushels, bushels, bushels."*

One day the bugs in the little bug houses opened the bug doors and looked out of the bug windows and said to each other, "They are washing their shirts and sewing on buttons—there is going to be a wedding."

And the next day the bugs said, "They are going to have a wedding and a wedding breakfast for Jack Knife and Kindling Wood. They are asking everybody in the kitchen, the cellar, and the backyard to come."

The wedding day came. The people came. From all over the kitchen, the cellar, the backyard, they came. The Rag Doll and the

Broom Handle were there. Hammer and Nails and all the little Hammers and all the little Nails were there. The Ice Tongs, the Coal Bucket, the Potato Sack, were all there—and the Bushel Basket going and coming and saying under his breath, *"Bushels, bushels, bushels."* And, of course, the Hot Cookie Pan was there hopping up and down with hot cookies.

So Jack Knife and Kindling Wood began living in the corner house. A child came. They named her Splinters. And the Hot Cookie Pan and Splinters met and kissed each other and sat together in cozy corners close to each other.

And the bugs high up in the corners in the little bug houses, they opened the bug doors, looked out of the bug windows, and said, "They are washing their shirts and sewing on buttons. There is a wedding again—the Hot Cookie Pan and Splinters."

And now they have many, many children, the Hot Cookie Pan and Splinters. Their children have gone all over the world, and everybody knows them.

"Whenever you find a splinter or a sliver or a shiny little shaving of wood in a hot cookie," the bugs in the little bug houses say, "whenever you find a splinter or a sliver or a shiny little shaving of wood in a hot cookie, it is the child of the Hot Cookie Pan and the girl named Splinters, the daughter of Jack Knife and Kindling Wood, who grew up and married the Hot Cookie Pan."

And sometimes if a little bug asks a big bug a queer, quivvical, quizzical question hard to answer, the big bug opens a bug door, looks out of a bug window, and says to the little bug, "If you don't believe what we tell you, go and ask Hammer and Nails or any of the little Hammers and Nails. Then run and listen to the Bushel Basket going and coming and saying under his breath, *'Bushels, bushels, bushels.'* "

SHUSH SHUSH, THE BIG BUFF BANTY HEN WHO LAID AN EGG IN THE POSTMASTER'S HAT

SHUSH SHUSH WAS a big buff banty hen. She lived in a coop. Sometimes she marched out of the coop and went away and laid eggs. But always she came back to the coop.

And whenever she went to the front door and laid an egg in the doorbell, she rang the bell once for one egg, twice for two eggs, and a dozen rings for a dozen eggs.

Once Shush Shush went into the house of the Sniggers family and laid an egg in the piano. Another time she climbed up in the clock and laid an egg in the clock. But always she came back to the coop.

One summer morning Shush Shush marched out through the front gate, up to the next corner and the next, till she came to the post office. There she walked into the office of the postmaster and laid an egg in the postmaster's hat.

The postmaster put on his hat, went to the hardware store, and bought a keg of nails. He took off his hat, and the egg dropped into the keg of nails.

The hardware man picked up the egg, put it in *his* hat, and went out to speak to a policeman. He took off his hat, speaking to the policeman, and the egg dropped on the sidewalk.

The policeman picked up the egg and put it in *his* police hat. The postmaster came past; the policeman took off his police hat, and the egg dropped down on the sidewalk.

The postmaster said, "I lost that egg—it is my egg," picked it up, put it in his postmaster's hat, and forgot all about having an egg in his hat.

Then the postmaster, a long, tall man, came to the door of the post office, a short, small door. And the postmaster didn't stoop low, didn't bend under, so he bumped his hat and his head on the top of the doorway. And the egg *broke* and ran down over his face and neck.

And long before that happened, Shush Shush was home in her coop, standing in the door saying, "It is a big day for me because I laid one of my big buff banty eggs in the postmaster's hat."

There Shush Shush stays, living in a coop. Sometimes she marches out of the coop and goes away and lays eggs in pianos, clocks, hats. But she always come back to the coop.

And whenever she goes to the front door and lays an egg in the doorbell, she rings the bell once for one egg, twice for two eggs, and a dozen rings for a dozen eggs.

❀ ❀ ❀

Five Stories About Hatrack the Horse, Six Pigeons, Three Wild Babylonian Baboons, Six Umbrellas, Bozo the Button Buster

PEOPLE: *Hatrack the Horse*
Peter Potato Blossom Wishes
Ragbag Mammy
Gimmes

Wiffle the Chick
Chickamauga
Chattanooga
Chattahoochee
Blue Mist
Bubbles
Wednesday Evening in the Twilight and the Gloaming
Telegrams

The three wild Babylonian Baboons
Three umbrellas
The night policeman

Six umbrellas
The big umbrella
Straw hats
Dippy the Wisp

Bozo the Button Buster
A mouse
Deep Red Roses
The Beans Are Burning
Sweeter Than the Bees Humming

HOW RAGBAG MAMMY KEPT HER SECRET
WHILE THE WIND BLEW AWAY
THE VILLAGE OF HATPINS

THERE WAS A horseface man in the Village of Cream Puffs. People called him Hatrack the Horse.

The skin stretched tight over his bones. Once a little girl said, "His eyes look like lightning bugs lighting up the summer night coming out of two little doors."

When Hatrack the Horse took *off* his hat, he reached his hand around behind and hung the hat *on* a shoulder bone sticking out.

When he wanted to put *on* his hat, he reached his hand around and took it *off* from where it was hanging on the shoulder bone sticking out behind.

One summer Hatrack said to Peter Potato Blossom Wishes, "I am going away up north and west in the Rootabaga Country to see the towns different from each other. Then I will come back east as far as I went west, and south as far as I went north, till I am back again where my little pal, Peter Potato Blossom Wishes, lives in the Village of Cream Puffs."

So he went away, going north and west and coming back east and south till he was back again in his home town, sitting on the front steps of his little red shanty, fixing a kite to fly.

"Are you glad to come back?" asked Peter.

"Yes, this is home; this is the only place where I know how the winds act up so I can talk to them when I fly a kite."

"Tell me what you saw and how you listened and if they handed you any nice packages."

"They handed me packages, all right, all right," said Hatrack the Horse.

"Away far to the west I came to the Village of Hatpins," he went on. "It is the place where they make all the hatpins for the hats to be pinned on in the Rootabaga Country. They asked me about the Village of Cream Puffs and how the winds are here, because the winds here blow so many hats off that the Village of Hatpins sells more hatpins to the people here than anywhere else.

"There is an old woman in the Village of Hatpins. She walks across the town and around the town every morning and every afternoon. On her back is a big ragbag. She never takes anything out of the ragbag. She never puts anything in. That is, nobody ever sees her put anything in or take anything out. She has never opened the ragbag telling people to take a look and see what is in it. She sleeps with the ragbag for a pillow. So it is always with her, and nobody looks into it unless she lets them. And she never lets them.

"Her name? Everybody calls her Ragbag Mammy. She wears aprons with big pockets. And though she never speaks to big grown-up people, she is always glad to meet little growing people, boys and girls. And especially, most of all, she likes to meet boys and girls who say, 'Gimme' (once, like that) or 'Gimme, gimme' (twice, like that) or 'Gimme, gimme, gimme' (three times) or 'Gimme, gimme, gimme, gimme, gimme, gimme' (more times than we can count). She likes to meet the gimmes because she digs into her pockets and brings out square chocolate drops and round chocolate drops and chocolate drops shaped like a half-moon, barber-pole candy with red and white stripes wrapped around it, all-day suckers so long they last not only all day but all this week and all next week, and different kinds of jackstones, some that say chink-chink on the sidewalks and some that say teentsy-weentsy chink-chink when they all bunch together on the sidewalk. And sometimes if one of the gimmes is crying and feeling bad, she gives the gimme a doll only as big as a child's hand, but the doll can say the alphabet and sing little Chinese-Assyrian songs.

"Of course," said Hatrack the Horse, reaching his hand around to see if his hat was hanging on behind, "of course, you have to have sharp ears and listen close up and be nice when you are listening if you are going to hear a doll say the alphabet and sing little Chinese-Assyrian songs."

"I could hear them," said Peter Potato Blossom Wishes. "I am a nice listener. I could hear those dolls sing the little Chinese-Assyrian songs."

"I believe you, little pal of mine," said Hatrack. "I know you have the ears, and you know how to put your ears so you hear."

"Of course, every morning and every afternoon when Ragbag Mammy walks across the town and around the town in the Village of Hatpins, people ask her what is in the ragbag on her back. And she answers, 'It is a nice day we are having,' or, 'I think the rain will stop when it stops raining, don't you?' Then if they ask again and beg and plead, *What* is in the ragbag? What *is* in the ragbag?' she tells them, 'When the wind blows away the Village of Hatpins and blows it so far away it never comes back, then—then, then, then—I will tell you what is in the ragbag.' "

"One day the wind came along and blew the Village of Hatpins loose and, after blowing it loose, carried it high off in the sky. And the people were saying to each other, 'Well, now we are going to hear Ragbag Mammy tell us what is in the ragbag.'

"And the wind kept blowing, carrying the Village of Hatpins higher and farther and farther and higher. And when at last it went away so high it came to a white cloud, the hatpins in the village all stuck out and fastened the village to the cloud so the wind couldn't blow it any farther.

"And—after a while they pulled the hatpins out of the cloud—and the village dropped back right down where it was before.

"And Ragbag Mammy goes every morning and every afternoon with the ragbag on her back across and around the town. And sometimes people say to her, 'The next time the wind blows us away—the next time the wind will blow us so far there won't be any cloud to fasten hatpins in—and you will have to tell us what is in the ragbag.' And Ragbag Mammy just answers, 'Yes, yes—yes—yes,' and goes on her way looking for the next boy or girl to say, 'Gimme' (once, like that) or 'Gimme, gimme' (twice, like that) or 'Gimme, gimme, gimme, gimme, gimme' (more times than we can count).

"And if a child is crying, she digs into her pockets and pulls out the doll that says the alphabet and sings little Chinese-Assyrian songs."

"And," said Peter Potato Blossom Wishes, "you have to listen close up with your ears and be nice when you are listening."

"In the Village of Hatpins that the wind nearly blew away forever," said Hatrack the Horse.

And Peter Potato Blossom Wishes skipped away down from the little red shanty, skipped down the street, and then began walking slow saying to herself, "I love Hatrack the Horse like a granduncle—his eyes look like lightning bugs lighting up the summer night coming out of two little doors."

HOW SIX PIGEONS CAME BACK TO HATRACK THE HORSE AFTER MANY ACCIDENTS AND SIX TELEGRAMS

SIX CROOKED LADDERS stood against the front of the shanty where Hatrack the Horse lived.

Yellow roses all on fire were climbing up and down the ladders, up and down and crossways.

And leaning out on both sides from the crooked ladders were vines of yellow roses, leaning, curving, nearly falling.

Hatrack the Horse was waiting. This was the morning Wiffle the Chick was coming.

"Sit here on the cracker box and listen," he said to her when she came; "listen and you will hear the roses saying, 'This is climbing time for all yellow roses, and climbing time is the time to climb; how did we ever learn to climb only by climbing? Listen and you will hear—st

. . . th . . . st . . . th . . . st . . . th . . . it is the feet of the yellow roses climbing up and down and leaning out and curving and nearly falling . . . st . . . th . . . st . . . th . . .' "

So Wiffle the Chick sat there, early in the summer, enjoying herself, sitting on a cracker box, listening to the yellow roses climb around the six crooked ladders.

Hatrack the Horse came out. On his shoulders were two pigeons, on his hands two pigeons. And he reached his hand around behind his back where his hat was hanging, and he opened the hat and showed Wiffle the Chick two pigeons in the hat.

"They are lovely pigeons to look at, and their eyes are full of lessons to learn," said Wiffle the Chick. "Maybe you will tell me why you have their feet wrapped in bandages, hospital liniment bandages full of hospital liniment smells? Why do you put soft mittens on the feet of these pigeons so lovely to look at?"

"They came back yesterday; they came back home," was the answer. "They came back limping on their feet with the toes turned in so far they nearly turned backward. When they put their bleeding feet in my hands one by one each one, it was like each one was writing his name in my hand with red ink."

"Did you know they were coming?" asked Wiffle.

"Every day the last six days I get a telegram, six telegrams from six pigeons—and at last they come home. And ever since they come home, they are telling me they come because they love Hatrack the Horse and the yellow climbing roses climbing over the six crooked ladders."

"Did you name your pigeons with names?" asked Wiffle.

"These three, the sandy and golden brown, all named themselves by where they came from. This is Chickamauga, here is Chattanooga, and this is Chattahoochee. And the other three all got their names from me when I was feeling high and easy. This is Blue Mist, here is Bubbles, and last of all take a look at Wednesday Evening in the Twilight and the Gloaming."

"Do you always call her Wednesday Evening in the Twilight and the Gloaming?"

"Not when I am making coffee for breakfast. If I am making coffee for breakfast, then I just call her Wednesday Evening."

"Didn't you tie the mittens on her feet extra special nice?"

"Yes—she is an extra special nice pigeon. She cries for pity when she wants pity. And she shuts her eyes when she doesn't want to look at you. And if you look deep in her eyes when her eyes are open, you will see lights there exactly like the lights on the pastures and the meadows when the mist is drifting on a Wednesday evening just between the twilight and the gloaming.

"A week ago yesterday they all went away. And they won't tell why they went away. Somebody clipped their wings, cut off their flying feathers so they couldn't fly—and they won't tell why. They were six hundred miles from home—but they won't tell how they counted the six hundred miles. A hundred miles a day they walked, six hundred miles in a week, and they sent a telegram to me every day, one writing a telegram one day and another writing a telegram the next day —all the time walking a hundred miles a day with their toes turned in like pigeon toes turn in. Do you wonder they needed bandages, hospital liniment bandages on their feet—and soft mittens?"

"Show me the telegrams they sent you, one every day, for six days while they were walking six hundred miles on their pigeon toes."

So Hatrack the Horse got the six telegrams. The reading on the telegrams was like this:

1. "Feet are as good as wings if you have to. CHICKAMAUGA."

2. "If you love to go somewhere, it is easy to walk. CHATTANOOGA."

3. "In the night sleeping you forget whether you have wings or feet or neither. CHATTAHOOCHEE."

4. "What are toes for if they don't point to what you want? BLUE MIST."

5. "Anybody can walk hundreds of miles putting one foot ahead of the other. BUBBLES."

6. "Pity me. Far is far. Near is near. And there is no place like home when the yellow roses climb up the ladders and sing in the early summer. Pity me. WEDNESDAY EVENING IN THE TWILIGHT AND THE GLOAMING."

"Did they have any accidents going six hundred miles walking with their little pigeon toes turned in?" asked Wiffle.

"Once they had an accident," said Hatrack, with Chattahoochee standing in his hat, Chickamauga on his right shoulder, Chattanooga on his left, and holding Blue Mist and Bubbles on his wrists. "They came to an old wooden bridge. Chattahoochee and Wednesday Evening both cried out, 'The bridge will fall if we all walk on it the same time!' But they were all six already on the bridge, and the bridge began sagging and tumbled them all into the river. But it was good for them all to have a footbath for their feet, Wednesday Evening explained."

"I got a suspicion you like Wednesday Evening in the Twilight and the Gloaming best of all," spoke up Wiffle.

"Well, Wednesday Evening was the only one I noticed making any mention of the yellow roses in her telegram," Hatrack the Horse explained as he picked up Wednesday Evening and reached her around and put her to perch on the shoulder bone on his back.

Then the old man and the girl sat on the cracker box saying nothing, only listening to the yellow roses all on fire with early summer climbing up the crooked ladders, up and down and crossways, some of them leaning out and curving and nearly falling.

HOW THE THREE WILD BABYLONIAN BABOONS WENT AWAY IN THE RAIN EATING BREAD AND BUTTER

ONE MORNING WHEN Hatrack the Horse went away from his shanty, he put three umbrellas in the corner next to the front door.

His pointing finger pointed at the three umbrellas as he said, "If the three wild Babylonian Baboons come sneaking up to this shanty and sneaking through the door and sneaking through the house, then all you three umbrellas open up like it was raining, jump straight at the baboons, and fasten your handles in their hands. Then, all three of you stay open as if it was raining—and hold those handles in the hands of the baboons and never let go till I come."

Hatrack the Horse went away. The three umbrellas stood in the corner next to the front door. And when the umbrellas listened, they could hear the three wild Babylonian Baboons sneaking up to the shanty. Soon the baboons, all hairy all over, bangs down their foreheads, came sneaking through the door. Just as they were sneaking through the door, they took off their hats to show they were getting ready to sneak through the house.

Then the three umbrellas in the corner opened up as if it was raining; they jumped straight at the three wild Babylonian Baboons; and they fastened their handles tight in the hands of the baboons and wouldn't let go.

So there were the three wild Babylonian Baboons, each with a hat in his left hand and an open umbrella in his right hand.

When Hatrack the Horse came home, he came, quiet. He opened the front door, quiet. Then he looked around inside the house, quiet.

In the corner where he had stood the three umbrellas, he saw the three wild Babylonian Baboons on the floor, sleeping, with umbrellas over their faces.

"The umbrellas were so big they couldn't get through the door," said Hatrack the Horse. For a long time he stood looking at the bangs hanging down the foreheads of the baboons while they were sleeping. He took a comb and combed the bangs down the foreheads of the baboons. He went to the cupboard and spread bread and butter. He took the hats out of the left hands of the baboons and put the hats on their heads. He put a piece of bread and butter in the hand of each baboon.

After that he snipped each one across the nose with his finger (*snippety-snip!* just like that). They opened their eyes and stood up. Then he loosened the umbrella handles from their right hands and led them to the door.

They all looked out. It was raining. "Now you can go," he told the baboons. And they all walked out of the front door, and they seemed to be snickering and hiding the snickers.

The last he saw of them they were walking away in the rain eating bread and butter. And they took off their hats so the rain ran down and slid off on the bangs of their foreheads.

Hatrack the Horse turned to the umbrellas and said, "We know how to make a surprise party when we get a visit from the Babylonian Baboons with their bangs falling down their foreheads—don't we?"

That is what happened as Hatrack the Horse told it to the night policeman in the Village of Cream Puffs.

HOW SIX UMBRELLAS TOOK OFF THEIR STRAW HATS TO SHOW RESPECT TO THE ONE BIG UMBRELLA

WHEREVER DIPPY THE Wisp went, she was always changing hats. She carried two hatboxes with big picture hats on her *right* arm. And she carried two hatboxes with big picture hats on her *left* arm. And she changed from green and gold hats to purple and gray hats and then back to green and gold whenever she felt like it.

Now the hill that runs down from the shanty of Hatrack the Horse toward the Village of Cream Puffs is a long, long hill. And one morning the old man sat watching, and away down at the bottom of the long, long hill he saw four hatboxes. Somebody was coming to call on him. And he knew it was Dippy the Wisp.

The hatboxes came up the hill. He saw them stop once, stop twice, stop more times. So he knew Dippy the Wisp was changing hats, changing from green and gold to purple and gray and then back to green and gold.

When at last she got to the top of the hill and came to the shanty of Hatrack the Horse, she said to him, "Make up a story and tell me. Make up the story about umbrellas. You have traveled all over the Rootabaga Country; you have seen so many umbrellas, and such wonderful umbrellas. Make me up a big elegant story about umbrellas."

So Hatrack the Horse took his hat *off* his head, reached around, and hung it *on* one of the shoulder bones sticking out behind on his back. And the old man looked with a faraway look down the long, long hill running from his shanty toward the Village of Cream Puffs. Then he told her this story:

"One summer afternoon I came home and found all the umbrellas sitting in the kitchen, with straw hats on, telling each other who they are.

"The umbrella that feeds the fishes fresh buns every morning stood up and said, 'I am the umbrella that feeds the fishes fresh buns every morning.'

"The umbrella that fixes the clocks free of charge stood up and said, 'I am the umbrella that fixes the clocks free of charge.'

"The umbrella that peels the potatoes with a pencil and makes a pink ink with the peelings stood up and said, 'I am the umbrella that peels the potatoes with a pencil and makes a pink ink with the peelings.'

"The umbrella that eats the rats with pepper and salt and a clean napkin every morning stood up and said, 'I am the umbrella that eats the rats with pepper and salt and a clean napkin every morning.'

"The umbrella that washes the dishes with a wiper and wipes the dishes with a washer every morning stood up and said, 'I am the umbrella that washes the dishes with a wiper and wipes the dishes with a washer every morning.'

"The umbrella that covers the chimney with a dishpan before it rains stood up and said, 'I am the umbrella that covers the chimney with a dishpan before it rains.'

"The umbrella that runs to the corner to get corners for the hand-kerchiefs stood up and said, 'I am the umbrella that runs to the corner to get corners for the handkerchiefs.'

"Now while the umbrellas are all sitting in the kitchen with their straw hats on telling each other who they are, there comes a big black stranger of an umbrella walking into the kitchen without opening the door, walking in without knocking, without asking anybody, without telling anybody beforehand.

" 'Since we are telling each other who we are,' said the stranger, 'since we are telling each other who we are, I am going to tell you who I am.

" 'I am the umbrella that holds up the sky. I am the umbrella the rain comes through. I am the umbrella that tells the sky when to begin raining and when to stop raining.

" 'I am the umbrella that goes to pieces when the wind blows and then puts itself together again when the wind goes down. I am the first umbrella, the last umbrella, the one and only umbrella all other um-brellas are named after, first, last, and always.'

"When the stranger finished this speech telling who he was and where he came from, all the other umbrellas sat still for a little while, to be respectful.

"Then they all got up, took off their straw hats, walked up to the stranger, and laid those straw hats at his feet. They wanted to show him they had respect for him. Then they all walked out, first the um-brella that feeds the fishes fresh buns every morning, then the um-brella that fixes the clocks free of charge, then the umbrella that peels the potatoes with a pencil and makes pink ink with the peelings, then the umbrella that eats the rats with pepper and salt and a clean nap-kin, then the umbrella that washes the dishes with a wiper and wipes the dishes with a washer, then the umbrella that covers the chimney with a dishpan before it rains, then the umbrella that runs to the cor-ner to get corners for the handkerchiefs. They all laid their straw hats at the feet of the stranger because he came without knocking or tell-ing anybody beforehand and because he said he is the umbrella that holds up the sky, that big umbrella the rain goes through first of all, the first and the last umbrella."

That was the way Hatrack the Horse finished his story for Dippy the Wisp. She was changing hats, getting ready to go.

The old man put his loose, bony arms around her and kissed her for a good-by. And she put her little dimpled arms around his neck and kissed him for a good-by.

And the last he saw of her that day she was walking far away down at the bottom of the long, long hill that stretches from Hatrack's shanty toward the Village of Cream Puffs.

And twice going down the long hill she stopped and changed hats, opening and shutting the hatboxes and changing hats from green and gold to purple and gray and back to green and gold.

HOW BOZO THE BUTTON BUSTER BUSTED ALL HIS BUTTONS WHEN A MOUSE CAME

ONE SUMMER EVENING the stars in the summer sky seemed to be moving with fishes, cats, and rabbits.

It was that summer evening three girls came to the shanty of Hatrack the Horse. He asked each one, "What is your name?" And they answered, first, "Me? My name is Deep Red Roses"; second, "Me? My name is The Beans are Burning"; and last of all, "Me? My name is Sweeter Than the Bees Humming."

And the old man fastened a yellow rose for luck in the hair of each one and said, "You ought to be home now."

"After you tell us a story," they reminded him.

"I can only tell you a sad story all mixed up tonight," he reminded them, "because all day today I have been thinking about Bozo the Button Buster."

"Tell us about Bozo the Button Buster," said the girls, feeling in their hair and fixing the yellow roses.

The old man sat down on the front steps. His eyes swept away off toward a corner of the sky heavy with mist, where it seemed to be moving with firetails, fishes, cats, and rabbits of slow changing stars.

"Bozo had buttons all over him," said the old man. "The buttons on Bozo fitted so tight, and there were so many buttons, that sometimes when he took his lungs full of new wind to go on talking, a button would bust loose and fly into the face of whoever he was speaking to. Sometimes when he took new wind into his lungs, two buttons would bust loose and fly into the faces of two people he was speaking to.

"So people said, 'Isn't it queer how buttons fly loose when Bozo fills his lungs with wind to go on speaking?' After a while everybody called him Bozo the Button Buster.

"Now, you must understand, Bozo was different from other people. He had a string tied to him. It was a long string hanging down with a knot in the end. He used to say, 'Sometimes I forget where I am; then I feel for the string tied to me, and I follow the string to where it is tied to me; then I know where I am again.'

"Sometimes when Bozo was speaking and a button busted loose, he would ask, 'Was that a mouse? Was that a mouse?' And sometimes he said to people, 'I'll talk with you—*if you haven't got a mouse in your pocket.*'

"The last day Bozo ever came to the Village of Cream Puffs, he stood on the public square, and he was all covered with buttons, more buttons than ever before, and all the buttons fitting tight, and five, six buttons busting loose and flying into the air whenever he took his lungs full of wind to go on speaking.

" 'When the sky began to fall, who was it ran out and held up the sky?' he sang out. 'It was me, it was me ran out and held up the sky when the sky began to fall.

" 'When the blue came off the sky, where did they get the blue to put on the sky to make it blue again? It was me, it was me picked the bluebirds and the blue pigeons to get the blue to fix the sky.

" 'When it rains now, it rains umbrellas first, so everybody has an umbrella for the rain afterward. Who fixed that? I did—Bozo the Button Buster.

" 'Who took the rainbow off the sky and put it back again in a hurry? That was me.

" 'Who turned all the barns upside down and then put them right side up again? I did that.

" 'Who took the salt out of the sea and put it back again? Who took the fishes out of the sea and put them back again? That was me.

" 'Who started the catfish fighting the cats? Who made the slippery elms slippery? Who made the King of the Broken Bottles a wanderer, wandering over the world mumbling, "Easy, easy"? Who opened the windows of the stars and threw fishes, cats, and rabbits all over the frames of the sky? I did, I did, I did.'

"All the time Bozo kept on speaking, the buttons kept on busting because he had to stop so often to fill his lungs with new wind to go on speaking. The public square was filled with piles of buttons that kept busting off from Bozo the Button Buster that day.

"And at last a mouse came, a sneaking, slippery, quick little mouse. He ran with a flash to the string tied to Bozo, the long string hanging down with a knot in the end. He bit the knot and cut it loose. He slit the string with his teeth as Bozo cried, 'Ai! Ai! Ai!'

"The last of all the buttons busted loose off Bozo. The clothes fell off. The people came up to see what was happening to Bozo. There was nothing in the clothes. The man inside the clothes was gone. All that was left was buttons and a few clothes.

"Since then whenever it rains umbrellas first so everybody has an umbrella for the rain afterward, or if the sky looks like it is falling, or if a barn turns upside down, or if the King of the Broken Bottles comes along mumbling, 'Easy, easy,' or if firetails, fishes, cats, and rabbits come on the sky in the night, or if a button busts loose and flies into somebody's face, people remember Bozo the Button Buster."

When the three girls started home, each one said to Hatrack the Horse, "It looks dark and lonesome on the prairie, but you put a yellow rose in my hair for luck—and I won't be scared after I get home."

❀ ❀ ❀

Two Stories About Four Boys Who Had Different Dreams

PEOPLE: *Googler*
Gaggler
Twins
The family doctor
The father of the twins
The mother of the twins
Pen wipers and pencil sharpeners
Smokestacks and monkey wrenches
Monkey faces on the monkey wrenches
Left-handed monkey wrenches

Potato Face Blind Man
Ax Me No Questions
Johnny the Wham
Joe the Wimp
Grasshoppers
Thousand dollar bills
Brass doors
Lizzie Lazarus

HOW GOOGLER AND GAGGLER, THE TWO CHRISTMAS BABIES, CAME HOME WITH MONKEY WRENCHES

1

TWO BABIES CAME one night in snowstorm weather, came to a tar-paper shack on a cinder patch next the railroad yards on the edge of the Village of Liver-and-Onions.

The family doctor came that night, came with a bird of a spizz car throwing a big spotlight of a headlight through the snow of the snow-storm on the prairie.

"Twins," said the doctor. "Twins," said the father and mother. And the wind as it shook the tar-paper shack and shook the doors and the padlocks on the doors of the tar-paper shack, the wind seemed to be howling softly, "Twins, twins."

Six days and Christmas Eve came. The mother of the twins lit two candles, two little two-for-a-nickel candles in each little window. And the mother handed the father the twins and said, "Here are your Christmas presents." The father took the two baby boys and laughed. "Twice times twice is twice."

The two little two-for-a-nickel candles sputtered in each little win-dow that Christmas Eve and at last sputtered and went out, leaving the prairies dark and lonesome. The father and the mother of the twins sat by the window, each one holding a baby.

Every once in a while they changed babies so as to hold a different twin. And every time they changed they laughed at each other. "Twice times twice is twice."

One baby was called Googler, the other Gaggler. The two boys grew up, and hair came on their bald red heads. Their ears, wet be-hind, got dry. They learned how to pull on their stockings and shoes and tie their shoestrings. They learned at last how to take a handker-chief and hold it open and blow their noses.

Their father looked at them growing up and said, "I think you'll make a couple of peanut-wagon men pouring hot butter into popcorn sacks."

The family doctor saw the rashes and the itches and the measles and the whooping cough come along one year and another. He saw the husky Googler and the husky Gaggler throw off the rashes and the itches and the measles and the whooping cough. And the family doc-tor said, "They will go far and see much, and they will never be any good for sitting with the sitters and knitting with the knitters."

Googler and Gaggler grew up and turned handsprings going to school in short pants, whistling with school books under their arms. They went barefooted and got stickers in their hair and teased cats and killed snakes and climbed apple trees and threw clubs up walnut trees and chewed slippery ellum. They stubbed their toes and cut their feet on broken bottles and went swimming in brickyard ponds and came home with their backs sunburnt so the skin peeled off. And before they went to bed every night, they stood on their heads and turned flip-flops.

One morning early in spring the young frogs were shooting silver spears of little new songs up into the sky. Strips of fresh young grass were beginning to flick the hills and spot the prairie with flicks and spots of new green. On that morning, Googler and Gaggler went to school with fun and danger and dreams in their eyes.

They came home that day and told their mother, "There is a war between the pen wipers and the pencil sharpeners. Millions of pen

wipers and millions of pencil sharpeners are marching against each other, marching and singing, *'Hayfoot, strawfoot, bellyful o' bean soup.'* The pen wipers and the pencil sharpeners, millions and millions, are marching with drums, drumming, *'Ta rum, ta rum, ta rum tum tum.'* The pen wipers say, 'No matter how many million ink spots it costs and no matter how many million pencil sharpeners we kill, we are going to kill and kill till the last of the pencil sharpeners is killed.' The pencil sharpeners say, 'No matter how many million shavings it costs, no matter how many million pen wipers we kill, we are going to kill and kill till the last of the pen wipers is killed.' "

The mother of Googler and Gaggler listened, her hands folded, her thumbs under her chin, her eyes watching the fun and the danger and the dreams in the eyes of the two boys. And she said, "Me, oh, my— but those pen wipers and pencil sharpeners hate each other." And she turned her eyes toward the flicks and spots of new green grass coming on the hills and the prairie, and she let her ears listen to the young frogs shooting silver spears of little songs up into the sky that day.

And she told her two boys, "Pick up your feet now and run. Go to the grass, go to the new green grass. Go to the young frogs and ask them why they are shooting songs up into the sky this early spring day. Pick up your feet now and run."

2

At last Googler and Gaggler were big boys, big enough to pick the stickers out of each other's hair, big enough to pick up their feet and run away from anybody who chased them.

One night they turned flip-flops and handsprings and climbed up on top of a peanut wagon where a man was pouring hot butter into popcorn sacks. They went to sleep on top of the wagon. Googler dreamed of teasing cats, killing snakes, climbing apple trees, and stealing apples. Gaggler dreamed of swimming in brickyard ponds and coming home with his back sunburnt so the skin peeled off.

They woke up with heavy gunnysacks in their arms. They climbed off the wagon and started home to their father and mother lugging the heavy gunnysacks on their backs. And they told their father and mother:

"We ran away to the Thimble Country where the people wear thimble hats, where the women wash dishes in thimble dishpans, where the men go to work with thimble shovels.

"We saw a war, the left-handed people against the right-handed. And the smokestacks did all the fighting. They all had monkey wrenches, and they tried to wrench each other to pieces. And they had monkey faces on the monkey wrenches—to scare each other.

"All the time they were fighting, the Thimble people sat looking on, the thimble women with thimble dishpans, the thimble men with thimble shovels. They waved handkerchiefs to each other, some left-hand handkerchiefs and some right-hand handkerchiefs. They sat looking till the smokestacks with their monkey wrenches wrenched each other all to pieces."

Then Googler and Gaggler opened the heavy gunnysacks. "Here," they said, "here is a left-handed monkey wrench; here is a right-handed monkey wrench. And here is a monkey wrench with a monkey face on the handle—to scare with."

Now the father and mother of Googler and Gaggler wonder how they will end up. The family doctor keeps on saying, "They will go far and see much, but they will never sit with the sitters and knit with the knitters." And sometimes when their father looks at them, he says what he said the Christmas Eve when the two-for-a-nickel candles stood two by two in the windows, "Twice times twice is twice."

HOW JOHNNY THE WHAM SLEEPS IN MONEY ALL THE TIME AND JOE THE WIMP SHINES AND SEES THINGS

ONCE THE POTATO Face Blind Man began talking about arithmetic and geography, where numbers come from and why we add and subtract before we multiply, when the first fractions and decimal points were invented, who gave the rivers their names and why some rivers have short names slipping off the tongue easy as whistling and why other rivers have long names wearing the stub ends off lead pencils.

The girl, Ax Me No Questions, asked the old man if boys always stay in the home towns where they are born and grow up, or whether boys pack their packsacks and go away somewhere else after they grow up. This question started the old man telling about Johnny the Wham and Joe the Wimp and things he remembered about them.

"Johnny the Wham and Joe the Wimp are two boys who used to live here in the Village of Liver-and-Onions before they went away. They grew up here, carving their initials, J.W., on wishbones and peanuts and wheelbarrows. And if anybody found a wishbone or a peanut or a wheelbarrow with the initials J.W. carved on it, he didn't know whether it was Johnny the Wham or Joe the Wimp.

"They met on summer days, put their hands in their pockets, and traded each other grasshoppers learning to say yes and no. One kick and a spit meant yes. Two kicks and a spit meant no. One two three, four five six of a kick and a spit meant the grasshopper was counting and learning numbers.

"They promised what they were going to do after they went away from the village. Johnny the Wham said, 'I am going to sleep in money up to my knees with thousand dollar bills all over me for a blanket.' Joe the Wimp said, 'I am going to see things and shine, and I am going to shine and see things.'

"They went away. They did what they said. They went up into the grasshopper country near the Village of Eggs Over where the grasshoppers were eating the corn in the fields without counting how much. They stayed in those fields till those grasshoppers learned to say yes and no and learned to count. One kick and a spit meant yes. Two kicks and a spit meant no. One two three, four five six meant the grasshoppers were counting and learning numbers. The grasshoppers, after that, eating ears of corn in the fields were counting how many and how much.

"Today Johnny the Wham sleeps in a room full of money in the big bank in the Village of Eggs Over. The room where he sleeps is the room where they keep the thousand dollar bills. He walks in thousand dollar bills up to his knees at night before he goes to bed on the floor. A bundle of thousand dollar bills is his pillow. He covers himself, like a man in a haystack or a strawstack, with thousand dollar bills. The paper money is piled around him in armfuls and sticks up and stands out around him the same as hay or straw.

"And Lizzie Lazarus, who talked with him in the Village of Eggs Over last week, she says Johnny the Wham told her, 'There is music in thousand dollar bills. Before I go to sleep at night and when I wake up in the morning, I listen to their music. They whisper and cry, they sing little oh-me, oh-my songs as they wriggle and rustle next to each other. A few with dirty faces, with torn ears, with patches and finger and thumb prints on their faces, they cry and whisper so it hurts to hear them. And often they shake all over, laughing.

" 'I heard one dirty thousand dollar bill say to another, spotted with patches and thumb prints, "They kiss us welcome when we come; they kiss us sweet good-by when we go."

" 'They cry and whisper and laugh about things and special things and extra extra special things—pigeons, ponies, pigs, special pigeons, ponies, pigs, extra extra special pigeons, ponies, pigs—cats, pups, monkeys, big bags of cats, pups, monkeys, extra extra big bags of special cats, pups, monkeys—jewelry, ice cream, bananas, pie, hats, shoes, shirts, dustpans, rattraps, coffee cups, handkerchiefs, safety pins—diamonds, bottles, and big front doors with bells on. They cry and whisper and laugh about these things—and it never hurts unless the dirty thousand dollar bills with torn ears and patches on their faces say to each other, "They kiss us welcome when we come; they kiss us sweet good-by when we go." ' "

The old Potato Face sat saying nothing. He fooled a little with the accordion keys as if trying to make up a tune for the words, "They kiss us welcome when we come; they kiss us sweet good-by when we go."

Ax Me No Questions looked at him with a soft look and said softly, "Now maybe you'll tell about Joe the Wimp." And he told her:

"Joe the Wimp shines the doors in front of the bank. The doors are brass, and Joe the Wimp stands with rags and ashes and chamois skin keeping the brass shining.

" 'The brass shines slick and shows everything on the street like a looking glass,' he told Lizzie Lazarus last week. 'If pigeons, ponies, pigs come past, or cats, pups, monkeys, or jewelry, ice cream, bananas, pie, hats, shoes, shirts, dustpans, rattraps, coffee cups, handkerchiefs, safety pins, or diamonds, bottles, and big front doors with bells on, Joe the Wimp sees them in the brass.

" 'I rub on the brass doors, and things begin to jump into my hands out of the shine of the brass. Faces, chimneys, elephants, yellow humming birds, and blue cornflowers, where I have seen grasshoppers sleeping two by two and two by two, they all come to the shine of the brass on the doors when I ask them to. If you shine brass hard, and wish as hard as the brass wishes, and keep on shining and wishing, then always things come jumping into your hands out of the shine of the brass.' "

"So you see," said the Potato Face Blind Man to Ax Me No Questions, "sometimes the promises boys make when they go away come true afterward."

"They got what they asked for—now will they keep it or leave it?" said Ax Me.

"Only the grasshoppers can answer that," was the old man's reply.

"The grasshoppers are older. They know more about jumps. And especially grasshoppers that say yes and no and count one two three, four five six."

And he sat saying nothing, fooling with the accordion keys as if trying to make up a tune for the words, "They kiss us welcome when we come; they kiss us sweet good-by when we go."

❀ ❀ ❀

Two Stories Told by the Potato Face Blind Man About Two Girls with Red Hearts

PEOPLE: *Blixie Bimber*
The Potato Face Blind Man
Shoulder Straps
High High Over
Six Bits
Deep Red Roses
A clock
A looking glass
Baggage

Pink Peony
Spuds the ballplayer
Four moons
Peacocks
Frogs
Oranges
Yellow silk handkerchiefs

HOW DEEP RED ROSES GOES BACK
AND FORTH BETWEEN THE CLOCK
AND THE LOOKING GLASS

ONE MORNING WHEN big white clouds were shouldering each other's shoulders, rolling on the rollers of a big blue sky, Blixie Bimber came along where the Potato Face Blind Man sat shining the brass bickerjiggers on his accordion.

"Do you like to shine up the brass bickerjiggers?" asked Blixie.

"Yes," he answered. "One time a long time ago the brass bickerjiggers were gold, but they stole the gold away when I wasn't looking."

He blinked the eyelids over his eyeballs and said, "I thank them because they took gold they wanted. Brass feels good to my fingers the same as gold." And he went on shining up the brass bickerjiggers on the accordion, humming a little line of an old song, "Tomorrow will never catch up with yesterday because yesterday started sooner."

"Seems like a nice morning with the sun spilling bushels of sunshine," he said to Blixie, who answered, "Big white clouds are shouldering each other's shoulders, rolling on the rollers of a big blue sky."

"Seems like it's April all over again," he murmured, almost like he wasn't talking at all.

"Seems just that way—April all over again," murmured Blixie, almost like she wasn't talking at all.

So they began drifting, the old man drifting his way, the girl drifting her way, till he drifted into a story. And the story he told was like this and in these words:

"Deep Red Roses was a lovely girl with blue skylights like the blue skylights of early April in her eyes. And her lips reminded people of deep red roses waiting in the cool of the summer evening.

"She met Shoulder Straps one day when she was young yet. He promised her. And she promised him. But he went away. One of the long wars between two short wars took him. In a faraway country, then, he married another girl. And he didn't come back to Deep Red Roses.

"Next came High High Over, one day when she was young yet. A dancer he was, going from one city to another city to dance, spending his afternoons and evenings and late nights dancing, and sleeping in the morning till noon. And when he promised, she promised. But he went away to another city and after that another city. And he married one woman and then another woman. Every year there came a new story about one of the new wives of High High Over, the dancer. And while she was young yet, Deep Red Roses forgot all about her promise and the promise of High High Over, the dancer who ran away from her.

"Six Bits was the next to come along. And he was not a soldier, nor a dancer, nor anything special. He was a careless man, changing from one job to another, changing from paperhanging to plastering, from fixing shingle roofs where the shingles were ripped to opening cans with can openers.

"Six Bits gave Deep Red Roses his promise, and she gave him her promise. But he was always late keeping his promise. When the wedding was to be Tuesday, he didn't come till Wednesday. If it was Friday, he came Saturday. And there wasn't any wedding.

"So Deep Red Roses said to herself, 'I am going away and learn; I am going away and talk with the wives of High High Over, the dancer, and maybe if I go far enough, I will find the wife of Shoulder Straps, the soldier—and maybe the wives of the men who promised me will tell me how to keep promises kept.'

"She packed her baggage till her baggage was packed so full there was room for only one more thing. So she had to decide whether to put a *clock* or whether to put a *looking glass* in her baggage.

" 'My head tells me to carry the clock so I can always tell if I am early or late,' she said to herself. 'But my heart tells me to carry a looking glass so I can look at my face and tell if I am getting older or younger.'

"At last she decides to take the clock and leave the looking glass —because her head says so. She starts away. She goes through the door, she is out of the house, she goes to the street, she starts up the street.

"Then her heart tells her to go back and change the clock for the looking glass. She goes back up the street, through the door, into the house, into her room. Now she stands in front of the clock and the looking glass saying, 'Tonight I sleep home here one more night, and tomorrow morning I decide again.'

"And now every morning Deep Red Roses decides with her head to take the clock. She takes the clock and starts away and then comes back because her heart decides she must have the looking glass.

"If you go to her house this morning, you will see her standing in the doorway with blue skylights like the blue sky of early April in her eyes, and lips that remind you of deep red roses in the cool of the evening in summer. You will see her leave the doorway and go out of the gate with the clock in her hands. Then if you wait, you will see her come back through the gate, into the door, back to her room, where she puts down the clock and takes up the looking glass.

"After that she decides to wait until tomorrow morning to decide again what to decide. Her head tells her one thing; her heart tells her another. Between the two she stays home. Sometimes she looks at her face in the looking glass and says to herself, 'I am young yet, and while I am young, I am going to do my own deciding.' "

Blixie Bimber fingered the end of her chin with her little finger and said, "It is a strange story. It has a stab in it. It would hurt me if I couldn't look up at the big white clouds shouldering their shoulders, rolling on the rollers of the big blue sky."

"It is a good story to tell when April is here all over again—and I am shining up the brass bickerjiggers on my accordion," said the Potato Face Blind Man.

HOW PINK PEONY SENT SPUDS, THE BALLPLAYER, UP TO PICK FOUR MOONS

EARLY ONE SUMMER evening the moon was hanging in the treetops. There was a lisp of leaves. And the soft shine of the moon sifting down seemed to have something to say to the lisp of the leaves.

The girl named Blixie Bimber came that particular summer evening to the corner where the Potato Face Blind Man sat with his accordion. She came walking slow and thoughtful to where he was sitting in the evening shadows. And she told him about the summer moon in the treetops, the lisp of the leaves, and the shine of the moon trying to tell something to the lisp of the leaves.

The old man leaned back, fumbled the keys of his accordion, and said it loosened up things he remembered far back.

"On an evening like this, every tree has a moon all of its own for itself—if you climb up in a thousand trees this evening, you can pick a thousand moons," the old man murmured. "You remind me tonight about secrets swimming deep in me."

And after hesitating a little—and thinking a little—and then hesitating some more—the old man started and told this story:

"There was a girl I used to know, one time, named Pink Peony. She was a girl with cheeks and lips the peonies talked about.

"When she passed a bush of peonies, some of the flowers would whisper, 'She is lovelier than we are.' And the other peonies would answer in a whisper, 'It *must* be so, it . . . must . . . be . . . *so.*'

"Now there was a ballplayer named Spuds came one night to take her riding, out to a valley where the peacocks always cry before it rains, where the frogs always gamble with the golden dice after midnight.

"And out in that valley they came to a tall tree shooting spraggly to the sky. And high up in the spraggly shoots, where the lisp of the leaves whispers, there a moon had drifted down and was caught in the branches.

" 'Spuds, climb up and pick *that* moon for me,' Pink Peony sang reckless. And the ballplayer jumped out of the car, climbed up the tall tree, up and up till he was high and far in the spraggly branches where the moon had drifted down and was caught.

"Climbing down, he handed the girl a silver hat full of peach-color pearls. She laid it on the backseat of the car where it would be safe. And they drove on.

"They came to another tall tree shooting spraggly to the sky. And high up the moon was caught.

" 'Pick *that* one, Spuds,' Peony sang reckless again. And when he came climbing down, he handed her a circle of gold with a blood-color autumn leaf. And they put it on the backseat of the car where it would be safe. Then they drove on.

" 'Spuds, you are good to me,' said Pink Peony when he climbed another tree shooting spraggly high in the sky and came down with a brass pansy sprinkled with two rainbows for her. She put it on the backseat where it would be safe. And they drove on.

"One time more Spuds climbed up and came down with what he picked, up where the moon was caught in the high spraggly branches. 'An Egyptian collar frozen in diamond cobwebs, for you,' he said. 'You are a dear, Spuds,' she said, reckless, with a look into his eyes. She laid the Egyptian collar frozen in diamond cobwebs on the back-seat of the car where it would be safe—and they drove on.

"They listened a while; they stopped the car and listened a longer while, to the frogs gambling with golden dice after midnight.

"And when at last they heard the peacocks crying, they knew it was going to rain. So they drove home.

"And while the peacocks were crying, and just before they started home, they looked in the backseat of the car at the silver hat full of peach-color pearls, the circle of gold with a blood-color autumn leaf, the brass pansy sprinkled with two rainbows, the Egyptian collar frozen in diamond cobwebs.

"Driving home, the spray of a violet dawn was on the east sky. And it was nearly daylight when they drove up to the front door of Pink Peony's home. She ran into the house to get a basket to carry the presents in. She came running out of the house with a basket to carry the presents in.

"She looked in the backseat; she felt with her hands and fingers all over the backseat.

"In the backseat she could find only four oranges. They opened the oranges, and in each orange they found a yellow silk handkerchief.

"Today, if you go to the house where Pink Peony and Spuds are living, you will find four children playing there, each with a yellow silk handkerchief tied around the neck in a mystic slipknot.

"Each child has a moon face and a moon name. And sometimes their father and mother pile them all into a car, and they ride out to the valley where the peacocks always cry before it rains—and where the frogs always gamble with golden dice after midnight.

"And what they look longest at is a summer moon hanging in the treetops when there is a lisp of leaves, and the shine of the moon and the lisp of the leaves seem to be telling each other something."

So the Potato Face came to a finish with his story. Blixie Bimber kissed him good night on the nose, saying, "You loosened up beautiful tonight."

❀ ❀ ❀

Three Stories About Moonlight, Pigeons, Bees, Egypt, Jesse James, Spanish Onions, the Queen of the Cracked Heads, the King of the Paper Sacks

PEOPLE:
Dippy the Wisp
Slip Me Liz
The Potato Face Blind Man
Egypt
Jesse James
Spanish Onions
The Queen of the Cracked Heads
The King of the Paper Sacks
The Queen of the Empty Hats
Hot Balloons
A snoox
A gringo
Sweetheart dippies
Nail-eating rats

HOW DIPPY THE WISP AND SLIP ME LIZ CAME IN THE MOONSHINE WHERE THE POTATO FACE BLIND MAN SAT WITH HIS ACCORDION

THE SKY SHOOK a rain down one Saturday night over the people, the post office, and the peanut stand in the Village of Liver-and-Onions.

And after the rain, the sky shook loose a moon so a moonshine came with gold on the rainpools.

And a west wind came out of the west sky and shook the moonshine gold on the tops of the rainpools.

Dippy the Wisp and Slip Me Liz came, two tough pony girls, two limber prairie girls, in the moonshine humming little humpty dumpty songs.

They came to the post office corner where the Potato Face Blind Man sat hugging his accordion, wondering what was next and who and why.

He was saying to himself, "Who was it told me the rats on the moon in the middle of the winter lock their mittens in iceboxes?"

And just then Dippy the Wisp and Slip Me Liz came flipping along saying, "It is a misty, moisty evening in the moonshine, isn't it?"

And he answered, "The moon is a round gold door with silver transoms tonight. Bumblebees and honeybees are chasing each other over the gold door of the moon and up over the silver transoms."

Dippy the Wisp took out a bee bag, took bees out of the bee bag, bal-

anced the bees on her thumb, humming a humpty dumpty song. And
Slip Me Liz, looking on, joined in on the humpty dumpty song. And,
of course, the bees began buzzing and buzzing their *bee* humpty
dumpty song.

"Have you fastened names on them?" asked the Potato Face.

"These three on my thumb, these three special blue-violet bees, I
put their names on silk white ribbons and tied the ribbons to their
knees. This is Egypt—she has inkwells in her ears. This is Jesse
James—he puts postage stamps on his nose. This is Spanish Onions
—she likes pearl-color handkerchiefs around her yellow neck."

"Bees belong in bee bags, but these are different," the old man murmured.

"Runaway bees, these are," Dippy the Wisp went on. "They buzz
away, they come buzzing back, buzzing home, buzzing secrets, syllables, snitches.

"Today Egypt came buzzing home with her inkwells in her ears.
And Egypt buzzed, 'I flew and flew and I buzzed and buzzed far, far
away, till I came where I met the Queen of the Cracked Heads with
her head all cracked. And she took me by the foot and took me to the
palace of the Cracked Heads with their heads all cracked.

" 'The palace was full of goats walking up and down the stairs,
sliding on the banisters eating bingety bing clocks. Before he bites the

clock and chews and swallows and eats the bingety bing clock, I noticed, each goat winds up the clock and fixes it to go off bling bling bingety bing, after he eats it down. I noticed that. And the fat, fat, puffy goats, the fat, fat, waddly goats, had extra clocks hung on their horns—and the clocks, tired of waiting, spoke to each other in the bingety bing clock talk. I noticed that too.

" 'I stayed all morning, and I saw them feed the big goats big hunks and the little goats little hunks and the big clocks big bings and the little clocks little bings. At last in the afternoon, the Queen of the Cracked Heads came with her cracked head to say good-by to me. She was sitting on a ladder feeding baby clocks to baby alligators, winding the clocks and fixing the bingety bings, so after the baby alligators swallowed the clocks, I heard them singing bling bling bingety bing.

" 'And the Queen was reading the alphabet to the littlest of the baby alligators—and they were saying the alligator A B C while she was saying the A B C of the Cracked Heads. At last she said good-by to me, good-by and come again soon, good-by and stay longer next time.

" 'When I went out of the door, all the baby alligators climbed up the ladder and bingety blinged good-by to me. I buzzed home fast because I was lonesome. I am so, *so* glad to be home again.' "

The Potato Face looked up and said, "This is nice as the rats on the moon in the middle of the winter locking their mittens in the icebox. Tell us next about that blue-violet bumblebee, Jesse James."

"Jesse James," said Dippy the Wisp, "Jesse James came buzzing home with a postage stamp on his nose. And Jesse James buzzed, 'I flew and I flew and buzzed and buzzed far, far away till I came where I met the King of the Paper Sacks who lives in a palace of paper sacks. I went inside the palace expecting to see paper sacks everywhere. But instead of paper sacks, the palace was full of pink and purple peanuts walking up and down the stairs washing their faces, stitching handkerchiefs.

" 'In the evening all the pink and purple peanuts put on their overshoes and make paper sacks. The King of the Paper Sacks walks around and around among them saying, "If anybody asks you who I am, tell them I am the King of the Paper Sacks." And one little peanut flipped up one time in the King's face and asked, "Say it again— *who* do you think you are?" And it made the King so bitter in his feelings he reached out his hand and with a sweep and a swoop he swept fifty pink and purple peanuts into a paper sack and cried out,

"A nickel a sack, a nickel a sack." And he threw them into a trash pile of tin cans.

" 'When I went away, he shook hands with me and said, "Good-by, Jesse James, you old buzzer. If anybody asks you, tell them you saw the King of the Paper Sacks where he lives."

" 'When I went away from the palace, the doors and the windowsills, the corners of the roofs and the eave troughs where the rain runs off, they were all full of pink and purple peanuts standing in their over-shoes washing their faces, stitching handkerchiefs, calling good-by to me, good-by and come again, good-by and stay longer next time. Then I came buzzing home because I was lonesome. And I am so, *so* glad to be home again.' "

The Potato Face looked up again and said, "It *is* a misty, moisty evening in the moonshine. Now tell us about that blue-violet honey-bee, Spanish Onions."

And Dippy the Wisp tied a slipknot in the pearl-color handkerchief around the yellow neck of Spanish Onions and said, "Spanish Onions came buzzing back home with her face dirty and scared, and she told us, 'I flew and flew and I buzzed and buzzed till I came where I met the Queen of the Empty Hats. She took me by the foot and took me across the City of the Empty Hats, saying under her breath, "There is a screw loose somewhere; there is a leak in the tank." Fat rats, fat bats, fat cats, came along under empty hats, and the Queen always said under her breath, "There is a screw loose somewhere; there is a leak in the tank." In the houses, on the street, riding on the rattlers and the razz cars, the only people were hats, empty hats. When the fat rats changed hats with the fat bats, the hats were empty. When the fat bats changed *those* hats with the fat cats, the hats were empty. I took off my hat and saw it was empty. *I began to feel like an empty hat myself.* I got scared. I jumped loose from the Queen of the Empty Hats and buzzed back home fast. I am so, *so* glad to be home again.' "

The Potato Face sat hugging his accordion. He looked up and said, "Put the bees back in the bee bag—they buzz too many secrets, sylla-bles, and snitches."

"What do you expect when the moon is a gold door with silver tran-soms?" asked Slip Me Liz.

"Yes," said Dippy the Wisp. "What do you expect when the bumble-bees and the honeybees are chasing each other over the gold door of the moon and up over the silver transoms?"

And the two tough pony girls, the two limber prairie girls, went away humming a little humpty dumpty song across the moonshine gold on the tops of the rainpools.

HOW HOT BALLOONS AND HIS PIGEON DAUGHTERS CROSSED OVER INTO THE ROOTABAGA COUNTRY

HOT BALLOONS WAS a man who lived all alone among people who sell slips, flips, flicks, and chicks by the dozen, by the box, by the boxcar job lot, back and forth to each other.

Hot Balloons used to open the window in the morning and say to the ragpickers and the rag handlers, "Far, far away the pigeons are calling; far, far away the white wings are dipping in the blue, in the sky blue."

And the ragpickers and the rag handlers looked up from their rag-bags and said, "Far, far away the rags are flying; far, far away the rags are whistling in the wind, in the sky wind."

Now two pigeons came walking up to the door, the doorknob and the doorbell under the window of Hot Balloons. One of the pigeons rang the bell. The other pigeon, too, stepped up to the bell and gave it a ring.

Then they waited, tying the shoestrings on their shoes and the bonnet strings under their chins, while they waited.

Hot Balloons opened the door. And they flew into his hands, one pigeon apiece in each of his hands, flipping and fluttering their wings, calling, "Ka loo, ka loo, ka lo, ka lo," leaving a letter in his hands and then flying away fast.

Hot Balloons stepped out on the front steps to read the letter where the light was good in the daylight because it was so early in the morning. The letter was on paper scribbled over in pigeon-foot blue handwriting with many secrets and syllables.

After Hot Balloons read the letter, he said to himself, "I wonder if those two pigeons are my two runaway daughters, Dippy the Wisp and Slip Me Liz. When they ran away, they said they would cross the Shampoo River and go away into the Rootabaga Country to live. And I have heard it is a law of the Rootabaga Country whenever a girl crosses the Shampoo River to come back where she used to be, she changes into a pigeon—and she stays a pigeon till she crosses back over the Shampoo River into the Rootabaga Country again."

And he shaded his eyes with his hands and looked far, far away in the blue, in the sky blue. And by looking long and hard, he saw far, far away in the sky blue the two white pigeons dipping their wings in the blue, flying fast, circling and circling higher and higher, toward the Shampoo River, toward the Rootabaga Country.

"I wonder, I guess, I think so," he said to himself, "I wonder, I think so, it must be those two pigeons are my two runaway daughters, my two girls, Dippy the Wisp and Slip Me Liz."

He took out the letter and read it again right side up, upside down, back and forth. "It is the first time I ever read pigeon-foot blue handwriting," he said to himself. And the way he read the letter, it said to him:

Daddy, daddy, daddy, come home to us in the Rootabaga Country where the pigeons call ka loo, ka loo, ka lo, ka lo, where the squirrels carry ladders and the wildcats ask riddles and the fish jump out of the rivers and speak to the frying pans, where the baboons take care of the babies and the black cats come and go in orange and gold stockings, where the birds wear rose and purple hats on Monday afternoons up in the skylights in the evening.

(Signed) DIPPY THE WISP,
SLIP ME LIZ.

And reading the letter a second time, Hot Balloons said to himself, "No wonder it is scribbled over the paper in pigeon-foot blue handwriting. No wonder it is full of secrets and syllables."

So he jumped into a shirt and a necktie, he jumped into a hat and a vest, and he jumped into a steel car, starting with a snizz and a snoof till it began running smooth and even as a catfoot.

"I will ride to the Shampoo River faster than two pigeons fly," he said. "I will be there."

Which he was. He got there before the two pigeons. But it was no use, for the rain and the rainstorm was working—and the rain and the rainstorm tore down and took and washed away the steel bridge over the Shampoo River.

"Now there is only an air bridge to cross on, and a *steel* car drops down, falls off, falls through, if it runs on an *air* bridge," he said.

So he was all alone with the rain and the rainstorm all around him —and far as he could see by shading his eyes and looking, there was only the rain and the rainstorm across the river—and the *air* bridge.

While he waited for the rain and the rainstorm to go down, two pigeons came flying into his hands, one apiece into each hand, flipping and fluttering their wings and calling, "Ka loo, ka loo, ka lo, ka lo." And he could tell by the way they began tying the shoestrings on their shoes and the bonnet strings under their chins, they were the same two pigeons ringing the doorbell that morning.

They wrote on his thumbnails in pigeon-foot blue handwriting, and he read their handwriting asking him why he didn't cross over the Shampoo River. And he explained, "There is only an *air* bridge to cross on. A *steel* car drops down, falls off, falls through, if it runs on an *air* bridge. Change my *steel* car to an *air* car. Then I can cross the *air* bridge."

The pigeons flipped and fluttered, dipped their wings and called, "Ka loo, ka loo, ka lo, ka lo." And they scribbled their pigeon feet on his thumbnail—telling him to wait. So the pigeons went flying across the Shampoo River.

They came back with a basket. In the basket was a snoox and a gringo. And the snoox and the gringo took hammers, jacks, flanges, nuts, screws, bearings, ball bearings, axles, axle grease, ax handles, spits, spitters, spitballs and spitfires, and worked.

"It's a hot job," said the snoox to the gringo.

"I'll say it's a hot job," said the gringo, answering the snoox.

"We'll give this one the merry razoo," said the snoox to the gringo, working overtime and double time.

"Yes, we'll put her to the cleaners and shoot her into high," said the gringo, answering the snoox, working overtime and double time.

They changed the steel to air, made an *air* car out of the *steel* car, put Hot Balloons and the two pigeons into the air car, and *drove the air car across the air bridge*.

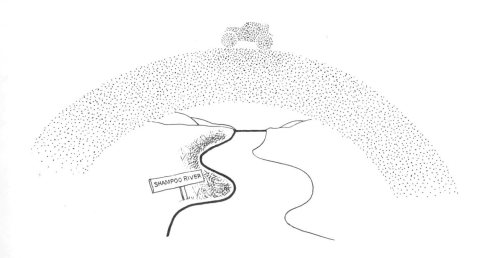

SHAMPOO RIVER

And nowadays when people talk about it in the Rootabaga Country, they say, "The snoox and the gringo drove the air car across the air bridge clean and cool as a whistle in the wind. As soon as the car got off the bridge and over into the Rootabaga Country, the two pigeons changed in a flash. And Hot Balloons saw they were his two daughters, his two runaway girls, Dippy the Wisp and Slip Me Liz, standing and smiling at him and looking fresh and free as two fresh fish in a free river, fresh and free as two fresh bimbos in a bamboo tree.

He kissed them both, two long kisses, and while he was kissing them, the snoox and the gringo worked double time and overtime and changed the *air* car back into a *steel* car.

And Dippy the Wisp and Slip Me Liz rode in that car—starting with a snizz and a snoof till it began running smooth and even as a catfoot —showing their father, Hot Balloons, where the squirrels carry ladders and the wildcats ask riddles and the fish jump out of the rivers and speak to the frying pans, where the baboons take care of the babies and the black cats come and go in orange and gold stockings, where the birds wear rose and purple hats on Monday afternoons up in the skylights in the evening.

And often on a Saturday night or a New Year Eve or a Christmas morning, Hot Balloons remembers back how things used to be, and he tells his two girls about the ragpickers and the rag handlers back among the people who sell slips, flips, slicks, and chicks, by the dozen, by the box, by the boxcar job lot, back and forth to each other.

HOW TWO SWEETHEART DIPPIES SAT IN THE MOONLIGHT ON A LUMBERYARD FENCE AND HEARD ABOUT THE SOONERS AND THE BOOMERS

NOT SO VERY far and not so very near the Village of Liver-and-Onions is a dippy little town where dippy people used to live.

And it was long, long ago the sweetheart dippies stood in their windows and watched the dips of the star dippers in the dip of the sky.

It was the dippies who took the running wild oleander and the running wild rambler rose and kept them so the running wild winters let them alone.

"It is easy to be a dippy . . . among the dippies . . . isn't it?" the sweetheart dippies whispered to each other, sitting in the leaf shadows of the oleander, the rambler rose.

The name of this dippy town came by accident. The name of the town is Thumbs Up, and it used to be named Thumbs Down and expects to change its name back and forth between Thumbs Up and Thumbs Down.

The running wild oleanders and the running wild rambler roses grow there over the big lumberyards where all the old lumber goes.

The dippies and the dippy sweethearts go out there to those lumberyards and sit on the fence moonlight nights and look at the lumber.

The rusty nails in the lumber get rustier and rustier till they drop out. And whenever they drop out, there is always a rat standing under to take the nail in his teeth and chew the nail and eat it.

For this is the place the nail-eating rats come to from all over the Rootabaga Country. Father rats and mother rats send the young rats there to eat nails and get stronger.

If a young rat comes back from a trip to the lumberyards in Thumbs Up and he meets another young rat going to those lumberyards, they say to each other, "Where have you been?" "To Thumbs Up." "And how do you feel?" *"Hard as nails."*

Now one night two of the dippies, a sweetheart boy and girl, went out to the big lumberyards and sat on the fence and looked at the lumber and the running wild oleanders and the running wild rambler roses.

And they saw two big rusty nails, getting rustier and rustier, drop out of the lumber and drop into the teeth of two young rats.

And the two young rats sat up on their tails there in the moonlight under the oleanders, under the roses, and one of the young rats told the other young rat a story he made up out of his head.

Chewing on the big rusty nail and then swallowing, telling more of the story after swallowing and before beginning to chew the nail again, this is the story he told—and this is the story the two dippies, the two sweethearts sitting on the fence in the moonlight, heard:

Far away where the sky drops down, and the sunsets open doors for the nights to come through—where the running winds meet, change faces, and come back—there is a prairie where the green grass grows all around.

And on that prairie the gophers, the black and brown-striped ground squirrels, sit with their backs straight up, sitting on their soft paddy tails, sitting in the spring song murmur of the south wind, saying to each other, "This is the prairie, and the prairie belongs to us."

Now far back in the long time, the gophers came there, chasing each other, playing the-green-grass-grew-all-around, playing cross tag, hop tag, skip tag, billy-be-tag, billy-be-it.

The razorback hogs came then, eating pig nuts, potatoes, paw paws, pumpkins. The wild horse, the buffalo, came. The moose, with spraggly branches of antlers spreading out over his head, the moose came—and the fox, the wolf.

The gophers flipped a quick flip-flop back into their gopher holes when the fox, the wolf, came. And the fox, the wolf, stood at the holes and said, "You *look* like rats, you *run* like rats, you *are* rats, rats with stripes. Bah! You are only *rats*. Bah!"

It was the first time anybody said "Bah!" to the gophers. They sat in a circle with their noses up asking, *"What* does this 'Bah!' mean?" And an old-timer, with his hair falling off in patches, with the stripes on his soft paddy tail patched with patches, this old-timer of a gopher said, " 'Bah!' speaks more than it means whenever it is spoken."

Then the sooners and the boomers came, saying "Bah!" and saying it many new ways, till the fox, the wolf, the moose, the wild horse, the buffalo, the razorback hog picked up their feet and ran away without looking back.

The sooners and boomers began making houses, sod houses, log, lumber, plaster-and-lath houses, stone, brick, steel houses, but most of the houses were lumber with nails to hold the lumber together to keep the rain off and push the wind back and hold the blizzards outside.

In the beginning the sooners and boomers told stories, spoke jokes, made songs, with their arms on each other's shoulders. They dug wells, helping each other get water. They built chimneys together helping each other let the smoke out of their houses. And every year the day before Thanksgiving they went in cahoots with their posthole diggers and dug all the postholes for a year to come. That was in the morning. In the afternoon they took each other's cistern cleaners and cleaned all the cisterns for a year to come. And the next day on Thanksgiving they split turkey wishbones and thanked each other they had all the postholes dug and all the cisterns cleaned for a year to come.

If the boomers had to have broomcorn to make brooms, the sooners came saying, "Here is your broomcorn."

If the sooners had to have a gallon of molasses, the boomers came saying, "Here is your gallon of molasses."

They handed each other big duck eggs to fry, big goose eggs to boil, purple pigeon eggs for Easter breakfast. Wagonloads of buff banty eggs went back and forth between the sooners and boomers. And they took big hayracks full of buff banty hens and traded them for hayracks full of buff banty roosters.

And one time at a picnic, one summer afternoon, the sooners gave the boomers a thousand golden ice tongs with hearts and hands carved on the handles. And the boomers gave the sooners a thousand silver wheelbarrows with hearts and hands carved on the handles.

Then came pigs, pigs, pigs, and more pigs. And the sooners and boomers said the pigs had to be painted. There was a war to decide whether the pigs should be painted pink or green. Pink won.

The next war was to decide whether the pigs should be painted checks or stripes. Checks won. The next war after that was to decide whether the checks should be painted pink or green. Green won.

Then came the longest war of all, up till that time. And this war decided the pigs should be painted both pink and green, both checks and stripes.

They rested then. But it was only a short rest, for then came the war to decide whether peach pickers must pick peaches on Tuesday mornings or on Saturday afternoons. Tuesday mornings won. This was a short war. Then came a long war—to decide whether telegraph pole climbers must eat onions at noon with spoons, or whether dishwashers must keep their money in pig's ears with padlocks pinched on with pincers.

So the wars went on. Between wars they called each other goofs and snoofs, grave robbers, pickpockets, porch climbers, pie thieves, pie-face mutts, bums, big bums, big greasy bums, dummies, mummies, rummies, sneezicks, bohunks, wops, snorkies, ditchdiggers, peanuts, fatheads, sapheads, pinheads, pickle faces, horse thieves, rubbernecks, big pieces of cheese, big bags of wind, snabs, scabs, and dirty sniveling snitches. Sometimes when they got tired of calling each other names, they scratched in the air with their fingers and made faces with their tongues out twisted like pretzels.

After a while, it seemed, there was no corn, no broomcorn, no brooms, not even teeny sweepings of corn or broomcorn or brooms. And there were no duck eggs to fry, goose eggs to boil, no buff banty eggs, no buff banty hens, no buff banty roosters, no wagons for wagonloads of buff banty eggs, no hayracks for hayrack loads of buff banty hens and buff banty roosters.

And the thousand golden ice tongs the sooners gave the boomers, and the thousand silver wheelbarrows the boomers gave the sooners, both with hearts and hands carved on the handles, they were long ago broken up in one of the early wars deciding pigs must be painted both pink and green with both checks and stripes.

And now, at last, there were no more pigs to paint either pink or green or with checks or stripes. The pigs, pigs, pigs, were gone.

So the sooners and boomers all got lost in the wars, or they screwed wooden legs on their stump legs and walked away to bigger, bigger prairies, or they started away for the rivers and mountains, stopping always to count how many fleas there were in any bunch of fleas they met. If you see anybody who stops to count the fleas in a bunch of fleas, that is a sign he is either a sooner or a boomer.

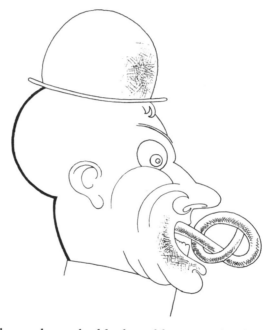

So again the gophers, the black and brown striped ground squirrels, sit with their backs straight up, sitting on their soft paddy tails, sitting in the spring song murmur of the south wind, saying, "This is the prairie, and the prairie belongs to us."

Far away today where the sky drops down and the sunsets open doors for the nights to come through—where the running winds meet, change faces, and come back—there the gophers are playing the-green-grass-grew-all-around, playing cross tag, skip tag, hop tag, bil-ly-be-tag, billy-be-it. And sometimes they sit in a circle and ask, "What does this 'Bah!' mean?" And an old-timer answers, " 'Bah!' speaks more than it means whenever it is spoken."

That was the story the young rat under the oleanders, under the roses, told the other young rat, while the two sweetheart dippies sat on the fence in the moonlight looking at the lumber and listening.

The young rat who told the story hardly got started eating the nail he was chewing, while the young rat that did the listening chewed up and swallowed down a whole nail.

As the two dippies on the fence looked at the running wild oleander and the running wild rambler roses over the lumber in the moonlight, they said to each other, "It's easy to be a dippy . . . among the dippies . . . isn't it?" And they climbed down from the fence and went home in the moonlight.

❀ ❀ ❀

Two Stories Out of the Tall Grass

PEOPLE: *John Jack Johannes Hummadummaduffer*
Feed Box
Eva Evelyn Evangeline Hummadummaduffer
Sky Blue
The harvest moon
A haystack cricket

Baby Moon
Half Moon
Silver Moon

Doorbells, chimneys, cellars

The night policeman in the Village of Cream Puffs
Butter Fingers
Three Strikes
Cub ballplayers

THE HAYSTACK CRICKET AND HOW THINGS ARE DIFFERENT UP IN THE MOON TOWNS

THERE IS AN old man with wrinkles like wrinkled leather on his face living among the cornfields on the rolling prairie near the Shampoo River.

His name is John Jack Johannes Hummadummaduffer. His cronies and the people who know him call him Feed Box.

His daughter is a cornfield girl with hair shining the way corn silk shines when the corn is ripe in the fall time. The tassels of corn silk hang down and blow in the wind with a rusty dark gold, and they seem to get mixed with her hair. Her name is Eva Evelyn Evangeline Hummadummaduffer. And her chums and the people who know her call her Sky Blue.

The eleventh month, November, comes every year to the corn belt on that rolling prairie. The wagons bring the corn from the fields in the harvest days, and the cracks in the corncribs shine with the yellow and gold of the corn.

The harvest moon comes, too. They say it stacks sheaves of the November gold moonshine into gold corn shocks on the sky. So they say.

On those mornings in November that time of the year, the old man they call Feed Box sits where the sun shines against the boards of a corncrib.

The girl they call Sky Blue, even though her name is Eva Evelyn Evangeline Hummadummaduffer, she comes along one November morning. Her father is sitting in the sun with his back against a corncrib. And he tells her he always sits there every year listening to the mice in the cornfields getting ready to move into the big farmhouse.

"When the frost comes and the corn is husked and put in the corncribs, the fields are cleaned and the cold nights come. Papa mouse and mama mouse tell the little ones it is time to sneak into the cellar and the garret and the attic of the farmhouse," said Feed Box to Sky Blue.

"I am listening," she said, "and I can hear the papa mouse and the mama mouse telling the little ones how they will find rags and paper and wool and splinters and shavings and hair, and they will make warm nests for the winter in the big farmhouse—if no kits, cats, nor kittycats get them."

The old man, Feed Box, rubbed his back and his shoulders against the boards of the corncrib and washed his hands almost as if he might be washing them in the gold of the autumn sunshine. Then he told this happening:

"This time of the year, when the mouse in the fields whispers so I can hear him, I remember one November when I was a boy.

"One night in November when the harvest moon was shining and stacking gold cornshocks in the sky, I got lost. Instead of going home, I was going away from home. And the next day and the next night instead of going home, I was going away from home.

"That second night I came to a haystack where a yellow and gold cricket was singing. And he was singing the same songs the crickets sing in the haystacks back home where the Hummadummaduffers raise hay and corn, in the corn belt near the Shampoo River.

"And he told me, this cricket did, he told me when he listened soft if everything was still in the grass and the sky, he could hear golden crickets singing in the cornshocks the harvest moon had stacked in the sky.

"I went to sleep listening to the singing of the yellow and gold crickets in that haystack. It was early in the morning, long before daylight, I guess, the two of us went on a trip away from the haystack.

"We took a trip. The yellow and gold cricket led the way. 'It is the call of the harvest moon,' he said to me in a singing whisper. 'We are going up to the moon towns where the harvest moon stacks the cornshocks on the sky.'

"We came to a little valley in the sky. And the harvest moon had slipped three little towns into that valley, three little towns named Half Moon, Baby Moon, and Silver Moon.

"In the town of Half Moon they *look* out of the doors and *come in* at the windows. So they have taken all the doorbells off the doors and put them on the windows. Whenever we rang a doorbell, we went to a window.

"In the town of Baby Moon they had windows on the chimneys so the smoke can look out of the window and see the weather before it comes out over the top of the chimney. And whenever the chimneys get tired of being stuck up on the top of the roof, the chimneys climb down and dance in the cellar. We saw five chimneys climb down and join hands and bump heads and dance a laughing chimney dance.

"In the town of Silver Moon the cellars are not satisfied. They say to each other, 'We are tired of being under, always under.' So the cellars slip out from being under, always under. They slip out and climb up on top of the roof.

"And that was all we saw up among the moon towns of Half Moon, Baby Moon, and Silver Moon. We had to get back to the haystack so as to get up in the morning after our night sleep."

"This time of the year I always remember that November," said the old man, Feed Box, to his daughter, Sky Blue.

And Sky Blue said, "I am going to sleep in a haystack sometime in November just to see if a yellow and gold cricket will come with a singing whisper and take me on a trip to where the doorbells are on the windows and the chimneys climb down and dance."

The old man murmured, "Don't forget the cellars tired of being under, always under."

WHY THE BIG BALLGAME BETWEEN HOT GROUNDERS AND THE GRAND STANDERS WAS A HOT GAME

UP NEAR THE Village of Cream Puffs is a string of ball towns hiding in the tall grass. Passengers in the railroad trains look out of the windows, and the tall grass stands up so they can't see the ball towns. But the ball towns are there, and the tall grass is full of pitchers, catchers, basemen, fielders, shortstops, sluggers, southpaws, and backstops. They play ball till dark, and after dark they talk ball. The big, fast ballplayers in the Rootabaga Country all come from these ball towns in the tall grass.

The towns used to have names like names in books. But now the names are all like ball talk: Knock the Cover Off, Home Plate, Chest Protector, Grand Stand, Nine Innings, Three Balls and Two Strikes, Bases Full and Two Out, Big League, Bush League, Hot Grounder, Out Drop, Bee Liner, Muffs and Pick Ups, Slide Kelly Slide, Paste It on the Nose.

Now the night policeman in the Village of Cream Puffs stopped in at the cigar store one night, and a gang of cub ballplayers loafing and talking ball talk asked him if there was anything in the wind. And he told them this happening:

"I was sitting on the front steps of the post office last night thinking how many letters get lost and how many letters never get answered. A ballplayer came along with a package and said his name was Butter Fingers and he was the heavy hitter, the hard slugger, for the Grand Stand ball team playing a championship game the day before with the Hot Grounders ball team. He came to the Village of Cream Puffs the

day before the game, found a snoox and a gringo and got the snoox and the gringo to make him *a home run shirt*. Wearing a home run shirt, he told me, you knock a home run every time you come to bat. He said he knocked a home run every time he came to bat, and it was his home runs won the game for the Grand Standers. He was carrying a package and said the home run shirt was in the package and he was taking it back to the snoox and the gringo because he promised he wouldn't keep it, and it belonged to the snoox and the gringo and they only rented it to him for the championship game. The last I saw of him he was hotfooting it pitty-pat pitty-pat up the street with the package.

"Well, I just said tra-la-loo to Butter Fingers when along comes another ballplayer. He had a package too, and he said his name was Three Strikes, and he was the left-handed southpaw pitcher for the Hot Grounders team the day before playing a game against the Grand Stand team. He said he knew unless he put over some classy pitching, the game was lost and everything was goose eggs. So he came to the Village of Cream Puffs the day before the game, found a snoox and a gringo, and got the snoox and the gringo to make him *a spitball shirt*. A spitball looks easy, he told me, but it has smoke and whiskers and nobody can touch it. He said he handed the Grand Standers a line of inshoots close to their chins, and they never got to first base. Three Strikes was carrying a package, and he said the spitball shirt was in the package, and he was taking it back to the snoox and the gringo because he promised he wouldn't keep it and it belonged to the snoox and the gringo and they only rented it to him. The last I saw of him he was hot-footing it pitty-pat pitty-pat up the street with a package."

The gang of cub ballplayers in the cigar store asked the night policeman, "Who won the game? Was it the Grand Standers or the Hot Grounders took the gravy?"

"You can search me for the answer," he told the boys. "If the snoox and the gringo come past the post office tonight when I sit on the front steps wondering how so many letters get lost and how so many never get answered, I will ask the snoox and the gringo, and if they tell me tonight, I'll tell you tomorrow night."

And ever since then when they talk ball talk in the ball towns hiding in the tall grass, they say the only sure way to win a ballgame is to have a pitcher with a spitball shirt and over that a home run shirt, both made by a snoox and a gringo.

❀ ❀ ❀

Two Stories Out of Oklahoma and Nebraska

THE HUCKABUCK FAMILY AND HOW THEY RAISED POPCORN IN NEBRASKA AND QUIT AND CAME BACK

JONAS JONAS HUCKABUCK was a farmer in Nebraska with a wife, Mama Mama Huckabuck, and a daughter, Pony Pony Huckabuck.

"Your father gave you two names the same in front," people had said to him.

And he answered, "Yes, two names are easier to remember. If you call me by my first name Jonas and I don't hear you, then when you call me by my second name Jonas, maybe I will.

"And," he went on, "I call my pony-face girl Pony Pony because if she doesn't hear me the first time, she always does the second."

And so they lived on a farm where they raised popcorn, these three, Jonas Jonas Huckabuck, his wife Mama Mama Huckabuck, and their pony-face daughter Pony Pony Huckabuck.

After they harvested the crop one year, they had the barns, the cribs, the sheds, the shacks, and all the cracks and corners of the farm, all filled with popcorn.

"We came out to Nebraska to raise popcorn," said Jonas Jonas, "and I guess we got nearly enough popcorn this year for the popcorn poppers and all the friends and relations of all the popcorn poppers in these United States."

And this was the year Pony Pony was going to bake her first squash pie all by herself. In one corner of the corncrib, all covered over with popcorn, she had a secret, a big round squash, a fat yellow squash, a rich squash all spotted with spots of gold.

She carried the squash into the kitchen, took a long, sharp, shining knife, and then she cut the squash in the middle till she had two big half squashes. And inside just like outside, it was rich yellow spotted with spots of gold.

And there was a shine of silver. And Pony Pony wondered why silver should be in a squash. She picked and plunged with her fingers till she pulled it out.

"It's a buckle," she said, "a silver buckle, a Chinese silver slipper buckle."

She ran with it to her father and said, "Look what I found when I cut open the golden yellow squash spotted with gold spots—it is a Chinese silver slipper buckle."

"It means our luck is going to change, and we don't know whether it will be good luck or bad luck," said Jonas Jonas to his daughter, Pony Pony Huckabuck.

Then she ran with it to her mother and said, "Look what I found when I cut open the yellow squash spotted with spots of gold—it is a Chinese silver slipper buckle."

"It means our luck is going to change, and we don't know whether it will be good luck or bad luck," said Mama Mama Huckabuck.

And that night a fire started in the barns, crib, sheds, shacks, cracks, and corners, where the popcorn harvest was kept. All night long the popcorn popped. In the morning the ground all around the farmhouse and the barn was covered with white popcorn so it looked like a heavy fall of snow.

All the next day the fire kept on, and the popcorn popped till it was up to the shoulders of Pony Pony when she tried to walk from the house to the barn. And that night in all the barns, cribs, sheds, shacks, cracks, and corners of the farm, the popcorn went on popping.

In the morning when Jonas Jonas Huckabuck looked out of the upstairs window, he saw the popcorn popping and coming higher and higher. It was nearly up to the window. Before evening and dark of that day, Jonas Jonas Huckabuck, and his wife Mama Mama Huckabuck, and their daughter Pony Pony Huckabuck, all went away from the farm saying, "We came to Nebraska to raise popcorn, but this is too much. We will not come back till the wind blows away the popcorn. We will not come back till we get a sign and a signal."

They went to Oskaloosa, Iowa. And the next year Pony Pony Huckabuck was very proud because when she stood on the sidewalks in the street, she could see her father sitting high on the seat of a coal wagon, driving two big spanking horses hitched with shining brass harness in front of the coal wagon. And though Pony Pony and Jonas Jonas were proud, very proud all that year, there never came a sign, a signal.

The next year again was a proud year, exactly as proud a year as they spent in Oskaloosa. They went to Paducah, Kentucky, to Defiance, Ohio; Peoria, Illinois; Indianapolis, Indiana; Walla Walla, Washington. And in all these places Pony Pony Huckabuck saw her father, Jonas Jonas Huckabuck, standing in rubber boots deep down in a ditch with a shining steel shovel shoveling yellow clay and black mud from down in the ditch high and high up over his shoulders. And though it was a proud year, they got no sign, no signal.

The next year came. It was the proudest of all. This was the year Jonas Jonas Huckabuck and his family lived in Elgin, Illinois, and Jonas Jonas was watchman in a watch factory watching the watches.

"I know where you have been," Mama Mama Huckabuck would say of an evening to Pony Pony Huckabuck. "You have been down to the watch factory watching your father watch the watches."

"Yes," said Pony Pony. "Yes, and this evening when I was watching father watch the watches in the watch factory, I looked over my left shoulder and I saw a policeman with a star and brass buttons, and he was watching me to see if I was watching Father watch the watches in the watch factory."

It was a proud year. Pony Pony saved her money. Thanksgiving came. Pony Pony said, "I am going to get a squash to make a squash pie." She hunted from one grocery to another; she kept her eyes on the farm wagons coming into Elgin with squashes.

She found what she wanted, the yellow squash spotted with gold spots. She took it home, cut it open, and saw the inside was like the outside, all rich yellow spotted with gold spots.

There was a shine like silver. She picked and plunged with her fingers and pulled and pulled till at last she pulled out the shine of silver.

"It's a sign; it is a signal," she said. "It is a buckle, a slipper buckle, a Chinese silver slipper buckle. It is the mate to the other buckle. Our luck is going to change. Yoo hoo! Yoo hoo!"

She told her father and mother about the buckle. They went back to the farm in Nebraska. The wind by this time had been blowing and blowing for three years, and all the popcorn was blown away.

"Now we are going to be farmers again," said Jonas Jonas Huckabuck to Mama Mama Huckabuck and to Pony Pony Huckabuck. "And we are going to raise cabbages, beets, and turnips; we are going to raise squash, rutabaga, pumpkins, and peppers for pickling. We are going to raise wheat, oats, barley, rye. We are going to raise corn such as Indian corn and kaffir corn—but we are *not* going to raise any popcorn for the popcorn poppers to be popping."

And the pony-face daughter, Pony Pony Huckabuck, was proud because she had on new black slippers, and around her ankles, holding the slippers on the left foot and the right foot, she had two buckles, silver buckles, Chinese silver slipper buckles. They were mates.

Sometimes on Thanksgiving Day and Christmas and New Year's, she tells her friends to be careful when they open a squash.

"Squashes make your luck change good to bad and bad to good," says Pony Pony.

YANG YANG AND HOO HOO, OR THE SONG
OF THE LEFT FOOT OF THE SHADOW
OF THE GOOSE IN OKLAHOMA

YANG YANG AND HOO HOO were two girls who used to live in Battle Ax, Michigan, before they moved to Wagon Wheel Gap, Colorado, and back to Broken Doors, Ohio, and then over to Open Windows, Iowa, and at last down to Alfalfa Clover, Oklahoma, where they say, "Our Oklahoma home is in Oklahoma."

One summer morning Yang Yang and Hoo Hoo woke up saying to each other, "Our Oklahoma home is in Oklahoma." And it was that morning the shadow of a goose flew in at the open window, just over the bed where Yang Yang and Hoo Hoo slept with their eyes shut all night and woke with their eyes open in the morning.

The shadow of the goose fluttered a while along the ceiling, flickered a while along the wall, and then after one more flutter and flicker put itself on the wall like a picture of a goose put there to look at, only it was a living picture—and it made its neck stretch in a curve and then stretch straight.

"Yang yang," cried Yang Yang. "Yang yang."

"Hoo hoo," sang Hoo Hoo. "Hoo hoo."

And while Hoo Hoo kept on calling a soft, low coaxing hoo hoo, Yang Yang kept on crying a hard, noisy, nagging yang yang till everybody in the house upstairs and down and everybody in the neighbor houses heard her yang-yanging.

The shadow of the goose lifted its left wing a little, lifted its right foot a little, got up on its goose legs, and walked around and around in a circle on its goose feet. And every time it walked around in a circle, it came back to the same place it started from, with its left foot or right foot in the same foot spot it started from. Then it stayed there in the same place like a picture put there to look at, only it was a living picture with its neck sometimes sticking up straight in the air and sometimes bending in a long curving bend.

Yang Yang threw the bedcovers off, slid out of bed, and ran downstairs yang-yanging for her mother. But Hoo Hoo sat up in bed laughing, counting her pink toes to see if there were ten pink toes the same as the morning before. And while she was counting her pink toes, she looked out of the corners of her eyes at the shadow of the goose on the wall.

And again the shadow of the goose lifted its left wing a little, lifted its right foot a little, got up on its goose legs, and walked around and around in a circle on its goose feet. And every time it walked around in a circle, it came back to the same place it started from, with its left foot or right foot back in the same foot spot it started from. Then it stayed there in the same place where it put itself on the wall like a picture to look at, only it was a living picture with its neck sticking up straight in the air and then changing so its neck was bending in a long curving bend.

And all the time little Hoo Hoo was sitting up in bed counting her pink toes and looking out of the corners of her eyes at the shadow of the goose.

By and by little Hoo Hoo said, "Good morning—hoo hoo for you —and hoo hoo again, I was looking at the window when you came in. I saw you put yourself on the wall like a picture. I saw you begin to walk and come back where you started from with your neck sticking straight up and your neck bending in a bend. I give you good morning. I blow a hoo hoo to you. I blow two of a hoo hoo to you."

Then the shadow of a goose, as if to answer good morning, and as if to answer what Hoo Hoo meant by saying, "I blow two of a hoo hoo to you," stretched its neck sticking up straight and long, longer than any time yet, and then bended its neck in more of a bend than any time yet.

And all the time Hoo Hoo was sitting in bed feeling of her toes with her fingers to see if she had one toe for every finger, and to see if she had one pink little toe to match her one pink little finger, and to see if she had one fat, flat big toe to match her one fat, flat thumb.

Then when the room was all quiet, the shadow of the goose lifted its left foot and began singing—singing just as the shadow of a goose always sings—with the left foot—very softly with the left foot—so softly you must listen with the softest little listeners you have deep inside your ears.

And this was the song, this was the old-time, old-fashioned left foot song the shadow of the goose sang for Hoo Hoo:

> Be a yang yang if you want to.
> Be a hoo hoo if you want to.
>
> The yang yangs always yang in the morning.
> The hoo hoos always hoo in the morning.
>
> Early in the morning the putters sit putting,
> Putting on your nose, putting on your ears,
> Putting in your eyes and the lashes on your eyes,
> Putting on the chins of your chinny chin chins.

And after singing the left-foot song the shadow of the goose walked around in a long circle, came back where it started from, stopped and stood still with the proud standstill of a goose, and then stretched its neck sticking up straight and long, longer than any time yet, and then bended its neck bent and twisted in longer bends than any time yet.

Then the shadow took itself off the wall, fluttered and flickered along the ceiling and over the bed, flew out of the window and was gone, leaving Hoo Hoo all alone sitting up in bed counting her pink toes.

Out of the corners of her eyes she looked up at the wall of the room, at the place where the shadow of the goose put itself like a picture. And there she saw a shadow spot. She looked and saw it was a left foot, the same left foot that had been singing the left-foot song.

Soon Yang Yang came yang-yanging into the room holding to her mother's apron. Hoo Hoo told her mother all the happenings that happened. The mother wouldn't believe it. Then Hoo Hoo pointed up to the wall, to the left foot, the shadow spot left behind by the shadow of the goose when it took itself off the wall.

And now when Yang Yang and Hoo Hoo sleep all night with their eyes shut and wake up in the morning with their eyes open, sometimes they say, "Our Oklahoma home is in Oklahoma," and sometimes they sing:

> Be a yang yang and yang yang if you want to.
> Be a hoo hoo and hoo hoo if you want to.

❀ ❀ ❀

One Story About Big People Now and Little People Long Ago

PEOPLE: *Peter Potato Blossom Wishes*
Three whispering cats
Hannah
Hannah More
Susquehannah

Hoom Slimmer

HOW A SKYSCRAPER AND A RAILROAD TRAIN GOT PICKED UP AND CARRIED AWAY FROM PIG'S EYE VALLEY FAR IN THE PICKAX MOUNTAINS

PETER POTATO BLOSSOM Wishes sat with her three cats, Hannah, Hannah More, and Susquehannah, one spring morning.

She was asking different kinds of questions of the three cats. But she always got the same answers no matter what she asked them.

They were whispering cats. Hannah was a yes-yes cat and always whispered yes-yes and nothing else. Hannah More was a no-no cat and always whispered no-no and nothing else. And Susquehannah was a stuttering cat and whispered halfway between yes and no, always hesitating and nothing else.

"The bye-low is whistling his bye-low and bye-low again," Peter said to herself with a murmur. "It is spring in the tall timbers and over the soft black lands. The hoo hoo and the biddywiddies come north to make a home again. The booblow blossoms put their cool white lips out into the blue mist. Every way I point my ears, there is a bye-low whistling his bye-low and bye-low again. The spring in the timbers and black lands calls to the spring aching in my heart."

Now the three whispering cats heard what Peter Potato Blossom Wishes was murmuring to herself about the spring heartache.

And Hannah, the yes-yes cat, answered yes-yes. Hannah More, the no-no cat, answered no-no. And Susquehannah, the stuttering cat, hesitated halfway between yes-yes and no-no.

And Peter rubbed their fur the right way, scratched them softly between the ears, and murmured to herself, "It is a don't-care morning —I don't care."

And that morning her heart gave a hoist and a hist when she saw a speck of a blackbird spot far and high in the sky. Coming nearer, it hummed, zoomed, hong whonged . . . shut off the hong whong . . . stoplocked and droplocked . . . and came down on the ground like a big easy bird with big wings stopped.

Hoom Slimmer slid out, wiped his hands on the oil rags, put a smear of axle grease on Peter's chin, kissed her on the nose, patted her ears two pats—and then they went into the house and had a late breakfast, which was her second breakfast and his first.

"I flew till I came to Pig's Eye Valley in the Pickax Mountains," Hoom Slimmer told her. "The pickax pigs there run digging with their pickax feet and their pickax snouts. They are lean, long-legged pigs with pockets all over, fat pocket ears ahead and fat pocket tails behind, and the pockets full of rusty dust. They dip their noses in their pockets, sniff their noses full of rusty dust, and sneeze the rusty dust in each other's wrinkly, wriggly, wraggly faces.

"I took out a buzz shovel and scraper, pushed on the buzzer, and watched it dig and scrape out a city. The houses came to my ankles. The factories came to my knees. The top of the roof of the highest skyscraper came up to my nose.

"A spider ran out of a cellar. A book fell out of his mouth. It broke into rusty dust when I took hold of it. One page I saved. The reading on it said millions of people had read the book and millions more would read it."

Hoom Slimmer reached into a pocket. He took out in his hand a railroad train with an engine hooked on ahead, and a smoking car, coaches, and sleeping cars hooked on behind.

"I cleaned it nice for you, Peter," he said. "But the pickax pigs sneezed rusty dust on it. Put it in your handkerchief."

"And now," he went on, "I will wrap off the wrappers on the skyscraper. . . . Look at it! . . . It is thirty stories high. On top is a flagpole for a flag to go up. Halfway down is a clock, with the hands gone. On the first floor is a restaurant with signs, 'Watch Your Hats and Overcoats.' Here is the office of the building, with a sign on the wall, 'Be Brief.' Here the elevators ran up and down in a hurry. On doors are signs, bankers, doctors, lawyers, life insurance, fire insurance, steam hoist and operating engineers, bridge and structural iron and steel construction engineers, stocks, bonds, securities, architects, writers, detectives, window cleaners, jewelry, diamonds, cloaks, suits, shirts, sox, silk, wool, cotton, lumber, brick, sand, corn, oats, wheat, paper, ink, pencils, knives, guns, land, oil, coal, one door with a big sign, 'We Buy and Sell Anything,' another door, 'We Fix Anything,' and more doors, 'None Such,' 'The World's Finest,' 'The Best in the World,' 'Oldest Establishment in the World,' 'The World's Greatest,' 'None Greater,' 'Greatest in the World,' 'Greatest Ever Known.' ''

And Hoom Slimmer put his arms around the skyscraper, lifted it on his shoulder, and carried it upstairs where Peter Potato Blossom Wishes said to put it, in a corner of her sleeping room. And she took out of her handkerchief the railroad train with the engine hooked on ahead and the smoking car, coaches, and sleeping cars hooked on behind. And she put the railroad train just next to the bottom floor of the skyscraper so people on the train could step off the train and step right into the skyscraper.

"Little railroad trains and little skyscrapers are just as big for little people as big railroad trains and big skyscrapers are for big people— is it not such?" she asked Hoom Slimmer.

And for an answer he gave her a looking glass half as long as her little finger and said, "The women in that skyscraper used to look at themselves from head to foot in that looking glass."

Then Peter sang out like a spring birdsong, "Now we are going to forget the pickax pigs sneezing rusty dust, and the Pig's Eye Valley and the Pickax Mountains. We are going out where the bye-low is whistling his bye-low and bye-low again, where it is spring in the tall timbers and over the soft black lands, where the hoo hoo and the biddywiddies come north to make a home again and the booblow blossoms put their cool white lips out into the blue mist."

And they sat under a tree where the early green of spring crooned in the black branches, and they could hear Hannah, Hannah More, and Susquehannah whispering yes-yes, no-no, and a hesitating stutter halfway between yes-yes, and no-no, always hesitating.

❀ ❀ ❀

Three Stories About the Letter X and How It Got into the Alphabet

PEOPLE: *An oyster king*
        Shovel Ears
        Pig Wisps
        The men who change the alphabets

        A river lumber king
        Kiss Me
        Flax Eyes
        Wildcats

        A rich man
        Blue Silver
        Her playmates, singing

There are six hundred different stories told in the Rootabaga Country about the first time the letter X got into the alphabet and how and why it was. The author has chosen three of the shortest and strangest of those stories, and they are told in the next and following pages.

PIG WISPS

THERE WAS AN oyster king far in the south who knew how to open oysters and pick out the pearls.

He grew rich, and all kinds of money came rolling in on him because he was a great oyster opener and knew how to pick out the pearls.

The son of this oyster king was named Shovel Ears. And it was hard for him to remember.

"He knows how to open oysters, but he forgets to pick out the pearls," said the father of Shovel Ears.

"He is learning to remember worse and worse and to forget better and better," said the father of Shovel Ears.

Now in that same place far in the south was a little girl with two braids of hair twisted down her back and a face saying, "Here we come—where from?"

And her mother called her Pig Wisps.

Twice a week Pig Wisps ran to the butcher shop for a soupbone. Before starting, she crossed her fingers and then the whole way to the butcher shop kept her fingers crossed.

If she met any playmates and they asked her to stop and play cross-tag or jackstones or all-around-the-mulberry-bush or the-green-grass-grew-all-around or drop-the-handkerchief, she told them, "My fingers are crossed, and I am running to the butcher shop for a soupbone."

One morning running to the butcher shop, she bumped into a big queer boy and bumped him flat on the sidewalk.

"Did you look where you were running?" she asked him.

"I forgot again," said Shovel Ears. "I remember worse and worse. I forget better and better."

"Cross your fingers like this," said Pig Wisps, showing him how.

He ran to the butcher shop with her, watching her keep her fingers crossed till the butcher gave her the soupbone.

"After I get it, then the soupbone reminds me to go home with it," she told him. "But until I get the soupbone, I keep my fingers crossed."

Shovel Ears went to his father and began helping his father open oysters. And Shovel Ears kept his fingers crossed to remind him to pick out the pearls.

He picked a hundred buckets of pearls the first day and brought his father the longest slippery, shining rope of pearls ever seen in that oyster country.

"How do you do it?" his father asked.

"It is the crossed fingers—like this," said Shovel Ears, crossing his fingers like the letter X. "This is the way to remember better and forget worse."

It was then the oyster king went and told the men who change the alphabets just what happened.

When the men who change the alphabets heard just what happened, they decided to put in a new letter, the letter X, near the end of the alphabet, the sign of the crossed fingers.

On the wedding day of Pig Wisps and Shovel Ears, the men who change the alphabets all came to the wedding with their fingers crossed.

Pig Wisps and Shovel Ears stood up to be married. They crossed their fingers. They told each other they would remember their promises.

And Pig Wisps had two ropes of pearls twisted down her back and a sweet young face saying, "Here we come—where from?"

KISS ME

MANY YEARS AGO when pigs climbed chimneys and chased cats up into the trees, away back, so they say, there was a lumber king who lived in a river city with many wildcats in the timbers nearby.

And the lumber king said, "I am losing my hair and my teeth, and I am tired of many things; my only joy is a daughter who is a dancing shaft of light on the ax handles of morning."

She was quick and wild, the lumber king's daughter. She had never kissed. Not her mother nor father nor any sweetheart ever had a love print from her lips. Proud she was. They called her Kiss Me.

She didn't like that name, Kiss Me. They never called her that when she was listening. If she happened to be listening, they called her Find Me, Lose Me, Get Me. They never mentioned kisses because they knew she would run away and be what her father called her, "a dancing shaft of light on the ax handles of morning."

But—when she was not listening, they asked, "Where is Kiss Me today?" Or they would say, "Every morning Kiss Me gets more beautiful—I wonder if she will ever in her young life get a kiss from a man good enough to kiss her."

One day Kiss Me was lost. She went out on a horse with a gun to hunt wildcats in the timbers nearby. Since the day before, she was gone. All night she was out in a snowstorm with a horse and a gun hunting wildcats. And the storm of the blowing snow was coming worse on the second day.

It was then the lumber king called in a long, loose young man with a leather face and hay in his hair. And the king said, "Flax Eyes, you are the laziest careless man in the river lumber country—go out in the snowstorm now, among the wildcats, where Kiss Me is fighting for her life, and save her."

"I am the hero. I am the man who knows how. I am the man who has been waiting for this chance," said Flax Eyes.

On a horse, with a gun, out into the snowstorm Flax Eyes rode that day. Far, far away he rode to where Kiss Me, the quick, wild Kiss Me, was standing with her back against a big rock fighting off the wildcats.

In that country the snowstorms make the wildcats wilder—and

Kiss Me was tired of shooting wildcats, tired of fighting in the snow, nearly ready to give up and let the wildcats have her.

Then Flax Eyes came. The wildcats jumped at him, and he threw them off. More wildcats came, jumping straight at his face. He took hold of those wildcats by the necks and threw them over the big rock, up into the trees, away into the snow and the wind.

At last he took all the wildcats one by one and threw them so far they couldn't come back. He put Kiss Me on her horse, rode back to the lumber king, and said, lazy and careless, "This is us."

The lumber king saw the face of Flax Eyes was all covered with cross marks like the letter X. And the lumber king saw the wildcats had torn the shirt off Flax Eyes, and on the skin of his chest, shoulders, arms, were the cross marks of the wildcats' claws, cross marks like the letter X.

So the king went to the men who change the alphabets, and they put the cross marks of the wildcats' claws for a new letter, the letter X, near the end of the alphabet. And at the wedding of Kiss Me and Flax Eyes, the men who change the alphabets came with wildcat claws crossed like the letter X.

BLUE SILVER

LONG AGO WHEN the years were dark and the black rains used to come with strong winds and blow the front porches off houses, and pick chimneys off houses and blow them onto other houses, long ago when people had understanding about rain and wind, there was a rich man with a daughter he loved better than anything else in the world.

And one night when the black rain came with a strong wind blowing off front porches and picking off chimneys, the daughter of the rich man fell asleep into a deep sleep.

In the morning they couldn't wake her. The black rain with the strong wind kept up all that day while she kept on sleeping in a deep sleep.

Men and women with music and flowers came in, boys and girls, her playmates, came in—singing songs and calling her name. And she went on sleeping.

All the time her arms were crossed on her breast, the left arm crossing the right arm like a letter X.

Two days more, five days, six, seven days went by—and all the time the black rain with a strong wind blowing—and the daughter of the rich man never woke up to listen to the music nor to smell the flowers nor to hear her playmates singing songs and calling her name.

She stayed sleeping in a deep sleep—with her arms crossed on her breast—the left arm crossing the right arm like a letter X.

So they made a long silver box, just long enough to reach from her head to her feet.

And they put on her a blue silver dress and a blue silver band around her forehead and blue silver shoes on her feet.

There were soft blue silk and silver sleeves to cover her left arm and her right arm—the two arms crossed on her breast like the letter X.

They took the silver box and carried it to a corner of the garden where she used to go to look at blue lilacs and climbing blue morning glories in patches of silver lights.

Among the old leaves of blue lilacs and morning glories they dug a place for the silver box to be laid in.

And men and women with music and flowers stood by the silver box, and her old playmates singing songs she used to sing—and calling her name.

When it was all over and they all went away, they remembered one thing most of all.

And that was her arms in the soft silk and blue silver sleeves, the left arm crossing over the right arm like the letter X.

Somebody went to the king of the country and told him how it all happened, how the black rains with a strong wind came, the deep sleep, the singing playmates, the silver box—and the soft silk and blue silver sleeves on the left arm crossing the right arm like the letter X.

Before that there never was a letter X in the alphabet. It was then the king said, "We shall put the crossed arms in the alphabet; we shall have a new letter called X, so everybody will understand a funeral is beautiful if there are young singing playmates."

❀ EARLY MOON

❀ ❀ ❀

Short Talk on Poetry

with different kinds of explanations for young people as to how little anybody knows about poetry, how it is made, what it is made of, how long men have been making it, where it came from, when it began, who started it and why, and who knows all about it.

WHAT IS POETRY? Is the answer hidden somewhere? Is it one of those answers locked in a box and nobody has the key? There are such questions and answers.

Once a man reading a newspaper clipped a poem written by a small boy in a school in New York City. The lines read:

> There stands the elephant.
> Bold and strong—
> There he stands chewing his food.
> We are strengthless against his strength.

And the man has kept this poem for many years. He has a feeling the boy did a good, honest piece of writing. The boy stood wondering and thinking before the biggest four-legged animal on earth today. And the boy put his wonder and thought, his personal human secret, a touch of man's fear in the wilderness, into the nineteen words of the poem. He asked, "What does the elephant do to me when I look at him? What is my impression of the elephant?" Then he answered his own questions.

Once there was a boy went to school and learned that any two-legged animal is a biped. And he said, "Here I've been a biped all the time and I didn't know it." So there are people sometimes who talk poetry without writing it but they don't know they are talking poetry. And every child, every boy and girl, sometimes has poetry in his head and heart—even though it doesn't get written.

Once there was a wee, curly-headed boy tugged at a cornstalk, tugged till he pulled the cornstalk up all by himself and told about it to his father, who said, "I guess you're getting to be a pretty strong boy now." The little one answered, "I guess I am. The whole earth had a hold of the other end of the cornstalk and was pulling against me." Should we say this boy had imagination and what he told his father was so keen and alive it could be called poetry? Perhaps he was a poet without knowing it just like the boy who was a biped without knowing it.

Poetry is old, ancient, goes far back. It is among the oldest of human things. So old is it that no man knows how and why the first poems came.

When it shall happen sometime that men gather their gifts and go to work and write a history of language, then it may be that we shall have at the same time a history of poetry. For the first poems of man probably came about the same time the first men, women and children spoke the first human words on the earth.

Is anyone surprised to hear that we do not have a history of poetry? Shall we believe that the learned men have written histories of all the important things of mankind? Surely there are many big histories yet to be written on big subjects. We do not have, for instance, a history of Money that goes back to when money first began, telling how and why. We do not have a history of Language which goes far back, telling how and why men first began to talk.

Yes, poetry is old. The first men that walked the earth, before men had learned to write, must have talked poetry to each other sometimes. Among the oldest things we have today which tell us about the Indians, the Chinese, the Egyptians, how they lived and talked, thousands of years ago, are writings we know to be poetry. These writings have words that go along with timebeats, with rhythm, one-two, one-two, or one-two-three-four, one-two-three-four. They had drums among the Indians, the Chinese, the Egyptians, thousands of years ago. And the words of their poetry move along like drum-beats, keeping time, now fast, now slow, drumming easy and slow at the opening of a war dance, drumming faster and faster, wild and furious, till it is so swift only the best-trained warriors can stand the speed of the dance that is drummed.

We have old poems, some so old no man knows how far they go back in time. One beautiful ancient English poem has no author, whose name we know. Where it came from no history books tell us. It goes like this—

On a misty moisty morning, when cloudy was the weather,
I chanced to meet an old man all clothed in leather.

He began to compliment and I began to grin,
"How do you do? and how do you do? and how do you do again?"

This is only one of many fine and strange poems we have out of the long ago. Nobody knows who wrote them or whether they were first spoken centuries before they were written down to meet our eyes in books.

What is poetry? This question no man has ever answered in such a way that all men have said, "Yes, now we know what poetry is." Many men have tried to explain what poetry is. Some men have written thick books so the question might be settled and made clear for all time. But they have all failed. Several fine poets have written essays and papers on what they believe poetry to be. Yet these poets did not do what they started out to do. They meant to explain in prose what poetry is, and they ended up with writing poetry to explain poetry. This is like a man inside of a strange house trying to tell people outside who have never been in the house exactly how it feels to be in that house, which is not scientific nor exact and which is like saying, "The way to write poems is to write poems." It is only clear and understandable to those who already understand and therefore need no explanations.

When Walt Whitman says, "The poet is the answerer," we are interested. If we could know just what he means by "the answerer" we would know what he means by "the poet." One poet says poetry must be "cold, lonely and distant," not knowing that some readers of poetry are glad to have books which are warm, friendly and so near that they almost breathe with life. Another poet has said poetry is "emotion remembered in tranquillity." What does that mean? It is anybody's guess what that means. To know exactly what it means we would have to know exactly what is emotion, what is tranquillity, and what we do when we remember. Otherwise it is an escape from words into words, "passing the buck," or winding like a weasel through language that ends about where it begins. "He came out of the same hole he went in at."

There is a science called "esthetics." It is the science which tries to find the laws of beauty. If as a science it ever became perfect then the books dealing with that science would become very important. Then when a builder finished a house and wished to know whether it was a beautiful house, he would only have to open the books on esthetics and the books would tell him.

What is beauty? And when shall we call a thing beautiful? These, too, are questions no man has ever answered in such a way that all men have said, "Yes, now we know what beauty is and now we know how to tell the beautiful when we find it." The nearest that men have come to answering the question, "What is the beautiful?" has been in their saying the beautiful is *the appropriate,* that which serves. No hat is a beautiful hat which does not fit you and which the wind can easily blow off your head. A Five-gallon Hat on a cowboy riding a horse on an Arizona ranch is beautiful—but the same hat on a crowded city street car would be out of place, inappropriate. No song is beautiful in a room where persons desire complete quiet. No polite behavior has beauty unless it has thought and consideration for others. The most beautiful room is the one which best serves those who live in it.

The most beautiful skyscrapers are those without extras stuck on after the real structure is finished. Why should a good, honest skyscraper have a dome or a mosque or a cement wedding cake plastered on top of it? Nearly always, what serves, what is appropriate to human use, is beautiful enough—without extras. A farm silo, a concrete grain elevator, a steel barge hauling iron ore on the Great Lakes, or a series of tall coal chutes rising as silhouettes on a moonlight night, may any one of them have as complete a beauty as the Greek Parthenon or a Gothic cathedral. Steichen, the photographer, declares he occasionally meets newspaper photographs which in design and as works of art are superior to many of the proclaimed masterpieces of painting and etching.

Now, poetry is supposed to be the esthetic art which gathers the beautiful into words. The first stuff for making poetry is words. No poems, strictly speaking, have ever been made without words. To make poems without words would be like a painter painting without paint or a bricklayer bricklaying without bricks. Of course, a feeling or a thought, or both must come to a poet before he begins using the words that make a poem. But the right words, the special and particular words for the purpose in view, these must come. For out of them the poem is made.

The words for a poem sometimes come swiftly and easily so that at last when the poem is put down on paper, the writer of them says, "I do not know how these words came. What is here was not my own absolute doing any more than a dream that should come to me in a night of sleep." Yet again the words may come slowly, out of years of toil and sometimes anguish of changing phrases and arrangements.

While we do not know very much in an absolute way about the questions, "What is poetry? How is a poem made?" we do know the one little fact that poems are made of words and without words there can be no poetry. Beyond this we do not know much. However, there is one other little scientific fact we know about poetry. That is, what is poetry for any given individual depends on the individual and what his personality requires as poetry. This links up with one of the few accepted propositions of the science of esthetics: Beauty depends on personal taste. What is beauty for one person is not for another. What is poetry for one person may be balderdash or hogwash for another.

Each of us has a personality different from all others. It has even been said that as no two leaves in a forest are the same no two human characters are precisely alike. This personality that each of us has is strangely woven of millions of little facts, events, impressions out of the past and present. Your personality and mine go back to many mysterious human connections before we were born—and since. And what any one of us loves today with depth of passion, and what each of us tries to shape his life by, goes back to strange things in personality, things so darkly mixed and baffling that it is not easy for any of us at a given time to answer the question, "Why do you love this and not that? Why do you want those and not them?" The old song with its line, "I want what I want when I want it," is not entirely comic in its backgrounds.

We do not know the start of the old folk saying, "Every one to his taste as the old woman said when she kissed the cow." We are sure a blunt Indiana philosopher knew his ground well when he wrote, "What is one man's lettuce is another man's poison ivy." These are humorous comments on the deeply serious and involved reality known as human personality. They connect directly with the fact that what is poetry for some is not poetry for others. They indicate that sometimes we cannot help it that we do not merely *dislike* some poetry; we go farther and *hate* it. And why we should hate any particular poem, thing or person is no more clear than why we love others, for hate is usually expensive in many ways and is a waste of time that belongs elsewhere. Charles Lamb said he believed an old story he had heard about two men, who had never before seen each other, meeting one day in a street in London—and the moment they saw each other's faces they leaped and began fighting.

Lamb said those two men who began hitting at each other's faces the moment they saw those faces, had "imperfect sympathies." Something clicked in each one saying, "Hit him! Kill him!" They couldn't help it. Though they met in a crowded street of a great city, and there was no war on, they attacked each other like two soldiers with bayonets in front-line trenches.

And exactly like those two men meeting in a London street, some of us register instantly—though not so violently—to faces we meet, buildings, colors, neckties, gowns, designs, pictures, books, plays—and poems. Something clicks in us and we know like a flash whether we like this or that new thing we meet for the first time.

And then may happen afterward a slow change of our viewpoint. What we saw nothing in to begin with takes on a glint or two we had not noticed at first; then as time passes, we gather values, intentions, gleams, that interest us and lead us on till we know we were ignorant, possessed of "imperfect sympathies," in our first impression of hate or dislike. This change of viewpoint from dislike to interest, from indifference to enthusiasm, often has happened with the finest of men and women in respect to great masterpieces of literature. Sometimes we do not know what a writer is talking about in his books because in life we have not met the people, facts, impressions which he is trying to deliver his mind and heart about in his book. Said a great modern artist, "Going along a railroad one day I see a thing I have seen many times. But this day I suddenly *see*. 'Tisn't that you *see* new, but things have prepared you for *a new vision.*"

As the years pass by and experience writes out new records in our mind life, we go back to some works of art that we rejected in the early days and find values we missed. Work, love, laughter, pain, death, put impressions on us as time passes, and as we brood over what has happened.

Out of songs and scars and the mystery of personal development, we get eyes that pick out intentions we had not seen before in people, in works of art, in books and poetry.

Naturally, too, the reverse happens. What we register to at one period of life, what we find gay and full of fine nourishment at one time, we find later has lost interest for us. A few masterpieces may last across the years but we usually discard some. A few masterpieces are enough. Why this is so we do not know. For each individual his new acquisitions and old discards are different.

The books and poems at hand ready for each of us are so many and so different that we use and throw away, acquire and discard, according to personal taste, and often merely guided by whim like the man in the song, "I want what I want when I want it." Too often both among young people and grownups, there is a careless drifting and they take the easiest way in books and poetry. Millions read without asking themselves why they read and whether in all their reading they have learned anything worth the spending of their time.

It was not for nothing Thoreau said an old newspaper would do for him just as well as a new one. Each of us can sit alone with our conscience for a while on the proposition of Robert Louis Stevenson that the intelligent man can find an Iliad of the human race in a newspaper. And any kindly philosopher could write a thick book on why the shrewd, tolerant reader enjoys even a stupid, vain, hypocritical book because the writer of the book is etching his own portrait on every page, stepping forth and talking off lines like one of the fools, clowns or pretenders in a Russian play. Healthy questions for each of us: "Why do I read books? What do books do to me? Can I improve my form as a reader? What does poetry do to me? Why do I need this or that poetry?"

We have heard much in our time about free verse being modern, as though it is a new-found style for men to use in speaking and writing, rising out of the machine age, skyscrapers, high speed and jazz. Now, if free verse is a form of writing poetry without rhyme, without regular meters, without established and formal rules governing it, we can easily go back to the earliest styles of poetry known to the human family —and the style is strictly free verse. Before men invented the alphabet, so that poems could be put down in writing, they spoke their poems. When one man spoke to another in a certain timebeat and rhythm, if it happened that his words conveyed certain impressions and moods to his listeners, he was delivering poetry to them, whether he knew it or they knew it, and whether he or they had a name for an art which the poet was practicing on himself and them.

We may go through thousands of pages of the reports of songs, poems and spoken dreams of American Indians as recorded in the volumes of the Bureau of Ethnology of the Smithsonian Institution at Washington, and we find it all to be in the free verse style. The poems of the ancient Chinese writers Li Po, Tu Fu and others, as read in translations, and as notated by the translators, show how strange and marvelous moments of life can be captured and compressed in the manner called free verse. The Bible is one of the sublime sources of free verse. The orations of Moses, the Book of Proverbs, Ecclesiastes, the Sermon on the Mount, the "love chapter" of the Apostle Paul, these are in the free verse style of writing poetry.

If those who write in the free verse style fail at getting onto paper any lines worth reading twice, they are in the same class with those who in regular, ordered, formal verse fail to get onto paper lines worth reading twice. The crimes of free verse have been many. The same goes for sonnets, ballads, ballades, triolets, rondeaus, villanelles, and the forms of verse which are governed by hexameters, pentameters, iambics, strophes and by laws which dictate how many syllables shall be permitted to perch on each line of the poem.

Perhaps no wrong is done and no temple of human justice violated in pointing out here that each authentic poet makes a style of his own. Sometimes this style is so clearly the poet's own that when he is imitated it is known who is imitated. Shakespeare, Villon, Li Po, Whitman —each sent forth his language and impress of thought and feeling from a different style of gargoyle spout. In the spacious highways of great books each poet is allowed the stride that will get him where he wants to go.

Should children write poetry? Yes, whenever they feel like it. If nothing else happens they will find it a training for writing and speaking in other fields of human work and play. No novelist has been a worse writer for having practiced at poetry. Many a playwright, historian, essayist, editorial writer, could have improved his form by experimenting with poetry.

At what age should a child begin writing poetry? Any age. Poems are made of words and when a child is learning to talk, to shape words on its tongue, is a proper time for it to speak poetry—if it can.

Does it help a child poet to have praise for his poems? The child should be told that poetry is first of all for the poet, that great poets usually die saying their best work is not written. Perhaps it is wise for every child to be told that it is a mistake for either a child or a grown-up accomplished artist to be satisfied with any past performance.

The foremost American woman poet, Emily Dickinson, had scarcely any of her poetry published in her lifetime. What she wrote had to be. And it is doubtful if her poems would have had the same complete glory they have if she had been taken up and praised. On the other hand, there have been poets saved to live and write beautiful pages because they found friends, an audience, and enough money to keep the wolf from sniffing round their little doorways.

The father of a great Irish poet once remarked, "What can be explained is not poetry." There are people who want a book of verse to be like the arithmetic—you turn to the back of the book and find the answers. Ken Nakazawa notes, "The poems that are obvious are like the puzzles that are already solved. They deny us the joy of seeking and creating."

Once a little girl showed to a friend a poem she had written. "Why didn't you make it longer?" asked the friend. "I could have," she answered, "but then it wouldn't have been a poem." She meant she left something in the air for the reader of the poem to linger over, as any of us do over a rose or a sunset or a face. Roses, sunsets, faces, have mystery. If we could explain them, then after having delivered our explanations we could say, "Take it from me, that's all there is to it, and there's no use your going any further for I've told you all there is and there isn't any more."

If poems could be explained, then poets would have to leave out roses, sunsets, faces, from their poems. Yet it seems that for thousands of years poets have been writing about roses, sunsets, faces, because they have mystery, significance, and a heavy or a light beauty, an appeal, a lesson and a symbolism that stays with us long as we live. It was something like this in the heart of the philosopher who declared, "What can be explained is not poetry."

❁ ❁ ❁

Pictures of Today

POTOMAC TOWN IN FEBRUARY

The bridge says: Come across, try me; see how good I am.
The big rock in the river says: Look at me; learn how to stand up.
The white water says: I go on; around, under, over, I go on.
A kneeling, scraggly pine says: I am here yet; they nearly got me last
    year.
A sliver of moon slides by on a high wind calling: I know why;
    I'll see you tomorrow; I'll tell you everything tomorrow.

PEOPLE WHO MUST

I painted on the roof of a skyscraper.
I painted a long while and called it a day's work.
The people on a corner swarmed and the traffic cop's whistle never let
    up all afternoon.

They were the same as bugs, many bugs on their way—
Those people on the go or at a standstill;
And the traffic cop a spot of blue, a splinter of brass,
Where the black tides ran around him
And he kept the street. I painted a long while
And called it a day's work.

SKY PIECES

PROUDLY the fedoras march on the heads of the somewhat
  careless men.
Proudly the slouches march on the heads of the still more
  careless men.
Proudly the panamas perch on the noggins of dapper
  debonair men.
Comically somber the derbies gloom on the earnest solemn
  noodles.
And the sombrero, most proud, most careless, most dapper and debonair
  of all, somberly the sombrero marches on the heads of important
  men who know what they want.
Hats are sky pieces; hats have a destiny; wish your hat
  slowly; your hat is you.

NEW FARM TRACTOR

Snub nose, the guts of twenty mules are in your cylinders and
  transmission.

The rear axles hold the kick of twenty Missouri jackasses.

It is in the records of the patent office and the ads there is twenty
  horsepower pull here.

The farm boy says hello to you instead of twenty mules—he sings to
  you instead of ten span of mules.

A bucket of oil and a can of grease is your hay and oats.

Rain proof and fool proof they stable you anywhere in the fields with
the stars for a roof.

I carve a team of long ear mules on the steering wheel—it's good-by
now to leather reins and the songs of the old mule skinners.

DAN

Early May, after cold rain the sun baffling cold wind.
Irish setter pup finds a corner near the cellar door,
                  all sun and no wind,
Cuddling there he crosses forepaws and lays his skull
Sideways on this pillow, dozing in a half-sleep,
Browns of hazel nut, mahogany, rosewood, played off
                  against each other on his paws
                  and head.

EVEN NUMBERS

1

A house like a man all lean and coughing,
a man with his two hands in the air at a cry,
"Hands up."

A house like a woman shrunken and stoop-shouldered,
shrunken and done with dishes and dances.

These two houses I saw going uphill in Cincinnati.

2

Two houses leaning against each other like drunken
brothers at a funeral,

Two houses facing each other like two blind wrestlers
hunting a hold on each other,

These four scrawny houses I saw on a dead level
cinder patch in Scranton, Pennsylvania.

3

And by the light of a white moon in Waukesha, Wisconsin,
I saw a lattice work in lilac time . . . white-mist lavender
. . . a sweet moonlit lavender . . .

SLOW PROGRAM

The iron rails run into the sun.
The setting of the sun chooses an hour.
The red rail ribbons run into the red ball sun.
The ribbons and the ball change like red water lights.
The picture floats with a slow program of red haze lights.

PHIZZOG

This face you got,
This here phizzog you carry around,
You never picked it out for yourself,
   at all, at all—did you?
This here phizzog—somebody handed it
   to you—am I right?
Somebody said, "Here's yours, now go see
   what you can do with it."
Somebody slipped it to you and it was like
   a package marked:
"No goods exchanged after being taken away"—
This face you got.

AGAIN?

Old Man Woolworth put up a building.
There it was; his dream; all true;
The biggest building in the world.
Babel, the Nineveh Hanging Gardens,
Karnak, all old, outclassed.
And now, here at last, what of it?
What about it? Well, every morning
We'll walk around it and look up.
And every morning we'll ask what
It means and where it's going.
It's a dream; all true; going somewhere,
That's a cinch; women buying mousetraps,
Wire cloth dishrags, ten cent sheet music,
They paid for it; the electric tower
Might yell an electric sign to the inbound
Ocean liners, "Look what the washerwomen
Of America can do with their nickels," or
"See what a nickel and a dime can do,"
And that wouldn't clear Old Man Woolworth's

Head; it was a mystery, a dream, the biggest
Building in the world; Babel, the Nineveh
Hanging Gardens, Karnak, all old,
Outclassed. So the old man cashes in,
The will of the old man is dug out,
And the widow gets thirty million dollars,
Enough to put up another building,
Another bigger than any in the world,
Bigger than Babel, the Nineveh Hanging Gardens,
Karnak, another mystery, another dream
To stand and look up at
And ask what it means.

BUFFALO DUSK

The buffaloes are gone.
And those who saw the buffaloes are gone.
Those who saw the buffaloes by thousands and how they pawed the
   prairie sod into dust with their hoofs, their great heads down paw-
   ing on in a great pageant of dusk,
Those who saw the buffaloes are gone.
And the buffaloes are gone.

PLUNGER

Empty the last drop.
Pour out the final clinging heartbeat.
Great losers look on and smile.
Great winners look on and smile.

Plunger:
Take a long breath and let yourself go.

Children

CHILD MOON

The child's wonder
At the old moon
Comes back nightly.
She points her finger
To the far silent yellow thing
Shining through the branches
Filtering on the leaves a golden sand,
Crying with her little tongue, "See the moon!"
And in her bed fading to sleep
With babblings of the moon on her little mouth.

UPSTAIRS

I too have a garret of old playthings.
I have tin soldiers with broken arms upstairs.
I have a wagon and the wheels gone upstairs.
I have guns and a drum, a jumping-jack and a magic lantern.
And dust is on them and I never look at them upstairs.
I too have a garret of old playthings.

WINTER MILK

The milk-drops on your chin, Helga,
Must not interfere with the cranberry red of your cheeks
Nor the sky winter blue of your eyes.

Let your mammy keep hands off the chin.
This is a high holy spatter of white on the reds and blues.

Before the bottle was taken away,
Before you so proudly began today
Drinking your milk from the rim of a cup
They did not splash this high holy white on your chin.

There are dreams in your eyes, Helga.
Tall reaches of wind sweep the clear blue.
The winter is young yet, so young.
Only a little cupful of winter has touched your lips.
Drink on . . . milk with your lips . . . dreams with your eyes.

FIVE CENT BALLOONS

Pietro has twenty red and blue balloons on a string.
They flutter and dance pulling Pietro's arm.
A nickel apiece is what they sell for.

Wishing children tag Pietro's heels.

He sells out and goes the streets alone.

BABY TOES

There is a blue star, Janet,
Fifteen years' ride from us,
If we ride a hundred miles an hour.

There is a white star, Janet,
Forty years' ride from us,
If we ride a hundred miles an hour.

Shall we ride
To the blue star
Or the white star?

THEME IN YELLOW

I spot the hills
With yellow balls in autumn.
I light the prairie cornfields
Orange and tawny gold clusters
And I am called pumpkins.
On the last of October
When dusk is fallen
Children join hands
And circle round me
Singing ghost songs
And love to the harvest moon;
I am a jack-o'-lantern
With terrible teeth
And the children know
I am fooling.

HELGA

The wishes on this child's mouth
Came like snow on marsh cranberries;
The tamarack kept something for her;
The wind is ready to help her shoes.
The north has loved her; she will be
A grandmother feeding geese on frosty
Mornings; she will understand
Early snow on the cranberries
Better and better then.

SLIPPERY

The six month child
Fresh from the tub

Wriggles in our hands.
This is our fish child.
Give her a nickname: Slippery.

BABY FACE

White Moon comes in on a baby face.
The shafts across her bed are flimmering.

Out on the land White Moon shines,
Shines and glimmers against gnarled shadows,
All silver to slow twisted shadows
Falling across the long road that runs from the house.

Keep a little of your beauty
And some of your flimmering silver
For her by the window tonight
Where you come in, White Moon.

PRIMER LESSON

Look out how you use proud words.
When you let proud words go, it is
  not easy to call them back.
They wear long boots, hard boots; they
  walk off proud; they can't hear you
  calling—
Look out how you use proud words.

❁ ❁ ❁

Wind and Sea

YOUNG SEA

The sea is never still.
It pounds on the shore
Restless as a young heart,
Hunting.

The sea speaks
And only the stormy hearts
Know what it says:
It is the face
        of a rough mother speaking.

The sea is young.
One storm cleans all the hoar
And loosens the age of it.
I hear it laughing, reckless.

They love the sea,
Men who ride on it
And know they will die
Under the salt of it.

Let only the young come,
   Says the sea.
Let them kiss my face
   And hear me.
I am the last word
   And I tell
Where storms and stars come from.

I AM CHICAGO

from THE WINDY CITY

The lean hands of wagon men
put out pointing fingers here,
picked this crossway, put it on a map,
set up their sawbucks, fixed their shotguns,
found a hitching place for the pony express,
made a hitching place for the iron horse,
the one-eyed horse with the fire-spit head,
found a homelike spot and said, "Make a home,"
saw this corner with a mesh of rails, shuttling
   people, shunting cars, shaping the junk of
   the earth to a new city.

The hands of men took hold and tugged
And the breaths of men went into the junk
And the junk stood up into skyscrapers and asked:
Who am I? Am I a city? And if I am what is my name?
And once while the time whistles blew and blew again
The men answered: Long ago we gave you a name,
Long ago we laughed and said: You? Your name is Chicago.

Early the red men gave a name to a river,
   the place of the skunk,
   the river of the wild onion smell,
   Shee-caw-go.

Out of the payday songs of steam shovels,
Out of the wages of structural iron rivets,

The living lighted skyscrapers tell it now as a name,
Tell it across miles of sea blue water, gray blue land:
I am Chicago, I am a name given out by the breaths of working men,
    laughing men, a child, a belonging.

So between the Great Lakes,
The Grand De Tour, and the Grand Prairie,
The living lighted skyscrapers stand,
Spotting the blue dusk with checkers of yellow,
    streamers of smoke and silver,
    parallelograms of night-gray watchmen,
Singing a soft moaning song: I am a child, a belonging.

                 * * *

Winds of the Windy City, come out of the prairie,
    all the way from Medicine Hat.
Come out of the inland sea blue water, come where
    they nickname a city for you.

Corn wind in the fall, come off the black lands,
    come off the whisper of the silk hangers,
    the lap of the flat spear leaves.

Blue water wind in summer, come off the blue miles
    of lake, carry your inland sea blue fingers,
    carry us cool, carry your blue to our homes.

White spring winds, come off the bag wool clouds,
    come off the running melted snow, come white
    as the arms of snow-born children.

Gray fighting winter winds, come along on the tear-
    ing blizzard tails, the snouts of the hungry
    hunting storms, come fighting gray in winter.

Winds of the Windy City,
Winds of corn and sea blue,
Spring wind white and fighting winter gray,
Come home here—they nickname a city for you.

The wind of the lake shore waits and wanders.
The heave of the shore wind hunches the sand piles.

The winkers of the morning stars count out cities
And forget the numbers.

LOST

Desolate and lone
All night long on the lake
Where fog trails and mist creeps,
The whistle of a boat
Calls and cries unendingly,
Like some lost child
In tears and trouble
Hunting the harbor's breast
And the harbor's eyes.

WIND HORSES

Roots, go deep: wrap your coils; fasten your knots:
Fix a loop far under, a four-in-hand far under:
The wind drives wild horses, gnashers, plungers:
   Go deep, roots.
Hold your four-in-hand knots against all wild horses.

SAND SCRIBBLINGS

The wind stops, the wind begins.
The wind says stop, begin.

A sea shovel scrapes the sand floor.
The shovel changes, the floor changes.

The sandpipers, maybe they know.
Maybe a three-pointed foot can tell.
Maybe the fog moon they fly to, guesses.

The sandpipers cheep "Here" and get away.
Five of them fly and keep together flying.

Night hair of some sea woman
Curls on the sand when the sea leaves
The salt tide without a good-by.

Boxes on the beach are empty.
Shake 'em and the nails loosen.
They have been somewhere.

SEA SLANT

On up the sea slant,
On up the horizon,
This ship limps.

The bone of her nose fog-gray,
The heart of her sea-strong,
She came a long way,
She goes a long way.

On up the horizon,
On up the sea-slant,
She limps sea-strong, fog-gray.

She is a green-lit night gray
She comes and goes in the sea fog.
Up the horizon slant she limps.

SKETCH

The shadows of the ships
Rock on the crest
In the low blue lustre
Of the tardy and the soft inrolling tide.

A long brown bar at the dip of the sky
Puts an arm of sand in the span of salt.

The lucid and endless wrinkles
Draw in, lapse and withdraw.

Wavelets crumble and white spent bubbles
Wash on the floor of the beach.

Rocking on the crest
In the low blue lustre
Are the shadows of the ships.

FOG

The fog comes
on little cat feet.

It sits looking
over harbor and city
on silent haunches
and then moves on.

SANDPIPERS

Ten miles of flat land along the sea.
Sandland where the salt water kills the sweet potatoes.
Homes for sandpipers—the script of their feet is on the sea shingles
    —they write in the morning, it is gone at noon—they write at
    noon, it is gone at night.

Pity the land, the sea, the ten mile flats, pity anything but the sandpipers' wire legs and feet.

SEA-WASH

The sea-wash never ends.
The sea-wash repeats, repeats.
Only old songs? Is that all the sea knows?
    Only the old strong songs?
    Is that all?
The sea-wash repeats, repeats.

BITTER SUMMER THOUGHTS

The riders of the wind
Weave their shadows,
Trample their time-beats,
Take their time-bars,
Shake out scrolls,
And run over the oats, the barley,
Over the summer wheat-fields.

The farmer and the horse,
The steel and the wagon
Come and clean the fields
And leave us stubble.
The time-bars of the wind are gone;
The shadows, time-beats, scrolls,
They are woven away, put past,
Into the hands of threshers,
Into chaff, into dust,
Into rust and buff of straw stacks,
Into sliding, shoveling oats and wheat.
Over the wheat-fields,
Over the oats,
Summer weaves, is woven away, put past,
Into dust, into rust and buff.

Indian runners ran along this river road.
They cleaned the wind they clutched in ribs and lungs,
Up over the clean ankles, the clean elbows.
The Frenchmen came with lessons and prayers.
The Scotchmen came with horses and rifles.
Cities, war, railroads came.

In the rain storms, in the blizzards,
This river road is clean.

❁ ❁ ❁

Portraits

WINTER WEATHER

It is cold.
The bitter of the winter
whines a story.
It is the colder weather when the truck
drivers sing it would freeze the whiskers
off a brass monkey.
It is the bitterest whining of the winter
now.

Well, we might sit down now, have a cup of coffee
apiece, and talk about the weather.
We might look back on things that happened long
ago, times when the weather was different.
Or we might talk about things ahead of us, funny
things in the days, days, days to come, days when
the weather will be different again.

Yes, a cup of coffee apiece.
Even if this winter weather is bitter,
The truck drivers are laughing:
It would freeze the whiskers off a brass monkey.

MYSTERIOUS BIOGRAPHY

Christofo Colombo was a hungry man,
hunted himself half way round the world;
he began poor, panhandled, ended in jail,
Christofo so hungry, Christofo so poor,
Christofo in the chilly, steel bracelets,
honorable distinguished Christofo Colombo.

FISH CRIER

I know a Jew fish crier down on Maxwell Street with a voice like a
north wind blowing over corn stubble in January.
He dangles herring before prospective customers evincing a joy identi-
cal with that of Pavlowa dancing.
His face is that of a man terribly glad to be selling fish, terribly glad
that God made fish, and customers to whom he may call his wares
from a pushcart.

JAZZ FANTASIA

Drum on your drums, batter on your banjoes,
sob on the long cool winding saxophones.
Go to it, O jazzmen.

Sling your knuckles on the bottoms of the happy
tin pans, let your trombones ooze, and go husha-
husha-hush with the slippery sand-paper.

Moan like an autumn wind high in the lonesome treetops, moan soft
like you wanted somebody terrible, cry like a racing car slipping away
from a motorcycle cop, bang-bang! you jazzmen, bang altogether
drums, traps, banjoes, horns, tin cans—make two people fight on the
top of a stairway and scratch each other's eyes in a clinch tumbling
down the stairs.

Can the rough stuff . . . now a Mississippi steamboat pushes up the
night river with a hoo-hoo-hoo-oo . . . and the green lanterns calling
to the high soft stars . . . a red moon rides on the humps of the low
river hills . . . go to it, O jazzmen.

TO BEACHEY, 1912

Riding against the east,
A veering, steady shadow
Purrs the motor-call
Of the man-bird
Ready with the death-laughter
In his throat
And in his heart always
The love of the big blue beyond.

Only a man,
A far fleck of shadow on the east
Sitting at ease

With his hands on a wheel
And around him the large gray wings.
Hold him, great soft wings,
Keep and deal kindly, O wings,
With the cool, calm shadow at the wheel.

WEEDS

From the time of the early radishes
To the time of the standing corn
Sleepy Henry Hackerman hoes.

There are laws in the village against weeds.
The law says a weed is wrong and shall be killed.
The weeds say life is a white and lovely thing
And the weeds come on and on in irrepressible regiments.
Sleepy Henry Hackerman hoes; and the village law uttering a ban on
    weeds is unchangeable law.

STREET WINDOW

The pawn-shop man knows hunger,
And how far hunger has eaten the heart
Of one who comes with an old keepsake.
Here are wedding rings and baby bracelets,
Scarf pins and shoe buckles, jeweled garters,
Old-fashioned knives with inlaid handles,
Watches of old gold and silver,
Old coins worn with finger-marks.
They tell stories.

ILLINOIS FARMER

Bury this old Illinois farmer with respect.
He slept the Illinois nights of his life after days of work in Illinois
    cornfields.

Now he goes on a long sleep.

The wind he listened to in the cornsilk and the tassels, the wind that combed his red beard zero mornings when the snow lay white on the yellow ears in the bushel basket at the corncrib,

The same wind will now blow over the place here where his hands must dream of Illinois corn.

CHICAGO POET

I saluted a nobody.
I saw him in a looking-glass.
He smiled—so did I.
He crumpled the skin on his forehead,
    frowning—so did I.
Everything I did he did.
I said, "Hello, I know you."
And I was a liar to say so.

Ah, this looking-glass man!
Liar, fool, dreamer, play-actor,
Soldier, dusty drinker of dust—
Ah! he will go with me
Down the dark stairway
When nobody else is looking,
When everybody else is gone.

He locks his elbow in mine,
I lose all—but not him.

MANUAL SYSTEM

Mary has a thingamajig clamped on her ears
And sits all day taking plugs out and sticking plugs in.
Flashes and flashes—voices and voices
                calling for ears to pour words in
Faces at the ends of wires asking for other faces
                at the ends of other wires:

All day taking plugs out and sticking plugs in,
Mary has a thingamajig clamped on her ears.

PSALM OF THOSE WHO GO FORTH BEFORE DAYLIGHT

The policeman buys shoes slow and careful; the teamster buys gloves slow and careful; they take care of their feet and hands; they live on their feet and hands.

The milkman never argues; he works alone and no one speaks to him; the city is asleep when he is on the job; he puts a bottle on six hundred porches and calls it a day's work; he climbs two hundred wooden stairways; two horses are company for him; he never argues.

The rolling-mill men and the sheet-steel men are brothers of cinders; they empty cinders out of their shoes after the day's work; they ask their wives to fix burnt holes in the knees of their trousers; their necks and ears are covered with a smut; they scour their necks and ears; they are brothers of cinders.

SOUP

I saw a famous man eating soup.
I say he was lifting a fat broth
Into his mouth with a spoon.
His name was in the newspapers that day
Spelled out in tall black headlines
And thousands of people were talking about him.

When I saw him,
He sat bending his head over a plate
Putting soup in his mouth with a spoon.

Birds and Bugs

LAUGHING CORN

There was a high majestic fooling
Day before yesterday in the yellow corn.

And day after tomorrow in the yellow corn
There will be a high majestic fooling.

The ears ripen in late summer
And come on with a conquering laughter,
Come on with a high and conquering laughter.

The long-tailed blackbirds are hoarse.
One of the smaller blackbirds chitters on a stalk
And a spot of red is on its shoulder
And I never heard its name in my life.

Some of the ears are bursting.
A white juice works inside.
Cornsilk creeps in the end and dangles in the wind.
Always—I never knew it any other way—
The wind and the corn talk things over together.
And the rain and the corn and the sun and the corn
Talk things over together.

Over the road is the farmhouse.
The siding is white and a green blind is slung loose.
It will not be fixed till the corn is husked.
The farmer and his wife talk things over together.

BUG SPOTS

This bug carries spots on his back.
Last summer he carried these spots.
Now it is spring and he is back here again
With a domino design over his wings.
All winter he has been in a bedroom,
In a hole, in a hammock, hung up, stuck away,
Stashed while the snow blew over
The wind and the dripping icicles,
The tunnels of the frost.
Now he has errands again in a rotten stump.

PEARL COBWEBS

from SMOKE AND STEEL

Pearl cobwebs in the windy rain,
in only a flicker of wind,
are caught and lost and never known again.

A pool of moonshine comes and waits,
but never waits long: the wind picks up
loose gold like this and is gone.

A bar of steel sleeps and looks slant-eyed
on the pearl cobwebs, the pools of moonshine;
sleeps slant-eyed a million years,
sleeps with a coat of rust, a vest of moths,
a shirt of gathering sod and loam.

The wind never bothers . . . a bar of steel.
The wind picks only . . . pearl cobwebs . . . pools of moonshine.

SPRING GRASS

Spring grass, there is a dance to be danced
   for you.
Come up, spring grass, if only for young feet.
Come up, spring grass, young feet ask you.

Smell of the young spring grass,
You're a mascot riding on the wind horses.
You came to my nose and spiffed me. This is
   your lucky year.

Young spring grass just after the winter,
Shoots of the big green whisper of the year,
Come up, if only for young feet.
Come up, young feet ask you.

PEOPLE OF THE EAVES,
I WISH YOU GOOD MORNING

The wrens have troubles like us. The house of a wren will not run itself
any more than the house of a man.

They chatter the same as two people in a flat where the laundry came
back with the shirts of another man and the shimmy of another woman.

The shirt of a man wren and the shimmy of a woman wren are a trouble in the wren house. It is this or something else back of this chatter a
spring morning.

Trouble goes so quick in the wren house. Now they are hopping wren
jigs beaten off in a high wren staccato time.

People of the eaves, I wish you good morning, I wish you a thousand
thanks.

JUST BEFORE APRIL CAME

The snow-piles in dark places are gone.
Pools by the railroad tracks shine clear.
The gravel of all shallow places shines.
A white pigeon reels and somersaults.

Frogs plutter and squdge—and frogs beat
       the air with a recurring thin
       steel sliver of melody.
Crows go in fives and tens; they march their
       black feathers past a blue pool; they
       celebrate an old festival.
A spider is trying his webs, a pink bug sits
       on my hand washing his forelegs.
I might ask: Who are these people?

MAROON WITH SILVER FROST

Whispers of maroon came on the little river.
The slashed hill took up the sunset,
Took up the evening star.
The brambles crackled in a fire call
To the beginnings of frost.
"It is almost night," the maroon whispered
   in widening blood rings on the little river.
"It is night," the sunset, the evening star
   said later over the hump of the slashed hill.
"What if it is?" the brambles crackled across
   the sure silver beginnings of frost.

RAT RIDDLES

There was a gray rat looked at me
with green eyes out of a rathole.

"Hello, rat," I said,
"Is there any chance for me
to get on to the language of the rats?"

And the green eyes blinked at me,
blinked from a gray rat's rathole.

"Come again," I said,
"Slip me a couple of riddles;
there must be riddles among the rats."

And the green eyes blinked at me
and a whisper came from the gray rathole:
"Who do you think you are and why is a rat?
Where did you sleep last night and why do
  you sneeze on Tuesdays? And why is the
  grave of a rat no deeper than the grave
  of a man?"

And the tail of a green-eyed rat
Whipped and was gone at a gray rathole.

CRICKET MARCH

As the corn becomes higher
The one shrill of a summer cricket
Becomes two and ten
With a shrilling surer than last month.

As the banners of the corn
Come to their highest flying in the wind,
The summer crickets come to a marching army.

SPLINTER

The voice of the last cricket
across the first frost

is one kind of good-by.
It is so thin a splinter of singing.

EVENING WATERFALL

What was the name you called me?—
And why did you go so soon?

The crows lift their caw on the wind,
And the wind changed and was lonely.

The warblers cry their sleepy-songs
Across the valley gloaming,
Across the cattle-horns of early stars.

Feathers and people in the crotch of a treetop
Throw an evening waterfall of sleepy-songs.

What was the name you called me?—
And why did you go so soon?

SMALL HOMES

The green bug sleeps in the white lily ear.
The red bug sleeps in the white magnolia.
Shiny wings, you are choosers of color.
You have taken your summer bungalows wisely.

Night

MILK-WHITE MOON,
PUT THE COWS TO SLEEP

Milk-white moon, put the cows to sleep.
Since five o'clock in the morning,
Since they stood up out of the grass,
Where they slept on their knees and hocks,
They have eaten grass and given their milk
And eaten grass again and given milk,
And kept their heads and teeth at the earth's face.
   Now they are looking at you, milk-white moon.
   Carelessly as they look at the level landscapes,
   Carelessly as they look at a pail of new white milk,
   They are looking at you, wondering not at all, at all,
   If the moon is the skim face top of a pail of milk,
   Wondering not at all, carelessly looking.
   Put the cows to sleep, milk-white moon,
   Put the cows to sleep.

GOOD NIGHT

Many ways to spell good night.

Fireworks at a pier on the Fourth of July
   spell it with red wheels and yellow spokes.
They fizz in the air, touch the water and quit.
Rockets make a trajectory of gold-and-blue
   and then go out.

Railroad trains at night spell with a smokestack mushrooming a white
  pillar.

Steamboats turn a curve in the Mississippi crying in a baritone that
  crosses lowland cottonfields to a razorback hill.

It is easy to spell good night.
              Many ways to spell good night.

LUMBER YARD POOLS AT SUNSET

The rain pools in the old lumber yard
change as the sky changes.

No sooner do lightfoot sunset maroons
cross the west than they cross the rain
pools too.

So now every blue has a brother
and every singing silver a sister.

SUMMER STARS

Bend low again, night of summer stars.
So near you are, sky of summer stars,
So near, a long-arm man can pick off stars,
Pick off what he wants in the sky bowl,
So near you are, summer stars,
So near, strumming, strumming,
          So lazy and hum-strumming.

NOCTURN CABBAGE

Cabbages catch at the moon.
It is late summer, no rain, the pack of the soil
  cracks open, it is a hard summer.

In the night the cabbages catch at the moon, the
leaves drip silver, the rows of cabbages are
series of little silver waterfalls in the moon.

SLEEPYHEADS

Sleep is a maker of makers. Birds sleep. Feet cling to a perch. Look
at the balance. Let the legs loosen, the backbone untwist, the head go
heavy over, the whole works tumbles a done bird off the perch.

Fox cubs sleep. The pointed head curls round into hind legs and tail.
It is a ball of red hair. It is a muff waiting. A wind might whisk it in
the air across pastures and rivers, a cocoon, a pod of seeds. The
snooze of the black nose is in a circle of red hair.

Old men sleep. In chimney corners, in rocking chairs, at wood stoves,
steam radiators. They talk and forget and nod and are out of talk
with closed eyes. Forgetting to live. Knowing the time has come useless for them to live. Old eagles and old dogs run and fly in the
dreams.

Babies sleep. In flannels the papoose faces, the bambino noses, and dodo, dodo the song of many matushkas. Babies—a leaf on a tree in the spring sun. A nub of a new thing sucks the sap of a tree in the sun, yes a new thing, a what-is-it? A left hand stirs, an eyelid twitches, the milk in the belly bubbles and gets to be blood and a left hand and an eyelid. Sleep is a maker of makers.

SMOKE ROSE GOLD

The dome of the capitol looks to the Potomac river.
      Out of haze over the sunset,
      Out of a smoke rose gold:
One star shines over the sunset.
Night takes the dome and the river, the sun and the smoke rose gold,
The haze changes from sunset to star.
The pour of a thin silver struggles against the dark.
A star might call: It's a long way across.

EARLY MOON

The baby moon, a canoe, a silver papoose canoe, sails and sails in
    the Indian west.
A ring of silver foxes, a mist of silver foxes, sit and sit around the In-
    dian moon.
One yellow star for a runner, and rows of blue stars for more runners,
    keep a line of watchers.
O foxes, baby moon, runners, you are the panel of memory, fire-white
    writing tonight of the Red Man's dreams.
Who squats, legs crossed and arms folded, matching its look against the
    moon-face, the star-faces, of the West?
Who are the Mississippi Valley ghosts, of copper foreheads, riding wiry
    ponies in the night?—no bridles, love-arms on the pony necks, rid-
    ing in the night a long old trail?
Why do they always come back when the silver foxes sit around the
    early moon, a silver papoose, in the Indian west?

SUNSETS

There are sunsets who whisper a good-by.
It is a short dusk and a way for stars.
Prairie and sea rim they go level and even
And the sleep is easy.

There are sunsets who dance good-by.
They fling scarves half to the arc,
To the arc then and over the arc.
Ribbons at the ears, sashes at the hips,
Dancing, dancing good-by. And here sleep
Tosses a little with dreams.

VALLEY SONG

The sunset swept
To the valley's west, you remember.

The frost was on.
A star burnt blue.
We were warm, you remember,
And counted the rings on a moon.

The sunset swept
To the valley's west
And was gone in a big dark door of stars.

✿ ✿ ✿

End Thoughts

HAPPINESS

I asked professors who teach the meaning of life to tell me what is
  happiness.
And I went to famous executives who boss the work of thousands of
  men.
They all shook their heads and gave me a smile as though I was
  trying to fool with them.
And then one Sunday afternoon I wandered out along the Desplaines
  river
And I saw a crowd of Hungarians under the trees with their women
  and children and a keg of beer and an accordion.

PRAYERS OF STEEL

Lay me on an anvil, O God.
Beat me and hammer me into a crowbar.
Let me pry loose old walls.
Let me lift and loosen old foundations.

Lay me on an anvil, O God.
Beat me and hammer me into a steel spike.
Drive me into the girders that hold a skyscraper together.
Take red-hot rivets and fasten me into the central girders.
Let me be the great nail holding a skyscraper through blue nights into
  white stars.

TRINITY PLACE

The grave of Alexander Hamilton is in Trinity yard at the end of Wall
 Street.

The grave of Robert Fulton likewise is in Trinity yard where Wall
 Street stops.

And in this yard stenogs, bundle boys, scrubwomen, sit on the tomb-
 stones, and walk on the grass of graves, speaking of war and
 weather, of babies, wages and love.

An iron picket fence . . . and streaming thousands along Broadway
 sidewalks . . . straw hats, faces, legs . . . a singing, talking, hustling
 river . . . down the great street that ends with a Sea.

 . . . easy is the sleep of Alexander Hamilton.
 . . . easy is the sleep of Robert Fulton.
 . . . easy are the great governments and the great steamboats.

DO YOU WANT AFFIDAVITS?

There's a hole in the bottom of the sea.
      Do you want affidavits?
There's a man in the moon with money for you.
      Do you want affidavits?
There are ten dancing girls in a sea-chamber off Nantucket waiting
 for you.
There are tall candles in Timbuctoo burning penance for you.
There are—anything else?
Speak now—for now we stand amid the great wishing windows—and
 the law says we are free to be wishing all this week at the windows.
Shall I raise my right hand and swear to you in the monotone of a no-
 tary public? this is "the truth, the whole truth, and nothing but the
 truth."

✿ WIND SONG

To John Carl and Karlen Paula

Dear young folks:

Some poems may please you for half a minute & you don't care whether you keep them or not. Other poems you may feel to be priceless & you hug them to your heart & keep them for sure. Here in this book poems of each kind may be found: you do the finding.

I sign this book for you saying love & blessings: may luck stars ever be over you.

Carl Sandburg

✿ ✿ ✿

New Poems

BLUEBIRD, WHAT DO YOU FEED ON?

Bluebird, what do you feed on?
It is true you gobble up worms, you
　swallow bugs,
And your bill picks up corn, seed,
　berries.
This is only part of the answer.
Your feathers have captured a piece of
　smooth sky.
Your wings are burnished with
　lake-morning blue.

It is not a worm blue nor a bug
  blue nor the blue
Of corn or berry you shine with.
Bluebird, we come to you for facts,
  for valuable
Information, for secret reports.
Bluebird, tell us, what do you
    feed on?

NEVER TWO SONGS THE SAME

the light on the leaves
in girlish early spring
    the deep green of the matron leaves
    in the stride of high summer suns
the colors of the turning oak and maple
when October crosses gold and brown
    there is winter then to wait for
    when trees wear frost of a morning
            wear snow of an evening
    when bare branches often reach out
    saying they would be lonely
    only for the wind coming
    with never two songs the same
    with changes always in the old songs

DAYBREAK

Daybreak comes first
  in thin splinters shimmering.
Neither is the day here
  nor is the night gone.
Night is getting ready to go
And Day whispers, "Soon now, soon."

BEE SONG

Bees in the late summer sun
Drone their song
Of yellow moons
Trimming black velvet,
Droning, droning a sleepysong.

BUBBLES

Two bubbles found they had rainbows on their curves.
They flickered out saying:
"It was worth being a bubble just to have held that
  rainbow thirty seconds."

OLD DEEP SING-SONG

in the old deep sing-song of the sea
in the old going-on of that sing-song
in that old mama-mama-mama going-on
of that nightlong daylong sleepsong
we look on   we listen
we lay by and hear
too many big bells   too many long gongs
too many weepers over a lost gone gold
too many laughs over light green gold
woven and changing in the wash and the heave
moving on the bottoms   winding in the waters
sending themselves with arms and voices
up in the old mama-mama-mama music
up into the whirl of spokes of light

FOURTH OF JULY NIGHT

The little boat at anchor
in black water sat murmuring
to the tall black sky.
   . . .

 A white sky bomb fizzed on a black line.
 A rocket hissed its red signature into the west.
 Now a shower of Chinese fire alphabets,
 a cry of flower pots broken in flames,
 a long curve to a purple spray,
 three violet balloons—
   Drips of seaweed tangled in gold,
   shimmering symbols of mixed numbers,
   tremulous arrangements of cream gold folds
   of a bride's wedding gown—
    . . .

A few sky bombs spoke their pieces,
then velvet dark.

The little boat at anchor
in black water sat murmuring
to the tall black sky.

SEA WISDOM

 The sea was always the sea
 and a maker was the sea always.
 What the sea was making you may know
 by asking the sea and getting an answer.
 Well the sea knows its own importance.
 Well the sea will answer you when it knows
      your importance.

NIGHTSONG

bring me now the bright flower
of the moongold grass—
let me have later on the horizon
the black gold of moonset—
spill for me then the bowl of dawn
overshot and streaming—
for men have often seen and taken
night as a changing scene
priceless yet paid for

PORTRAIT OF A CHILD SETTLING DOWN FOR AN AFTERNOON NAP

Marquita had blossom fists
   and bubble toes.
I saw them, touched them,
the same as an oak gnarled and worn
when the wind bends it down
to a frail hope of an oak
and their leaves touch
and branch whispers to branch.

"Baby say blossom for you are a blossom,
Baby say bubble for you are a bubble,"
   I said to Marquita.
And as she lay ready
and prepared to spit at the sky,
I told her to spit in the face of the wind,
not yet having learned what happens.

   San Francisco lay in silver tones
   and the Golden Gate swaddled
   in frames of blue mountains

while Marquita lay swathed as a sweet pig,
pink as a fresh independent pig
                    ready to spit at the sky.

STARS

The stars are too many to count.
The stars make sixes and sevens.
The stars tell nothing—and everything.
The stars look scattered.
Stars are so far away they never speak
    when spoken to.

BE READY

Be land ready
for you shall go back to land.

Be sea ready
for you have been nine-tenths water
and the salt taste shall cling to your mouth.

Be sky ready
for air, air, has been so needful to you—
you shall go back, back to the sky.

AUCTIONEER

Now I go down here and bring up a moon.
How much am I bid for the moon?
You see it a bright moon and brand-new.
What can I get to start it?   how much?
What! who ever ever heard such a bid for a moon?
    Come now, gentlemen, come.
This is a solid guaranteed moon.
You may never have another chance
    to make a bid on such a compact
    eighteen-carat durable gold moon.
You could shape a thousand wedding rings
    out of this moongold.
I can guarantee the gold and the weddings
    will last forever
    and then a thousand years more.
Come gentlemen, no nonsense, make me a bid.

SLEEP SONG

Into any little room
may come a tall steel bridge
and a long white fog,
changing lights and mist,
moving as if a great sea
and many mighty waters
had come into that room
easy with bundles of sleep,
bundles of sea-moss sheen,
shapes of sunset cunning,
shifts of moonrise gold—
    slow talk of low fog
    on your forehead,
    hands of cool fog
    on your eyes—

so let a sleep song be spoken—
let spoken fog sheets come
out of a long white harbor—
let a slow mist deliver
long bundles of sleep.

ALICE CORBIN IS GONE

Alice Corbin is gone
and the Indians tell us where.
  She trusted the Indians
  and they kept a trust in her.
She took a four-line Indian song
  and put it into English.
You can sing it over and over:

The wind is carrying me round the sky;
The wind is carrying me round the sky.
  My body is here in the valley—
The wind is carrying me round the sky.

LINES WRITTEN FOR GENE KELLY TO DANCE TO

Spring is when the grass turns green and glad.
Spring is when the new grass comes up and says, "Hey, hey!
  Hey, hey!"
Be dizzy now and turn your head upside down and see how
  the world looks upside down.
Be dizzy now and turn a cartwheel, and see the good earth
  through a cartwheel.

Tell your feet the alphabet.
Tell your feet the multiplication table.
Tell your feet where to go, and watch 'em go and come back.

Can you dance a question mark?
Can you dance an exclamation point?

Can you dance a couple of commas?
And bring it to a finish with a period?

Can you dance like the wind is pushing you?
Can you dance like you are pushing the wind?
Can you dance with slow wooden heels
   and then change to bright and singing silver heels?
Such nice feet, such good feet.

So long as grass grows and rivers run
Silver lakes like blue porcelain plates
Silver snakes of winding rivers.
You can see 'em on a map.

Why we got geography?
Because we go from place to place. Because the earth used to be flat
   and had four corners, and you could jump off from any of the corners.
But now the earth is not flat any more. Now it is round all over. Now
   it is a globe, a ball, round all over, and we would all fall off it and
   tumble away into space if it wasn't for the magnetic poles. And
   when you dance it is the North Pole or the South Pole pulling on
   your feet like magnets to keep your feet on the earth.
And that's why we got geography.
And it's nice to have it that way.

Why does duh Mississippi River wind and wind?
Why, dat's easy. She wind so she git where she wanna go.
Mississippi, Rappahannock, Punxatawney. Spell out their names with
   your heels.

Where duh towns uh Punxatawney and Mauk Chunk? Why, yeanh day's
   bof in Pennsylvan-ee-eye-ay.
   And dat's why we got geography.

Left foot, tweedle-dum—right foot tweedle-dee, here they go.

When Yankee Doodle come to town, wot wuz he a-ridin' on?
A buffalo? A elephant? A horse?
No, no, no, no. A pony it wuz, a pony.
That's right—

Giddi-ap, Giddi-ap, Giddi-ap, Giddi-ap.
Whoa! Whoa!

❀ ❀ ❀

Little People

LITTLE GIRL, BE CAREFUL WHAT YOU SAY

Little girl, be careful what you say
when you make talk with words, words—
for words are made of syllables
and syllables, child, are made of air—
and air is so thin—air is the breath of God—
air is finer than fire or mist,
finer than water or moonlight,
finer than spider-webs in the moon,
finer than water-flowers in the morning:
    and words are strong, too,
    stronger than rocks or steel
stronger than potatoes, corn, fish, cattle,
and soft, too, soft as little pigeon-eggs,
soft as the music of hummingbird wings.
    So, little girl, when you speak greetings,
when you tell jokes, make wishes or prayers,
    be careful, be careless, be careful,
    be what you wish to be.

CHILDREN OF THE DESERT

from THE PEOPLE, YES

1.

The old timer on the desert was gray
and grizzled with ever seeing the sun:

"For myself I don't care whether it rains.
I've seen it rain.
But I'd like to have it rain
pretty soon sometime.
Then my son could see it.
He's never seen it rain."

2.

"What is the east? Have you been in the east?"
the New Jersey woman asked the little girl
the wee child growing up in Arizona who said:
"Yes, I've been in the east,
the east is where trees come
between you and the sky."

BUFFALO BILL

Boy heart of Johnny Jones—aching today?
Aching, and Buffalo Bill in town?
Buffalo Bill and ponies, cowboys, Indians?

Some of us know
All about it, Johnny Jones.
Buffalo Bill is a slanting look of the eyes,
    A slanting look under a hat on a horse.
He sits on a horse and a passing look is fixed
    On Johnny Jones, you and me, barelegged,
A slanting, passing, careless look under a hat on a horse.

Go clickety-clack, O pony hoofs along the street.
Come on and slant your eyes again, O Buffalo Bill.
Give us again the ache of our boy hearts.
Fill us again with the red love of prairies, dark nights, lonely wagons,
    and the crack-crack of rifles sputtering flashes into an ambush.

WE MUST BE POLITE

(Lessons for children on how to behave under
peculiar circumstances)

1

If we meet a gorilla
what shall we do?
Two things we may do
if we so wish to do.

Speak to the gorilla,
very, very respectfully,
"How do you do, sir?"

Or, speak to him with less
distinction of manner,
"Hey, why don't you go back
where you came from?"

2

If an elephant knocks on your door
and asks for something to eat,
there are two things to say:

Tell him there are nothing but cold
victuals in the house and he will do
better next door.

Or say: We have nothing but six bushels
of potatoes—will that be enough for
your breakfast, sir?

ARITHMETIC

Arithmetic is where numbers fly like pigeons in and out of your
head.

Arithmetic tells you how many you lose or win if you know how many you had before you lost or won.

Arithmetic is seven eleven all good children go to heaven—or five six bundle of sticks.

Arithmetic is numbers you squeeze from your head to your hand to your pencil to your paper till you get the answer.

Arithmetic is where the answer is right and everything is nice and you can look out of the window and see the blue sky—or the answer is wrong and you have to start all over and try again and see how it comes out this time.

If you take a number and double it and double it again and then double it a few more times, the number gets bigger and bigger and goes higher and higher and only arithmetic can tell you what the number is when you decide to quit doubling.

Arithmetic is where you have to multiply—and you carry the multiplication table in your head and hope you won't lose it.

If you have two animal crackers, one good and one bad, and you eat one and a striped zebra with streaks all over him eats the other, how many animal crackers will you have if somebody offers you five six seven and you say No no no and you say Nay nay nay and you say Nix nix nix?

If you ask your mother for one fried egg for breakfast and she gives you two fried eggs and you eat both of them, who is better in arithmetic, you or your mother?

BOXES AND BAGS

The bigger the box the more it holds.

Empty boxes hold the same as empty heads.

Enough small empty boxes thrown into a big empty box fill it full.

A half-empty box says, "Put more in."

A big enough box could hold the world.

Elephants need big boxes to hold a dozen elephant handkerchiefs.

Fleas fold little handkerchiefs and fix them nice and heat in flea handkerchief-boxes.

Bags lean against each other and boxes stand independent.

Boxes are square with corners unless round with circles.

Box can be piled on box till the whole works comes tumbling.

Pile box on box and the bottom box says, "If you will kindly take notice you will see it all rests on me."
Pile box on box and the top one says, "Who falls farthest if or when
we fall? I ask you."
Box people go looking for boxes and bag people go looking for bags.

SIXTEEN MONTHS

On the lips of the child Janet float changing dreams.
It is a thin spiral of blue smoke,
A morning campfire at a mountain lake.

On the lips of the child Janet,
Wisps of haze on ten miles of corn,
Young light blue calls to young light gold of morning.

MARGARET

Many birds and the beating of wings
Make a flinging reckless hum
In the early morning at the rocks
Above the blue pool
Where the gray shadows swim lazy.

In your blue eyes, O reckless child,
I saw today many little wild wishes,
Eager as the great morning.

LAUGHING CHILD

from THREE SPRING NOTATIONS ON BIPEDS

The child is on my shoulders.
In the prairie moonlight the child's legs
    hang over my shoulders.

She sits on my neck and I hear her calling
  me a good horse.
She slides down—and into the moon silver of
  a prairie stream.
She throws a stone and laughs at the clug-clug.

SWEEPING WENDY: STUDY IN FUGUE

Wendy put her black eyes on me
and swept me with her black eyes—
sweep on sweep she swept me.
    Have you ever seen Wendy?
    Have you ever seen her sweep
    Keeping her black eyes on you
    keeping you eyeswept?

CHILD MARGARET

The child Margaret begins to write numbers on a Saturday morning,
    the first numbers formed under her wishing child fingers.
All the numbers come well-born, shaped in figures assertive for a
    frieze in a child's room.
Both 1 and 7 are straightforward, military, filled with lunge
    and attack, erect in shoulder-straps.
The 6 and 9 salute as dancing sisters, elder and younger, and
    2 is a trapeze actor swinging to handclaps.
All the numbers are well-born, only 3 has a hump on its back
    and 8 is knock-kneed.
The child Margaret kisses all once and gives two kisses to 3 and 8.
(Each number is a brand-new rag doll. . . . O in the wishing fin-
    gers . . . millions of rag dolls, millions and millions of new rag
    dolls!!)

PAPER I

Paper is two kinds, to write on, to wrap with.
If you like to write, you write.
If you like to wrap, you wrap.
Some papers like writers, some like wrappers.
Are you a writer or a wrapper?

PAPER II

I write what I know on one side of the paper
    and what I don't know on the other.
Fire likes dry paper and wet paper laughs at
    fire.
Empty paper sacks say, "Put something in me,
    what are we waiting for?"
Paper sacks packed to the limit say, "We hope
    we don't bust."
Paper people like to meet other paper people.

DOORS

An open door says, "Come in."
A shut door says, "Who are you?"
Shadows and ghosts go through shut doors.
If a door is shut and you want it shut,
    why open it?
If a door is open and you want it open,
    why shut it?
Doors forget but only doors know what it is
    doors forget.

❁ ❁ ❁

Little Album

NAMES

from Prologue *to* THE FAMILY OF MAN

There is only one horse on the earth
and his name is All Horses.

There is only one bird in the air
and his name is All Wings.
There is only one fish in the sea
and his name is All Fins.
There is only one man in the world
and his name is All Men.
There is only one woman in the world
and her name is All Women.
There is only one child in the world
and the child's name is All Children.
　　There is only one Maker in the world
　　and His children cover the earth
　　and they are named All God's Children.

PROVERBS

from THE PEOPLE, YES

We'll see what we'll see.
Time is a great teacher.
Today me and tomorrow maybe you.
This old anvil laughs at many broken hammers.
What is bitter to stand against today may be sweet to remember tomor-
　row.
Fine words butter no parsnips. Moonlight dries no mittens.
Whether the stone bumps the jug or the jug bumps the stone it is bad
　for the jug.
One hand washes the other and both wash the face.
Better leave the child's nose dirty than wring it off.
We all belong to the same big family and have the same smell.
Handling honey, tar or dung some of it sticks to the fingers.
　The liar comes to believe his own lies.
He who burns himself must sit on the blisters.
　God alone understands fools.
　　　　　　　　　* * *
The sea has fish for every man.
Every blade of grass has its share of dew.
　The longest day must have its end.
Man's life? A candle in the wind, hoar-frost
　　on stone.

Nothing more certain than death and nothing
      more uncertain than the hour.
Men live like birds together in a wood; when
      the time comes each takes his flight.
As wave follows wave, so new men take old
      men's places.

HOME

from POEMS DONE ON A LATE NIGHT CAR

Here is a thing my heart wishes the world had more of:
I heard it in the air of one night when I listened
To a mother singing softly to a child restless and angry in the dark-
      ness.

GOLDWING MOTH

A goldwing moth is between the scissors and the ink bottle on the desk.
Last night it flew hundreds of circles around a glass bulb and a flame
      wire.
The wings are a soft gold; it is the gold of illuminated initials in man-
      uscripts of the medieval monks.

SO TO SPEAK

Dreams, graves, pools, growing
flowers, cornfields—these are
silent, so to speak.

Northwest blizzards, sea rocks
apounding in high wind, southeast
sleet after a thaw—these are heard,
so to speak.

CIRCLES

from THE PEOPLE, YES

The white man drew a small circle in the sand
and told the red man, "This is what the Indian
knows," and drawing a big circle around the
small one, "This is what the white man knows."
The Indian took the stick and swept an immense
ring around both circles: "This is where the
white man and the red man know nothing."

MY PEOPLE

My people are gray,
   pigeon gray, dawn gray, storm gray.
I call them beautiful,
   and I wonder where they are going.

BASKET

Speak, sir, and be wise.
Speak choosing your words, sir,
   like an old woman over a bushel
   of apples.

HATS

Hats, where do you belong?
   what is under you?

On the rim of a skyscraper's forehead
I looked down and saw: hats: fifty thousand hats:

Swarming with a noise of bees and sheep, cattle and waterfalls,
Stopping with a silence of sea grass, a silence of prairie corn.
Hats: tell me your high hopes.

UNDER A HAT RIM

While the hum and the hurry
Of passing footfalls
Beat in my ear like the restless surf
Of a wind-blown sea,
A soul came to me
Out of the look on a face.

Eyes like a lake
Where a storm-wind roams
Caught me from under
The rim of a hat.
I thought of a midsea wreck
and bruised fingers clinging
to a broken state-room door.

HITS AND RUNS

I remember the Chillicothe ball players grappling the Rock Island
ball players in a sixteen-inning game ended by darkness.
And the shoulders of the Chillicothe players were a red smoke against
the sundown and the shoulders of the Rock Island players were a
yellow smoke against the sundown.
And the umpire's voice was hoarse calling balls and strikes and outs
and the umpire's throat fought in the dust for a song.

NEW HAMPSHIRE AGAIN

I remember black winter waters,
I remember thin white birches,
I remember sleepy twilight hills,
I remember riding across New
  Hampshire lengthways.
I remember a station named
  "Halcyon," a brakeman call-
  ing to passengers "Halcyon!!
  Halcyon!! "
I remember having heard the
  gold diggers dig out only
  enough for weddings rings.
I remember a stately child tell-
  ing me her father gets letters
  addressed "Robert Frost, New
  Hampshire."
I remember an old Irish saying,
  "His face is like a fiddle and
  every one who sees him must
  love him."

I have one remember, two re-
    members, ten remembers; I
    have a little handkerchief
    bundle of remembers.

One early evening star just over
    a cradle moon,
One dark river with a spatter of
    later stars caught,
One funnel of a motorcar head-
    light up a hill,
One team of horses hauling a
    bobsled load of wood,
One boy on skis picking himself
    up after a tumble—
I remember one and a one and a
    one riding across New Hamp-
    shire lengthways: I have a lit-
    tle handkerchief bundle of re-
    members.

NIAGARA

from THE PEOPLE, YES

The tumblers of the rapids go white, go green,
go changing over the gray, the brown, the rocks.
The fight of the water, the stones,
the fight makes a foam laughter
before the last look over the long slide
down the spread of a sheen in the straight fall.
    Then the growl, the chutter,
    down under the boom and the muffle,
    the hoo hoi deep,
    the hoo hoi down,
    this is Niagara.

CHEAP BLUE

Hill blue among the leaves in summer,
Hill blue among the branches in winter—
Light sea blue at the sand beaches in winter,
Deep sea blue in the deep deep waters—
Prairie blue, mountain blue—
   Who can pick a pocketful of these blues,
     a handkerchief of these blues,
   And go walking, talking, walking as though
   God gave them a lot of loose change
   For spending money, to throw at the birds,
   To flip into the tin cups of blind men?

MOTHER AND CHILD

from THE PEOPLE, YES

   "I love you,"
said a great mother.
"I love you for what you are
knowing so well what you are.
And I love you more yet, child,
deeper yet than ever, child,
for what you are going to be,
knowing so well you are going far,
knowing your great works are ahead,
ahead and beyond,
yonder and far over yet."

❀ ❀ ❀

Corn Belt

IMPROVED FARM LAND

Tall timber stood here once, here on a corn belt farm along the
Monon.

Here the roots of a half mile of trees dug their runners deep in the
loam for a grip and a hold against wind storms.

Then the axmen came and the chips flew to the zing of steel and
handle—the lank railsplitters cut the big ones first, the beeches and
the oaks, then the brush.

Dynamite, wagons and horses took the stumps—the plows sunk their
teeth in—now it is first class corn land—improved property—and
the hogs grunt over the fodder crops.

It would come hard now for this half mile of improved farm land
along the Monon corn belt, on a piece of Grand Prairie, to remember once it had a great singing family of trees.

PLOWBOY

After the last red sunset glimmer,
Black on the line of a low hill rise,
Formed into moving shadows, I saw
A plowboy and two horses lined against the gray,
Plowing in the dusk the last furrow.
The turf had a gleam of brown,
And smell of soil was in the air,
And, cool and moist, a haze of April.

I shall remember you long,
Plowboy and horses against the sky in shadow.

I shall remember you and the picture
You made for me,
Turning the turf in the dusk
And haze of an April gloaming.

FROG SONGS

The silver burbles of the frogs wind and swirl.
The lines of their prongs swing up in a spray.
They cut the air with bird line curves.
The eye sees nothing, the ear is filled, the head remembers
The beat of the swirl of frog throat silver prongs
In the early springtime when eggs open, when feet learn,
When the crying of the water begins a new year.

SHE OPENS THE BARN DOOR
EVERY MORNING

Open the barn door, farm woman,
It is time for the cows to be milked.
Their udders are full from the sleep night.
Open the door with your right hand shuttling a cleat,
Your left hand pulling a handle.
The smell of the barn is let out to the pastures.
Dawn lets itself in at the open door.
A cow left out in the barnyard all the night
Looks on as though you do this every morning.
Open the barn door, farm woman, you do it
As you have done it five hundred times.
As a sleep woman heavy with the earth,
Clean as a milk pail washed in the sun,
You open the barn door a half mile away
And a cow almost turns its head and looks on.

SUMMER MORNING

from PRAIRIE

A wagonload of radishes on a summer morning.
Sprinkles of dew on the crimson-purple balls.
The farmer on the seat dangles the reins on the rumps of dapple-gray
    horses.
The farmer's daughter with a basket of eggs dreams of a new hat to
    wear to the county fair.

BROWN GOLD

The time of the brown gold comes softly.
Oat shocks are alive in brown gold belts,
    the short and the shambling oat shocks
    sit on the stubble and straw.
The timothy hay, the fodder corn, the cabbage
    and the potatoes, across their leaves are
    footsteps.
There is a bold green up over the cracks in
    the corn rows where the crickets go criss-
    cross errands, where the bugs carry pack-
    ages.

Flutter and whirr, you birdies, you newcomers
    in lines and sashes, tellers of harvest
    weather on the way, belts of brown gold
    coming softly.
It is very well the old time streamers take
    up the old time gold haze against the west-
    ern timber line.
It is the old time again when months and birds
    tell each other, "Oh, very well," and repeat it
    where the fields and the timber lines meet
    in belts of brown gold hazes, "Oh, very
    well, Oh, very well."

RIPE CORN

The wind blows. The corn leans. The corn leaves go rustling. The
march time and the windbeat is on October drums. The stalks of fodder bend all one way, the way the last windstorm passed.

"Put on my winter clothes; get me an ulster; a yellow ulster to lay
down in January and shut my eyes and cover my ears in snow drifts."

The wind blows. The corn leans. The fodder is russet. October says to
the leaves, "Rustle now to the last lap, to the last leg of the year."

CORNHUSKERS

from PRAIRIE

The frost loosens cornhusks.
The sun, the rain, the wind
    loosen cornhusks.
The men and women are helpers.
They are all cornhuskers together.
I see them late in the western evening
    in a smoke-red dust.

HAYSTACKS

from PRAIRIE

After the sunburn of the day
handling a pitchfork at a hayrack,
after the eggs and biscuit and coffee,
the pearl-gray haystacks
in the gloaming
are cool prayers
to the harvest hands.

HARVEST SUNSET

Red gold of pools,
Sunset furrows six o'clock,
And the farmer done in the fields
And the cows in the barns with bulging udders.

Take the cows and the farmer,
Take the barns and bulging udders.
Leave the red gold of pools
And sunset furrows six o'clock.
The farmer's wife is singing.
The farmer's boy is whistling.
I wash my hands in red gold of pools.

PRAIRIE BARN

from THE PEOPLE, YES

For sixty years the pine lumber barn
had held cows, horses, hay, harness, tools, junk,
amid the prairie winds of Knox County, Illinois

and the corn crops came and went, plows and wagons,
and hands milked, hands husked and harnessed
and held the leather reins of horse teams
in dust and dog days, in late fall sleet
till the work was done that fall.
And the barn was a witness, stood and saw it all.
    "That old barn on your place, Charlie,
    was nearly falling last time I saw it,
    how is it now?"
    "I got some poles to hold it on the east side
    and the wind holds it up on the west."

LIMITED CROSSING WISCONSIN

from PRAIRIE

A headlight searches a snowstorm.
A funnel of white light shoots from over the pilot of the Pioneer Limited crossing Wisconsin.

In the morning hours, in the dawn,
The sun puts out the stars of the sky
And the headlight of the Limited train.

The fireman waves his hand to a country school teacher on a bobsled.
A boy, yellow hair, red scarf and mittens, on the bobsled, in his lunch
   box a pork chop sandwich and a V of gooseberry pie.

The horses fathom a snow to their knees.
Snow hats are on the rolling prairie hills.
The Mississippi bluffs wear snow hats.

SONGS

from PRAIRIE

When the morning sun is on the trumpet-vine blossoms, sing at the
   kitchen pans: Shout All Over God's Heaven.

When the rain slants on the potato hills and the sun plays a silver shaft
on the last shower, sing to the bush at the backyard fence: Mighty
Lak a Rose.

When the icy sleet pounds on the storm windows and the house lifts to
a great breath, sing for the outside hills: The Ole Sheep Done
Know the Road, the Young Lambs Must Find the Way.

* * *

Spring slips back with a girl face calling always: "Any new songs for
me? Any new songs?"

CORNFIELD RIDGE AND STREAM

The top of the ridge is a cornfield.
It rests all winter under snow.
It feeds the broken snowdrifts in spring
To a clear stream cutting down hill to the river.
Late in summer the stream dries; rabbits run and
  birds hop along the dry mud bottom.
Fall time comes and it fills with leaves; oaks and
  shagbark hickories drop their summer hats,
  ribbons, handkerchiefs.
"This is how I keep warm all winter," the stream
  murmurs, waiting till the snowdrifts melt and
  the ice loosens and the clear singing babble
  of spring comes back.

❀ ❀ ❀

Night

NIGHT

from THE WINDY CITY

Night gathers itself into a ball of dark yarn.
Night loosens the ball and it spreads.

The lookouts from the shores of Lake Michigan
  find night follows day, and ping! ping! across
  sheet gray the boat lights put their signals.
Night lets the dark yarn unravel, Night speaks and the yarns change
  to fog and blue strands.

PRAIRIE WATERS BY NIGHT

Chatter of birds two by two raises a night song joining a litany of
  running water—sheer waters showing the russet of old stones remembering many rains.

And the long willows drowse on the shoulders of the running water,
  and sleep from much music; joined songs of day-end, feathery
  throats and stony waters, in a choir chanting new psalms.

It is too much for the long willows when low laughter of a red moon
  comes down; and the willows drowse and sleep on the shoulders of
  the running water.

TIMBER MOON

There is a way the moon looks into the timber at night
And tells the walnut trees secrets of silver sand—
There is a way the moon makes a lattice work
Under the leaves of the hazel bushes—
There is a way the moon understands the hoot owl
Sitting on an arm of a sugar maple throwing its
One long lonesome cry up the ladders of the moon—
There is a way the moon finds company early in the fall-
      time.

NIGHT TOO HAS NUMBERS

from THE PEOPLE, YES

In the long flat panhandle of Texas
far off on the grassland of the cattle country
near noon they sight a rider coming toward them
and the sky may be a cold neverchanging gray
or the sky may be changing its numbers
back and forth all day even and odd numbers
and the afternoon slides away somewhere
and they see their rider is alive yet
their rider is coming nearer yet
and they expect what happens and it happens again
he and his horse ride in late for supper
yet not too late
and night is on and the stars are out
and night too slides away somewhere
night too has even and odd numbers.

RIVER MOONS

The double moon, one on the high backdrop of the west, one on the
  curve of the river face,

The sky moon of fire and the river moon of water, I am taking these home in a basket, hung on an elbow, such a teeny weeny elbow, in my head.

I saw them last night, a cradle moon, two horns of a moon, such an early hopeful moon, such a child's moon for all young hearts to make a picture of.

The river—I remember this like a picture—the river was the upper twist of a written question mark.

I know now it takes many many years to write a river, a twist of water asking a question.

And white stars moved when the moon moved, and one red star kept burning, and the Big Dipper was almost overhead.

SLEEP IMPRESSION

The dark blue wind of early autumn
ran on the early autumn sky
in the fields of yellow moon harvest.
    I slept, I almost slept,
    I said listening:
Trees you have leaves rustling like rain
When there is no rain.

NOCTURNE IN A DESERTED BRICKYARD

    Stuff of the moon
Runs on the lapping sand
Out to the longest shadows.
Under the curving willows,
And round the creep of the wave line,
Fluxions of yellow and dusk on the waters
Make a wide dreaming pansy of an old pond in the night.

BETWEEN TWO HILLS

Between two hills
The old town stands.
The houses loom
And the roofs and trees
And the dusk and the dark,
The damp and the dew
   Are there.

The prayers are said
And the people rest
For sleep is there
And the touch of dreams
   Is over all.

WINDOW

Night from a railroad car window
Is a great, dark, soft thing
Broken across with slashes of light.

PODS

Pea pods cling to stems.
Neponset, the village,
Clings to the Burlington railway main line.
Terrible midnight limiteds roar through
Hauling sleepers to the Rockies and Sierras.
The earth is slightly shaken
And Neponset trembles slightly in its sleep.

DROWSY

Sleep is the gift of many spiders
The webs tie down the sleepers easy.

SHEEP

Thousands of sheep, soft-footed, black-nosed sheep—one by one going up the hill and over the fence—one by one four-footed pattering up and over—one by one wiggling their stub tails as they take the short jump and go over—one by one silently unless for the multitudinous drumming of their hoofs as they move on and go over—thousands and thousands of them in the gray haze of evening just after sundown—one by one slanting in a long line to pass over the hill—

I am the slow, long-legged Sleepyman and I love you sheep in Persia, California, Argentina, Australia, or Spain—you are the thoughts that help me when I, the Sleepyman, lay my hands on the eyelids of the children of the world at eight o'clock every night—you thousands and thousands of sheep in a procession of dusk making an endless multitudinous drumming on the hills with your hoofs.

❀ ❀ ❀

Blossom Themes

BLOSSOM THEMES

1

Late in the winter came one day
When there was a whiff on the wind,
a suspicion, a cry not to be heard
   of perhaps blossoms, perhaps green
   grass and clean hills lifting rolling shoulders.
Does the nose get the cry of spring
   first of all? is the nose thankful
   and thrilled first of all?

2

If the blossoms come down
so they must fall on snow
because spring comes this year
before winter is gone,
then both snow and blossoms look sad;
peaches, cherries, the red summer apples,
all say it is a hard year.
The wind has its own way of picking off
the smell of peach blossoms and then
carrying that smell miles and miles.
    Women washing dishes in lonely farmhouses
    stand at the door and say, "Something is
    happening."
A little foam of the summer sea
    of blossoms,
    a foam finger of white leaves,
    shut these away—
    high into the summer wind runners.
Let the wind be white too.

GRASSROOTS

Grass clutches at the dark dirt with finger holds.
Let it be blue grass, barley, rye or wheat,
Let it be button weed or butter-and-eggs,
Let it be Johnny-jump-ups springing clean blue streaks.
Grassroots down under put fingers into dark dirt.

LANDSCAPE

See the trees lean to the wind's way of learning.
See the dirt of the hills shape to the water's
    way of learning.
See the lift of it all go the way the biggest
    wind and the strongest water want it.

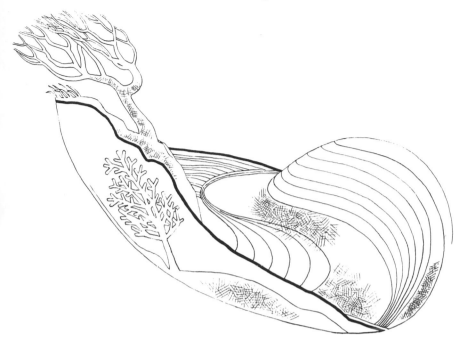

LITTLE SKETCH

There are forked branches of trees
Where the leaves shudder obediently,
Where the hangover leaves
Flow in a curve downward;
And between the forks and leaves,
In patches and angles, in square handfuls,
The orange lights of the done sunset
Come and filter and pour.

FLOWERS TELL MONTHS

Gold buttons in the garden today—
Among the brown-eyed susans the golden spiders are
  gamboling.
The blue sisters of the white asters speak to each other.

After the travel of the snows—
Buttercups come in a yellow rain,
Johnny-jump-ups in a blue mist—
Wild azaleas with a low spring cry.

CRISSCROSS

Spring crosses over into summer.
This is as it always was.

Buds on the redhaw, beetles in the loam,
And the interference of the green leaves
At the blue roofs of the spring sky
Crossing over into summer—
These are ways, this is out and on.
This always was.

The tumble out and the push up,
The breaking of the little doors,
The look again at the mother sun,
The feel of the blue roofs over—
This is summer? This always was?

The whispering sprigs of buds stay put.
The spiders are after the beetles.
The farmer is driving a tractor turning furrows.
The hired man drives a manure spreader.
The oven bird hops in dry leaves.
The woodpecker beats his tattoo.
Is this it? Is spring crossing over?
Is it summer? And this always was?
The whispering pinks, the buds on the redhaw,
The blue roofs of the sky . . . stay put.

SUMMER GRASS

Summer grass aches and whispers.

It wants something; it calls and sings; it pours
out wishes to the overhead stars.

The rain hears; the rain answers; the rain is slow
  coming; the rain wets the face of the grass.

RIVER ROADS

Let the crows go by hawking their caw and caw.
They have been swimming in midnights of coal mines somewhere.
Let 'em hawk their caw and caw.

Let the woodpecker drum and drum on a hickory stump.
He has been swimming in red and blue pools somewhere hundreds of
  years
And the blue has gone to his wings and the red has gone to his head.
Let his red head drum and drum.

Let the dark pools hold the birds in a looking-glass.
And if the pool wishes, let it shiver to the blur of many wings, old
  swimmers from old places.

Let the redwing streak a line of vermilion on the green wood lines.
And the mist along the river fix its purple in lines of a woman's shawl
  on lazy shoulders.

ON A RAILROAD RIGHT OF WAY

    Stream, go hide yourself.
    In the tall grass, in the cat-tails,
    In the browns of autumn, the last purple
      asters, the yellow whispers.
    On the moss rock levels leave the marks
      of your wave-lengths.
    Sing in your gravel, in your clean gully.
    Let the moaning railroad trains go by.
    Till they stop you, go on with your song.

    The minnies spin in the water gravel,
    In the spears of the early autumn sun.

There must be winter fish.
Babies, you will be jumping fish
In the first snow month.

CRABAPPLES

Sweeten these bitter wild crabapples, Illinois
October sun. The roots here came from the
wilderness, came before man came here. They
are bitter as the wild is bitter.

Give these crabapples your softening gold,
October sun, go through to the white wet
seeds inside and soften them black. Make
these bitter apples sweet. They want you, sun.

The drop and the fall, the drop and the fall,
the apples leaving the branches for the black
earth under, they know you from last year,
the year before last year, October sun.

HAZE GOLD

Sun, you may send your haze gold
Filling the fall afternoon
With a flimmer of many gold feathers.
Leaves, you may linger in the fall sunset
Like late lingering butterflies before frost.
Treetops, you may sift the sunset cross-lights
Spreading a loose checkerwork of gold and shadow.
Winter comes soon—shall we save this, lay it by,
Keep all we can of these haze gold yellows?

WINTER GOLD

The same gold of summer was on the winter hills,
the oat straw gold, the gold of slow sun change.

The stubble was chilly and lonesome,
the stub feet clomb up the hills and stood.

The flat cry of one wheeling crow faded and came,
ran on the stub gold flats and faded and came.

Fade-me, find-me, slow lights rang their changes
on the flats of oat straw gold on winter hills.

❁ ❁ ❁

Wind, Sea, and Sky

WINDS OF THE WINDY CITY

from THE WINDY CITY

Winds of the Windy City, come out of the prairie,
   all the way from Medicine Hat.
Come out of the inland sea blue water, come where
   they nickname a city for you.

Corn wind in the fall, come off the black lands,
   come off the whisper of the silk hangers,
   the lap of the flat spear leaves.

Blue water wind in summer, come off the blue miles
   of lake, carry your inland sea blue fingers,
   carry us cool, carry your blue to our homes.

White spring winds, come off the bag wool clouds,
   come off the running melted snow, come white
   as the arms of snow-born children.

Gray fighting winter winds, come along on the tearing blizzard tails, the snouts of the hungry
   hunting storms, come fighting gray in winter.

Winds of the Windy City,
Winds of corn and sea blue,
Spring wind white and fighting winter gray,
Come home here—they nickname a city for you.

CHILDREN OF THE WIND

from THE PEOPLE, YES

On the shores of Lake Michigan
high on a wooden pole, in a box,
two purple martins had a home
and taken away down to Martinique
and let loose, they flew home,
thousands of miles to be home again.
  And this has lights of wonder
  echo and pace and echo again.
The birds let out began flying
north north-by-west north
till they were back home.
How their instruments told them
of ceiling, temperature, air pressure,
how their control-boards gave them
reports of fuel, ignition, speeds,
is out of the record, out.
  Across spaces of sun and cloud,
in rain and fog, through air pockets,
wind with them, wind against them,
stopping for subsistence rations,
whirling in gust and spiral,
these people of the air,
these children of the wind,
had a sense of where to go and how,
how to go north north-by-west north,
till they came to one wooden pole,
till they were home again.

DOCKS

Strolling along
By the teeming docks,
I watch the ships put out.
Black ships that heave and lunge
And move like mastodons
Arising from lethargic sleep.

The fathomed harbor
Calls them not nor dares
Them to a strain of action,
But outward, on and outward,
Sounding low-reverberating calls,
Shaggy in the half-lit distance,
They pass the pointed headland,
View the wide, far-lifting wilderness
And leap with cumulative speed
To test the challenge of the sea.

Plunging,
Doggedly onward plunging,
Into salt and mist and foam and sun.

FROM THE SHORE

A lone gray bird,
Dim-dipping, far-flying,
Alone in the shadows and grandeurs and tumults
Of night and the sea
And the stars and storms.

Out over the darkness it wavers and hovers,
Out into the gloom it swings and batters,
Out into the wind and the rain and the vast,
Out into the pit of a great black world,
Where fogs are at battle, sky-driven, sea-blown,

Love of mist and rapture of flight,
Glories of chance and hazards of death
On its eager and palpitant wings.

Out into the deep of the great dark world,
Beyond the long borders where foam and drift
Of the sundering waves are lost and gone
On the tides that plunge and rear and crumble.

FLUX

Sand of the sea runs red
Where the sunset reaches and quivers.
Sand of the sea runs yellow
Where the moon slants and wavers.

SKY PRAYERS

from GOOD MORNING, AMERICA

Sea sunsets, give us keepsakes.
Prairie gloamings, pay us for prayers.
Mountain clouds on bronze skies—
    Give us great memories.
Let us have summer roses.
Let us have tawny harvest haze in pumpkin time.
Let us have springtime faces to toil for and play for.
Let us have the fun of booming winds on long waters.
Give us dreamy blue twilights—of winter evenings—to wrap us in a
    coat of dreaminess.
Moonlight, come down—shine down, moonlight—meet every bird
    cry and every song calling to a hard old earth, a sweet young earth.

ROLLING CLOUDS

from SKY TALK

Wool white horses and their heads sag and roll,
Snow white sheep and their tails drag far,
Impossible animals ever more impossible—
    They walk on the sky to say How do you do?
    Or Good-by or Back-soon-maybe.

Or would you say any white flowers come
    more lovely than certain white clouds?
Or would you say any tall mountains beckon,
rise and beckon beyond certain tall walking clouds?

Is there any roll of white sea-horses equal to
    the sky-horse white of certain clouds rolling?

BABY SONG OF THE FOUR WINDS

    Let me be your baby, south wind.
    Rock me, let me rock, rock me now.
    Rock me low, rock me warm.
    Let me be your baby.

    Comb my hair, west wind.
    Comb me with a cowlick.
    Or let me go with a pompadour.
    Come on, west wind, make me your baby.

    North wind, shake me where I'm foolish.
    Shake me loose and change my ways.
    Cool my ears with a blue sea wind.
    I'm your baby, make me behave.

    And you, east wind, what can I ask?
    A fog comfort? A fog to tuck me in?
    Fix me so and let me sleep.
    I'm your baby—and I always was.

BROKEN SKY

The sky of gray is eaten in six places,
Rag holes stand out.
It is an army blanket and the sleeper
slept too near the fire.

SANTA FE SKETCH

The valley was swept with a blue broom to the west.

And to the west, on the fringes of a mesa sunset,
there are blue broom leavings, hangover blue wisps—
bluer than the blue floor the broom touched
before and after it caught the blue sweepings.

The valley was swept with a blue broom to the west.

SILVER POINT

The silver point of an evening star
dropping toward the hammock of new moon
over Lake Okoboji, over prairie waters in Iowa—
it was framed in the lights just after twilight.

WIND SONG

Long ago I learned how to sleep,
In an old apple orchard where the wind swept by counting its money
and throwing it away,
In a wind-gaunt orchard where the limbs forked out and listened or
never listened at all,

In a passel of trees where the branches trapped the wind into whis-
tling, "Who, who are you?"
I slept with my head in an elbow on a summer afternoon and there I
took a sleep lesson.
There I went away saying: I know why they sleep, I know how they
trap the tricky winds.
Long ago I learned how to listen to the singing wind and how to for-
get and how to hear the deep whine,
Slapping and lapsing under the day blue and the night stars:
Who, who are you?

> Who can ever forget
> listening to the wind go by
> counting its money
> and throwing it away?

✸ PRAIRIE-TOWN BOY

To John Carl and Karlen Paula

❀ ❀ ❀

Prologue : Prairie Town

PEOPLE FROM NEW England and their children owned much of the town of Galesburg, Illinois, and set the main tone in politics, churches, schools and colleges. Up from Kentucky and Tennessee had come English and Scotch-Irish breeds. Many Swedes had become voters and a power in politics and business. In the two and a half blocks between our house and the railroad yards the Swedes were largest in number, then the "native-born," two or three Yankees, two English families, a sprinkling of Irish and Germans, and in the early 1890's a flood of Italians, some thirty men, women, and children in two houses next to the Narrow Gauge railroad tracks.

Often in the 1890's I would get to thinking about what a young prairie town Galesburg was—nearly twenty thousand people, and they had all come in fifty years. Before that it was empty rolling prairie. There was no standard pioneer cut to a regular pattern. Most of them could stand hard work and streaks of back luck. They had broken the prairie, laid the first roads and streets, built the first schools and churches, colored the traditions of the town and country where I was born and raised. As a boy I saw some of these old-timers in their seventies or eighties, hard-bitten, grizzled and fading. I tried in my boy mind to picture them standing where there wasn't a wall or a roof on Main Street not yet a street—no streets anywhere and no houses —looking around and deciding where to clear for the first row of houses, the Public Square, the church, the blacksmith shop, the general store—and the college to be the focus of light and hope for the youth and the coming generations. They saw their little town rise to be a place and a name where before had been silence broken only by wild-animal cries, by the recurring rains and winds.

They had left Ohio, New York, Tennessee, or Kentucky in a wagon holding family—sometimes six, eight, or ten children—and household goods. They had driven their horses over wilderness trails where often the feet of horses, the rims and spokes of wheels, tangled in underbrush. They camped where night found them and took up their journey again at daylight. Some had made part of their trip on flatboats or paddle-wheel steamboats—the generation who arrived before the railroad came to Knox County in 1854.

At the time I was born, one pioneer stood out above all others in the town and county—George W. Brown, then mayor of Galesburg. A farm boy in Saratoga County, New York, he learned the carpenter's trade, and worked on the earliest railroads of the Mohawk Valley. He heard from relatives of good land cheap in Illinois, and in 1836, at twenty-one, he and his wife rode a covered wagon west for weeks on weeks while the rains came nearly every day and the wagon wheels stuck in mud and clay and had to be lifted or pried loose. In July, some nine miles from Galesburg, he traded his team of horses for an eighty of land. His wife ran the farm while he built houses. In later years, in Galesburg, Knoxville, Henderson Grove, they pointed to houses well built by George W. Brown. He laid by what he could of his earnings while thinking and studying and experimenting with a machine to plant corn.

In the spring of 1852 he planted with his machine sixteen acres of corn for himself and eight acres for a neighbor. That year he planned and hoped to finish ten machines, and he completed only one. He sold livestock, then his last horse, for means to clinch his patents. In order to go on and produce and sell his cornplanters, he sold his farm and borrowed money at ten per cent interest. In 1856 he got his shops in Galesburg going and made six hundred cornplanters and the next year a thousand. His machines spread over the Midwest during the war years, 1861–1865, and they were credited with food-production increase that helped the North in winning the war.

When I was growing up the Brown Cornplanter Works produced and sold eight thousand machines a year. He had two hundred men working for him, his shops covering all of a city block except the corner lot he reserved for the new Methodist Church of which he was a regularly attending member.

When we walked the four and a half dusty miles of the Knoxville Road to the County Fair, we passed the old home of Isaac Guliher. Born in Christian County, Kentucky, he had moved to Sangamon County, Illinois, in 1830, and at seventeen years of age in 1832 had enlisted for the Black Hawk War and served as a private under Captain Abraham Lincoln, moving to Knox County in 1833. In 1858 when Lincoln was on his way from Knoxville to Galesburg to debate with Douglas, he was told this was the house where Isaac Guliher lived and Lincoln got out of his buggy and a mile of buggies and wagons stopped for ten minutes while Lincoln walked in and drank a dipper of cold water with old Sangamon County friends.

Out on the Seminary Street road was the five-hundred-and-forty-seven-acre farm of Daniel Green Burner. He had come to Knox County from New Salem, Illinois, where he had lived four years and had seen young Abraham Lincoln march off to the Black Hawk War. He had traded at the grocery where Lincoln served customers and he had noticed young Lincoln's ways with people. Mr. Burner told a reporter for a Galesburg paper that "Lincoln was as full of fun as a dog is of fleas. . . . He would back up against a wall and stretch out his arms; I never saw a man with so great a stretch. He did little things like that to please people. . . . He did not go to others for his amusement, but if they wanted fun, they came to him and found him full of it . . ." It would have been nice if I could have worked on Mr. Burner's farm in hay harvest and sat at table and heard him talk about Lincoln and New Salem days.

Knox College, Lombard College, and Brown's Business College gave Galesburg the nickname of "College City." Several times when carrying a two-gallon can of milk I met on streets near Knox College a little man who would nod to me without speaking and to whom I would nod without speaking. He wore a tight-fitting, square-cornered, single-breasted black coat to his knees with buttons running up to his chin. You couldn't see his collar from in front because of his white beard that spread like a fan and covered jaws, chin, and upper lip. Once on Main Street I heard a man say, "That fellow used to know Abe Lincoln." I learned he had been elected Superintendent of Public Instruction of the State of Illinois seven times and served fourteen years, that his room in the State House at Springfield was next to one Lincoln used when a candidate and he and Lincoln had had friendly talks.

This was Newton Bateman, sometimes called "Little Newt," president of Knox College. He said that Lincoln would introduce him as "My little friend, the big schoolmaster of Illinois," and that Lincoln once brought him a letter asking if there should be any corrections in grammar, saying, "I never was very strong on grammar." He saw Lincoln walk back and forth, he said, troubled about the storm that was to sweep the country, saying, "I am nothing but truth is everything." He said too he was the last man to shake hands and say good-by to President-elect Lincoln before the train pulled out from Springfield bound for Washington.

Newton Bateman was born in New Jersey in 1822. His father, a weaver and a cripple, took his wife and five children West to Illinois in a covered wagon in 1833. Near Jacksonville the Asiatic cholera struck down the mother, and people in a panic fear of the plague saw to it that she was buried in fast time, so fast that the grave wasn't marked. Her youngest son Newton in after years made searches for it but couldn't locate the grave. In his struggle toward an education, he lived for a time on mush and milk at eleven cents a week, walked with a peddler's pack on his back and sold pins, needles, thread, "notions." He had aimed at being a minister, and then changed to teaching. He was principal of the Jacksonville schools and organized the State Teachers Association. He was president of Knox from 1875 to 1892, the longest time any president of Knox had stayed. It was said that under him more graduates went out into the world and made big names for themselves than under any president before him. "He had character," I heard one man say, "and it reached the students."

Little Newt dropped out as president of Knox when he was seventy, went on teaching a few classes while a new president took the chair —John Huston Finley, twenty-nine years old and "the youngest college president in the United States." I met Finley several times, carrying my two-gallon can of milk, but he passed by, his head down, his mind far away. Finley made Knox known over the country as a college where Lincoln and Douglas had debated. He put on an Anniversary celebration of the debate on October 7, 1896. I got away from the milk wagon in time to wedge through the crowd for a good look at Chauncey M. Depew in a Prinz Albert coat, with a fedora on his head as he spoke. The day was cold and men on the platform wore overcoats with the collars turned up. I don't remember a word Chauncey Depew said, but I could say I had seen the president of the New York Central Railway and a man who in 1864 made stump speeches over all of New York State for Lincoln for President.

Robert Todd Lincoln, the son of Abraham Lincoln, made a short speech that afternoon. I wondered what kind of talks he had had with his father in the White House, what kind of a Secretary of War he had been in the cabinets of Presidents Garfield and Arthur. I had read of how at one Republican National Convention after another some delegate always nominated him for President and he would get one vote. In his short speech he didn't say anything I went away thinking about.

In those years as a boy in that prairie town I got education in scraps and pieces of many kinds, not knowing they were part of my education. I met people in Galesburg who were puzzling to me, and later when I read Shakespeare I found those same people were puzzling to him. I met little wonders of many kinds among animals and plants that never lost their wonder for me, and I found later that these same wonders had a deep interest for Emerson, Thoreau, and Walt Whitman. I met superstitions, folk tales, and folklore while I was a young spalpeen, "a broth of a boy," long before I read books about them. All had their part, small or large, in the education I got outside of books and schools.

❁ ❁ ❁

One : Home Folks

OF THE HOUSE where I was born I remember nothing—a three-room frame house on Third Street, the second house east of the Chicago, Burlington & Quincy Railroad tracks, in Galesburg, Illinois. The date was January 6, 1878, a little after midnight. The first baby, some three years earlier, was my sister Mary. They wanted a boy. I was a welcome man-child.

Mary once pointed to the cradle in later years and said, "When they took me out, they put him in." The cradle stood on three legs at each end, and mother told Mary that father had made it. A year and a half later they took me out to put Mart in.

I was born on a cornhusk mattress. Until I was past ten or more years, when we became a family of nine, the mattresses were bedticking filled with cornhusks. As we all slept well on cornhusks and never knew the feel of feather beds till far later years, we were in favor of what we had. Of the slats on which the mattress rested, we sometimes murmured. One would break, then another, till finally the mattress crashed to the floor—and we were suspicious of the new slats.

We moved to another three-room one-story house, on the north side of South Street, three doors west of Pearl. Here I wore dresses and watched my father spade a garden and plant and dig potatoes and carrots. I liked the feel of potatoes and carrots as my fingers brushed the black loam off them and I threw them into baskets. Here we had the mare Dolly—a small bay, old, fat and slow—kept in a shed at the end of the lot. Dolly pulled us in a four-wheeled, two-seater wagon out from the town streets and houses to where we saw for the first time the open country, rolling prairie and timber, miles of zigzag rail fences, fields of corn and oats, cows, sheep, and horses feeding in pastures. Grazing animals in the open had wonder for me.

We were regular at Swedish Lutheran Church services, though about once a month of a Sunday morning father would throw the harness on old Dolly and the word was, "We are going to the Kranses." Out seven miles near a small coal-mine crossroads with a post office named Soperville, on a thirty-acre farm, lived John and his wife Lena Krans. Lena was a cousin of my mother. Those four Swedish-born Americans had warm kinship. Their faces lighted on seeing each other, and their talk ran warm and pleasant. They were all strong for work, liked it, and talked it in those years of their thirties. The Swedish language was hurled back and forth, too swift for us children to be sure what they were saying. But when they talked of the steerage trip from Sweden, six to ten weeks on a sailing ship, their food only the black bread and cheese and baloney they brought along, we knew it was rugged going. Often we heard from father and mother, "In the old country we had *white* bread only at Easter and Christmas. Here in America we have *white* bread every day in the year!"

The Kranses were the nearest kinfolk we had in America except for the Holmes family in Galesburg. When John and Lena Krans bought their farm in the early 1870's, they worked from daylight to dark eight or nine months of the year till at last the mortgages were paid off. They had help from neighbors in getting in their crops and in turn helped the neighbors. The Kranses became part of the land they owned. Their feet wore paths that didn't change over the years—in the cow pasture with a small creek winding over it, the corn and oat fields, the vegetable garden, the potato patch. John Krans was a landsman, his thoughts never far from his land, the animals, the crops. He could talk about *hästarna,* meaning "horses," so to my mind he seemed part horse.

He was a medium-sized man, but he had a loose, easy way of carrying his shoulders with his head flung back so he gave the impression of being a big man. His eyes had gleam and his lips had a smile you could see through the beard. Even amid the four walls of a room his head, hair, and beard seemed to be in a high wind. When I sat on his knee and ran my five-year-old hand around in his beard, he called me *min lille gosse* ("my little boy") and there was a ripple of laughter and love in it. He read his Bible and sometimes a newspaper, though most often he liked to read the land and the sky, the ways of horses

and corn. He wasn't an arguing man except that with a plow he could argue against stubborn land and with strong hands on leather reins he could argue with runaway horses.

Not often on Sunday did he miss hitching a horse to a light wagon and taking the family to the Lutheran church a mile or two away. I doubt whether he ever listened to a preacher who had less fear and more faith than he had. I have sometimes thought that John Krans pictured God as a Farmer whose chores were endless and inconceivable, that in this world and in worlds beyond God planted and tended and reaped His crops in mysterious ways past human understanding.

The Kranses had a wooden barn with a dirt floor and three horses and four cows that were driven to and from the near-by pasture night and morning. Here we saw hands at udders and milk streaming into pails. The pails were carried up a slope to the house thirty yards away, where the cellar had a clean, hard dirt floor and plank shelves with a long line of crocks into which the milk was poured. We saw the yellow cream at the top of the crocks and once saw cream churned into butter. Here for the first time we drank milk from cows we saw give the milk and ate fried eggs having seen the hens that laid the eggs.

When I was about four we moved two blocks over to Berrien Street and a ten-room house with a roomy third-story garret running the length of the house and a four-room cellar that had floors in the two front rooms. A two-compartment privy had a henhouse back of it. The lot was three times the size of the South Street place and had a big garden with several gooseberry bushes, a front yard with five tall soft-maple trees, a picket fence, a brick sidewalk, and a ditch in front. It was really two houses and lots. Two sign numbers said we lived at 622 and 624 East Berrien Street. Here the emigrant Swede August Sandburg set himself up, with due humility and constant anxiety, as a landlord. The two east rooms of the first floor, along with the two cellar rooms under them, were rented to different families across the years, never vacant for more than a day or two. And the large upstairs east rooms always had a renter.

My father had never learned to write. His schooling had only taught him to read when his father and mother died in Sweden and he went to work as a chore boy in a distillery. He became a teamster at the distillery and laid by enough money for steerage passage to America. When he arrived in New York, Swedes who had kinfolk at Herkimer, New York, sent him to a job in a cheese factory there. After a few months at cheese-making he read a letter from his cousin in Galesburg, Illinois, Magnus Holmes, who wrote that the chances were all good out there. Magnus Holmes had arrived by rail in 1854, the first year the C.B.&Q. reached Galesburg, and joined a gang that built a bridge over the Rock River. He was nineteen. Had he stayed two years longer in Sweden, he would have had to serve two years in the Swedish army. His father had spent all his years after he was twenty-one in the Swedish army, till he was retired. And Magnus Holmes had seen army life close up, didn't want to be a soldier, and at nineteen skipped Sweden, took steerage passage for New York on a sailing vessel that buffeted stormy seas for ten weeks and, blown off its course, landed at Quebec.

He reached Albany, took the Erie Canal to Buffalo and railroads to Chicago and Galesburg. There in Galesburg he kept his name of Magnus and changed Holm to Holmes because Holm sounded Swedish and Holmes sounded English. He worked with a railroad construction gang out of Hannibal, Missouri. At a Methodist camp meeting he fell in love with a Swedish girl, a housemaid living with a family that kept slaves. She moved from Hannibal to Galesburg, and Holmes used to call on her when she worked at the Ladies' Dormitory of Lombard College and he had a job in the Q. blacksmith shop forging and hammering bolts. He was interested that she was not merely good-looking and handy as a cook but that she owned a book she was reading, a translation of *Faust*. They were married.

They went to the Knox College campus the afternoon of October 7, 1858, and stood for three hours in a cold northwest wind, in a crowd of twenty thousand, listening to Abraham Lincoln and Stephen Douglas debate. Magnus Holmes voted for Lincoln, but refused to answer Lincoln's call for troops because he hated war and had a conscience about it. So because Holmes hated military service and left Sweden early, to end up at work in a C.B.&Q. Railroad shop, he was there to advise a newcomer cousin to come on West and get a job. The first job my father had was on the Q. railroad with a construction gang at a dollar a day. They lived in bunk cars, cooked their own meals, did their own washing, worked six days a week, ten hours a day.

My mother—young Clara Mathilda Anderson who married my father—told of her mother dying early and her father marrying again. Her mother was a gooseherd in Appuna, and she helped her mother in working with geese and ducks in two ponds on their place. When her stepmother came, "We didn't get along so good. I left Sweden because she was so different from my mother. Letters came from Swedes in America about how things were better there and I managed to save the money to come over and do my best. There was a chum, like you say, a good friend of mine, came with me and I wasn't lonely."

How my father and mother happened to meet I heard only from my mother. I had asked her how they came to marry and she said: "I was working in a hotel in Bushnell [Illinois], making the beds and helping in the kitchen. He came to Bushnell with the railroad gang. He came to the hotel and saw me and we talked and he said he wanted to marry me. I saw it was my chance and soon went to Galesburg and the Reverend Lindahl married us and we started housekeeping." A smile spread over her face half-bashful and a bright light came to her eyes as she said, "I saw it was my chance." She was saying this years after the wedding and there had been hard work always, tough luck at times, and she had not one regret that she had jumped at her "chance" when she saw it.

My father's hair was straight and black and his eyes, black with a hint of brown, were deep-set in the bone, the skin around them crinkling with his smile or laugh. He was below medium height, weighed about a hundred and forty-eight, was well muscled, and the skin of his chest showed a pale white against the grime when his collar was turned down. No sports interested him, though he did make a genuine sport of work that needed to be done. He was at the C.B. & Q. black-smith shop, rated as "a helper," the year round, with no vacations. He left home at six forty-five in the morning, walked to arrive at the Q. shop at seven, and was never late. He mauled away at engine and car parts till twelve, then walked home, ate the noon "dinner," walked back to the shop to begin work at one and go on till the six o'clock whistle, when he stood sledge alongside anvil and walked home.

It would take him ten or fifteen minutes to get the grime off hands, face, and neck before supper. He poured the cistern rain water from a pail into a tin basin on a washstand, twice throwing the used water into another pail on the floor before the final delicious rinsing at a third basin of the water that had run off the roof into the cistern. The calluses inside his hands were intricate with hollows and fissures. To dig out the black grit from the deep cracks took longer than any part of the washing, and still black lines of smudge failed to come out.

In late spring, summer, and early fall, he would often work in the garden till after dark, more than one night in October picking tomatoes and digging potatoes by the light of a moon. In the colder months he always found something to fix or improve. He liked to sew patches on his jeans pants or his work coat and had his own strong thread and large needle for replacing lost buttons. In those early years he read a weekly paper from Chicago, *Hemlandet,* Swedish for Homeland. Regularly he or mother read aloud, to each other and the children, from the Swedish Bible.

My mother had fair hair, between blond and brown—the color of oat straw just before the sun tans it—eyes light-blue, skin white as fresh linen by candlelight, the mouth for smiling. She had ten smiles for us to one from our father. Her nose was retroussé, not snub. She was five feet five inches high and weighed perhaps one hundred and forty. She had tireless muscles on her bones and was tireless about her housework. She did the cooking, washing, and sew-ing, bedmaking, and housecleaning for her family of nine. At six in the morning she was up to get breakfast for her man and later break-fast for the children. There were meals for all again at noon and at evening. Always there were clothes to be patched, the boys sometimes wearing out a third seat of trousers. As we got into long pants, the knees usually needed patching. Playing marbles in the spring, wrestling, and scuffling, we wore holes at the knees, which went bare till "Mama" patched the holes. That was always our name for her when we spoke to her or of her in the family circle.

My father had respect and affection for Magnus Holmes, older by fifteen years, and his close friend and adviser. He was well Americanized when August Sandburg arrived at the Holmes house in the early 1870's. He had been in Galesburg more than fifteen years; the men he worked with were mostly Irish and English, and he and Mrs. Holmes learned English so well that they made it the one language spoken in their house. So their four sons never learned to speak Swedish and their daughter Lily learned her Swedish speech by going one summer to the Swedish Lutheran parish school.

From Magnus Holmes, August Sandburg learned many simple and important English words he needed. And this cousin explained where to go and what papers to sign in order to become an American citizen. For years the Holmeses came to the Sandburgs for Thanksgiving dinner, and the Sandburgs went to the Holmeses on New Year's Day. Once in our house on Thanksgiving I heard Mr. Holmes talk on the Declaration of Independence and then make clear to my father the Constitution of the United States.

In the Sandburg family the first three children, Mary, Carl August, and Martin Godfrey, learned Swedish fairly well. I am sure that while I was still in dresses, I used only Swedish words to tell what I was wanting. But while the two boys, Emil and Fred, and the two girls, Esther and Martha, who came later knew that *mjölk* was milk, they couldn't count to six in Swedish.

Among the younger church members later there were grumblings and mutterings. "Why must we listen to sermons in Swedish when we can't understand what the preacher is telling us?" After a time there were occasional sermons in English, and changes went on in many churches till all the preaching was in English. This didn't come easy for gray-bearded old-timers who could remember when they sat in their pews two hours with their ears drinking in the beloved syllables of the speech of the homeland that still had its hold over them.

For all that was unjust in living conditions in Sweden that had sent them to America, my father and mother kept a warmth of feeling, a genuine affection, for Swedish people and the language of *gamla hemlandet* (the old country). It stayed deep in their hearts. But they told us little about the Old Country. In their first years in America they had their minds set on making a go of it in the New Country, and perhaps it was a help to forget the Old Country. Then as the years passed they spoke the language of the new land and made many friends and acquaintances who spoke no Swedish, their own later children speaking only English. They became part of the new land.

❀ ❀ ❀

Two : The House on Berrien Street

IN THE BERRIEN Street house I was to live growing, formative years from 1882 to 1899, from dresses to short pants to long pants. In that house came babies across ten years, the bright companionable boy Emil, the vague younger one Fred, the beautiful girl Esther and her plain and modest sister Martha.

The ten-room house was a challenge to August Sandburg. He couldn't see himself paying for repairs, and he became carpenter, bricklayer, house painter, paper-hanger, cabinetmaker, truck gardener. I was his chore boy, Mart later throwing in. When the roof needed shingling I went up the ladder bringing him shingles. When a cistern had its yearly cleaning, I was let down barelegged to shovel mud and silt into the bucket he drew up with a rope. A chair or table getting wobbly, my father brought it down to his cellar workbench and had me holding a kerosene lamp to light him while he chiseled, fitted, mortised, and hammered. I might after supper have taken my place at the kitchen table to read J. T. Headley's *Napoleon and His Marshals,* from the Seventh Ward school library. And when he called me, I might be saying, "It's a good book and I want to know about Napoleon." But father would say, "Sholly (Charlie), you let Napoleon go for tonight and hold de lamp for me."

Though I had been solemnly christened, with holy water sprinkled on my infant head, by the name of Carl August Sandberg, I decided in the first year or two of school, to use the name Charles. It could have been I had a feeling the name Carl would mean one more Poor Swede Boy while the name Charles had them guessing. Also it was about this time that Mary, Mart, and I decided to write "burg" instead of "berg" in our surname.

Those two letters *ch* bothered many a Swede boy. In our third-grade Sheldon's reader was a story titled "Charlie's Chickens," about a boy named Charlie who planted feathers and expected a crop of chickens.

One after another, Swede boys Johnson, Nelson, Bostrom, and Hillstrom stood up to read the story aloud. One after another they blurted out "Sharlie's Shickens." The teacher would ask for it again, herself pronouncing it distinctly correct. But from each again came, "Sharlie's Shickens" and the good and patient teacher gave it up. In my seat I laughed inside myself because I had picked the name Charles and had a noble and correct way to fill my mouth with it.

Monday was washday. When I was strong enough, I carried pails of water, from the cistern in the yard, to fill two washtubs. One tub had warm water and a washboard for soaping and rubbing; the other cold water for rinsing, and a wringer attached. On summer and vacation Mondays I often turned the wringer while mother fed the clothes into it. On many winter Mondays I carried the basket of wash out to the back-yard clothesline. Often the clothes would get frozen stiff. Coaxing those frozen pieces of cloth to go around the rope clothesline to be fastened with a wooden clothespin was a winter sport with a challenge to your wit and numb fingers in Illinois zero weather, with sometimes a wild northwest wind knocking a shirt stiff as a board against your head. More than once I had to take the basket into the kitchen for the clothes to thaw out while my fingers thawed out.

After the wash was hung, three or four of us would climb on the kitchen table. Mama threw soapy water on the floor and scrubbed and mopped while we played we were on an island or on a housetop floating down a river. After supper or the next morning I would go out and pile the frozen clothes high into the basket and bring them into the house. The noon dinner and the evening supper on Monday, never failing for years, were boiled herring and boiled potatoes, *sill och potatis,* for generations a simple classic menu of which they said with straight faces, "This is what makes the Swedes so strong."

Mama saw to it when we had been too long without a bath. She half filled a washtub with warm water, gave us soap, and told us to scrub. The three sisters would clear out of the kitchen while Mart and I took our washtub bath. Then we would go to bed and the girls would take over.

Mama watched carefully the cellar corner where the cabbage heads were piled in October so that in part of the winter there would be slaw and boiled cabbage. If we forgot, she reminded Mart and me in February of the garden where we could pound, dig, and rassle out one or two bushels of parsnips from the frozen ground.

In the triangle closet under the stairs from the first floor to the cellar Papa used to keep a barrel of apples in winter months, when he could afford it. He put a lock on the door and hid the key. He had seen that when a barrel of apples stood where everyone could get at it, we would soon be at the barrel bottom. He would have put a board over the gap above the door had he known what Mart and I were doing. By hard wriggling our boy bodies could squeeze through the gap and drop down to the apple barrel. We took two apples at a time and only every other day. What we stole wasn't noticed and we said, "When two of us steal two apples and divide them, that's only stealing one apple apiece and stealing one apple isn't really stealing, it's snooking."

Of all our renters I like to think of Joe Elser. He came to our house with a carpenter's tool chest on one shoulder. His belongings had arrived by wagon, and he moved into the two upstairs east rooms, reached by the outside wooden stairway with the coalbin under it.

Joe Elser didn't drink, smoke, or chew tobacco. He didn't go to religious services of any kind. He didn't have any books in his rooms and didn't take any from the Public Library. He never complained, and we never knew him to be sick. He did his own cooking and washing; he darned his socks, mended his clothes, and kept his rooms neat and shipshape.

Joe was tall, strong, spare of build, and we saw him often with his tool chest on his shoulder, carrying it as though he liked it. He was in his early fifties, and his face and hair were grayish, his mustache close-trimmed. He never hurried; in any work he was doing he seemed to have a knack for the next motion after the one now. Joe had fairly regular work as a carpenter across the year. Sometimes because of weather or when a foundation was not finished on a house, he would have days off for sharpening tools and washing bedsheets and pillow-cases.

Many a winter night Mart and I went up to see him. He always made us welcome. We began calling him "Uncle Joe" and he enjoyed that. He never referred to his being lonely in any way, and we couldn't believe he had anything sad in his loneliness. We would come up to his kitchen after our supper and he would be setting his table with its oilcloth cover for his supper. He would set chairs for us at the table, then step to the oven and bring out a fresh-baked pie. He would cut the pie and put a quarter of it on my plate and another quarter on Mart's plate. He was proud of the pies he could bake. So were Mart

and I. When we told him we had never tasted such good pie, his face had a quiet shine.

Mother said we were going up too often and too early: "You should leave him some pie for himself." And when we came up to see him finished with supper, he would get out a couple of flatirons, hand us a hammer apiece, and bring out a canvas sack of black walnuts, hickory nuts, or hazelnuts. While he joined us in cracking and eating nuts—though we always ate more than he—he did most of the talking.

Joe Elser had been in The War. There was only one war then a man could have been in, the war over the Union and the slaves. Joe had had nearly four years of it. He went in as a private and came out as a private. He had been in battles, and he would take stove wood, put one piece on the floor "where they were lined up" and another "where we stood." Then he would change the wood to show "where they came at us" and "where we counter-charged." He had never been wounded, "but once I had malarial fever bad for six weeks." He didn't make himself out any kind of hero. "You enlisted and then you took what come." The eating was mostly "sowbelly and beans, though sometimes in enemy territory we had rich living on cattle we took and butchered and sometimes there was a sight of pigs and chickens we caught and roasted and fried." They had knapsacks and haversacks at first but threw them away and put everything into a blanket roll. On the march, over the left shoulder went the blanket roll and on the right shoulder the rifle—and a cartridge belt around the middle.

This or that was "issued"—uniforms, shoes, socks, rations. You didn't need to buy anything, but if you wanted something special there was the "sutler," who followed the army and set up a store where the army stopped.

When Joe Elser moved away after three or four years, we missed him. Out of what he had he made a pretty good life. He had his carpenter's wage of two dollars a day, and thirty dollars a month pension from the government. He liked his work and took pride in being a good carpenter. He was temperate and never talked about temperance. He was lonely and prized his loneliness. Joe Elser never showed any signs of being afraid. He learned somehow to get along without being afraid of what is or of what is to come.

When my father bought the Berrien Street house I am sure he had talked over with his cousin Magnus Holmes the advantages of having enough rooms so you could rent them and have cash coming in every month. Mr. Holmes had bought a used lumberyard office, had it moved on rollers pulled by horses to a vacant lot he owned next to his home, and fixed it over into a house to rent. And when August Sandburg went in for buying a quarter section of land out in Pawnee County, Kansas, he was keeping pace with his cousin, who had bought a quarter section near Holdrege, Nebraska.

Payments he owed on the big house were a load on Papa's mind. So were the payments on that first quarter section of land. He sold this land at some kind of profit and bought another quarter section. I came to know by heart the numbers of the range and the township, because once a year I would write the letter to the County Treasurer of Pawnee County, enclosing a postal money order for the year's taxes. To write that letter Papa would hand me a pencil he prized. Just why he had that pencil, we never knew. The lead was purple and indelible, and Papa called it "indebible." He liked it that you couldn't erase what you wrote.

For several years those one hundred and sixty acres of Kansas farm land haunted the family. Papa talked vaguely about leaving Galesburg and trying his hands on that land way out there. Folders with pictures came from railroads and speculators, showing what bumper crops of wheat and corn, even of pears and apples, could be raised there. "Independent"—we learned that word. The farmer never starves, he can live on what he raises, he is his own boss, he can't be fired from his job, he is "independent."

Then came the crash, the Panic of 1893 and the Hard Times. We heard how corn went to ten cents a bushel in Kansas. We read of Kansas farmers burning corn for fuel. Kansas land went down in price. What father sold his land for I never heard. But we quit our family discussions about whether a man is more independent working for a railroad or taking his chances as a farmer.

A panic—people running to the banks to find the banks closed, men out of work, charity balls, Coxey's Army in the news for months, men marching on Washington to ask Congress to get them work—and the Hard Times definitely reached Galesburg. Except for watchmen, the railroad shopmen went from a ten-hour to a four-hour day, the checks on payday less than half what they were used to.

We learned to eat bread spread with lard sprinkled with salt, and we liked it. When lard was short we put molasses or sorghum on the bread, which was not so good. We were lucky in our garden giving a bumper crop of potatoes. The land laughed with spuds. As Mart and I helped father dig potatoes and carry the bushel baskets into the cellar, we saw him do the only writing of his we ever witnessed. For each bushel brought in he would chalk on a ceiling rafter a straight vertical line. When there were four verticals he would cross them with a diagonal line, meaning we had five more bushels, by golly.

A little co-operative of neighbors sprang up. They borrowed a horse and wagon and hauled to town a hog from John Krans, "the price near nothing," laughed Krans. Two lots away from us, in front of a small barn in open daylight of a winter day, I first saw a hog killing. The butchering was a drama to us kids. I carried home a bucket of blood from which Mama made a tasty "blood pudding." Mart and I hustled home with a ham and hog sections from which we had across the weeks that winter pork chops, pork loins, side meat, spareribs, cracklings, sowbelly, pig's knuckles, lard for frying and for bread spread.

We learned about "slack" that winter, screenings of coal with no lumps, much cheaper than regular soft coal or bituminous. Into our small heating stove in the kitchen we would shovel it and then keep watch on it, breaking its cinder formations with a poker. If not carefully tended there would be clinkers too large to pass through the grate below. With poker and shovel we would bring up the clinker and put it in its special galvanized iron bucket.

I learned to stoop going through the door to our coalbin under the stairs. I learned to stoop swinging a hammer breaking big lumps into little lumps so they would fit into the coalhod and the stove door. Hands black, nose and ears filled with coal dust, I felt I was earning my board and keep. I would have thought my fate a hard one if I hadn't been reading the *Youth's Companion* with its stories about miners and breaker boys who worked all day and came out with black faces and coal dust in layers. Once I rigged up a small tin can, fastened it to my cap, and went into the dark coalbin playing it was a mine and I had a head lamp like a regular miner.

The kitchen was the only room heated during the cold months. The second-floor bedrooms got what heat went through the door and up the stairs. No heat reached the third-floor garret where Mart and I slept. But we enjoyed, on a below-zero night, standing by the warm kitchen stove, stripping to our underwear and then dashing up two floors and getting under the quilts and snuggling into the cornhusks before Old Mister Zero Fahrenheit could tag us.

The kitchen at first was heated by a stove with lids. At the stove end was a small oblong tank holding water warmed by the hot coals. At first we children called this, as Papa and Mama did, "the rissy-warn." When we learned it was a reservoir we went on calling it "rissy-warn" out of habit. Later this cookstove went to the cellar, where it served on washdays during the warmer months. Improvements then modern came to the kitchen—a gasoline stove for cooking, and a heating stove with an isinglass door and an ashpan at the bottom. Was it a thousand times or two thousand that I took that ashpan out to the ends of the potato rows to dump one more pan of ashes on the honorable Ashpile?

The kitchen was fifteen feet long and twelve wide, and with cupboard and pantry, sink, gasoline stove and heating stove, a table, eight chairs, and a baby high chair, any passageway was narrow. There we were, a family of, at one time, nine persons in that one room—kitchen, dining room, study room, playroom, workshop. We saw mother mix flour and knead dough, put it in the oven, and bring out brown loaves of bread. We saw coats and trousers patched and socks and stockings darned. We saw father during Hard Times cut leather and peg half-soles on our shoes and cut boy's hair with the family scissors—a ragged-edged haircut but it saved the barber's two bits.

We popped corn and made taffy. We put a flatiron bottom up on the knees, and with a hammer cracked hazelnuts and walnuts we had picked in October. We made cocked hats out of newspapers. When the lamp needed tending, we went to the cellar for the kerosene can and filled the lamp after trimming the wick. To light the lamp we scratched a blue sulphur match, waited till the blue light was gone and the yellow blaze came, then ran it along the wick and put on the chimney.

We tried a cat once or twice, but it took up too much room and got in the way. Papa was looking on the bright side of things when one day he said Mama could buy a canary and a cage. As it hung high over our heads it didn't get in our way. The canary stayed a year or two but the babies were coming along and each of them was plenty of a pet to look after. In such a room as our kitchen you come to know each other. You learn to mind your own business or there is trouble.

Papa shaved at the kitchen sink before a small looking glass. A serious father with lather over cheeks, chin, and neck looks less serious to his children. The sound of the scraping razor mowing down the three days' growth of whiskers had a comic wonder for us. He couldn't shave without making faces at himself. There were times that his face took on so fearful and threatening a look we were a little scared.

We saw his razor travel over cheeks, chin, upper lip, below the jaws, everywhere except a limited area under his chin. There he left a small tuft of hair. At intervals over a few weeks we would see him take scissors and trim this goatee. Father didn't mind Mart and me singing the popular song that ended each verse, "With the little bunch of whiskers on his chin."

The pump in the back yard was wooden and stood about fifteen steps from the foot of the stairs going down from the back door. In the warm months water standing in a pail an hour or two didn't taste good and the call was for fresh water, father saying, *"Friskt vatten,* Sholly," I would take an empty galvanized iron pail from the side of the kitchen sink, set the pail under the pump spout, put my two hands on the wooden pump handle, push down, pull up, and go on pumping till water poured out of the spout and filled the pail. Others did this chore at times but I was counted the oldest boy, the handy strong boy who was called on.

In a summer dry spell when the pump handle came up light and loose, pulling up no water, I knew the water was low and the pump needed "priming." I would go back to the kitchen for a pail of cistern rain water and pour it down to the leather sucker and the tubing. Then I would push and pull at the pump handle till at last the pump spout was running glad and free saying, "Here is your water!" And on sweltering summer days when butter melted in the kitchen, mother would put it in a small tin pail, tie a doubled grocery string to the handle, and I would let the butter down the well to become cool and hard again.

There were winter mornings when my hands in mittens went round the pump handle and I couldn't budge it. Watching from the kitchen window, they were ready with a pail of hot water. I would skip back to the kitchen for this and pour it down the pump, sometimes running back for a second pail of hot water. After the pump was thawed out, I pumped and carried in two pails of water to last the family till the next morning, when again we thawed out the pump. And this meant carrying extra pails of water from the cistern, where there was no pump and you let down your galvanized iron pail and broke the thin ice and pulled the pail up with a rope.

Three or four times when I pushed and pulled at the pump handle no water came. Papa looked it over, then cut leather and shaped a new sucker. He let me down into the well on a rope, told me what to do, and stood looking down telling me more what to do. I was glad when he pulled me up and we could say the new sucker worked.

In our early years every house and lot in our block and the near-by blocks had a fence in front, in back, and on the sides. The front fences had gates. Slowly and little by little the fences and gates were taken away. The front-yard fences went first, then the side and back-yard fences. It began on such streets as North Broad and North Prairie where the rich and the well-to-do had their homes. One theory of why the fences and gates came and vanished goes back to the early days when people, rich and poor, kept horses, cows, pigs, and chickens that were always straying, and if you didn't have your house and yard fenced they would stray in and forage and trample your garden. As the roving livestock became fewer, the North side set the style of tearing fences away and the rest of the town slowly followed. The year came when we tore down our front-yard fence and burned it for kindling wood, saving good boards for repair jobs. But the side and backyard fences stayed the seventeen years we lived in that house.

❁ ❁ ❁

Three : A Young Republican

I WAS SIX years old on the October night I walked holding my father's hand to Seminary Street near South. It was the first time I saw politics run hot in the blood of men. Hundreds of men were standing in line, two by two. The line ran farther than my eyes could see. Each man had a pole over his shoulder. At the end of the pole swung a lighted torch. I had never seen one torch in my life, and now of a sudden I saw hundreds of torches in a straight line. Over his shoulders each man had a red, white, and blue oilskin cape. Drippings from the kerosene lamp of the torch fell on the oilskin. My father told me it was "a Republican rally." The sidewalk edges were filled with people waiting to see the march.

We walked north and came to men carrying flambeaus. When the order was given each man blew into a pipe that ran high over his head and they sent up into the air tongues of fire three or four feet high, spreading and weaving like big flowers of fire. I had never seen one flambeau before, and now to see twenty of them blaze up at once was a wonder. When the long red and yellow tongues slowed down and flickered out, the darkness was darker.

We walked farther north to the brass band heading the procession. Leading them as they turned into Main Street was a tall man in yellow pants with a red coat and a red-velvet hat nearly as tall as I. He had a stick with a big gold ball on the end and with this stick he motioned the parade how to make the turn. West on Main Street they marched, blowing horns and pounding drums.

On a Main Street corner we watched the parade go by. Every man marching was a Republican. By marching he was showing the Democrats he was a Republican. My father explained that to me. I heard the marching men holler to people along the sidewalks, and most often it was "Hurrah for Blaine!" or "Blaine for President!" Sometimes a hundred of them would be keeping time with their feet to "Blaine, Blaine, James G. Blaine."

I heard a man on the sidewalk yell, "Hurrah for Cleveland!" Right away came howls from the procession, "And a rope to hang him!" I asked my father about it and he said, "Cleveland is a Democrat. He is against Blaine."

On the way home I asked my father more questions. He gave me the idea that Republicans are good men and Democrats are either bad men, or good men gone wrong, or sort of dumb. And I had a feeling that Cleveland was an ugly man, and if the Republicans got a rope and hanged him, I wouldn't be sorry. Nobody had ever explained to me exactly how you hang a man, but if hanging was what the Republicans wanted for Cleveland then I was for it. I was a young Republican, a six-year-old Republican.

A few months later came election. I was told that Grover Cleveland, instead of being hanged, had been elected President. And when Cleveland named a new postmaster for Galesburg it was William Twohig, who lived only two blocks from us in a plain frame house. We called him Billy Twohig. In his back yard he had a sand pile, and when my father had bricklaying to do he sent me with a wheelbarrow over to Billy Twohig's for ten cents' worth of sand. On these trips I came to know him, and I thought he was a pretty good man even though he was a Democrat, even though the ugly Grover Cleveland had named him Galesburg postmaster and boss of all the mail carriers. My father too liked Billy Twohig. I was so mixed up in my head about the Republicans and the Democrats that I didn't ask my father any more questions about it.

I was seven and a half years old when General Ulysses S. Grant died and I went to his funeral. He had died far from Galesburg, I didn't hear where. But Main Street stores closed for the afternoon and the Q. shops and the Brown Cornplanter Works and Frost's foundry shut down too. A parade began at the Q. depot on Seminary Street and moved to Main Street, turned west, and marched to the Public Square. They said it was the longest parade Galesburg had ever seen.

The five long blocks of Main Street sidewalks from Seminary to the Square were crowded with people. It was a hot July afternoon in 1885. My father had been pushed and squeezed and had done some pushing and squeezing himself till at last we stood about three or four feet from the curb in front of the big O. T. Johnson dry-goods store. It was good they had made me put on shoes and stockings, because the way I got tramped on would have been worse if I had been barefoot. I tried to see the parade looking between the legs of men ahead of me but all I saw was more legs of more men. I pulled my father's hand and blubbered, "I can't see! I can't see!"

My father lifted me up, stuck his head between my legs, and there I sat straddle of him, and only a giant could see the parade better than I could. There was the marshal at the head of the parade on a skittish sorrel horse with a shiny bridle and with brass buttons, each bigger than a silver dollar, on the saddle. Then came two rows of policemen with nickel-plated stars shining on their blue coats, each with a club hanging from his belt. A fife-and-drum corps followed. The pounding noise they made seemed to shake the buildings and I took a better grip on my father's hat to make sure I wouldn't fall off. Then came a long line of men dressed like they might be going to church on Sunday, marching four in a row.

The Galesburg Marine Band marched past, men walking and blowing into their horns. One man had a big horn that seemed to be wrapped around him and I was puzzled how he got into it. They had on blue coats and blue pants with a stripe down the sides. Their music was slow and sad. It was only twenty years since the war had ended and General Grant was the greatest general in the war and they wanted to show they were sad because he was dead.

Marching past came men wearing dark-blue coats and big black hats tied round with a little gold cord having a tassel. They were the G.A.R., the Grand Army of the Republic, and I heard that some of these men had been in the war with General Grant and could tell how he looked on a horse and what made him a great general. Eight or ten of them walked along the sides of a long black box on a black cart

pulled by eight black horses. The body of General Grant wasn't in the box, but I could see everybody was even more quiet when this part of the parade passed.

I remember a couple of cannon came past with six or eight horses pulling them. The Negro Silver Cornet Band marched. Their music too was slow and sad. They were the only black faces in the parade, and as they passed I saw faces of men and women light up. I had heard from my father and Mr. Holmes that the war where Grant was the big general was a war for the black people to be free. I didn't quite understand what it was for people to be not free, to be bought and sold like horses. There was nothing like it in Galesburg. But whatever it was it was terrible, and men would shake their heads talking about it. So there was something people liked about seeing the black men playing sad music because General Grant, who had helped them get free, was dead.

A big flag was swinging high over the chunky man carrying it. The end of the pole holding the flag came to some kind of pocket the man had in a belt around his middle. It looked heavy and I could see the sweat rolling on his puffed-out cheeks.

The parade was different from other parades. I had seen a circus parade and people on the sidewalks laughing and hollering at the clowns and elephants and wild animals in cages. I had seen the Republican rally parade with torchlights, and the Democrats on the sidewalks hooted the marching Republicans and the Republicans hooted back. But in this General Grant funeral parade the men marching had straight faces and so did the people on the sidewalks. What boys and girls I saw stood still with straight faces like the old folks. They knew, like I did, it was a day that meant something. Except for the two bands and the fife-and-drum corps and the sound of feet and horse hoofs and wheels on the street stones, you couldn't hear much of anything. Even the slow sad music seemed quiet. I think the only smile I saw while the parade was passing was once when my father turned his face up toward me and felt good over the way he had fixed it so I could see the parade.

I remember how hard I tried to think about what the war was and what General Grant did that made him the greatest general of all. And I heard he had been President. I heard too he was one of the high men of the Republican party and the Republicans would miss him, and that some Democrats who had been in the war with him liked the way he did things and the way he treated them and these Democrats were sorry along with the Republicans.

The parade over, my father let me down. We walked along Main Street among thousands of people, and then home. I could see it was a day that meant something to my father. In some store windows I noticed pictures of General Grant with black cloth hung around them. I couldn't see that he looked so different from other men with whiskers over the whole face and the hairs cut close. He didn't look much different from Mr. Grubb, the Lombard professor who lived across the street from us and milked his Jersey cow each morning before starting out for his classes. And then I said to myself that even though Professor Grubb's face was nearly exactly like General Grant's face, if he should die there wouldn't be any parade as we had seen for General Grant. I went to bed that night saying I hoped sometime I would know more about the war, about the black people made free, about Grant the general and what it was like to be President and the head man of the government in Washington.

⚘ ⚘ ⚘

Four : Hungry to Learn

ONE OF MY most vivid early memories is our first home Bible, a small Swedish-language Bible. I was about four years old, and it was in the Berrien Street house, in the second-floor bedroom of my father and mother. It was winter, with winds howling outside. Mary and I heard father read a chapter by the light of a small kerosene lamp. Several times that week I went to where the Book lay on top of a bureau, and I opened it and turned the pages. I asked my mother to point out certain words I remembered. I took comfort in mother saying it would be clear to me when I started school and learned to read.

The day came when I started off for the Fourth Ward school, four blocks from our house. But the next year our block on Berrien Street was moved over into the Seventh Ward and we had to walk six blocks more to school. The secrets of the alphabet were unlocked for me. We recited in class and we learned that every word has a right way to say it and a wrong way. It came clear that any language is a lot of words and if you know the words you know the language.

One winter Friday afternoon when I was in the fifth grade, I took home the first volume of John S. C. Abbot's *The History of Napoleon*

Bonaparte and most of Saturday and Sunday I sat in an overcoat at the north window of our third-floor garret and read the book. The next week I did the same with the second volume. I had heard about Napoleon so often I wanted to see what kind of fighter he was. I got a picture in my mind of what Napoleon was like and I buckled a leather strap around my middle, ran where the strap would hold it a sword I whittled from a lath, and walked from garret to cellar and back giving orders to my marshals like Napoleon.

In the sixth grade Miss Goldquist kept at us about getting "the reading habit," saying, "You don't know what good friends books can be till you try them, till you try many of them." One of her favorite words was "ed-u-ca-tion," and she said you could never get enough of it. I read a row of history books by Jacob Abbot and John S. C. Abbot, J. T. Headley's *Napoleon and His Marshals* and *Washington and His Generals*. I found Thomas W. Knox's *Boy Travellers* in different countries a little dry and not up to Hezekiah Butterworth's *Zigzag Journeys* over the world. What time I could steal from lessons I turned the pages of Champlin's *Young Folks' Cyclopaedia of Persons and Places,* and *Young Folks' Cyclopaedia of Common Things* from the school library.

Best of all was the American history series by Charles Carleton Coffin. *The Boys of '76* made me feel I could have been a boy in the days of George Washington and watched him on a horse, a good rider sitting easy and straight, at the head of a line of ragged soldiers with shotguns. I could see Paul Revere on a horse riding wild and stopping at farmhouses to holler the British were coming. I could see old curly-headed Israel Putnam, the Connecticut farmer, as the book told it: "Let 'em have it!" shouted Old Put, and we sent a lot of redskins head over heels into the lake . . . A few days later . . . the French and Indians ambushed us. We sprung behind trees and fought like tigers. Putnam shot four Indians . . . one of the Frenchmen seized Roger's gun, and the other was about to stab him, when Put up with his gun and split the fellow's head open."

I met General Nathanael Green and watched him fight and in the nick of time draw off his soldiers and then come back when the time was right to win. He was a whiz at retreating and then, when the enemy didn't expect him, making a comeback and crippling the enemy or breaking him. I read about Lord North, the British Head Minister who ran the war. I saw a picture of the fathead and agreed with another boy, "I could cut the guts out of him."

The Boys of '76 had me going through the book just for the pictures. Whoever drew them was as good for the book as the author, but all it said on the title page was ILLUSTRATED.

I was thankful to Mr. Coffin for other books like *Old Times in the Colonies.* You were right there with those people building huts and cabins, clearing timbers, putting wooden plows to new land and plowing around the stumps while keeping an eye on the shotguns ready for the Indians. In *The Story of Liberty* he tried to tell what went on over in Europe that sent people heading across the ocean to America. You learned about "tyrants" and "tyranny" and people slaughtered in fights and wars about religion.

When I took home Mr. Coffin's *The Boys of '61* and two or three more on the Civil War I found they were dry compared with *The Boys of '76* and his earlier books. I couldn't understand this because I read that Mr. Coffin had been a war correspondent in the Civil War, went with the armies and was on the spot when some of the hottest battles were fought. When he wrote about a war he had seen, it wasn't worth reading. I puzzled over this: "It was a bigger war in '61 than '76 and maybe so big he couldn't get his head around it. Or maybe following the armies he got sick of the war, so disgusted that when he started writing about it he tried to hide his disgust but it got into his book without his knowing it."

Every boy except the dumbest read those two books by James Otis, *Toby Tyler; or, Ten Weeks with a Circus* and *Tim and Tip; or, The Adventures of a Boy and a Dog.* The library copies were ragged, dog-eared, thumb-and-finger dirtied, and here and there a pencil had written, "Good" or "Gee whiz."

The detective-story books of those school days were mostly Old Cap Collier at a nickel apiece. We read them in the schoolroom behind a geography, and traded with each other. But soon I went back to Champlin's *Young Folks' Cyclopaedia of Persons and Places.* Later came Nick Carter and his sidekick Chick, keener than Old Cap Collier. The year came, though, when I decided that detective stories were mostly tricks.

We read *Huckleberry Finn* and *Tom Sawyer* by Mark Twain but they didn't get the hold on us that other books did. They seemed to be for a later time. It was the same with the novels of Charles Dickens.

We had a first book in physiology in school and then one or two more. We read about alcohol and saw what happens to a drunkard's stomach. But I wasn't worried about my father's stomach because never did he go into any of the town's dozen saloons. When on a cold winter night Papa took down his pint bottle of pure grain alcohol and poured a spoon or two into a cup of black coffee, we knew the bottle would be finished that winter and there wouldn't be another till the next winter. The Kranses, the Holmeses, and the Swedish Lutherans we knew kept away from beer, wine, and whisky if only for the money it wasted that they could spend for things they liked better.

There came the day I entered a declamation contest to speak a piece against the evils of alcohol. On Seminary two blocks south of Berrien Street an afternoon Sunday school named the Mission drew boys and girls, about a hundred, from Berrien and other streets. The frame building, painted brown but with the paint peeling away, stood across the street from the Q. machine shop, next to the Peoria branch of the Q. The meetings ran through the fall and winter, and the teachers were mostly students from Knox College. We had good times at the Mission. As a member of the Mission's Junior Epworth League, I was once a delegate to a convention in Monmouth, sixteen miles from Galesburg, the farthest I had ever been away from home. And we put on "entertainments." After rehearsing a program three or four times, we gave it of an evening for grownups and children. I sang once in a quartet and once I took the part of a tramp in a one-act play.

But it was the Demorest Silver Medal Declamation Contest that had all of us at the Mission buzzing. Mr. Demorest, a rich man in the East who had made his money getting out a magazine giving women ideas and patterns for dresses, was "a total-abstinence man." He never drank a drop of liquor himself and he wanted to see every saloon in America put out of business. So he had thought up the Demorest medal contests in which the young people of any school or neighborhood would speak pieces against alcohol. Mr. Demorest sent us each a book to pick out the piece to speak in the contest. I picked the shortest piece in the book, and the last line was: "The world moves!" I practiced many ways to say it and couldn't decide whether to give it slow and drawn out or fierce and fast like a shot in the dark.

It was all very exciting, because whoever won the silver medal in our contest would go into another contest with other silver-medal winners. Then whoever won that contest would get a gold medal. Then the gold-medal winners would go into a contest for a diamond medal. We talked about it and agreed that if any of us won a diamond medal that would be high enough and we would be satisfied.

The night of the contest came and there was the biggest crowd the Mission had ever seen. There we sat, a row of us on the platform looking at the audience and the audience looking at us. We picked out faces from them and they picked out faces from us. They smiled and we tried not to smile. When there is a silver medal hanging over you, you don't smile, or anyhow we thought you're not expected to.

Four boys and four girls stood up one by one and gave their declamations. About the middle of the program my name was called. I walked to the center of the platform feeling good that what I had to remember was only half as long as some of the others. I blurted out my opening sentences wondering how it sounded to the people out there. Near the middle of my declamation I had to stop.

I didn't know what was coming next. I reached up and around and somehow my mind pulled down what I wanted and I went on to the end and gave "The world moves!" fierce and fast like a shot in the dark and saw more faces laughing than sober.

The judges didn't make us wait long to hear who was the winner. I knew I had done a little worse than any of the others on the program, and I didn't expect to be excited or proud about whoever got the prize. But when one of the judges stood up and told us who was the winner, there I was, excited and proud. The judge was saying, "It gives us great pleasure to announce that the winner of the Demorest Silver Medal is Miss Mary Sandburg."

A book we owned each year till it got lost was *Hostetter's Illustrated United States Almanac,* given away every New Year's Day. Half the almanac was filled with good words for Hostetter's Stomach Bitters. There was advice too on how to get rid of warts, corns, boils, how to get a ring off a swollen finger, what to do about a rusty nail in the foot and other ailments. Five pages had funny drawings with jokes under them. We read Hostetter's out loud in the kitchen and talked over the points of the jokes and what the "wise sayings" meant.

We didn't know we were getting education while having fun, Mary, Mart and I, in that crowded kitchen when we read *Hostetter's Almanac* to each other. It was crammed with all sorts of facts new to us and interesting—the morning and evening stars from any month in the year, the ocean tides, the velocity of the earth, eclipses, and so on. We were hungry to learn.

The first biography I owned was of a size I could put in one of my vest pockets. I was going along to the Seventh Ward school when I found it on a sidewalk. It had been rained on and I brushed the dirt off and smoothed it where the top corner had been scorched. When I measured it later it was two and three-fourths inches long and one and one-half inches wide. The front cover had gloss paper and a color

picture of the head and shoulders of a two-star general in a Confeder-
ate gray uniform. The title read *A Short History of General P. T.
Beauregard.*

There were thirteen pages of reading in fine print. Inside the back
cover was a list of a "Series of Small Books," histories of Civil War
generals, fifty of them, with a notice of "other series in preparation."
And here you learned how to get these books. It said "Packed in
Duke's Cigarettes."

I couldn't think of buying ten-cent packages of Duke's Cameo or
Duke's Cross-cut cigarettes for the sake of filling my vest pockets with
histories, nice as they were. Cigarettes had a bad name among us
kids; we believed only "dudes" and "softies" smoked them. Our physiology books had warned us that tobacco had nicotine in it and nicotine is a poison. And with cigarettes you were supposed to inhale and
take the poison straight into your lungs. This could lead you into consumption, or anyhow it would weaken your wind and slow you down
as a runner or ballplayer. When we bought Virginia Cheroots at five
for a nickel or the ten little "cigaroos" for a nickel and smoked them,
we were like strong men ready to take a chance on what real tobacco
could do to us.

I scouted around and found three men who smoked Duke's Cigarettes "once in a while for a change." One of them was saving the
books for himself. The other two saved them for me. After a while I
had the histories of Beauregard, Cornelius Vanderbilt, and Sarah
Bernhardt, *The Life of T. De Witt Talmage,* and the lives of George
Peabody, James B. Eads, Horace B. Claflin, and Robert Ingersoll.
They changed from *History of* to *Life of.*

In the list I noticed John Ericsson, the inventor of the *Monitor,* the
Swede who helped the North win the war. I tried but couldn't scare
up a copy of the Ericsson. A Swede boy pulled one out of his vest
pocket one day and grinned at me. He knew I wanted it. I offered
him a penny for it and went as high as a nickel and he shook his
head. Then he let me borrow it and I let him borrow my Sarah Bernhardt. He had heard she kept a coffin in her bedroom and liked to
stretch out in it to rest. I showed him where the book told about that.
"Gee!" said the Swede boy, "I sure want to read that book." I offered
to trade him the Sarah Bernhardt for his John Ericsson. He said
maybe and next day told me he had talked it over with his Swede father and mother and they said, "No, you keep the John Ericsson."

So there was my vest-pocket library of biography and history.
There were days I carried the eight books, four in the upper right-

hand vest pocket and four in the upper left. I had books I didn't have to take back to the Seventh Ward school or the Public Library. I was a book-owner.

One Monday morning, a bright summer day, mother was doing a wash in the cellar. I came in to see a well-dressed man talking to her. She had quit washing and was listening to him. He was showing her a sample of a book. Here were the covers and here were sample pages —the real book was five times bigger. Mama's face and eyes were shining. He was saying that education is important. And how do you get education? Through books, the right kind of books. Now you have this *Cyclopedia of Important Facts of the World* around and the children can't help reading it. Knowledge—that is what counts when your children go out in the world—knowledge! "The more they learn the more they earn!"

Mother was a little dazed by now. He was speaking her own mind as to education and knowledge. Papa would have been scowling and shaking his head. Mother was more than interested. She took the sample and turned pages. She looked down into my face. Would I like the book? I said yes in several ways. She signed her name and she had the required seventy-five cents ten days later when the man came with the book.

About this *Cyclopedia* father grumbled—a waste of money, let the children get "eddication" in the schools. It was later he made a real fuss. This time I was there again when the book agent came, not the same man, but well dressed and polite, handy with his tongue, like the first one. His book was three times bigger than the *Cyclopedia,* bigger pages, two columns to the page, many pictures, *A History of the World and Its Great Events,* with special attention to the famous battles of all time. Mother was not quite so bright, not so sure, as the last time. But I was surer I would like this book. Mother signed again. This time it was a dollar and a half, more than a day's pay of my father. But mother had the money when the book came two weeks later.

I won't go into the scene father made when he saw the book and heard the price. We were heading for the Knoxville poorhouse. If it ever happened again he didn't know what he would do. It ended mother's listening to book agents.

Mother had visions and hopes. She could say with a lighted face, "We will hope for the best," as I bent my head over *A History of the World and Its Great Events*. Father would stand over me saying, "Wat good iss dat book, Sholly?" And I had no answer. I didn't like his saying such a thing, but I had some dim realization too that he had in mind mortgages on which payments must be made.

When I finished the Seventh Ward school, I could feel I was growing up, halfway toward being a man. It was a change to walk a mile twice a day to the Grammar School downtown and home again. They came from all ends of town to the Grammar School, many new faces to see, many more boys and girls from the well-off families.

The Grammar School stood a short block from the Public Square. Between stood the Old First Church, built more than forty years before by the First Settlers. Straight across the street from the Grammar School stood the two-story house of Henry R. Sanderson. He had a long white beard and a quiet face and had been mayor of Galesburg when Lincoln came to debate with Douglas in 1858. We heard he had taken Abraham Lincoln into his house as a guest and had helped with towels and warm water for Lincoln to take a bath.

In the eighth grade I had Miss Frances (Fanny) Hague, truly a great teacher. She knew books and would have loved them whether she taught them or not. She had traveled Europe and could make cities and ruins there come alive for us. The high spot for me under her teaching was *A Brief History of the United States;* the title page didn't tell who wrote it. It was for me the first book that tried to tell the story of our country from the time of the early Indians through Grant as President. It was stuffy and highfalutin in style, yet it made me see the American Story in new lights. Miss Hague knew history too and often gave color and good sense to passages in it.

When I left Miss Hague's room my mind kept going back to it. I wasn't sure what education was but I was sure that I got a little under her teaching. From then on until several years later, what schooling I got was outside of schools, from reading books, newspapers, and magazines, from watching and listening to many kinds of people and what they were doing and saying.

❀ ❀ ❀

Five : Days of Play and Sport

ON THE WOODEN sidewalks of Berrien Street we played one kind of mumble-peg and in the grass of the front yard or the grass between sidewalk and gutter ditch we played the more complicated and interesting kind with jump-the-fence, thread-the-needle, plow-forty-acres, and plow-eighty-acres. On the wooden sidewalks we spun tops, flipped jackstones, chalked tit-tat-toe. On the street we played baseball, two-old-cat, choose-up, knocking-up-flies. In shinny any kind of club would do for knocking a tin can or a block of wood toward a goal, though the fellow with a plow handle had the best of it. And duck-on-a-rock had its points—knocking a small rock off a large rock and then running to pick up your own rock to get back to taw without being tagged.

After we had seen the commencement Field Day on the Knox or Lombard campus, we put on our own field day, barefoot in the summer dust of Berrien Street. Some boy usually had a two-dollar-and-a-half Waterbury watch and timed us as we ran fifty yards, one hundred yards, a few seconds slower than the college runners, and five or six seconds under the world's record. We knew how near we came to the college records in the standing broad jump, the running broad jump, the hop-skip-and-a-step, the standing high jump and the running high jump. Whoever could throw a crowbar the farthest was counted put-and-shot "champeen." We did everything the college athletes did except the pole vault. The mile run we did afternoons, breaking no records except some of our own, yet satisfying ourselves that there is such a thing as "second wind" and if you can get it you can finish your mile.

Straight across the street from the house next east to ours was an average two-story frame house, with a porch. In the street in front of this house was our home base when playing ball. Often we saw on that porch in a rocking chair a little old woman, her hair snow-white with the years. She had a past, a rather bright though not dazzling past. She could lay claim to fame, if she chose. Millions of children reading the McGuffey and other school readers had met her name and memorized lines she had written. For there was in the course of her years no short poem in the English language more widely published, known, and recited than her lines about "Little Things":

Little drops of water,   Little deeds of kindness,
　Little grains of sand,   　Little words of love,
Make the mighty ocean   Help to make earth happy
　And the pleasant land . . .   　Like the heaven above.

She was Julia Carney. Her sons Fletcher and James were Universalists and Lombard graduates, Fletcher serving three or four terms as mayor of Galesburg. There she sat in the quiet of her backward-gazing thoughts, sometimes gently rocking, an image of silence and rest, while the air rang with boy screams, "Hit it bang on the nose now!" "Aw, he couldn't hit a balloon!" "Down went McGinty to the bottom of the sea!" Rarely she turned her head to see what we were doing. To us she was just one more nice old woman who wouldn't bother boys at play. We should have heard about her in school. We should have read little pieces about her in the papers. She has a tiny quaint niche in the history of American literature under which one line could be written: "She loved children and wrote poems she hoped children would love."

In early years we would stop our play and follow the lamplighter when he came along before dusk. He carried a small ladder he would set against the lamppost, and we would watch him climb up, swing open the door of the glass case holding a gas burner, turn on the gas, and with a lighted taper put the flame to the escaping gas. Then he would climb down and move on from the corner of Pearl and Berrien to the corner of Day and Berrien, a block east. Then came the electric lights, one arc lamp at every second corner, exactly in the center of the four street crossings, high enough so a man driving a load of hay couldn't reach up and touch the globe. The lamplighter was gone. We missed him.

It wasn't long before the fathers and mothers along Berrien Street had new troubles with their boys. Under that electric light at Day and Berrien the boys had a new playground. They could turn night into day. There was night baseball, night shinny, night duck-on-a-rock, night tug-of-war. There were winners yelling because they had won. There were losers yelling that next time they would make the winners eat dirt. Vehement remarks floated through windows into rooms where honest Q. shopmen and worthy railroad firemen and brakemen were trying for a little sleep.

One of the sleepers who couldn't sleep had a voice like a big-league umpire when one night he clamored from his bedroom window, "You boys shut up and go home with you. If you don't I'll get the police on you." The noise stopped. We sat cross-legged on a patch of grass next to a sidewalk and talked in whispers: "Do you s'pose he means it?" "Aw, we got a right to holler, this is a free country." "Yeah, but what if he means it? We'll get run in." "Yeah, I don't want no patrol-wagon ride." About then came a woman who wanted her sonny-boy; she took him by one ear and led him away and his face had a sheepish look. Then came two men, fathers. They spotted their boys, collared them, and led them away like two sheep for slaughter. Mart and I went home. If we didn't get into the house by nine o'clock we would get scoldings or worse.

On a later night the boys forgot themselves and the hullabaloo they made could be heard a block away. Then as promised, the patrol wagon came. Before it could stop, five or six boys skedaddled. That left five or six of us who weren't going to run and show we were scared. We stood in a huddle waiting. Out of the patrol wagon came two policemen, their nickel-plated stars shining on their coats. One of them, Frank Peterson, weighed about two hundred and twenty pounds, and looked like a battleship coming toward us. We expected hard words from Policeman Peterson. But he spoke in a soft voice like what he was saying was confidential. "Don't you boys know you're disturbing people who are trying to sleep?" What could we say to a quiet intelligent question like that? One boy said, "Yes," another, "Well, you know we were just trying to have some fun." "Yes," said Peterson, again quiet and confidential like, "but ain't there some way you can have your fun without keeping people awake that's trying to sleep?" We had come to like Policeman Peterson. We saw he wasn't mad at us and it didn't look like we were going to be put in the wagon and hauled to the calaboose. We said yes, we would try to have our fun without making so much noise.

Before walking away Peterson said, "Now that's a promise, boys, and I expect you to keep it. If you don't stop your noise, we'll have to run you in." And his voice got a little hard as he said, "Remember that. We don't like to arrest young fellows like you but sometimes we have to do it." That word "arrest" stuck in our ears. They could have arrested us. When you're arrested that means you're a criminal. And if you're a criminal, where are you?

The patrol wagon drove away. When the rumble of its wheels had died away, we sat on the grass and talked in low tones near a whisper. All of us agreed that from now on we had better try to have our fun without yelling. All agreed except the boy who had on another night said, "Aw, we got a right to holler, this is a free country." This boy guessed he'd rather stay away and have some other kind of fun than come around and be a nice boy like the police told him. And he did stay away and later he took to the poolrooms and the saloons and still later put in a year in the Pontiac reformatory for petty larceny.

We went on playing under the electric light and trying to keep quiet but it was a strain. I had a job where I had to report at six-thirty in the morning and had gone home early one night, leaving the boys in a hot game of shinny, back in their old hooting and yelling. They told me next day that a railroad fireman had come out in his nightshirt with a club and a revolver. He shot in the air twice to show the gun was loaded. He sent a bullet into a sidewalk plank and had them look at the bullet. He was wild-eyed, cursed them, slapped one of them, kicked another, then took out a watch and said if every last one of them wasn't gone in two minutes he would shoot to kill. Half the boys ran and the rest went away on a fast walk. From then on not as many boys came to that corner at night; it became reasonably quiet, and decent people could sleep. There was hate for the shooting-iron fireman. And Policeman Frank Peterson we would point out with, "He ain't a bad fellow, do you know?"

Four lots to the east of our house was a vacant double lot where later we laid out a small diamond. At the time a good-natured Jersey cow was pastured there. We never hit the cow but when the ball landed near her and the fielder ran toward her it disturbed her. Also it disturbed the owner of the cow, who said he would have the police on us. So we played in the street till the day the cow was gone and we heard it had been sold. Then we went back to our pasture.

On the narrow lot next to the pasture was Mrs. Moore's house. She was the widow of a Civil War veteran, living alone on a Federal pension. She was a tall woman with dark hair streaked with gray—a quiet woman, smoking her clay pipe, keeping to herself and raising vegetables and flowers. She had the nicest all-round flower garden in our block, the front of her lot filled with hollyhocks, begonias, salvia, asters, and morning-glories climbing the fences. First base was only ten feet from her fence and every so often a fly or a foul ball would go over into her potatoes, carrots, and hollyhocks. A boy would climb the fence and go stomping around hunting the lost ball. At such times as Mrs. Moore stood between the boy and the place where he believed the ball fell it was not pleasant for either party concerned. "Why must you boys do this to my place?" she would ask. When the boy answered, "We'll try never to do it again," her reply would come, "See that you don't do it again. I don't want to make trouble for you boys."

Again and again we sent the ball over into her well-kept yard. She tried scolding but she just naturally wasn't a scold. She quietly hinted she might have to go to the police, but she didn't go to the police or to our parents. She had property rights and we were trespassing on her property, and she forgave us our trespasses even though we went on trespassing. She was a woman of rare inner grace who had gathered wisdom from potatoes and hollyhocks.

In our early games played in the street, the bat was a broom handle, the ball handmade—a five-cent rubber ball wrapped round with grocery string. The home plate was a brick, first base a brick, second base a tin can, third another tin can. We played barehanded till we learned how to stuff a large man-sized glove with cotton, wool, or hair to take the sting out of a fast ball.

The days came when we played in the cow pasture with a Spalding big-league regulation ball. We gathered round the boy who first brought it. "Well, what do you know!" we said, "a dollar and a half." And we told it around as a kind of wonder, "We been playing today with a dollar and a half"—the same ball that Amos Rusie was throwing in the big league, the same ball Big Bill Lange was hitting with the Chicago team. When I carried Chicago newspapers and read sports news I learned about the "elusive pill" thrown by Amos Rusie. I was among those who grieved later to hear of Amos Rusie taking to drink, being dropped from major and minor clubs, and being found one day digging gas mains at a dollar-fifty a day. He was doing ten cents a day better than my father at the Q. shop but still I was more sorry for him than for my father.

When Galesburg played Chillicothe or Peoria or Rock Island on the Knox campus, the Berrien Street kids, lacking the two bits' admission, watched the games through knotholes in the fence. Or we climbed a tree fifty yards from the home plate, found a crotch to sit in, and had as much fun as though we were in the two-bit bleachers.

The most exciting baseball year the town had was when a City League was organized and played one or two games a week. The Main Street clerks had one team, the railroad shopmen another, and there were two other teams. Out of the tall grass around Victoria came a team that had surprises. Galesburg had picked the best nine in the town to meet them and the word was that maybe Galesburg would "goose-egg" them. But the country boys played fast ball, among them the Spratt brothers, Bob and Jack, who later went into minor-league clubs. Their center fielder was a tall gawk wearing a derby! As the game got going Victoria took the lead by one or two runs and kept the lead till near the closing inning, when Galesburg with one out got two men on bases and one of its heaviest sluggers came to bat. He hit the ball high and handsome and sent it sailing away out to deep center field. The tall gawk in the derby made a fast run, made a leap for it, caught it with one hand and threw it straight to second to catch a man off base—and Victoria was victorious in one of the craziest, sweetest pieces of baseball drama I have ever seen.

On many a summer day I played baseball starting at eight in the morning, running home at noon for a quick meal and again with fielding and batting till it was too dark to see the ball. There were times my head seemed empty of everything but baseball names and figures. I could name the leading teams and the tailenders in the National League and the American Association. I could name the players who led in batting and fielding and the pitchers who had won the most games. And I had my opinions about who was better than anybody else in the national game.

An idea began growing in me that if I played and practiced a lot I might become good enough to get on a team. Once on a minor-league team I would have my chance to show what I could do and I might end up in the majors—who knows about a thing like that? It was a secret ambition. In what spare time I could find I played with the boys and did fairly well in left field on a scrub team.

Then came an afternoon in early October when I was sixteen. I had managed to buy secondhand a fielder's glove, a regular big-league af-

fair I was proud of. Skinny Seeley and I went to a pasture and knocked up flies. He hit a high one to me and I was running top speed for it. I believed I would make a brilliant catch, the kind I would make when maybe one of the minor-league clubs had taken me on. Suddenly my right foot stashed into a hole and I fell on my face. When I looked at my foot I saw a gash in the shoe leather and blood oozing from the tangled yarn of the sock. In the hole there was a broken beer bottle, and into this my foot had crashed.

I limped across the pasture, about a block, to the house of Dr. Taggart. Out on his front porch he had me take off the shoe, then slowly the sock. He cleaned the cut, picked out yarn and glass, applied antiseptic. Then he brought out a curved needle and sewed four stitches at about the middle of the foot just below the instep. He bandaged my foot and I limped home. My mother spoke sorrow and pity. My father asked when would I ever learn any sense and quit wasting my time with baseball.

From that day on I was completely through with any and all hopes of becoming a big-time ballplayer. I went on playing occasional games, but those four stitches marked the end of my first real secret ambition.

❀ ❀ ❀

Six : Fair and Circus Days

WE WERE BETWEEN nine and twelve when we took in the Knox County Fair one year after another for three years. We walked the four and a half miles to the fair grounds just outside of Knoxville —Husky Larson, his brother Al, and one or two other boys. The dust lay thick on the road. We walked barefoot, carrying our shoes and putting them on when we came to the fair grounds so we wouldn't get our bare toes stepped on in the crowds. We walked to save the round-trip railroad fare and after paying twenty-five cents admission, we watched our few nickels.

One nickel went to the man who had the new and amazing Edison Talking Phonograph. Around the machine stood people watching what it did to the faces of those who clapped on the earphones and were listening. Some faces sober and doubting stayed sober and came away saying, "It works, doggone it, you can hear that brass band playing like it was right here on the fair grounds." Most faces, however, wore smiles, and came away saying, "It's pretty cute, I tell you. The machine talks like it's human."

We stepped up with our nickels. We plugged our ears with the phone ends. We watched the cylinder on the machine turning. We heard a voice saying this was the Edison Talking Phonograph and that next we would hear a famous brass band playing. We looked at one another and nodded and smiled, "It works! I can hear it! Ain't it the doggonedest thingamajig? I wouldn't believe it if I wasn't hearing it."

We watched the stallions and mares, bulls and cows, boars and sows, cocks and hens—and the judges awarding prizes and blue ribbons. We saw farmers proud of what they had bred and raised. We felt something in the air very different from a circus. Many a farmer and his boy had come to learn. Their work the year round was in trying to make the land and the animals bring bigger crops and more food. They had on their best clothes but their muscles stood out in little humps and bunches so that their coats hung on them. Their women carried the signs of hard work, some of them taking pride in the jellies and preserves they had entered for showing. The biggest Knox County potato of the year was worth seeing, as also the largest rutabaga.

We didn't have the two bits for grandstand seats to see the horse races. We stood at the board fence next to the grandstand and watched the fastest horses in Knox County—saddle horses, thoroughbreds, pacers and trotters, with drivers in sulkies with high wheels, spokes of wood, and the rims iron. Several of the drivers, like Fred Seacord, we had seen on the streets of Galesburg exercising their horses and getting them used to the sulkies.

There was a "special feature"—"The Only Pacing Dog in the World." Occasionally we had seen Mr. Redfield with his Irish setter on Main Street. And we knew it was no common dog. Now at last we saw Mr. Redfield come out on the track with his horse and sulky. Alongside the right wheel so the grandstand could see him was the Irish setter, handsome with his coat of brown hair gleaming, his gait that of a pacer, the legs in that peculiar continuous sidewise throw. Twice around the half-mile track went the pacing dog. He wasn't as fast as pacing horses but the crowd believed he was the only pacing dog in the world and they cheered him and Mr. Redfield.

That year we caught a ride in a hayrack from the fair grounds to Galesburg. Arriving home we talked most about having heard the first Edison Talking Phonograph in Knox County and having seen the only pacing dog in the world. About the dog Papa merely remarked that it was interesting. That Edison Talking Phonograph, however, giving you a band concert without bringing you the band, that was curious and he said, "Wat will dey tink up next?" When the talking machine later came to a vacant store on Main Street he spent several nickels listening to the newfangled contraption.

When the circus came to town, we managed to shake out of sleep at four o'clock in the morning, grab a slice of bread and butter, and make a fast walk to the Q. yards to watch the unloading in early daylight. A grand clear voice the man had who rode his horse a half-block ahead of the elephants in the parade and cried out, "The elephants are coming, watch your horses!" First to one side of the street and then the other he cried it and those who had skittish horses watched them.

The great P. T. Barnum himself never met my eyes but on a bright summer morning I did see Mr. Bailey of the firm of Barnum & Bailey in a black swallowtail coat giving orders and running the circus in the big green pasture that soon was subdivided into city lots. And with the other kids who had seen Bailey I joined in saying, "Wasn't he something to look at? And think of it, he's nearly as great a man as Barnum himself!"

After the unloading we went home for a quick breakfast and then a run to the circus grounds, a big pasture at Main and Farnham near the city limits. If we were lucky we got jobs at carrying water for the elephants or lugging to the big tent the boards for the audience to sit on. After three or four hours of this work we were presented with slips of paper that let us in to see the big show in the afternoon. If we hadn't been lucky and if we didn't have the fifty cents for a ticket we tried to slide under the canvas and crawl to where we could peek through boards and between legs to see the grand march, the acrobats, the trapezists, the clowns, the hippodrome chariot race given before our eyes as it was in the time of Nero in Rome. Once as I was nearly through the canvas a pair of strong hands caught me by the ankles, yanked me out and threw me for a fall, and a voice told me I could get going.

I walked around to the Side Show. There out front as a free show I saw the man with the elastic skin. He would pull it out from his face and neck and it would snap back into place. There I saw the tattooed man with fish, birds, brunette girls, ships, and many other shapes inked deep into his skin—and there too the Oriental Dancing Girl smiling to some giggling farm hands.

The spieler, a man with a thick uncurled mustache, turned to the crowd and let go in a smooth, loud voice: "La-deez and gen-tul-men, beneath yon canvas we have the curi-aw-si-ties and the mon-straw-si-ties—the Wild Man of Borneo, the smallest dwarf ever seen of man-kind and the tallest giant that ever came into existence, the most mar-velous snake ever brought to your fair city, a man-eating python captured in the darkest jungles of Africa ever penetrated by man. And I would call your particular attention to Jo Jo, the dogfaced boy born forty miles from land and forty miles from sea. The price of admis-sion, la-deez and gen-tul-men, is a dime, ten cents only, the tenth part of a dollar. Buy your tickets now before the big rush comes."

I had a dime and a nickel. With the dime, I bought a ticket. I went in and I saw the Wild Man of Borneo was a sad little shrimp and his whiskers messy. The Fat Woman, the Dwarf, the Giant seemed to me to be mistakes God had made, that God was absent-minded when he shaped them. I hung around the midget and his wife, watched them sign their names to photographs they sold at ten cents—and they were so pleasant and witty that I saw I had guessed wrong about them and they were having more fun out of life than some of the men in the Q. shops.

I stood a long while watching the Giant and noticed he was quiet and satisfied about things. If a smarty asked, "How's the weather up there?" he might lift one eyebrow and let it pass, for he had heard it often enough. Nor did I feel sorry for the python. He may have been a man-eater but he was sleeping as if he had forgotten whoever it was he had swallowed and digested. After a third or fourth time around, the only one I felt sorry for was the Wild Man of Borneo. He could have been the only lonely creature among all the freaks. The Oriental Dancing Girl certainly was no freak, an average good-looking show-girl, somewhat dark of skin and probably a gypsy.

Later it came over me that at first sight of the freaks I was sad be-cause I was bashful. Except at home and among playmates, it didn't come easy for me to be looked at. I would pass people on the street and when they had gone by, I would wonder if they had turned their heads for another look at me. Walking down a church aisle between hundreds of people, I had a feeling of eyes on me. This was silly, but when you're bashful you have that feeling of eyes following you and boring through you. And there at the side show were these people, the freaks—and the business, the work, of each one of them was to be looked at. Every week, day by day, they sat or stood up to be looked at by thousands of people and they were paid to be looked at. If some one of them was more looked at than any others there was danger of jealousy on the part of those who didn't get looked at as much as they wished. Only the Wild Man of Borneo and the python seemed to be careless about whether anyone looked at them or not.

I walked out of the side show with my nickel still in my pocket. I passed the cane stand where a man held out rings and spoke like his tongue was oiled, "Only ten cents for a ring and the cane you ring is the cane you get." I stopped where a man was cheerfully calling with no letup, "Lem-o-nade, ice-cold lem-o-nade, a nice cool refreshing drink for a nickel, five cents, the twentieth part of a dollar." I passed by him to hear a laughing voice, "Here's where you get your hot roasted peanuts, those big double-jointed humpbacked peanuts, five a sack." I passed him by and still had my nickel.

Then I came to a man sitting on the ground, a deep-chested man with a face that had quiet on it and wouldn't bawl at you. I noticed he was barefoot. I looked up from his bare feet to see only stumps of arms at his shoulders. Between the first two toes of his right foot he held a card and lifted it toward me and said, "Take it and read it." I read in perfect handwriting, "I can write your name for you on a card for you to keep. The charge is only ten cents." I said, "I would if I had the ten cents. All I've got is a nickel." I took out the nickel and turned my pockets inside out and showed him that besides the nickel there was only a knife, a piece of string, and a buckeye. He took the nickel in his left foot. He put a pen between the first two toes of his right foot and on the card wrote "Charles A. Sandburg," lifted the foot up toward me, and I took the card. It was the prettiest my name had ever been written. His face didn't change. All the time it kept that quiet look that didn't strictly belong with a circus. I was near crying. I said some kind of thanks and picked up my feet and ran.

❀ ❀ ❀

Seven : The Hangout

THERE WAS A row of buildings running west from Chambers Street on the north side of Berrien. On the corner stood the wooden grocery building of "Swan H. Olson & Bro." Swan had a red chin beard, always neatly trimmed, and waited on customers quietly and politely. He had arrived from Sweden in 1854, twenty years old, worked on

Knox County farms, enlisted in 1862, fought in the Atlanta campaign, marched with Sherman to the sea, across the Carolinas and on up to Washington for the Grand Review. Not until later years when I studied the marches and campaigns in which Swan Olson served did I come to a full respect for him. He was a foot soldier whose feet had taken him more than two thousand miles. He had been in wild and bloody battles, had waded creeks and rivers and marched in heavy rains day after day carrying rifle and blanket roll—but you couldn't tell it by seeing him measuring a quart of cranberries for Mrs. Nelson or hanging out a stockfish in front of the store on a winter morning to let the Swedes know their favorite holiday sea food had arrived.

His brother William, with the most elegantly spreading and curled red mustache in the Seventh Ward, was more of a talker than Swan. Both brothers hung their coats in the back of the store and put on black sleeves up to the elbows to keep their cuffs clean when they dipped into coffee sacks or dusty bins. Like all grocers, they fastened strong wire screens over the tops of apple baskets. At times one or two boys would watch inside the store and when the two brothers were busy with customers they would signal a boy outside who worked the wire screen loose and would run off with as many apples as his pockets and hat could hold.

I was six or seven when I learned a lesson about dealing at the Olson store. After Will Olson had wrapped what I was sent for, I handed him the book mother had given me and told him, "Put it on the book." He wrote in the book and handed it back to me. Then I asked how much would be a stick of licorice that caught my eye. "Five cents," said Will Olson and I said, "Put it on the book." Until then I had never bought anything for more than a penny. Now I had found a way to get something for nothing. I walked home hoping I would be sent often to the grocery with "the book." When I got home they saw my lips and chin black with licorice and asked about it. I said the grocery man gave me a big stick of licorice. "Did you pay him for it? Where did you get the money?" "I told him to put it on the book." It was then I heard the book was for the family, and not for me to be a mean little pig. My mother gave me a slap and told me, "Go and wash your dirty face," saying further that if it happened again I would get a licking I would remember.

On payday my father would take the book to the Olson store and they would figure up what he owed for the past month's groceries. After he paid they would give him a sack of candy for the children and a five-cent cigar for himself. He smoked an inch or two of the

cigar each Sunday and it lasted till the next payday, when he got an-other cigar. The only smoking he ever did was these payday cigars. He couldn't waste them, so he smoked them.

There was an alley next to the Olsons' wooden building. Then came a one-story brick building where Franz Nelson ran a butcher shop. Here we would stop in and ask Franz when he was going to do some butchering. We liked to go with him to the slaughterhouse south-east of town and watch him knock a sledge into the head of a steer or stick a knife into the neck of a hog. At first we shivered at seeing the blood gushing from the slit in the hog's throat—then we got used to it. We helped at bringing water and carrying things to Franz and we watched him cutting steaks and chops on a tree-trunk chopping block. He gave us calf or beef liver to take home, and when a customer asked, "How about a piece of liver?" Franz would hand over liver without charge. He was freehanded with us boys when it came to ba-loney. We cut what we wanted and stood around eating it.

Next to the Franz Nelson butcher shop, in the same brick building, was our favorite hangout, the Julius Schulz cigar shop. In the front room were a wide aisle and two glass showcases filled with Schulz-made cigars and a line of pipes and smoking tobaccos. Mr. Schulz we didn't see often; he was out drumming up trade. He was medium-sized, wore a heavy brown mustache and matching it a brown suit and a brown derby, a gold watch chain on his brown vest. He would come into the store, look over his account books, fill a valise with samples, and go away without a look at us kids whether there were two, five, or six of us hanging around. We all liked Mr. Schulz. He didn't know our names nor bother to speak to us, but summer or winter he let us hang around and use his place for a kind of clubroom.

The back room was the main hangout. There sat "Nig" Bohnenberger, whose folks spoke German but he hadn't learned it. "They got to calling me Nig because I'm dark-complected," he said. He had a hawk nose, a pale face, a thin body, and a mind that was always thinking things over. He read the papers and while he rolled cigars and licked the wrappers he told us what was wrong with the country and the town. He often ended what he said with, "Of that I can tell you I'm pos-i-tive." He liked to be positive and we liked him being pos-i-tive. We saw him in coughing spells and slowly fade away from consumption. One boy came from Nig's funeral saying, "He looked so natural in the coffin I couldn't keep from crying."

To the cigar shop came the boys in the between-times of work and play. In warmer weather on nights and Sundays when the cigar store was closed, we met on the sidewalk in front and sang. There was tall, skinny, bony John Hultgren, a Swede boy who worked in the Boyer broom factory, and chubby, cheek-puffed, bright-eyed John Kerrigan, an Irish lad learning the plumber's trade under his father—both of them tenors. There was Willis ("Bohunk") Calkins and myself who were fair at baritone and bass. This quartet could give "In the Evening by the Moonlight," "Swanee River," "Carry Me Back to Old Virginia," "I Found a Horseshoe"—and we said we were good and when Al Field's Minstrels came to town they ought to hear us. Bohunk a couple of nights brought his banjo.

One morning about nine I drifted into the Schulz store to find excitement. In the night someone had broken open a back window and taken what money there was, maybe eight or ten dollars. Heavy rain had been falling all night. The thief, it was said, probably counted on few people being on the street and they would be hurrying through the rain, not stopping to look in on the store. We had been reading Old Cap Collier and Nick Carter and we tried sleuthing for clues. We hoped to find something the thief had dropped, but he hadn't dropped anything. There was mud on the floor from his shoes when he stepped in from the window and then less and less mud on a line toward the money drawer—but not a clue!

Soon came a short man with quiet eyes and a fine black mustache. He wore a blue suit, with a star on his coat. We knew him but had never seen him working on a case. He was Marshal Hinman, chief of police, and he had with him one of his best uniformed policemen. We watched them work and we saw that inside the store they didn't find any more clues than we did. Then they stepped out the back door and went to work on what we had missed. There in the black mud were shoe tracks. Marshal Hinman studied the shoe tracks. His face was sober and earnest as he looked down into the mud. I was thinking, "Now I'm watching a real man hunter at work."

The marshal called for some cardboard and was handed an empty shoe box. He took the top of the box, pulled a knife from his pocket, and laying the shoe-box top over a shoe track in the mud he cut the cardboard to the shape of the thief's shoe sole. Then we saw him crouching again over another shoe track. He was slow and patient, I noticed, like all good sleuths and man hunters. His knife cut the shoe-box bottom to the shape of another shoe track in the mud. It came to me like a flash what he was doing. The first cardboard he cut was the left shoe and the second one was the right shoe of the thief. After this was over he studied the tracks some more and went inside the store again. Unless his keen eyes had caught some clue he wasn't telling us about, we could see that all he had to work on was to find some man whose shoes were the same left and right sizes as his cardboard cuttings. I reasoned to myself that it wouldn't do for him to stop a thousand people on Main Street and try his cardboard cuttings on their shoe bottoms. There would be maybe fifty or a hundred men wearing exactly that size shoe and since it had been a rainy night, they would know where they had been out of the rain and every one would prove an alibi.

We hoped Marshal Hinman would catch the thief. We saw him leave after saying, "We haven't got much to work on but we'll do the best we can." Then time went by and the years passed and the case was never solved.

From the Schulz store we went sometimes next door west into a cubbyhole of a house—one room maybe twelve feet by twelve. Here sat a man with a leather apron and a line of tools and leather in easy reach. We watched him cut leather for the half-sole of a shoe or boot, then fill his mouth with wooden pegs and, taking one peg at a time from his mouth, fit and hammer them into holes he made with an awl. Or if the customer wanted the half-sole stitched in, John Swedenborg could do it, carefully waxing the heavy threads before he stitched. He could glue a patch on or sew it, depending on what he thought was needed. He liked his work and was steady at it from eight in the morning till six in the evening. We looked in on him more often in the winter when his little place with its coal stove was cozy.

He was a long man with stooped shoulders, with a good face when quiet, and burning eyes and trembling lips when he spoke. Always John spoke to us the same lesson, keeping silence only when his mouth was filled with wooden pegs. I learned later the word for John. He was a Zealot. His zeal ran in every drop of his blood. So many times we heard him say: "I have Yesus in my heart. Yesus is with me all the time. I pray to my Yesus in the daytime and in the nighttime. You boys will never go wrong if you can get Yesus in your heart. He is my Saviour and He can be your Saviour. He is the Light of the World. When I have Him I am not afraid. I cannot be afraid, for He has told me to lean on Him when it is dark and things go wrong. You should learn to pray to Him, boys. You should learn to kneel at His blessèd feet and ask forgiveness and ask Him to take you in His arms." He had his own style of speaking straight from the heart.

The words would come from John Swedenborg with his eyes having a fire in them and his lips shaking as he shaped the words: "We are not long for this world. My Yesus is waiting for me in the next world and it will be blessèd to see Him." He lived sober, went to Wednesday-evening prayer meetings and special services, and took his family to church Sunday morning and night. We saw him several times in coughing spells. There were days his shop was closed. His end, like Nig Bohnenberger's next door, came from consumption. Neither of them was afraid to go but John was more sure than Nig that he was going where he would have more shining happiness than he ever had on earth.

❀ ❀ ❀

Eight : The Dirty Dozen

ONE SUNDAY AFTERNOON a bunch of us came together in front of the Olson store, most of us about sixteen or seventeen. We were going to have a photograph made. We counted and there were twelve of us. Someone said, "Then we can show people what the Dirty Dozen looks like." And the name Dirty Dozen stuck. It sounded like we were a gang and went in for gang fights. But the Dirty Dozen never fought another gang nor did we have any fights among ourselves. Seven of the twelve were sons of Americans from Sweden. Four were "native American." One was the son of a Frenchman.

Ed Rosenberg should have been counted with the Dirty Dozen. It was they who worked out his nickname. He was pale and slim, a little undersized, always cheery and with his own sense of humor. He muffed an easy fly once and from then on we called him "Muff," or more often "Muffa." When running a race on a cinder path one day he stumbled and fell and got up saying, "I hit de grit." From then on it was "Muffa de Grit." He knocked in a winning run in a ball game and strutted around with his head high crying, "Who won the game? Eddie Ampa! Eddie Ampa!" Where he picked up the "Ampa" we didn't know but it sounded right, and now his name was "Muffa de Grit Eddie Ampa." Out of some sidewalk scuffling with a bigger fellow Eddie came saying, "He gave me de grunt." So for a long while whenever Ed Rosenberg was seen coming to join the bunch he heard them calling all together, "Here comes Muffa de Grit Eddie Ampa de Grunt." We missed him when he went over to Moline to work in the Deere plow factory, where they called him by his right name.

Charles ("Frenchy") Juneau was one of the best chums I had. His father was a short, sturdy man with a head and beard like you see in portraits of Victor Hugo. And Frenchy himself had something of the Napoleon face and head. He could pull a lock of black hair down his forehead, stick his right hand into his coat below the lapels, and ask, "If I'm not Napoleon, who am I?" He had worked as a metal-polisher in a stove factory in Aurora and when the works shut down he came to his father's home in Galesburg, held down several jobs he didn't like, and after a time went back to Aurora as a metal-polisher when the stove factory opened again. He didn't care for books nor singing as I did but he had brightness and drollery and when we had nothing to talk about it was good just being together. We would go downtown, walk Main Street, buy a half-dozen cream puffs for a dime, walk Main Street eating our cream puffs, walk around the Public Square, and back to Berrien Street calling it a merry evening.

We went together to see William Jennings Bryan get off a train and get on a platform on Mulberry Street next to the Q. tracks and make a speech. Later when Bryan was speaking in Monmouth, sixteen miles from Galesburg on the Q., we rode the cowcatcher of an engine on a cold October night. We were chilled through and Frenchy bought a pint of blackberry brandy which warmed us. This was the only time we went in for booze. After we heard Bryan speak, we rode an engine cowcatcher back to Galesburg, and we went back to our old ways of walking Main Street eating cream puffs.

We went that fall to a big tent on the Knox campus and heard Bob Ingersoll give a speech lambasting the Democrats and Free Silver. But first Frenchy and I went for a sack of cream puffs, and standing on the edge of the crowd we listened to the famous Republican orator from Peoria and munched our cream puffs. One night when the bakery was out of cream puffs we tried chocolate éclairs and decided, "Never again if we can get cream puffs."

There was a summer Sunday afternoon that eight of the Dirty Dozen could never forget. We had met in front of Schulz's, the sun pouring down hot and sweltering. Someone said, "Let's go out to that pond on the Booth farm and have a swim." On the way, just inside the city limits, we came to the "Old Brick," as we called it, a pond about thirty yards long by twenty yards wide. Once a small brickyard had been there and it was all gone except the pond and a big wheel we used to dive from. The water at its deepest was up to our shoulders, and the bottom was slushy mud with broken bricks and pieces of tile and glass. We had grown tired of it and we had heard that the people in the new homes built near by didn't like to have the boys swimming so close. But it was nearly three miles to the Booth farm pond and we decided on this hot day we would have our swim in the Old Brick. We peeled off our clothes. All of us had stepped into the water except slow Ed Rosenberg. Then came the surprise. "Look!" yelled one of the boys, "there's Wiley!"

On Day Street we saw the patrol wagon and coming toward us big Policeman Frank Peterson and big Chief Wiley. The chief had his right hand raised and he was hollering, "Stay where you are, you're under arrest!" As he came closer we heard, "You boys ought to know you're not allowed to swim here. It's against the law and every one of you will get into the wagon and come along with me." We got into part of our clothes and finished dressing in the patrol wagon—all of us except Ed Rosenberg. He had grabbed his pants and shirt and the last seen of him he was nearly out of sight hot-footing it along the Narrow Gauge Railroad.

The patrol wagon had no top, and the seats ran lengthwise. Four of us sat on one side, three on the other, looking at each other and wondering, taking side glances at Wiley and Peterson at the wagon end. We were going to be hauled along streets where people knew us—arrested and on the way to the calaboose! And after a night in the calaboose we would be taken to court and there would be a trial and we wondered what would be the worst they could do to us—how did we know? The law is the law and anything can happen in the law. There was my nice brother Mart opposite me—the first time any Sandburg in Galesburg had been arrested! There were Bohunk Calkins and "Jiddy" Ericson and Charlie Bloomgreen from their nice homes and decent people on Berrien Street, now in a wagon watched by two policemen, being hauled in broad daylight to the Cherry Street calaboose.

Along Main Street we didn't see anybody we knew who knew us. At the calaboose we were locked up, three of us in one cell where four drunks were sobering up and the other four in a cell where three drunks were sobering up. There were no chairs, no cots; you sat on the stone floor or kept standing. It was about three o'clock when they locked us up. It was seven, when they were getting ready to feed the drunks, that they unlocked our cells and said we could go home. And they said more, "You're under orders to appear in court tomorrow morning before Justice of the Peace Holcomb at ten o'clock."

We walked to our Berrien Street homes, talking all the way about what Justice Holcomb would hand us in the morning. Most of us believed the justice wouldn't give us jail sentences but maybe he would give us light fines, "two dollars and costs." When Tom Beckum or Peg Hoey got their names in the papers for being drunk and disorderly Justice Holcomb fined them "two dollars and costs." The costs were five dollars and some of us wondered where we would dig up such money. I could pay the fine but not the costs. And I couldn't tell beforehand what my father would say if Mart or I told him, "You've got to let me have five dollars for costs or a son of August Sandburg goes to jail."

We stood before Justice Holcomb the next morning. We pleaded guilty to the charge that we had stripped naked and gone swimming in an old brickyard pond inside the city limits on yesterday's Sunday afternoon. Justice Holcomb gave us a talk like he was a good uncle of ours; we should understand it was against the law to do what we did. And he had us each promise we would never again go swimming in that pond.

We walked away, glad to be free and footloose again. What we agreed on was, "They didn't have to arrest us and throw us in that wagon and take us to the lockup. Not one of us had heard there was any law about not swimming in that pond. Why didn't they put up a sign 'Against the law to swim here'? We have been swimming in that pond

for years. If they had just got out of their wagon and told us we were breaking the law every one of us would have promised never to swim there again. What's the matter with the police?"

At home father and mother were quiet and decent about the whole affair. They didn't say so but they seemed to agree with us that the law and the police had been somewhat silly. Policeman Frank Peterson, who was with Chief Wiley, was then renting the second-story rooms of our house. I think Peterson, if he had been acting on his own, would have talked to us and given us warnings instead of hollering like Wiley, "Stay where you are, you're under arrest!" If you're a grown man and you hear a police chief say, "You're under arrest," it gives you at least a little shiver. And if you're sixteen there is something terrorizing about it—unless you're what they call an Old Offender who has been to reform schools.

I still refuse to feel the slightest guilt, and I am sure Muffa de Grit would agree with me. He ran out the Narrow Gauge Railroad till the police wagon was out of sight, put on his pants and shirt, sneaked back to the Old Brick, picked up his stockings, shoes and hat, and went home. He half expected the police would come for him but they didn't. The case wasn't that important. We all handed it to Muffa de Grit. He had quick wits and was fast on his feet.

Fellows two to four years older were putting on a dance once a month, renting a hall and hiring two fiddlers, and they picked for themselves the name of the Golden Rod Club. Husky Larson, Jiddy Ericson, and others of the Dirty Dozen said we could match the Golden Rod outfit, and we rented a hall and paid a couple of fiddlers. It came to twenty-five cents apiece each night we danced. We decided to call ourselves the Monarch Club. A fiddler called the quadrilles, and between we danced the waltz, two-step, polka and schottische with the Hanson sisters, Allie Harshbarger, Gertie Gent, and other lovely girls. The fiddlers played the sad "Home Sweet Home" at eleven o'clock.

Fatty Beckman, Skinny Seeley and I were the craziest at baseball. We began playing earlier in the spring and kept on later in the fall than the other boys—till the first frosts came and the last russet apple had fallen from the tree at the back fence of the pasture. We began playing earlier in the morning and played later in the evening than the others. Fatty wasn't fat; his cheeks puffed out a little. And Skinny wasn't skinny; he was merely lean and hard. I was "Cully," I suppose because it was considered an improvement on "Charlie." Fatty Beckman was the son of a widow and in September took days off from ballplaying to haul a wagon from house to house selling cabbages at five cents a head, earning fifty to sixty cents a day and jingling a pocket full of nickels when he came to the pasture for a last hour before supper. Skinny began hanging around the Auditorium, the new theater, helping the stage carpenter "Husky" Johnson, and the property man

"Cully" Rose. They trained him so when he went to Chicago he caught on as a stagehand.

The time came when I found other chums with different interests. There was Willis Calkins, a half-block away at Pearl and Berrien, his father a trolley-car motorman, clean and kindly, with a laughter for all weathers, his mother a beautiful woman whom we saw in one short year fade away from consumption. Willis was their only child. They were a singing family with Kentucky ancestors. Willis played the banjo, showed me the chords and how to accompany songs.

My first musical instrument had been a willow whistle I cut for myself. The pencil between the teeth and the tune rapped out by the right thumb followed. Then came the comb with paper over it and the mouth vocalizing—not so good. The ten-cent kazoo was better; you could imitate, in crude fashion, either a brass band or a rooster. A tin fife, a wooden flageolet, were interesting, and the ocarina surpassed all the wind instruments I fooled with. My first string instrument was a cigar-box banjo for which I cut and turned pegs and strung the wires myself; neither tunes nor chords could be coaxed from it. A slightly disabled concertina, at fifty cents from Mr. Gumbiner's New York Pawn Shop on Main Street, came next, developed wheezes, and was discarded. I tried the Old Man's accordion and it wheezed too often. Then came a two-dollar banjo from Mr. Gumbiner. This was a honey and from Willis I learned the chords. From the gracious Mrs. Schwartz on Ferris Street I had three banjo lessons at twenty-five cents a lesson. I should have gone on but it was Hard Times.

Willis could give the national popular songs, minstrel ditties, old ballads. He had a smooth baritone voice and put an easy charm into his singing. He had a long nose on a horse face, his good humor was irresistible, and he was welcome at all parties. He had a lumbering torso and a rolling gait. Someone nicknamed him "Bohunk" and it stuck.

One summer Bohunk and I walked a dozen times the three miles south and east to the pond on the Booth farm for the swimming there, "water up to your chin." It was in these fields out near town that we saw timothy hay growing, and oats and wheat. It was Indian corn, though, that hit me deepest. There was sweet corn for corn on the cob at the dinner table and there were acres of broomcorn and sorghum. But the Indian corn stood tallest and ran for miles on miles, food for men and horses, and there was a wonder about the little white soft ears of June becoming the tough, yellow, hard, and husky ears of late September that could lie on the frozen ground and wait to be used. We saw old zigzag rail fences go down and the Osage-orange hedge take its place. I picked hedge branches with the right crook to them and cut with a jackknife the club I wanted for playing shinny.

Walking back from the Booth farm pond Bohunk and I would make a decision where Farnham Street crossed the Peoria tracks. We could bear to the left, make a short cut across the Lombard campus, and on a hot day take a big cool drink of water from a cast-iron dipper chained to the Lombard pump. Or we could take a long walk on Farnham to Brooks Street and steal some luscious eating apples from Jon W. Grubb's orchard, tucking our pockets full and circling our shirts over the waistband of the pants with a line of apples. The question we discussed at Farnham and the Peoria tracks was simple: "What'll it be? A short cut and a drink or a long walk and apples?"

When the Calkins family moved out the Sjodins moved in—Swedes who had lived in Chicago fifteen years and lost their Swedish accent. Mr. Sjodin was a journeyman tailor, could measure, cut, and sew a suit of clothes. He walked with his head high and his shoulders erect and thrown back as if to say, "I am a free man and I bow to no masters or overlords. I cringe before no man." He was the first real radical I knew. He wanted a new society, a new world where no man had to cringe before another. He was an anarchist, a Populist, and a Socialist, at home with anyone who was against the government and the plutocrats who rob the poor. He was a skilled tailor who took good care of his wife, one daughter, and two sons and liked nothing better than a few glasses of beer with plenty of talk about politics and the coming revolution.

John Sjodin was two or three years older than I and had worked two years in a Milwaukee Avenue department store in Chicago. He had taken three lessons in clog dancing and from him I learned three steps to clog and never forgot them. He had absorbed much of Chicago's vivid and reckless flair and could give the feel of it in his talk. He had read widely. We lay on the grass next to the ditch in front of his home on summer nights. He could talk on and on about the exploits of a detective named Macon Moore. We both rated Macon Moore higher than Old Cap Collier and Nick Carter.

With John Sjodin and his brother Albert, another boy, and Mart, I chipped in and we bought one bonerack horse for two dollars and another for three dollars. We hitched them to light wagons we borrowed, drove some fifty miles to the Illinois River between Peoria and Chillicothe opposite Spring Green, where we camped, fished, and went swimming. The three-dollar horse died on us and we buried him with respect and many jokes. We scraped our pockets and raised five dollars that bought us another horse for the trip home to Galesburg, where we sold it for three dollars to the man who had sold us the three-dollar horse that died. The man who sold us the two-dollar horse wouldn't let us sell it back to him and I forget what we did with it, though we spoke highly of it as a willing horse that had staying power.

John at that time could be jolly, liked jokes and funny stories and had plenty of them. He was, like his father, a hard-and-fast political-action radical. "The big corporations" were running the country, as John saw it, and the time would come when the working people, farmers and laborers, would organize and get political power and take over the big corporations, beginning with the government ownership of railroads. Always John was sensitive about the extremes of the rich and the poor, the poor never knowing what tomorrow would bring and the rich having more than they knew what to do with.

I never saw John in a fight and I know he wouldn't have made any kind of a leader of a mob or riot. He would argue his points with anybody but he wouldn't let an argument or a debate run into a quarrel. He had his own reverence for life and said many a time that he couldn't hate a millionaire and most of the rich were sorry fools who didn't know what to do with their money except to put it to work making more money.

I asked John many questions and he nearly always had answers. I didn't argue with him. He believed deeply in a tide of feeling among the masses of the people. This tide would grow and become stronger and in generations to come the American people would challenge and break the power of the corporations, the interests of special privilege. John was not yet a voter but he favored the People's Party, the Populists. His main influence on me was to start me thinking. He made me know I ought to know more about what was going on in politics, industry, business, and crime over the widespread American scene.

✿ ✿ ✿

Nine : First Paydays

I WAS ELEVEN when I had the first regular job that paid me cash. There had been odd jobs for earning money and Saturdays and after school hours we took gunny sacks and went around streets, alleys, barns, and houses hunting in ditches and rubbish piles for rags, bones, scrap iron, and bottles, for which cash was paid us, my gunny sack one week bringing me eighteen cents. Now I was wearing long pants and every Friday was payday.

My employer was the real estate firm of Callender & Rodine on the second floor of a building on Main midway between Kellogg and Prairie. Mr. Callender was a heavy man with a large blond mustache. His head was wide between the ears and he had a smooth, round "bay window." Mr. Rodine was lean and had a pink face with blue eyes.

Their office was large and I would guess it was ten paces from the west wall where Mr. Callender had his desk to the east wall where Mr. Rodine also had a big roll-top desk with pigeonholes to stick papers in. It was Mr. Callender who told me about pigeonholes and what they are for. It came into my head, but I didn't mention it to Mr. Callender, that some of the pigeonholes were so thin you couldn't find a pigeon that could fly into one. Nor did I mention to him that it would be fun to bring in five or six pigeons and put them in the pigeonholes so that when Mr. Callender and Mr. Rodine rolled back the tops of their desks first thing in the morning, the office would be full of pigeons flapping and fluttering. This idea I liked to roll around in my head and I told other boys about it. One boy said, "If you did that, they would prosecute you." We made him tell us what it is to be prosecuted and for several weeks we saluted him, "Hello, Prosecutor" or "Here's Little Prosecutor again."

Mr. Callender and Mr. Rodine treated me fair. The longest talk I had with either of them was when Mr. Callender told me what my work was to be. After that, for month after month, about the only talk between us was on Friday morning when Mr. Callender handed me my pay, saying, "Here you are," and I said, "Thanks," and skipped.

They gave me a key to the office and I unlocked the door about a quarter to eight each morning, Monday through Friday. I swept the office, digging in for the dust in the corners and every crack in the floorboards, then sweeping the dust out into the hall and along the hall six or eight feet to the top of the wide stairway leading to the street. Reaching the bottom of the stairs I swept the accumulations of

my earnest and busy broom onto the sidewalk of Main Street and across the sidewalk. With two or three grand final strokes I swept a half-bushel of dust and paper and string and cigar butts out on the cobblestones to join other sweepings and layers of horse droppings. If a strong east wind was blowing, it would be no time until my sweepings were scattered all along Main Street.

Back upstairs, I carried the brass spittoon that stood at Mr. Callender's desk out in the hall to a cubbyhole with a faucet and running cold water. I dumped, washed, rinsed, and rinsed again and took the honorable and serviceable spittoon back to its place at Mr. Callender's desk. Then I did the same cleaning of Mr. Rodine's spittoon. About once in six or eight weeks I polished the spittoons till they were bright and shining.

This morning service of mine for Callender & Rodine took less than a half-hour. I was pleased and thankful when on Friday morning Mr. Callender would bring his right hand out of a pocket and, with a look on his face as though he had almost forgotten it, hand me a coin with "Here you are." And I would take the coin, say "Thanks," skip down the stairway, and on the sidewalk open my hand to look at what it held. There it was, twenty-five cents, a silver quarter of a dollar.

On the second floor a few doors west of the Callender & Rodine office was the printing press and office of the *Galesburg Republican-Register,* to which we carrier boys went as soon as school let out at half-past three. As the papers came off the flat bed press, we took them to a table and folded them. When I had folded the fifty or sixty papers for my route, I took them to a man who counted them again to make sure my count was correct, with one "extra" for myself. If a single paper seemed a little thick, the man would look to see whether one paper had been stuck inside of another, a trick some boys worked too often. Then with a bundle of papers under my arm, I went down the stairs to Main Street, turned north at the next corner, and went up Prairie Street. I learned how to cross-fold a paper so it could be thrown spang against a front door. If a house was near enough, I didn't have to leave the sidewalk to make my throw. On Prairie Street, however, the rich and the well-to-do lived, most of their houses set back so far from the sidewalk that I had to walk in halfway or more before making my throw.

At one house set well back a man would often be at home and expecting me—more yet, expecting the latest telegraphed news over America and the wide world. He would step out of the door to take the paper from my hand, the most roly-poly fat man in town. He was round everywhere you looked at him—a waddly barrel of a man, with a double chin, a round face, a gray mustache and goatee. This was the Honorable Clark E. Carr, mentioned often as the Republican Party boss of Knox County and having a hand in national politics. He had been appointed postmaster by Republican Presidents. He was to serve as United States Minister to Denmark.

Having left Mr. Carr with the latest news about how President Cleveland and the Democrats were ruining the country, I went along Prairie Street and threw a paper on the front porch of the biggest house in town. People said, "It cost more than any house ever put up in Galesburg, eighty thousand dollars." It was gray stone, three stories, with towers and fancy curves. Here lived the Honorable George A. Lawrence. He married a good woman who had a big fortune. He was a lawyer with brown sideburns that stood out and waved and shook in a strong wind.

I went on with my papers to the end of Prairie Street, went a block west to Cherry, turned south to Main, and had one copy of the *Republican-Register* left to take home. I had walked about two miles. When there was mud or snow or stormy weather it took about an hour and a half to carry my route and in good weather about an hour and a quarter. The *Republican-Register* paid me one dollar a week. I was more than satisfied with that weekly silver dollar.

Walking between rows of houses, many of them set widely apart—wider lots than at a later time—I came to know yards and trees—trees that I had seen in sun and rain in summer, and cloud and snow in winter, branches bending down with ice on them. Here and there in a back yard would be a tomato patch and carrots asking to be pulled out of the ground. Some yards had apple trees, and I helped myself to the windfalls.

For the little building in every back yard some said "backhouse," some said "privy." Carrying newspapers and later slinging milk I saw all the different styles of backhouses—the clean, roomy, elegant ones with latticework in front, those with leaky roofs and loose boards where the cold rain and wind came through, a few with soft paper that had no printing, but mostly it was newspapers neatly cut, or catalogues. When you had to go to the backhouse you stepped out into the weather—in rain or sleet. If the thermometer said zero you left your warm spot near the stove and the minute you were out the back door the cold put a crimp and a shiver in you.

About once a year a Negro we called Mister Elsey would come in the night with his wagon and clean the vault of our privy. He lived on Pine Street in a house he owned. We had respect for him and called him Mister. His work was always done at night. He came and went like a shadow in the moon.

I came to know the houses and yards of Prominent People. Their names were often in the paper. When they left for Kewanee, Peoria, or Chicago, I would read a "personal" about it in the paper. And I would notice the green blinds pulled over the front windows and three or four days of my papers waiting for them on the front porch when they came back from Kewanee, Peoria, or Chicago. If snow or rain was blowing in on the porch floor I would pull the doormat over the papers and have a feeling that I was not completely useless.

I had seen at his work one morning the man who went up and down Main Street and got the "personals," a short man with sandy hair, thin sandy sideburns, and a freckled face. He was writing in a notebook. I went closer and heard him asking a man how names were spelled. He thanked the man, put the book in his pocket, and went into Kellogg & Drake's dry-goods store. There I saw him speaking to Ed Drake, with the notebook again in his left hand as he wrote. Mr. Callender happening along, I asked him who was the man writing names in a book. "That's Fred Jeliff, reporter for the *Republican-Register*," said Mr. Callender.

I was fascinated. I could see Fred Jeliff walking back to the *Republican-Register* office and sitting at a table to write with a lead pencil on the same kind of paper the *Republican-Register* was printed on. Then he would carry the sheets to the man they called a "typesetter," and when the *Republican-Register* for that day was printed the names would be spelled like Fred Jeliff wrote them in his notebook up and down Main Street. I believed you could be a newspaper reporter if you could spell names and write them with a pencil on paper.

A year came when I was deep in the newspaper business. In addition to the afternoon route of the *Republican-Register* at a dollar a week, I carried a morning route of Chicago papers at seventy-five cents a week. Every morning, weekday and Sunday, I was on a Q. depot platform when the Fast Mail train from Chicago came in at seven-ten. Out of a mail car as the train slowed to a stop rolled the bundles we picked up and carried across Seminary Street to the front of the Crocker & Robbins grocery where a covered platform kept rain or snow off us.

We were working for Mr. Edwards, who had a store on Main Street where he sold books and stationery and kept a newsstand. He had long red whiskers and a Santa Claus look if he wasn't excited. When he told us what to do he wasn't bossy or fussed up. When two or three boys started scuffling he would step in like a mother hen who was going to have peace and no blood spilled.

We cut the ropes from the bundles, and there fresh as summer-morning dew or winter-daybreak frost were the *Chicago Tribune, Chicago Record, Chicago Inter-Ocean, Chicago Times, Chicago Herald,* and *Chicago Chronicle.* Each boy got his papers and started on his route, knowing well what he would catch if he threw a Democratic *Chicago Times* on the porch of a house where they were paying for the Republican *Chicago Tribune.* Where the other papers were two cents a copy, the *Chicago Record,* started by Victor Lawson, was one cent. You couldn't tell whether a man was taking the *Record* because it was cheapest or because it was the only Chicago paper independent in politics and giving what both sides had to say. When a house was taking two papers, one of them was the *Record.*

On the morning route I covered South and Mulberry streets and ended on Main. On Sunday mornings from seven-thirty till around noon, I pulled a little wagon of the Chicago papers, selling them at five cents a copy and getting one cent for myself out of each copy sold. I had about fifty regular customers and when there was extra-special big news, such as the assassination of Mayor Carter Harrison in Chicago, I sold ten or twenty more papers.

Along with the other boys I would end up about one o'clock at Mr. Edwards' store. After we turned in our money to Mr. Edwards, five or six of us would cross the street to a lunch counter. Always what we did was the same as the Sunday before. We climbed up on stools and each of us said with a grin, "One and a bun," meaning one fried egg laid between a split bun. We were hungry and we smacked and talked between bites of our five-cent snack. Each of us paid his nickel and felt chesty about it. It was like we were grown men and we had money we'd earned and could eat away from home. Some of us had pants that needed patching but we were little independent merchants spending a nickel of our profits.

What with spading two or three gardens, picking a pail or two of potato bugs, selling Pennsylvania Grit along Main Street, and other odd jobs, I made about twelve dollars a month. One odd job was "cleaning brick." A brick house or store torn down, we took trowels, knocked off the dried mortar and tried to make an old brick look new. Our pay ran so much a hundred of brick cleaned. I worked at it between my paper routes and averaged about fifteen cents an hour.

But it was more sport than work when we answered the cry, "The English sparrow must go!" The state was paying one cent for each dead English sparrow and I brought down more than thirty. I tried killing them with a "rubber gun" of my own make, a crotched stick with rubber bands holding a leather sling you put your stone in; then you pulled back the rubber, aimed at the sparrow, and let 'er go. Out of hundreds of rubber-gun shots I brought down one sparrow. Then I got an air rifle. I half believed a Swedish neighbor boy Axel Johnson when he said that an air rifle or a rubber gun was better for killing birds than a shotgun or a rifle using powder. "The birds can smell powder a mile off," said Axel, and he had me thinking hard about the smelling power of birds.

❁ ❁ ❁

Ten : Milk Wagon Days

I WAS FOURTEEN, near fifteen, in October of 1892. My mother would wake me at half-past five in the morning. She had ready for me when I came down from the garret a breakfast of buckwheat cakes, fried side pork, maybe applesauce or prunes, and coffee. I walked about two miles to the house and barn of George Burton, who had two milk wagons. I could have saved myself half the walk by taking a trolley but I saved instead the nickel carfare.

In this October were days I had a sore throat. I went to bed two days and sent word to Mr. Burton that I wasn't able to work. On reporting for work, I explained to him and he looked at me with suspicion and said not a word. I still had throat pains and was weak, but I didn't explain this to Mr. Burton; he looked suspicious enough.

That same week Mart went down with a sore throat and it was four days before he was up and around. Then the two youngest boys stayed in bed with throats so sore they couldn't eat. Freddie was two years old and Emil was seven. Emil had a broad freckled face, blue eyes, a quick beaming smile from a large mouth. He was strong for his age. He and I wrestled, scuffled, knocked off hats, and played tricks on each other. We liked the same stories and I read to him my favorites from the Grimm stories. He called often for "The Knapsack, the Hat, and the Horn."

We moved a narrow bed down to the kitchen, the one room that had a stove. Next to the west window, with afternoon sun pouring in, we put Emil and Freddie side by side in the bed, each with a throat looking queer. They seemed to be getting weaker, and though we knew it would be a dollar and a half for a call from Doctor Wilson, I walked to his Main Street office and told him to come as soon as he could.

Doctor Wilson came in about an hour, stepping into our kitchen in his elegant long black coat, white shirt and collar, and silk necktie. He had a good name as a doctor. He took a flat steel instrument from his case, put it on Emil's tongue and pressed down and looked keen and long at Emil's throat. He did the same for Freddie. Then Doctor Wilson stood up, turned to my father and mother and his face was sober and sorry as he said, "It is diphtheria."

Late that afternoon the city health commissioner nailed a big red card on our front door: DIPHTHERIA, warning people not to come to our house because it had a catching disease. I went to work next morning with a feeling that Mr. Burton wouldn't like it if I stayed home, that he would be suspicious like he was when I came back after two days off. I told him we had diphtheria at our house with a red card on the front door. He didn't say anything. So I went with my milk cans from one house to another across the town from seven in the morning till about one in the afternoon. The next two mornings again I peddled milk for Mr. Burton and there were houses where women were anxious, saying, "Do you think it right you should be handling our milk if you have diphtheria at your house?" I said I had told Mr. Burton about it, but he didn't say anything and I thought he wouldn't like it if I stayed home. And the women had worried faces and said, "It doesn't look right."

On the third day when Doctor Wilson made his third call, he said the boys were not making any improvement. He shook his head and said, "All we can do now is to hope. They might get better. They might get worse. I can't tell." Late that afternoon we were all there, with a west sun shining in on Emil and Freddie where they lay with their eyes closed. It was Freddie who first stopped breathing. Mother, touching his forehead and hands, her voice shaking and tears coming down her face, said, "He is cold. Our Freddie is gone." We watched Emil. He had had a rugged body and we hoped he might pull through. But his breathing came slower and in less than a half-hour he seemed to have stopped breathing. Mother put her hands on him and said with her body shaking, "Oh God, Emil is gone too."

The grief hit us all hard. In the Front Room the marble-topped center table with the big Family Bible was moved to a corner. In its place were two small white caskets. Neighbors and friends came, some with flowers. The Kranses and the Holmeses came to look at the faces of their two little relations. The Reverend Carl A. Nyblad spoke the Swedish Lutheran service. A quartet sang "Jesus, Lover of My Soul." The undertaker moved here and there as though it was what he did every day. Mother cried, but it was a quiet crying and she didn't shake her shoulders like when she said, "Oh God, Emil is gone too." Mart and I didn't cry. We kept our eyes dry and our faces hard. For two nights we had cried before going to sleep and waking in the night we had cried more, and it was our secret why we weren't crying at a public funeral.

We saw the two little white caskets carried out the front door and put in the black hearse with glass windows at the sides and end, four black tassels on the top corners.

We followed in a closed carriage. At the grave we heard the words, "Ashes to ashes, dust to dust," saw the two little coffins lowered and a handful of earth dropped on them, the sober faces of the Kranses and the Holmeses having grains of comfort for us.

We were driven home in the closed carriage, father and mother, sisters Mary and Esther, Mart and I. We went into the house. It was all over. The clock had struck for two lives and would never strike again for them. Freddie hadn't lived long enough to get any tangles in my heart. But Emil I missed; for years I missed him and had my wonderings about what a chum he would have made.

There were two days I didn't report to George Burton for work in that diphtheria and burial week. When I did report to him he was like before, not a word, not even "Hard luck," or "Too bad." Mr. Burton had a lean face with a brown mustache he liked to twirl in his fingers —and a "retreating" chin. He had a beautiful wife and his face lighted up at the sight of her. He had two or three fast horses he liked to drive with a sulky. One was a yearling bred from a glossy black mare he owned. The mare had a small head and her thin scrawny neck didn't match her heavy body. Mr. Burton said she was pedigreed and had class yet about half the time he had her hitched to his milk wagon. He enjoyed clucking at her to get a burst of speed and then pulling her in.

After Emil and Freddie died, doctor and undertaker bills, the cemetery lot, took regular cuts out of the month's wages of my father. We were now a family of seven, and besides money for food, clothes, coal, schoolbooks, Papa had to make his payments or lose the house. And Mary in her third and last year of high school had to have better clothes than in the grade schools. The twelve dollars a month George Burton paid me came in handy for the family. It was a hard winter and somehow I couldn't see my way to take out of my pay two dollars for a pair of felt boots, or even a dollar for overshoes. On my milk route I had wet feet, numb feet, and feet with shooting pains. If it

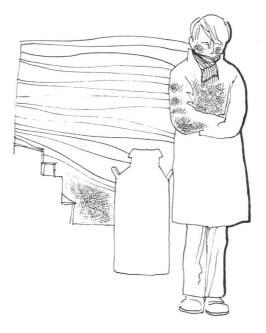

hadn't been for the five-minute stop at a grocery hot stove, or a housewife saying, "Poor boy, wouldn't you like to come in and warm yourself?" I would have had a case of bad feet for a long time. I learned a word for what my feet kept singing, "chilblains."

Once I was ten minutes late meeting Mr. Burton where he sat in his wagon in his felt boots. He said, "You're a slowpoke today." I told him, "My feet were near frozen and I had to stop to warm them." He said, "Why don't you get yourself a pair of felt boots like I have?" I said, "We're hard up at our house and I can't spare the two dollars." Mr. Burton sniffed a "humph" as though he couldn't understand what I was saying—which I'm sure he couldn't.

Mr. Burton never sang for himself or me, never joked to me, never told a funny story, never talked about what was in the newspapers or town gossip, never played any kind of music or talked about listening to it, never talked about men or women he liked or funny or mean customers. I wondered sometimes whether George Burton had ever been a boy. What few times I tried to talk with him like I thought a boy could talk with a man, he either cut me off short or he said nothing to me as though I had said nothing to him. But he would stop the horse and wagon for a ten- or fifteen-minute talk with a man in a sulky driving a racehorse. On and on they would talk horse talk.

I came to see that Mr. Burton wasn't ashamed of being a milkman and neither was he proud of it. What he was proud of were two or three horses he had that he hoped to build into a string of horses that would make a name for him. He hoped the milk business might make him enough money to get more horses to breed some world record-breakers. I caught myself saying one day, "He doesn't know boys and if you don't know boys you can't know colts and if you don't know colts you'll never be a big-time horse man."

I got tired of seeing him every day grumpy and frozen-faced, and sometime early in 1893 when he had paid me for my month's work I told him I guessed I didn't want to work for him any more. He said, "Well, I guess that'll be no loss to me." And I thought of two or three answers I could make but I played a hunch and walked away after saying only "Good-by, Mr. Burton."

❀ ❀ ❀

Eleven : In and Out of Jobs

THE TINNER HAD his shop on Seminary Street a half-block south of Main in a wooden building no bigger than a freight-train caboose, with the paint peeling off the boards. A sign in the window read, Tin Work of All Kinds. I had often seen the tinner going in and coming out. He was a medium-small man in clothes that hung loose on him and a slouch hat crumpled on his head. He needed a haircut and hair would stick out from a hole in the hat. I knew he had been in this shop a year or more and that people came to him for tinwork.

I opened the door and walked in one October day to ask if he had a job. He said, without asking whether I had any experience or recommendations or where I last worked, "You can start tomorrow morning at seven." He studied a knothole in the floor half a minute. "I can pay you three dollars a week. Come seven in the morning." He didn't ask my name and I didn't know his.

Next morning I was at the shop at seven. I found the door locked and stood around and waited. Near eight he came along in a one-horse wagon. We loaded an outfit on the wagon and drove out to Broad Street and the house of the well-known Galesburg photographer Osgood. We set up ladders and went up to the low sloping tin roof of the kitchen. I helped him pull loose old and worn tin sheets and carry them to the ladder and down to the ground.

At twelve the boss said we could knock off. I ate a lunch I had brought in a paper bag. It was near two when the boss came back. I hadn't been sure before, but this time I did get a whiff of his whisky breath. He was fumbly going up the ladder. His feet slipped once but his hands kept their hold and he made it to the roof. I followed him with a soldering outfit and made two trips bringing up new sheets of tin. He soldered two or three sheets, and near four said we would knock off for the day.

Next morning I was on hand at seven, and it was nine when my boss came in the wagon, the whisky breath still on him. We drove out to the Osgood house again and he soldered maybe three or four sheets on the roof. At twelve he said we would quit for the day. I was glad because he had slipped again on the ladder and had nearly slid down the roof once. The next morning I was at the shop at eight, waited till ten, walked up and down Main Street awhile, came back at eleven and again at twelve to find the door locked.

Then and there I decided I didn't want to learn the tinner's trade. I felt sorry for the tinner and I said, "I won't go back and ask him for my pay—he's too near his finish." A few weeks later I saw the place closed and the sign Tin Work of All Kinds gone.

When I took a job washing bottles in a pop bottling works one summer I knew the future in the job was the same as the past. You washed the same kind of bottles in the morning and afternoon today as you would be washing in the morning and afternoon tomorrow, and yesterday had been the same. You could see the used bottles coming in and the washed bottles going out and it was the same from seven in the morning till six at night. There was one point about the job they told you when they hired you; you could drink all the pop you wanted. I began drinking pop, bottle after bottle. On the fourth day I stopped drinking pop. I had had enough pop to last me a lifetime. At the end of two weeks I quit the job. I didn't like the sight of pop bottles coming in and going out and today the same as yesterday and tomorrow.

There was the late fall and winter I worked in the drugstore of Harvey M. Craig. I had a key and opened the front door at seven in the morning. I swept the floors of the store and prescription room and about half-past seven Mr. Hinman, the pharmacist, came in. I would take a chamois skin and go over the showcases. From the prescription room I took bottles that needed filling and went down in the cellar and turned the spigots of wine barrels and casks of rum and whisky and filled the bottles. There I had my first taste of port wine and claret and found they tasted better than I expected, though I was still leery of what they might do to me. I tasted whisky and decided it was not for me. From the carboys—the champion of all bottles, standing three or four feet high, and the glass two or three inches thick—I poured sulphuric acid and muriatic acid, wood alcohol, turpentine, and other stuff needed upstairs.

At nine o'clock Harvey Craig would come through the front door and nearly always his wife was with him. Mr. Craig was a fairly heavy man, though not big-bodied like his father, Justice A. M. Craig of the Illinois State Supreme Court. He had something of his father's face, the mouth stern and the lip ends pulled down a little. He was kindly with Mr. Hinman and me, though there was no fun or frolics when he was around. His wife was small alongside of him and had quiet and charm. She usually left before noon.

I liked working with Mr. Hinman. He was slim, somewhat dark-skinned, with a neat small dark mustache like Edgar Allan Poe. His eyes smiled when his mouth did. He took an interest in being a pharmacist, had pride about handling drugs and medicines, kept studying the latest finds in medicine. His sense of humor was always there. He liked to tell about a boy coming into a drugstore on a hot summer Sunday and asking for "ten cents' worth of asafoetida." The clerk climbed up to a shelf and brought down a bottle, weighed out ten cents' worth, and climbed up and put the bottle back, then climbed down and wrapped the asafoetida and handed it to the boy. The boy said, "Charge it." The clerk asked, "What's the name?" "August Schimmelderfer." At which the clerk blurted out "You little devil, run home with you. I wouldn't spell asafoetida and Schimmelderfer for ten cents!"

In the prescription room was the biggest and thickest book I had ever handled except *Webster's Unabridged Dictionary*. The name was on the front and back covers: *The Pharmacopoeia*. In it were the names of all the drugs there are and what they will do to you. I rambled here and there in it. I asked Mr. Hinman questions about what I read in the book and he was patient and kindly. He liked to share his learning with a younger fellow who had more hopes than he knew what to do with.

For a month or two one winter I took a whirl at the mail-order business. John Sjodin sold me on the idea. He had taken several weekly and monthly papers that were filled with mail-order advertising. He pointed to *Comofort* in Augusta, Maine, with a million subscribers, the biggest circulation of any paper in the country, its columns filled with ads for selling medicines, chickens, kazoos, eyewash, tool kit, knives, music boxes, toys, cheap watches, penny pencils, and more medicines. John said there had been fortunes made in the mail-order business; men now millionaires had started with just a little printing press. John had bought somewhere for five or ten dollars a set of type and a tricky little press that would print a sheet five inches by four. I threw into the scheme two or three dollars I had saved. I was the junior partner and would share in the profits the same percentage as I had put in.

We were going to print a "mail-order journal." John said, "We will have room in it for advertising only, so we can't expect to sell it. The subscription price will be not a cent; so that's what we will name our mail-order journal." We ran off fifty or sixty copies, and at the top of the first page was the name of this new publication in the advertising and selling field: *Not a Cent*. We followed the first issue with a second. I forget all that we advertised. But I do remember we offered for sale one Waterbury watch "slightly used," a couple of knives "slightly used," and we gave the names of several books "slightly used." We couldn't afford the postage to mail our "mail-order journal." We gave out here and there among friends and strangers over half the copies and kept the rest to look at and say, "We're publishers."

The Sjodin family had moved to the north side in a working-class neighborhood east of the Q. tracks. We did our printing in the hayloft of the barn, on cold days wearing our overcoats and running to the house once in a while to get warm. It was a mile walk across town for me and I ate with John in the Sjodin kitchen. John laughed from beginning to end of this plunge of ours in the mail-order business. Away back in our minds, of course, was a slim glimmering hope—that something would turn up, that a twist of chance might come along and all of a sudden, like it happens every once in a while in a business starting small, we would be on Easy Street. When we quit the business, when *Not a Cent* stopped publication, we laughed the same way as when we first got set for the plunge.

There was the summer I was going to learn the potter's trade. East of Day Street, next to the Peoria tracks, stood a pottery that had been going a year or two. On the ground floor were the turners. You had to be a real potter, who had learned his trade, to be a turner. A turner had a "ball pounder" next to him at the bench. The ball pounder— that was me—weighed on a wooden scale enough clay to make a jug. I would throw this clay on the bench without touching it with my fingers. The fingers wouldn't give the lift needed to carry it in the air and bring it down and cut it in two across a wire. It was a neat trick to learn how to brace your wrists and throw the lower half of the palms of the hands into the clay for this operation. I was warned that my wrists would be sore for a week or two, but after ten days the soreness was over and I could talk to the other ball pounders like I was one of them.

The "ball" you pounded out to a finish was cake-shaped, its size depending on the size of the jug to come. The turner threw it on a turning iron disk, sprinkled water on it, guided it with a hand scraper, and built it up into a jug. Then he stopped the turning disk and slicked out a handle that he smoothed onto the jug. Next, with my hands careful, I moved the jug off the disk and put it on a near-by rack to dry a little before it went for baking to a dome-shaped kiln outside the main building.

On the second floor were the molders, who didn't class up with the turners. They threw the clay into plaster-of-Paris molds on a turning wheel, scraped the inside of the crock or jar, and the mold and the wheel did the rest.

One morning I went down to breakfast to hear that the pottery had burned down in the night. I went out and walked around the smoking walls to see the fire had made a clean sweep of it. It was easy to decide I wouldn't be a potter.

On the main road running past the end of Lake George was a steep hill where the trolley-car motormen put on the brakes going downhill. On the uphill trip it was slow and hard going. So they decided to grade the hill. Men drove mule teams with scrapers, one man driving the mules, another man walking between the handles of the scraper. When the big shovel of the scraper filled up they turned around and dumped it lower down the hill. They went on with this till the hill was a long slope. I was a water boy on this job for three hot summer weeks. I carried two buckets of water from a pump, with two tin cups for each bucket. Some of the men called me "sonny," and it was, "This way, sonny," and "I can stand some of that, sonny," and "You come to the right man, sonny." Then between-times the mules had to have water. I would rather have been water boy just to the men and not to the mules. A mule would often drink nearly a whole pail of water, and it was a hundred yards to the pump.

And one summer I worked for Mr. Winfield Scott Cowan, who ran the boathouse and refreshment stand at Lake George near where the trolley cars stopped. Mr. Cowan had married a daughter of George W. Brown and lived in a big house across the street from the Brown Cornplanter Works. He was a medium-sized man with a dark-brown mustache, and he knew how the business should be run, down to such fine points that nearly always he was worrying about this or that not going to come out right. If anything went wrong, he acted as though something else was going to go wrong pretty soon.

My job was to let rowboats to people for twenty-five cents an hour. I would give them the oars, help them pick a boat, and then help them shove off. I had charge of the refreshments and sold ice cream and cake or cookies, pop, ginger ale, and a line of candies.

Mr. Bobbit had charge of the little steamboat that held ten or twelve people, twenty-five cents for a ride to the end of the lake and back. People said she was the prettiest steamboat in Knox County, and as there was no other steamboat in Knox County it was the solemn truth. Her name was *Lady Washington*. Mr. Bobbit kept up steam all day; on some days he had all the passengers he could handle and on other days nobody riding. A man-sized man, Mr. Bobbit, he was tall, broad-shouldered, thick through the body, quick in his motions, and always seemed to know what was going on and what to do. He had a blond mustache and keen eyes that could twinkle. He was English and had been a policeman somewhere, I heard. I am sure he was a first-class policeman. He was good company and said, "I worry when it's time to worry and what you don't know sometimes is a help."

It didn't come hard to leave Mr. Winfield Scott Cowan at the end of the season, him and his worrying. Leaving the company of Bobbit wasn't so good. He said he expected a night-watchman job in the fall and winter. I said I hoped I'd see him again, though I never did.

Two weeks of ice harvest on Lake George came one January, the thermometer from zero to fifteen above. I walked from home six blocks to catch a streetcar that ran the mile and a half out to the lake. The night gang worked from seven at night till six in the morning, with an hour off at midnight.

The ice was twelve to eighteen inches thick. Men had been over it with horse teams pulling ice cutters. In the first week on the job I was a "floater." Rafts of ice about fifteen feet long and ten feet wide had been cut loose. The floater stood on a raft and, pushing a pronged pole, he propelled the raft and himself to the chutes at the big ice-house. There the ice was broken into blocks or cakes, and a belt carried them up where they were stood in rows with sawdust sprinkled between to hold them cold till summer and warm weather.

I had overshoes and warm clothes and enjoyed the work. The air was crisp, and you could see a fine sky of stars any time you looked up, sometimes a shooting star and films of frost sparkles. I had never had a night job that kept me till the sun came up. I got acquainted with a little of what goes on over the night sky, how the Big Dipper moves, how the spread of the stars early in the night keeps on with slow changes into something else all night long. I did my wondering about that spread of changing stars and how little any one of us is standing and looking up at it.

The other floaters were good fellows and we hollered to each other over the dark water our warnings that if you fell in the water you'd find it cold. At midnight we went up a slope to the Soangetaha Clubhouse of the bon ton. On the porch, away from the windy side, we ate what we had carried out in paper bags.

The second week I was put in the icehouse, where a dozen of us worked on a footing of blocks or cakes of ice, the chute feeding us more cakes of ice. Each cake was about three feet long, two feet wide, and a foot thick. We threw our iron tongs into the end of a cake and then rassled and wrangled it twenty or thirty feet to where it stood even with a row of other cakes. Heavy work, it had my back and shoulder muscles pulling and hauling like a mule. I had never before felt so sure that what I was doing could be done better somehow by mules or machines. I went home the first morning with muscles from ankles to neck sore and aching. I ate breakfast, went to bed right

away, and lay abed trying to coax myself to sleep. But muscles would twitch and it was past noon before I went to sleep. Then three or four times I suddenly came awake with the muscles singing. When my mother woke me and said, "It's time to go to work," I was just beginning to sleep, it seemed. I had to unwind myself slowly to get out of bed and into my clothes.

The second night was worse. I would try for a rest by walking slow back to the chute. If I tried for a rest standing still two or three minutes, the foreman would come along, a quiet man saying in a voice that just carried over the noise of the rattling chute and the hustling men, "Better slide into it, Sandburg." If he had bawled or snarled it at me, I would have quit the job on the spot. He remembered my name and I wasn't just a number, I was a person. And he said "Better slide into it" nearly like my mother waking me out of sleep to go to work. I had respect for him and hoped sometime I could be a foreman and act and talk like him.

Near daybreak I thought to myself, "Come seven o'clock and I'm quitting." I stood still thinking about it and getting a rest when the foreman came along. "Better slide into it, Sandburg. You know there's only a few more days on this job. I think we'll be through this week." And that gave me a different feeling. I went home, slept better, ate better, and the muscles all round weren't as stiff. I lasted the week through, and at a dollar and twenty-five cents a night I had earned higher wages than in any work before. One thing I noticed. I hustled a little too much. Most of the other men on the job had been railroad section hands, ditch-diggers, pick-and-shovel men, and they knew what my father sometimes reminded me of on a piece of work, "Take your time, Sholly." They worked with a slow and easy swing I hadn't learned.

I was sixteen or seventeen when I carried water, ran errands, a few times helped sponge and dry a sweating horse, over six weeks of racing at the Williams racetrack. What I earned in quarters and half-dollars ran maybe up to ten dollars. But I had a pass to come in at any time and I saw up close the most famous trotting and pacing horses in the world.

C. W. Williams came to Galesburg from Independence, Iowa, where he had what they called a "kite-shaped" racetrack, though some said it was more like the figure eight. He had been a telegraph operator and had picked up, at prices that later looked silly, two mares. The world-famous stallions Axtell and Allerton were foaled from those two mares "bought for a song." In 1889 the three-year-old Axtell cut the world's trotting record for stallions down to two minutes and twelve seconds, and on the night of that day was sold to a syndicate for one hundred and fifty thousand dollars, said to be then the highest price ever paid for a horse of any breed. Two years later Mr. Williams could have sold his stallion Allerton for more than he got for Axtell. This was after Mr. Williams himself drove Allerton to cut down the world stallion record to two minutes and nine and three-quarters seconds.

So when Mr. Williams came to Galesburg in 1894 he had a reputation, organized the Galesburg District Association, and laid out a new racetrack on one hundred and twelve acres on the Knoxville Road east of Farnham Street. The new racetrack, Mr. Williams gave it out, was "the only dead-level track in the world." Shaped like a railroad coupling pin, the long sides of it were dead level, with the ends graded for the sulkies to make the turn. In the great six-weeks racing meet that Mr. Williams put on, there were rainy days when races had to be put off and other days when small crowds came, even though the trotters and pacers had national reputations. But there was one big week of good weather and one smashing big day in that week. That was the day we saw the black mare Alix come down the home stretch to break the world's record for trotters.

That day put Galesburg on the map for horsemen and horselovers over the whole country. At the center was Mr. Williams. He was a medium-sized man with an interesting face. He made a great name in the horse world and breeders came from the country over to see him. The blood of his stallions ran for many years in winning horses.

Then harness racing began to run down in style. Mr. Williams sold all his horses for good money and put it into Canada land dealings. I like to think of him as I saw him once on an October morning, a little frost still on the ground, in a sulky jogging around the only dead-level racetrack in the world, driving at a slow trot the stallion Allerton, being kind and easy with Allerton, whose speed was gone but whose seed were proud to call him grandsire.

❁ ❁ ❁

Twelve : Working for Fun

ONE NIGHT AT home we heard the Opera House was burning and I ran down to the corner of Main and Prairie to watch it. I stood across the street from the fire till midnight. I didn't like to see the place go, I could remember so much about it. There I had seen the Kickapoo Indians in buckskins and feather headdress, in dances stomping and howling their lonesome war songs which we tried to imitate. They stayed six weeks and I went once or twice a week, admission free. The white man they worked for was a slicker and would put in his spiels: If you had rheumatism or ached in muscles or bones, you eased it with Kickapoo Indian Snake Oil. If you had trouble with stomach or liver you took a few spoons of Kickapoo Indian Sagwa and your insides felt better and a bottle or two cured you. We listened and did imitations of him.

On the stage boards now burning Doctor O'Leary had lectured, admission free. Vegetarianism was his line. What he was selling I forget. He stayed three or four weeks telling what meat does to you, how you have a tired feeling most of the time and you don't have strength for your work. After he left town I didn't eat meat for two weeks, and I found I had the same tired feeling. I began eating meat again and I couldn't feel the poisons so I forgot about Doctor O'Leary.

There on five or six nights one month I had paid my ten cents to sit in the gallery and watch the first mesmerists I had seen. They looked in the eyes of fellows I knew, made passes in front of their faces, and had them fighting bumblebees, or swimming across a carpet. There I saw the body of a living man, his head on one table, his feet on another table, his torso and legs stiff as a hard oak log. A rock was laid on his body and the powerful blacksmith Ben Holcomb swung a sledge on the rock and split it. The body stayed stiff and straight through the whole act. Then the mesmerist snapped his fingers in the fellow's face, said something like "Right! right!," helped the fellow to his feet, and the two of them held hands and bowed to the applauding audience. "It wasn't a miracle but it was a wonder," we said.

The curving and sizzling tongues of fire licked away the stage curtain and boards where I had seen a diorama of the Battle of Gettysburg. They told us about it at Grammar School, admission five cents. One diorama curtain after another came down showing different parts of the battle. The curtains were dirty and worn. The man with a long pointer explaining the battle had short oily whiskers you couldn't tell the color of. His clothes looked like he had slept in them and never brushed them. His voice squeaked. What he was saying you could tell he had said so many times that it didn't interest him and his mind was somewhere else. I was so curious about how creepy and sad the man with the pointer looked that half the time I didn't see what he was pointing at.

Before my eyes the boards were burning where I had first seen Shakespeare's *Hamlet* and was interested only in the killings at the end. I had seen a man walk out on that stage that I was terribly curious about. I had seen cartoons of him in the Chicago papers, and from what I had read I expected he would tear the air and beat his chest and stamp his enemies under his feet. He was John Peter Altgeld and he was running for governor of Illinois. He just stood in the same foot tracks through his whole speech, about an hour and a half, and never sawed the air once with his hands. The few times he did lift his hands to make a point the motions were as if he could be running a hand along the forehead of a sick friend. He talked in a quiet way as though if we should be quiet too we could make up our minds about what he was saying. I wasn't sure of all he had said but I felt I would be more suspicious of his enemies than of him.

The new Auditorium was built at Broad Street and Ferris and often when out of work and puzzled where to go, I would end up there. It was an up-to-date theater with a main floor, a balcony, and a gallery that was called "Nigger Heaven." The seats nearest to the stage, ten or fifteen rows, were the "parkay." On the tickets it said "parquet." The stage was big enough to handle any show from Broadway, and nearly every Broadway hit heading straight west made a stop at Galesburg.

Some of my work at the Auditorium I got paid for. Mostly I got to see the show for a little work I liked to do. The stage carpenter was American-born of Swedish parents, Oscar Johnson, and everybody called him "Husky." He could drive us and shout at us when there was a rush to be on time with all the scenes and props for the next act, and we took it he had a right to blow off steam. The property man, Charles Rose, everybody called "Cully." He knew he knew everything a property man ought to know and if you wanted an argument he would give it to you. He believed in having props in order and on time. He could do quick headwork and we liked the way he ordered us around. Cully Rose hired the "supes." A supernumerary didn't travel with the show but they had to have their supes. I suped in *McFadden's Flats*. On the stage was an office scene on the eighth floor of a Chicago skyscraper. Off stage four supes watched the man in charge of us. When he went "Ahh-ahh-ahh" real loud and "Ohh-ohh-ohh" louder yet and "Umhh-umhh-umhh" softer, we did the same. What were we doing? We were making the clatter and the rumbling of the Chicago street eight floors below the office on the stage. When the play was showing the big Chicago fire of 1871, the supes ran across the stage with boxes, packages, and bundles, moaning and hollering. Then we ran back around the stage, got different boxes, packages, and bundles, and ran across the stage again trying to give out new moans and yells.

We worked as sceneshifters, and as we finished there might be at our elbows a few steps away a famous star waiting to make her entrance. We would see a comedian in his comic make-up, his face solemn, his eyes on the stage, waiting his cue to go on. A minute later he would be out before the footlights wriggling and twisting, his face and eyes lit up and the audience roaring. Sometimes there would be an actor saying in a low voice the first line he would say when he stepped out on the stage. They brushed by us after their exits, breathing hard after a heavy scene, sometimes limp and sweating.

When we worked in the "flies" we got ten cents a night. We were up thirty or forty feet, and on signals we would send up one curtain and let down another, pulling on ropes. If we got the wrong curtain we certainly heard from down below. Cully Rose could holler and he could be sarcastic. From where we were we could see parts of the play and if there was music or singing we caught it all.

We saw John L. Sullivan close-up playing in *Honest Hearts and Willing Hands*. We could see he liked stepping out on the stage and he wasn't afraid of any audience. In one scene he sat at a table playing he was in trouble and had to use his wits. He put his elbows on the table, dropped his chin into his cupped hands, and then in a whisper he was sure the audience could hear, "Now I must tink." When he took a curtain call he made a fine low bow to the audience, gave a little speech, ended it "I remain yours truly John L. Sullivan," and walked off the stage.

Fridtjof Nansen came. I had read his magazine articles that went into his book *Farthest North,* but I couldn't scrape up the fifty cents to hear him lecture. I was on hand when his train pulled in at the Q. depot, though. It was snowing and I thought he looked like a Scandinavian hero, tall in a long fur coat, as he walked the platform and through the station to where I watched him get into a Union Hotel hack.

When Henry M. Stanley, the African explorer, came to lecture, I was there again at the Q. depot to see him get off the train and tag at his heels through the depot. He wasn't as much to look at as Nansen. To me he was a Famous Writer while Nansen was a Great Norseman and a Viking with a heart for all human strugglers.

James J. Corbett, world's champion boxer, came in *Gentleman Jim,* and his bag-punching opened our eyes. I was following big-league baseball when I heard that Arlie Latham, the dandy second baseman of the Cincinnati Reds, would do a song and dance in a show, and I went to see it. The show wasn't much and Arlie Latham was no star at singing and dancing, but I had seen a hero. I didn't see Bob Fitzsimmons, another world's champion, in his show. But I did see him on the Q. depot platform, tall and lanky, with salmon hair and pink skin, leading a pet lion back and forth.

I helped on the stage when *Monte Cristo* came to town with James O'Neill the star. The sea that he swam when he made his escape, the rolling of that canvas sea, was made by some other boys and myself. There was the *Uncle Tom's Cabin* show I peddled bills for and got paid ten cents and a ticket to the show. The bills said there would be two Uncle Toms, two Evas, two Simon Legrees, two Elizas crossing the Ohio River, and two packs of bloodhounds. We were puzzled how there could be two of everything, and we went expecting something new and different. What we saw was just one more Uncle Tom show, with one of everything instead of two. The trick brought out a good crowd that would be suspicious about again paying cash to see two of everything.

We got used to melodramas where the mortgage hangs over the house and in the end the villain with the mortgage gets what is coming to him. Or it might be the will of a dead man and they poked here and there hunting for it, saying "The old will, the old will." Regular on the calendar came a Civil War play with a Union spy in love with a

Rebel girl or the other way around, but always wedding bells and appleblossoms in the end. I suped in one of these, *Shenandoah.*

Two famous theater names were Anna Held and John Drew. In cigar stores and saloons a picture hung on the wall showing a woman's hand holding five cards from a deck and the words "This is the hand that Anna Held." And under five cards in a man's hand were the words "This is the hand that John Drew."

If I was on a milk wagon or some other job when minstrels came to town I would manage to have two bits for a ticket to the top gallery. I would try to be on Main Street when the minstrels paraded in tan top hats matching their tan cutaway coats and tan spats, with horns and music in the lead. And when the curtain went up always there would be that Middleman, Mister In-ter-loc-u-tor—on one side six burnt-cork faces over white boiled shirts clicking the rattlebones, on the other side six more with tambourines opening with a song. More than once we heard an End Man ask the Middleman, "Why do the policemen in Monmouth wear rubber boots?" The Middleman couldn't think why in the world the policemen in Monmouth wear rubber boot, and the End Man would reply: "Why, everybody in Monmouth knows the policemen wear rubber boots so as not to wake up the other policemen." We laughed because Galesburg and Monmouth, sixteen miles apart, were jealous of each other and we liked any joke that made Monmouth look silly. We learned that over in Monmouth the minstrels asked why the policemen in Galesburg wore rubber boots! And we giggled at and passed on: "I have pants from Pantsylvania, a vest from Vest Virginia, a coat from Dacoata, and a hat from Manhattan—am I not an American?"

I missed none of Al Field's minstrel shows. I believed that Al Field was "the undisputed King of the Banjo." When I went to a minstrel show I was satisfied I got my two bits' worth in "Nigger Heaven." You could hear the peanut-eaters cracking the shells, and dropping the shells on the floor. That was expected in the top gallery. On the main floor and in the parquet nobody would dare to be seen eating a peanut. And down there they couldn't yell for a good act nor "mee-ouw" at a bad one.

❁ ❁ ❁

Thirteen : Learning a Trade

THEY KNEW AT home that I was a helper through the Hard Times, that what I earned counted. They knew I would rather have gone to school. When Mary graduated from high school it was the few dollars I threw in that gave her a nice white dress so she looked as good as any of them on Graduation Day when she stepped out and bowed and took her diploma. We knew that diploma would count. Now she could teach school and be a help and no longer an expense to the family. The next fall she had a country school at thirty dollars a month. Mary's high-school books were a help to me. I didn't study her algebra and Latin textbooks, but I thumbed back and forth in them and got glimmerings. I read Irving's *Sketch Book, Ivanhoe,* and *The Scarlet Letter* and talked with Mary about what the teachers said those novels meant. But the great book Mary brought home—great for what it did to me at that time, opening my eyes about law, government, history, and people—was *Civil Government in the United States* by John Fiske. Here for the first time I read answers to many questions: What are taxes? Who has the taxing power? What is the difference between taxation and robbery? Under what conditions may taxation become robbery? Why does a policeman wear a uniform? What is government? Here I first read the Constitution of the United States and tried to get my head around the English Magna Carta.

There were several months when I read every day in the *Galesburg Evening Mail* the column written in Washington by Walter Wellman. I did a lot of wondering about how one man could know so much about what the Government was doing, making plain to millions of people what was going on. From John Fiske's book I learned there are three branches of the Government—the Executive, the Legislative, and the Judicial. Walter Wellman made me think I knew what all three branches were doing.

It came over me often that I wasn't getting anywhere in particular. I wanted a job where I could learn a trade. I asked plumbers, carpenters, house painters, and they said there was no opening or I might come around later. When I asked Q. machinists and boilermakers what were the chances they said the Hard Times were still on, old hands waiting to go back. I heard that the Union Hotel barbershop wanted a porter. I said, "Barbering is a trade. A barber can travel, can work in other towns from coast to coast. At barbering you might be shaving a man who'll offer you a job with better money than you can ever make barbering."

I hired to Mr. Humphrey at three dollars a week, plus shoeshine money, and tips. The shop was under the Farmers' and Mechanics' Bank, in a half-basement with big windows that let you see the shoes of walkers on the sidewalk. By going up eight steps you could see the Public Square, down Broad Street to the courthouse park, and beyond that the Knox College campus. The floor of the shop was black and white square tiles which I mopped every morning. In rainy weather or snow, with mud tracked in, I gave the floor a once-over again in the afternoon. The big windows to the street I went over once a week with soap and water, sponge and chamois. And the four brass cuspidors had a brisk cleanout every day. Four barber chairs faced a long

wall mirror and three times a week I would put a white cleaning fluid on the glass, then with a chamois skin I would wipe off the white stuff.

Mr. Humphrey, Head Barber and Proprietor, had the first chair. At the second chair was a tall fellow with a mustache; his first name John. At the third chair was Frank Wykoff, smooth-faced, with silky golden hair. He had manners and a reputation as a dancer. The fourth chair was worked by Mr. Humphrey's eighteen-year-old son on Saturdays and before holidays when a rush was on.

Of what us kids called "the big bugs on the North Side," many came to the Union Hotel barbershop. "You will meet the bon ton of Galesburg while you work here, Charlie," Mr. Humphrey had said to me. "It's a bluestocking trade comes to our shop and we want to keep the place shipshape, everything clean as a whistle."

Mr. Humphrey was a barber and a gentleman. He would smile and in his pleasant voice say to a regular customer with a nod of the head and a bend of the back and shoulders that was nearly a bow, "Mister Higby, what is the good word with you?" or "Mister Applegreen, how does the world go round for you today?" or "Mister Hagenjos, it's about time we were seeing your good face again." He had a round face with a thin, straight-lined mouth. He was the Boss of the shop and ran it smooth and all had respect for him.

At half-past ten or eleven in the morning, when I saw there would be no customer out of a chair in ten or fifteen minutes, I would go up a back stairs, cross the big main office of the Union Hotel, and go into the most elegant saloon in that part of Illinois. There was a polished mahogany bar, a shining brass rail, tall brass spittoons, a long mirror so those standing at the bar could look at themselves or the other faces at the bar, and wood carving like lace or embroidery on the top and sides of the mirror. Near the end of the bar they set out the free lunch at halfpast ten—ham, cheese, pickles, rye and white bread, and sometimes deer or bear meat—and I helped myself. Then I went back to the barbershop thankful to the bartenders for not asking what a minor was doing in the place, and thankful to Solomon Frolich and Henry Gardt, the two German Jews who owned the saloon. I tried to do an extra-special job when I ran my whisk broom over them or gave them a shoeshine.

The Union Hotel got most of the big-time people who came to town, show people, lecturers, minstrels, star actors who had been playing on Broadway and were taking their play from Galesburg to Omaha, to Denver, to Salt Lake City, to San Francisco. Galesburg made a nice one-night stand for them—in the Auditorium across Broad Street from the hotel. In the hotel office, watching people come in and register, I would try to figure out whether they were traveling men or show people. And the pink-sheet *Police Gazette* in the barbershop which I read every week had me on the lookout for the high-class confidence men and gamblers who always stopped at high-class hotels.

At the desk was James or "Jimmy" Otway, an Englishman who reminded me of people and talk I had met in Dickens' novels. He was short with a blond face, blond hair combed back fancy and wavy, and a thick blond mustache that would have run out far only he kept it well curled, the curliest mustache in town, unless it was Will Olson's. He wore light tweed suits, stiff stand-up collars and stiff starched cuffs, colored neckties, and was spick-and-span. He bred blooded beagles and there might be two or three of his brown-and-white-haired dogs running around the office. Jimmy Otway belonged to the town and you were not quite a Galesburger unless you knew about him. I waited around sometimes to see whether he would drop his "aitches" and I learned there are Englishmen who don't drop their "aitches."

On my seventeenth birthday, January 6, 1895, General Philip Sidney Post died. He had served five terms as Congressman from our district, and was beginning his sixth when he died. Senators and Congressmen, old soldiers of the Civil War, politicians from far and near, came to his funeral. At the Q. depot I watched a noon train from Chicago pull in with a special car loaded with men wearing Prinz Albert coats and high silk hats. Then I walked to the Union Hotel barbershop to find every barber chair filled and a line of customers wearing Prinz Albert coats in the waiting chairs. The hatrack was filled with silk hats, and more of the same shiny hats were in a row on two window ledges.

I took to my shoeshine stand, where already the first customer was waiting. I shined the shoes of four Senators, eight Congressmen, two or three majors, and two pairs of knee-high boots of the same kind Lincoln wore. It was my banner day as a shoeshine boy. Most of them handed me the regular nickel pay. Some gave me a dime and two whose breath told me they could have been at the Union Hotel bar dropped a quarter into the hand I held out. For the first time I earned $1.40 in one day.

When I had seen Philip Sidney Post on the streets, I didn't think of him as any special hero. He was a man of stocky build, thick through the body, with a round head and face and a straight nose. He was a little bald over the forehead and had a longish dark mustache and a little goatee you had to look twice to see. Later I learned that Post was a great fighting man, one of the best soldiers who answered Lincoln's call for troops in '61. He was a young lawyer out in Wyandotte, Kansas, when the call came. He went east to Galesburg, enlisted, became second lieutenant of Company A, 59th Illinois Volunteer Infantry, and fought in some of the bloodiest battles of the war, taking wounds, getting honorable mentions, moving up to major, colonel, and brigadier general. Pea Ridge, Perryville, Murfreesboro, Chickamauga were bloody grounds, and Post was there. After the war his corps commander, General George H. Thomas, asked the Secretary of War to make him a colonel in the regular army.

Post had come back to Galesburg in 1879 after serving thirteen years as consul and then consul-general at Vienna, and he went into the real estate business. One day General Post with two other men came into the Union Hotel barbershop. All three had shaves and two had shines. One of the two whose shoes I shined was Philip Sidney Post. If I had known where those feet had been in their time I would have tried to turn out the best and brightest shine I ever put on shoe leather.

In the barbershop on Saturday I was here, there, and everywhere. Next to the shop was a bathroom with eight tubs and partitions between, twenty-five cents for a bath. For those who asked it I would get a tub of hot water ready. There were two or three regulars who would call me in to scrub their backs with a brush. Nearly always those I gave special help to paid me a quarter.

The worst mistake I made was one they guyed me about for a long time. The gentleman had had a shave, a haircut, and a shampoo. I gave him a shoe-shine. He looked good for a dime tip, at least a nickel. I swung my whisk broom over his Prinz Albert coat and his pants down to the shoes. Then I took his high silk hat off the hatrack. I began swinging my whisk broom up, down, and around his hat, the first hat of the kind I had ever handled. He had finished paying his bill to Mr. Humphrey when he looked over to where I was. He let out a howl and rushed over yelling, "You can't do that!" I saw at once what he meant; I had been an ignoramus about silk hats. I tried to mumble something about being sorry. I saw the two barbers trying to keep from laughing. Mr. Humphrey came up and I heard him say the only sharp words he ever said to me, ending up with talking natural,

"Charlie, you ought to have a soft brush for silk hats or a satin cloth." The customer had snatched his hat out of my hands and held it as though I might of a sudden jump at him and tear the hat away. He handed me a nickel for the shine and walked out as though he certainly would never come back to this place. The next day I had a soft satin cloth on hand and a brush with hairs so soft you could hardly feel them running over the palm of your hand. And after that when once in a while a silk hat came into the shop I was ready for it. I had what they call "confidence" because I had been through what they call "experience."

The barbers, among themselves as barbers, talked about razors. Most of them swore by the Wade & Butcher razor. It interested me that there was a razormaker whose name was Butcher. A fellow with a tough and tangled beard they called a "squirrel." One of them had just gone out the door when Frank Wykoff, who had shaved him, was saying, "He was a squirrel, all right. After I started on him I knew I had to lather him again and rub it in deep. I stropped my razor six times. You can't cut his whiskers. You have to whittle 'em."

Two or three times a week I would meet two other boys who were portering in barbershops. We talked about what blacking was best for a shoe, the rougher shoes that need two coats of blacking before you put on the brushes, and how to look at a customer or what to say that would make him think it would be a good idea to pay you a dime instead of a nickel. One of these boys, Harry Wade, thought he had a sidewise look up into the customer's face, along with a smile, that sometimes brought him an extra nickel. The other homely porter and I said to Harry, "You're a good-looker and wear smart clothes and that's more than half of why you get more tips than we do." Harry might not like the looks of a customer and after he gave him a brush-off that had everything, if he got no tip, he could say "Thank you" with a sarcastic sneer. The Head Barber caught on to this and said, "You're a good porter, Harry, but if you keep that up, we'll have to let you go."

Harry and the other porters used to dress in their fanciest clothes and Sunday noon walk into the Brown's Hotel dining room and order a fifty-cent dinner. They called it "classy." Their home folks set a good table, but after being barbershop porters all week they wanted to "sit with the bon ton." Harry Wade had the only snare drum in our neighborhood. He brought it to the Berrien Street pasture, where at night the boys sat on the grass while he stood and gave us all the drum taps he knew. Harry's arms and wrists were fast with the sticks;

he practiced hard and hoped to get on with a band and travel. Every one of us wished he had a classy snare drum and was good with the sticks like Harry. He had class enough without eating fifty-cent dinners at Brown's Hotel on Sundays.

Harry came along one night in 1893 to where we were sitting in the pasture. He had just got off a train from Chicago, where he had had three days at the World's Fair, the great Columbian Exposition. He sat down with us and talked for an hour about the fair. When he quit talking we put questions to him and he went on talking and gave us the feel of that World's Fair up in Chicago. We couldn't afford to go and Harry brought parts of it to us.

Spring came after fall and winter months in the barbershop and doubts had been growing in me that I wasn't cut out for a barber. Spring moved in with smells on the air, and Sam Barlow came into my life. He had sold his farm up near Galva and gone into the milk business. He was a jolly, laughing man, short, tough-muscled, a little stoop-shouldered, with a ruddy, well-weathered face, brown eyes, a thick sandy mustache, and a voice I liked. He had been a barn-dance fiddler, and still liked to play.

Barlow stopped his milk wagon one day, called me from a sidewalk, and asked if I wanted to go to work for him at twelve dollars a month and dinner with him and his wife every day. I took him up on it. It would be outdoor work; I would see plenty of sky every day. The barbershop had been getting stuffy. I parted from Mr. Humphrey and it wasn't easy to tell him, "You've been fine to me, Mr. Humphrey, but I've got to be leaving. I don't think I'm cut out for a barber."

❁ ❁ ❁

Fourteen : A Milk Route Again

EVERY MORNING FOR sixteen months or more I walked from home at half-past six, west on Berrien Street, crossing the Q. switchyard tracks, on past Mike O'Connor's cheap livery stable, past the Boyer broom factory, then across the Knox College campus and past the front of the Old Main building. Every morning I saw the east front of Old Main where they had put up the platform for Lincoln and Douglas to debate in October 1858. At the north front of Old Main many times I read on a bronze plate words spoken by Lincoln and by Douglas. They stayed with me, and sometimes I would stop to read those words only, what Lincoln said to twenty thousand people on a cold windy October day: "He is blowing out the moral lights around us, when he contends that whoever wants slaves has a right to hold them." I read them in winter sunrise, in broad summer daylight, in falling snow or rain, in all the weathers of a year.

Then I continued along South Street to Monmouth Boulevard to the house and barn of Samuel Kossuth Barlow. There I shook out straw and shoveled clean the stalls of three horses, sometimes packed mud into the sore foot of a horse, hitched a horse to a wagon. By that time Bill Walters, a good-looking husky with a brown mustache, would have come in from two farms west of town, bringing the day's milk to be delivered. Mr. Barlow would be out of the house, and Harry ("Fatty") Hart would show up. He wasn't fat but the boys had hung the nickname of "Fatty" on him and it stuck. He was straight and square-shouldered, with round cheeks maybe puffed out a little, and black hair, black eyes, and a bright quick smile. While Bill Walters went with his wagon and worked to the north, Mr. Barlow and Fatty and I covered the south side of town.

Sam Barlow was different from George Burton. He would take a two-gallon can of milk and walk a route of a few blocks while Fatty or I drove the wagon. He would keep telling us to pay respect to any complaints of customers, never to "sass" them, whereas Burton used to act as though it was something special for people to get their milk from him. Mr. Barlow had us keep an eye out for any house people were moving out of, and when new people came in we would be on the spot asking if they wouldn't like to have milk from us. Usually we got a new customer. From October on, when the cows didn't have pasture, we sold eighteen quart tickets for a dollar; then in summer twenty for a dollar. Starting in early June, till about the middle of September, we made two deliveries a day. Most customers didn't have iceboxes and didn't want their milk to sour over night. That meant Mr. Barlow and I would wash all the cans twice a day in the warm-weather months—the big eight-gallon cans that stayed on the wagon and the two- and three-gallon cans we carried and poured out the pints and quarts from. After washing up we always had a good dinner set out by Mrs. Barlow and her daughter.

To one house every day I carried a small can holding the milk of one cow. A doctor had ordered the baby in that house to have milk from one cow and every day the same cow. We were proud to be doing this because the father of the baby was Frank Bullard, whose name had been flashed to newspapers all over the country as the engineer on a fast mail train that set a new world's record for locomotive and train speed. I would see him walk out of his house and up the street carrying a wicker lunchbox, walking cool and taking it easy—a square-shouldered, upstanding man with black hair and a black mustache. We did the best we could to see that the baby never changed cows. But there were two or three times we couldn't help it; milk and cans got mixed up and the baby got the milk of several cows, and we never heard but the baby was doing well.

It was on my milk route that I had my "puppy love." Day and night her face would be floating in my mind. Her folks lived on Academy Street next to the Burlington tracks of the Q. They usually left a crock on the porch with a quart ticket in it. I would take the ticket out of the crock, tilt my can and pour milk into my quart measure, then pour it into the crock, well aware she was sometimes at the kitchen window watching my performance, ducking away if I looked toward the window. Two or three times a week, however, the crock wasn't there and I would call "Milk!" and she would come out with the crock in her hands and a smile on her face. At first she would merely say "Quart" and I would pour the quart and walk away. But I learned that if I spoke a smooth and pleasant "Good morning," she would speak me a "Good morning" that was like a blessing to be remembered. I learned too that if I could stumble out the words, "It's a nice day" or "It's a cold wind blowing" she would say a pert "Yes, it is" and I would go away wondering how I would ever get around to a one- or two-minute conversation with her.

It was a lost love from the start. It began to glimmer away after my first and only walk with her. I dropped in with another boy one summer night to revival services at the Knox Street Congregational Church. There I saw her with another girl. After the services my chum took the other girl and I found myself walking with the girl of my dreams. I had said, "See you home?" and she had said, "Certainly." And there we were walking in a moonlight summer night and it was fourteen blocks to her home. I said it was a mighty fine moonlight night. She said "Yes" and we walked a block saying nothing. I said it was quite a spell of hot weather we had been having. She said "Yes" and we walked another block. I said one of the solo singers at the church did pretty good. Again she agreed and we walked on without a word. I spoke of loose boards in the wooden sidewalk of the next block and how we would watch our step.

I had my right hand holding her left arm just above the elbow, which I had heard and seen was the proper way to take a girl home. And my arm got bashful. For blocks I believed maybe she didn't like the way I was holding her arm. After a few blocks it was like I had a sore wooden arm that I ought to take away and have some peace. Yet I held on. If I let go I would have to explain and I couldn't think of an explanation. I could have broken one of the blocks we walked without a word by saying, "Would you believe it, your face keeps com-

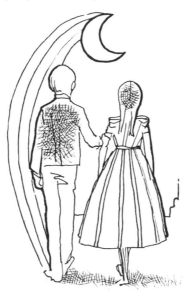

ing back to me when I'm away from you—all the time it keeps coming back as the most wonderful face my eyes ever met." Instead I asked her how her father, who was a freight-train conductor on the Q., liked being a conductor.

The fourteen blocks came to an end. At her gate I let go of her arm, said "Good night," and walked away fast, as if I had an errand. I didn't even stand to see if she made it to the front door. I had made the decision that we were not "cut out for each other." I had one satisfaction as I walked home. My bashful right arm gradually became less wooden.

After sixteen or eighteen months with Barlow, at twelve dollars a month and a good dinner every day, I asked him for a raise. He said the business couldn't stand it. I had to say, "I hate to leave you. You're the best man I ever worked for but I can't see I'm getting anywhere." He said, "If you have to go, then all right, Charlie. What has to be has to be. You've been a good boy and we've had some good times together. I hope you'll come around and see us once in a while." And I did. They put in a new Edison phonograph with a lot of cylinder records and I never got tired of hearing "Poet and Peasant." Sam Barlow and I stayed good friends as long as he lived.

❀ ❀ ❀

Fifteen : On the Road

I HAD MY bitter and lonely hours moving out of boy years into a grown young man. But I had been moving too in a slow way to see that to all the best men and women I had known in my life and especially all the great ones I had read about, life wasn't easy, life had often its bitter and lonely hours, and when you grow with new strengths of body and mind it is by struggle. I was through with *Tom the Bootblack, From Rags to Riches,* and the books by Horatio Alger. Every one of his heroes had a streak of luck. There was a runaway horse and the hero saved a rich man's daughter by risking *his* life to grab the reins and save *her* life. He married the daughter and from then on life was peaches and cream for him.

There was such a thing as luck in life but if luck didn't come your way it was up to you to step into struggle and like it. I read Ouida's *Under Two Flags.* The hero lost everything he had except a horse, lived a dirty and bloody life as a fighting man, with never a whimper. I read Olive Schreiner's *The Story of an African Farm,* sad lives on nearly every page, and yet a low music of singing stars and love too deep ever to be lost. I believed there were lives far more bitter and lonely than mine and they had fixed stars, dreams and moonsheens, hopes and mysteries, worth looking at during their struggles. I was groping.

I was nineteen years old, nearly a grown man. And I was restless. The jobs I'd had all seemed dead-end with no future that called to me. Among the boys I could hold my own. With the girls I was bashful and couldn't think of what to say till after I left them, and then I wasn't sure. I had never found a "steady."

I read about the Spanish General Weyler and his cruelties with the people of Cuba who wanted independence and a republic. I read about Gomez, Garcia, Maceo, with their scrabbling little armies fighting against Weyler. They became heroes to me. I tried to figure a way to get down there and join one of those armies. I would have signed up with any recruiting agent who could have got me there. Nothing came of this hope.

What came over me in those years 1896 and 1897 wouldn't be easy to tell. I hated my home town and yet I loved it. And I hated and loved myself about the same as I did the town and the people. I came to see that my trouble was inside of myself more than it was in the town and the people.

I decided in June of 1897 to head west and work in the Kansas wheat harvest. I would beat my way on the railroads; I would be a hobo and a "gaycat." I had talked with hoboes enough to know there is the professional tramp who never works and the gaycat who hunts work and hopes to go on and get a job that suits him. I would take my chances on breaking away from my home town where I knew every street and people in every block and farmers on every edge of town.

I had never been very far from Galesburg. I was sixteen when for the first time I rode a railroad train for fifty miles. I opened a little bank of dimes and found I had eighty cents. My father got me a pass on the Q. and I rode alone to Peoria and felt important and independent. I saw the State Fair and sat a long time looking at the Illinois River and the steamboats. I was a traveler seeing the world, and when I got home I couldn't help telling other people how Peoria looked to me.

I had made my first trip to Chicago only the year before, when I was eighteen. I had laid away one dollar and fifty cents and my father, after years of my begging for it, got me a pass on the Q. I was traveling light, no valise or bag. In my pockets I had my money, a knife, a piece of string, a pipe and tobacco and two handkerchiefs. John Sjodin had coached me how to live cheap in Chicago. The longer my dollar and a half lasted, the longer I could stay. I ate mostly at Pittsburgh Joe's on Van Buren near Clark Street, breakfast a high stack of wheat pancakes with molasses and oleo and coffee with a dash of milk in it, all for five cents. Dinner was a large bowl of meat stew, all the bread you wanted, and coffee, at ten cents. Supper was the same.

A room on the third floor of a hotel on South State Street was twenty-five cents a night. The rickety iron bedstead with its used sheets took up most of the bare wooden floor space. In the corners were huddles of dust and burnt matches. There were nails to hang my clothes on, and I went down a dark narrow hallway to a water closet and washroom with a roller towel.

I went two nights to the Variety Show, vaudeville, in a top gallery at ten cents. I mustn't miss at ten cents the Eden Musée on South State, John Sjodin had said, and there I saw in wax Jesse James and several murderers. I walked through the big State Street department stores I had heard about for years, Siegel Cooper's at Van Buren and north to Marshall Field's. I stood in front of the Daily News Building, the Tribune and Inter-Ocean buildings. I had carried and sold so many of their papers that I wanted to see where they were made. I had great respect for Victor Lawson and his *Record* and *Daily News* and I would have liked to go into his office and speak to him but I couldn't think of what I would say.

I walked miles and never got tired of the roar of the streets, the trolley cars, the teamsters, the drays, buggies, surreys, and phaetons, the delivery wagons high with boxes, the brewery wagons piled with barrels, the one-horse and two-horse hacks, sometimes a buckboard, sometimes a barouche with a coachman in livery, now and again a man in a saddle on horseback weaving his way through the traffic— horses, everywhere horses and here and there mules—and the cobblestone streets with layers of dust and horse droppings. I walked along Michigan Avenue and looked for hours to where for the first time in my life I saw shimmering water meet the sky. I walked around every block in the Loop, watched the frameworks of the Elevated lines shake and tremble and half expected a train to tumble down to the street. I dropped in at the Board of Trade and watched the grain gamblers throwing fingers and yelling prices.

The afternoon of my third day in Chicago I stopped in at a saloon with a free-lunch sign. I helped myself to slices of rye bread and hunks of cheese and baloney, paid a nickel for a glass of beer. I didn't care much for beer but I had heard so much about Chicago saloons that I wasn't going to leave without seeing the inside of one.

I had seen Chicago for three days on a dollar and a half. I rode home and tried to tell the folks what Chicago was like. None of them had ever been there except Papa and Mama and they had stayed only long enough to change trains. I was glad to be back in a room with a clean floor and a bed with clean sheets and it was good to have Mama's cooking after Pittsburgh Joe's. Yet there were times I wished I could be again in those street crowds and the roaring traffic.

Now I would take to The Road. The family didn't like the idea. Papa scowled. Mama kissed me and her eyes had tears after dinner one noon when I walked out of the house with my hands free, no bag or bundle, wearing a black-sateen shirt, coat, vest, and pants, a slouch hat, good shoes and socks, no underwear. In my pockets were a small bar of soap, a razor, a comb, a pocket mirror, two handkerchiefs, a piece of string, needles and thread, a Waterbury watch, a knife, a pipe and a sack of tobacco, three dollars and twenty-five cents.

It was the last week in June, an afternoon bright and cool. A little west of the Santa Fe station stood a freight train waiting for orders. As the train started I ran along and jumped into a boxcar. I stood at the open side door and watched the running miles of young corn. Crossing the long bridge over the Mississippi my eyes swept over it with a sharp hunger that the grand old river satisfied. Except for my father, when riding to Kansas to buy land, no one of our family had seen the Father of Waters. As the train slowed down in Fort Madison, I jumped out.

I bought a nickel's worth of cheese and crackers and sat eating and looking across the Mississippi. The captain of a small steamboat said I could work passage to Keokuk unloading kegs of nails, I slept on the boat, had breakfast, sailed down the river watching fields and towns go by—at Burlington, Quincy, and Keokuk shouldering kegs of nails to the wharves. At Keokuk I spread newspaper on green grass near a canal and slept in the open. I washed my face and hands at the canal, using soap from my pocket and drying with a handkerchief. Then I met a fellow who said, "On the road?" When I said "Yes," he led me to where he had been eating bread and meat unwrapped from a newspaper. "I got three lumps last night," he said, and handed me a lump. A lump was what you were handed if you got something to eat at a house where you asked for it. My new friend said, "I got a sitdown before I got the lumps." At one house he had been asked to sit at the kitchen table and eat. Then because he wanted to have this day free to look at the canal and the blue sky, he went from house to house for lumps, hiding them under wooden sidewalks so his hands were empty. The lump he gave me had four slices of buttered bread and two thick cuts of roast beef. "This is breakfast and dinner for me," I said.

His face and hands were pudgy as though your fingers would sink into them if you touched them. He had come out of a Brooklyn orphan asylum, had taken to The Road, and said he had never done a day's work in his life. He was proud he had found a way to live without working. He named Cincinnati Slim and Chicago Red and other professional tramps he had traveled with, as though they were big names known to all tramps and I must have heard of them. He named towns where the jail food was good and how in winter he would get a two or three months' sentence for vagrancy in those jails. "Or I might go South for the cold weather," he said, "keeping away from the towns where they're horstyle." Now I had learned that where they are hostile they are "horstyle" in tramp talk. He had a slick tongue and a fast way of talking, and soon I walked away, leaving him where he lay on the green grass looking at the blue sky. I would have felt sorry for him if he wasn't so sure he could take care of himself.

During a heavy rainstorm that night I slept in the dry cellar of a house the carpenters hadn't finished and I was up and out before they came to work. I had a fifteen-cent breakfast, found an old tomato can, bought a cheap brush, and had the can filled with asphaltum for a few nickels. Then I went from house to house in several blocks and got three jobs blacking stoves that were rusty, earning seventy-five cents, and two jobs where my pay was dinner and supper. I slept again in the house the carpenters hadn't finished and the next day went from house to house and got no jobs with pay brushing asphaltum on rusty stoves, though I did get breakfast, dinner, and supper for three jobs. The day after I bought a refill of asphaltum, earned three meals and twenty-five cents. The following day was the same as the day before. I found that the housewives were much like those for whom I had poured milk in Galesburg. I found, too, that if I said I was hoping to earn money to go to college they were ready to help me. The trouble was there were not enough rusty stoves.

The next day was the Fourth of July, with crowds pouring into Keokuk. I saw a sign "Waiter Wanted" in a small lunch counter near the end of Main Street. The owner was running the place by himself and said I could make myself useful at fifty cents a day and meals. He showed me the eggs, lard, and frying pan, the buns and ham for sandwiches, the doughnuts and the coffeepot. At ten o'clock he went out, telling me I was in charge and to be polite serving customers. Three or four people drifted in before eleven-thirty, when he came back, feeling good, he said, and he would help through the noon rush. Five or six customers came in the next two hours and he sat in a quiet corner taking a sleep while I handled the trade. There were not more than two customers at any one time and I flourished around, got them what they called for on our plain and simple bill of fare. I felt important. Maybe after a while I might work up to be a partner in the business.

The owner woke up and went out saying he would be back soon. At three o'clock he came in feeling better than the last time. He had forgotten to eat at noon and I offered to fix him two fried eggs, which I served him with a bun and coffee. He went out again saying he would be back soon. At five o'clock he came back "stewed to the gills," slumped himself in a corner on the floor, and went to sleep. I fried myself three eggs and ate them with two buns and coffee. I fixed two sandwiches with thick cuts of ham, put them in my coat pockets along with two doughnuts, opened the money drawer and took out a half-dollar. With my coat on one arm, I closed the front door softly, and that night slept in a boxcar that took me halfway across the State of Missouri. For a poor boy seeking his fortune I hadn't done so bad for one day.

Next was the railroad section gang at Bean Lake, Missouri. My Irish boss, Fay Connors, hired me at a dollar and twenty-five cents a day and I was to pay him three dollars a week for board and room in his four-room one-story house thirty feet from the railroad tracks. There were five of us in the gang and you would have known Connors was the boss. He liked his voice and his authority. At no time did he get mad and bawl out a man, but he had a frozen-faced way of letting men know he was once a section *hand* and was now a section *boss*. I tamped ties several days from seven till noon and from one till six. My muscles ached at night like they did when I worked in the ice harvest. Then came weed-cutting. We swung our scythes along the right of way; I had to train a new set of muscles and *they* ached at night.

At morning, noon, and evening, the meals at the Connors table were the same, fried side pork, fried potatoes, and coffee. Connors seemed to like it. So did his wife and three small children. At the end of two weeks, on a Sunday morning, I hopped a freight for Kansas City and left Boss Connors to collect for my board and room out of my paycheck.

In Kansas City Mrs. Mullin had a sign in the window of her restaurant on Armour Avenue, "Dishwasher Wanted." She took the sign out when the Swede boy from Illinois made himself at home in the kitchen. Noontime was the rush hour of the workers from the meatpacking plants near by. It was a fight in that dish trough to get enough dishes cleaned for serving the customers. I swept the eating room morning and afternoon and mopped it on Saturday. My sleeping place was the end of a hallway with my cot curtained off, and I washed and shaved, using my pocket mirror, at a sink in the hall.

I was up at six in the morning and had the eating room swept for customers who began coming at six-thirty when we opened. I worked every weekday till eight at night except for an hour or two in the afternoon. I had good times in that kitchen. The mulatto chef was fat, jolly, always cheerful and would fix me three good meals a day. He would ask what I wanted as though he was an uncle of mine and nothing was too good for me. The one waiter was also a mulatto. George was handsome and gay, could sing either oldtime songs or late hits, and would sing special songs I called for. I had Sunday off and walked miles around Kansas City.

In a week or so the wheat harvest in western Kansas would be ready. Mrs. Mullin paid me my second week's pay of one dollar and fifty cents and I said good-by and saw the sign "Dishwasher Wanted" whisked back into the window. Saying good-by to George and the chef wasn't easy. They were goodhearted men who had made everything easier and brighter for me.

I slept two nights in a fifteen-cent second-floor "flophouse" where forty men in one room each had a cot about an arm's length apart. A near neighbor might be snoring, and at two or three in the morning there might be a scream from a fellow waking out of a bad dream. Worst of all were the flat brown creepers who could bite into your skin so you were awake on the instant. They had homes in our blankets. We had no sheets.

Hopping freight trains on my way west I had one bad afternoon. A shack (hobo for brakeman) had ordered me off an open coal car where I was crouched. When the train started I got on again. The train was running full speed when he climbed down from the car ahead and another shack followed him. He put his face close to mine. "I told you to stay off this train. Now you'll come through with two bits or you'll take what you get." It was my first time with a shack of that kind. I had met brakemen who were not small-time grafters, and one who spotted me in a boxcar corner said, "If you're going to ride, keep out of sight." I figured I might owe the railroad money for fare but the shack wasn't a passenger-fare collector. So I didn't come through with two bits. He outweighed me by about forty pounds and when his right fist landed on my left jaw and his left fist slammed into my mouth

I went to the floor. As I slowly sat up, he snarled, "Stay where you are or you'll get more." Then as he and his partner turned to go he gave me a last look and laughed, "You can ride, you've earned it."

I stood up and watched the passing land. The trees were few, no such timber as in Illinois and Missouri. I had come to the Great Plains. I was traveling, though my handkerchief was splotched red from putting it to my mouth. When the train slowed down I got off and found myself at a hobo jungle, two men leaving to catch the train I had quit, two more washing their shirts in a shallow creek shaded by three cottonwood trees. I washed my shirt, socks, and handkerchief. The two men were gaycats, said they had spent their last nickel for a loaf of bread and a half-pound of Java and could I scrape the nickels for a few weenies? I said fair enough and went for the weenies and we ate well. I caught a freight that night that had me in Emporia, where I walked past the office of the *Emporia Gazette* but didn't have the nerve to step in and see the editor, William Allen White. After a big two-bit meal I went to the city park where I lay on the grass for a sleep and then talked with two men who got me to singing for them. They were professional tramps and wanted me to go along with them.

They were sure I could make money singing in saloons, and they had the idea we would all share in the money so made. It seemed a little queer to me.

That night a bright full moon was up in a clear sky and out past the Sante Fe water tank waiting their chances to catch a freight train west was a gay bunch of eight men, most of them heading toward the wheat harvest. In a windy rain I jumped out of the boxcar I caught in Emporia and found a sleeping place under a loading platform for stock cars. About seven in the morning I read the station sign and learned I was in Hutchinson, Kansas. I had heard it was better not to hit the houses near the railroad; they had been hit too often by 'boes. I walked eight or ten blocks and hit two houses. "Have you got any work I can do for breakfast?" At each they took one look at me and shut the door. At the third house a woman sent her daughter to get a saw, showed me a woodpile and a sawbuck. For an hour I kept the saw going, piled the wood, and went to the house. The smiling mother and daughter led me to the family table, set fried ham and potatoes, applesauce, bread and coffee, before me. After I had eaten they handed me a large lump. I thanked them, walked Main Street to see what Hutchinson was like, and went to my loading platform. Unwrapping the lump, I found fried chicken and bread that would make dinner and supper, along with two pocketsful of apples that had come down in the wind and rain the night before.

Lindsborg, Kansas, was Swedish, and Pastor Swenson, the head of Bethany College there, was a Lutheran Synod leader I had heard preach in Galesburg. It was either hay or broomcorn harvest I worked in with other Swedes on a farm near Lindsborg. I stayed three days at a dollar a day and meals, sleeping in a barn hayloft. On my third and last morning I had been awake a few minutes when I heard voices down below. One voice came clear, a Swede saying, "Is that bum up yet?" I said to myself, "Am I a bum?" And I had to answer, "Yes, I am a bum." I had bummed my way to Lindsborg; I had no baggage nor bundle and I expected to bum my way on a train out of Lindsborg. The first time in my life I heard myself referred to as a bum was among Swedes I had made a detour to see. I was getting no such hand of fellowship as from George and the chef in the Kansas City kitchen.

Newspapers said the country was pulling out of the Hard Times, yet there were many men still out of work, men who had left their homes hoping for jobs somewhere, riding the boxcars and sitting around the jungle hangouts. Some had learned hobo slang; some didn't care for it. There was always a small fraternity who knew each other at once by their slang. They were the professional tramps, who divided into panhandlers and petty thieves. Panhandlers talked about "how to work Main Street," what kind of faces to ask for a dime or a quarter. "Never mooch a goof wearing a red necktie," I heard. They would argue about the best kind of story to melt the heart of the citizen you walked along with. The longer you made your story, the more danger there was that the citizen would ask you questions and maybe while you were answering a cop would come along "and he sees you're a vag and jugs you." "I think I'll try the goat in this town," said one and I learned the goat was the Catholic priest. "I had a good snooze in a knowledge box last night," meant the fellow had slept in a country schoolhouse.

The petty thieves did less talking. The only one who got confidential with me wore a good brown suit, a brown shirt with a brown necktie. His face and mustache were like the pictures of the hero in the *Family Story Paper*. His quiet words to me were, "I'm a second-story man. I could use you." He would have me stand on his shoulders and climb up on a porch, go through a window, and search for money and jewels we would split. He hadn't been doing so well lately but he had seen good times and they would come again. He had a soft voice and he was polite. I told him I would think about it, but I managed to get away from him without telling him what I thought about it.

I was meeting fellow travelers and fellow Americans. What they were doing to my heart and mind, my personality, I couldn't say then nor later and be certain. I was getting a deeper self-respect than I had had in Galesburg, so much I knew. I was getting to be a better story-teller. You can be loose and easy when from day to day you meet strangers you will know only an hour or a day or two. What girls I was meeting on a job or at a sitdown usually wanted to know where I was from, where I was going, what kind of a home and folks I had, and I was working out of my bashfulness.

On one boxcar ride there was a young farm hand from Indiana I liked so much that I asked him how it would be for the two of us to travel together and share and share alike for a few weeks. He said he would shake hands on it if I would go with him to the Klondike. The gold rush was on and he was heading for Alaska. He had expected to stop for the Kansas wheat harvest and earn money he needed but now he figured that might make him a little late in getting to the Chilkoot Pass and the gold waiting for the early ones. We were sorry to part.

At Larned, Pawnee County, Kansas, I refused to regard myself as a hobo. My father had owned land in that county and had set foot in this town when he came to look at the land. I had written for my father the letters sending tax payments to the County Treasurer of Pawnee County. When I walked past the courthouse I felt like an important, respectable citizen. You could walk the few blocks of Main Street in about three minutes. You could see empty houses here and there; people had moved away because of Hard Times. The weekly paper was worth reading if only for its name, the *Tillers and Toilers Journal.*

For three days I worked at seventy-five cents a day helping a carpenter. I worked five days with a crew threshing wheat—three days on one farm and two days on another—pitchforking bundles of wheat onto the tables of the thresher. It was hard work but the crew was jolly, the meals good, the barns clean where four of us slept on hay, the pay a dollar and twenty-five cents a day and board. Then there was to be no more work till five days later. I decided to head west to Lakin, where I heard there was more doing.

In the days between work I had long talks and shared meals at the Santa Fe water tank with an odd bird from Kansas City. He said he had been a bookkeeper for a coal firm there several years. They had let him out because business was slow. He seemed to have money and he had a six-shooter that he took out once in a while and fingered. He had an interesting face with a hawknose, a good mouth, and a chin that pointed out. His blue eyes had some kind of danger that I couldn't make out. He was friendly with me and seemed to hint that maybe we could travel together.

But I went on alone to Lakin, which I noticed on a timetable was six hundred and eighty-four miles from Galesburg on the Santa Fe. I figured that with detours I had traveled a thousand miles since I left home. I worked with a threshing crew some three weeks around Lakin. The job finished on one farm, we moved to another farm with a different farmer and family.

A shack put me off the bumpers of a fast freight I had caught out of Lakin. A minute after I got off, I ran into the blue-eyed bird from Larned. It was near midnight. We went to a lunch counter and he insisted on paying. He had a roll of bills, and he said, "I'm flush." I told him I was catching the next freight out if there was an empty boxcar I could sleep in. He walked with me to the water tank, where he pulled the revolver from his hip pocket, saying, "This gat comes in handy, boy. It saves you a lot of hard work." Then it came out. He was sticking up harvest hands for their money. Once at a water tank and once

in a boxcar he had pulled his gun and, "I pushed the gat into his guts
and told him to come through with every dollar on him or I'd pull the
trigger and he came through." I had thirty-odd dollars on me and was
wondering why he didn't push the gat into my guts. I'm sure I would
have come through with my last dollar. I think he still hoped I might
buy a gun and go along with him as a partner. I left him when a
freight came along. He said, "I expect some nice pickings here the
next two or three days. Maybe I'll be seeing you in Rocky Ford on
Melon Day."

Thousands poured into Rocky Ford for the Melon Day celebration.
Watermelon and cantaloupe were handed out free. I rode a crowded
passenger train that evening—sitting on a small board over the rods
of a truck between the wheels. I changed for a freight train where I
had a boxcar sleep and got off in the morning not knowing where I
was. I didn't bother to go back and read the station sign. I ate a sandwich as I walked west on the railroad track. The day was sunny and
cool. My eyes caught high rises of tumbling land I had never met
before—the Rocky Mountains! Coming unexpectedly upon those rolling formations of rock and pine lifted away high, had me saying
"There's the Hand of God." I couldn't think of anything before in my
life that had me using that phrase.

I walked on to Canyon City, where I picked pears, earned meals
and a few half-dollars, went on to Salida, where I spent two days and
then took a Colorado Midland train heading back east, aiming for
Denver. There wasn't an empty boxcar on the train, and for the first
time I was riding the bumpers late at night. My feet were on the cou-
plers between two cars and my hands were on the brake rod so in case
my feet should slip I could hold on. Suddenly I was saying to myself,
"You darn fool, you've been asleep." My numb brain was telling me
that when you go to sleep on the bumpers you're in luck if your hands
don't loosen and topple you down under the moving train. I would
watch myself. But again I caught myself coming out of a sleep. From
then on I wouldn't trust myself to be still for a second. I kept changing my position. I kept moving my feet and hands. I beat the sides of
my head with a fist. I kicked one leg against the other. An hour of
that and the train stopped. I got off and thanked God and the everlasting stars over the Rockies.

I saw Pikes Peak so I could say I saw it. At the Windsor, a first-class
hotel in Denver, I washed dishes two weeks at a dollar and fifty cents
a week, had a cubbyhole for a room, and meals as good as were
served to the silk-hat guests. Then came the question, should I head

for the West coast or east to Galesburg? I admitted I was a little home-sick. A passenger train was on slow speed out of the yards one night and I hopped on the steps of a Pullman vestibule. A conductor and porter ordered me off. I got off and saw the train slow to a stop. I climbed on top of a Pullman car, lay with my head toward the engine, and swore a solemn oath I wouldn't go to sleep. The car rocked and shook going around curves and my hands held tight so I wouldn't slide off. It was a cool September night and the train speed made it cold. I still had no underwear. I buttoned my coat, turned the collar up and tied a handkerchief around my neck. I went to sleep twice and coming out of it kept hitting and kicking myself to stay awake.

Daybreak came. An early farmer waved to me. I saw we were pull-ing in to a division point, McCook, Nebraska. I climbed down and started to walk out of the yards. A one-eyed man in plain clothes with a club and a star stood in my way. "Where did you come from?" His tone was horstyle. "I just got off that train," I said. He gave me orders in a more horstyle tone: "We don't want the likes of you in this town. You get back on that train." There were no trainmen in sight as I climbed back to where I had been riding. I had a daylight view of the Nebraska landscape for thirty miles from McCook to the next stop at Oxford. No one was waiting for me at Oxford. I went to a lunch counter, where they let me into the kitchen to wash off the cinders and soot. Then I ordered a monster thirty-five cent breakfast of ham and eggs, fried potatoes, bread, coffee, and two pieces of pie.

Heading east I stopped three days in a jungle with five good fellows. Shirt, socks, and handkerchiefs got washed. We had several meals of corn we picked from fields near by to roast or boil and sat around a fire talking after our supper. I caught a freight that landed me in Ne-braska City. I chopped wood and picked apples for two sitdowns. At a large brick house where I chopped wood, the man of the house, a lawyer, seeing my suit of clothes somewhat ragged, asked me if I would like an old suit of his. He brought out an iron-gray all-wool suit, better than any I had had in my life. I offered to chop more wood but he laughed and said I'd better be on my way home. I found myself that night in a boxcar with four others. We spread newspapers under us, threw our coats over our shoulders, and tried for sleep. The night was clear and frosty. After a couple of hours we were saying, "It's too cold to sleep here." The five of us marched to the city cala-boose and asked the marshal to let us in. The cells had the expected stink, but we spread our newspapers on the stone floor, slept warm, and on leaving were told to get out of town that day.

I caught a freight for Omaha. In Omaha, as in Kansas City and Denver, I stood before the United States Army recruiting office and read many times the pay and conditions Uncle Sam offered his Regular Army boys. I came near enlisting. One year of service I could see, or maybe two years, but the required three years had me backing out. I would make my decision, walk away, and come back the next day, read the pay and conditions and make the same decision that three years was too long.

The Hotel Mercer took me on as dishwasher at a dollar and fifty cents a week. The hotel was leased and run by a fancily dressed tall man who was known as Wink Taylor. I didn't notice him wink at any time but he probably had the name because he was quick as a wink. At the end of the first week I didn't get my pay nor at the end of the second week. Then came word that the Hotel Mercer was foreclosed and Wink Taylor vanished, owing me three dollars and owing the chambermaids, the dining-room and kitchen hands too.

I had one last sleep in the Mercer, crossed over to Council Bluffs, had breakfast, then caught one freight train after another till I came in sight of Galesburg the afternoon of October fifteenth.

I walked along Berrien Street to the only house in the United States where I could open a door without knocking and walk in for a kiss from the woman of the house. They gave me a sitdown and as they had had only two or three letters from me, they asked questions about where I'd been. When I showed my father fifteen dollars and a few nickels, he said the money would come in handy and I should watch it. The clean bed sheets that night felt good.

Mart was suspicious of my fine suit of clothes. "I'll bet you didn't buy it new. If you bought it, it was a hockshop." So I told him how I got it. Mart said that along in August he had read in a newspaper about a hobo who fell off the bumpers in western Kansas and was mangled to death. The folks hadn't read it and he didn't tell them. "But I was afraid, Cully, that maybe it was you." Then I told him how in Colorado it could have been me.

What had the trip done to me? I couldn't say. It had changed me. I was easier about looking people in the eye. When questions came I was quicker at answering them or turning them off. I had been a young stranger meeting many odd strangers and I had practiced at having answers. At home and among my old chums of the Dirty Dozen they knew I had changed but they could no more tell how than I. Away deep in my heart now I had hope as never before. Struggles lay ahead, I was sure, but whatever they were I would not be afraid of them.

Sixteen : In the Army

I WENT TO work on the Schwarz farm three miles east of Galesburg. I was up at four-thirty in the morning, curried two horses, and Mr. Schwarz and I milked twenty-two cows. I milked eight while Mr. Schwarz, older and faster, milked fourteen. We put the milk into eight-gallon cans and loaded them into a milk wagon. After breakfast I drove the milk into town and poured it out in pints and quarts. I bought a *Chicago Record* every day and read in the wagon going back to the farm the two-column Home University series of lectures by University of Chicago professors on literature, history, politics, and government. The horses didn't mind. They liked going slow while I read.

After dinner I washed the cans and again Mr. Schwarz and I milked the cows. Mr. Schwarz was tall, somewhat stoop-shouldered, with a black beard—a kindly and gracious man, his people Pennsylvania Dutch. Mrs. Schwarz was robust, matronly, and when her fourteen-year-old daughter one evening at the supper table used the word "spondulix" she said sternly, "Why, Ethel, I'm surprised at you using such language." They were Methodists, well read, devout but not pious. You might have said they were a *Youth's Companion* family come true. Mrs. Schwarz had noticed that I spent the hour or two after supper reading among their books and magazines. She said to me one day with a beautifully serious look, "Charlie, I think you're going to make something of yourself." Until then Mary had been the only one to hand me anything like that. I was in bed every night at eight-thirty. I had come back to Galesburg weighing one hundred and thirty-six pounds and on the Schwarz farm I gained sixteen pounds.

About the middle of February I was sorry to leave the Schwarz home. I hired out to a blank-faced Swede to learn the painter's trade. At last it had come my way, a chance to learn a trade. A few of the ten-hour working days I was trusted to put on the first coat of paint. But most of the time I scraped and sandpapered. I climbed ladders outside of houses and stepladders inside and pushed sandpaper over wood to make it smooth for the painter. The boss was a man spare of words. My "Good morning" would bring a grunt from him. He believed in work without talk and toil without laughter. Once when he caught me singing his face had the look of a pickle fresh out of vinegar.

Each morning six days a week I was there at seven o'clock ready to wear out more sandpaper making more boards smooth for the boss and another painter. Not as much as a half-day a week did I swing a brush to put on a first coat. How long would this go on till they would let me put on a second and last coat?

On the night of February 15, 1898, I went to bed at nine-thirty. Not until later did I know that at two o'clock that morning the Secretary of the Navy in Washington heard a knock at the door that woke him and he was handed a telegram that nearly keeled him over. He got a White House watchman on the phone and told him to wake the President. On the phone Mr. McKinley heard the telegram read to him: "MAINE BLOWN UP IN HAVANA HARBOR AT NINE-FORTY TONIGHT. MANY WOUNDED AND DOUBTLESS MORE KILLED OR DROWNED." The *Maine* was a first-class battleship and of her three hundred and fifty-two officers and men, two hundred and sixty were dead and the ship had settled to the harbor bottom.

As the days went by and I went on sandpapering, I believed what I read and heard—that the same Spanish government whose General Weyler had killed thousands of Cuban patriots wanting independence and a republic had a hand in blowing up the *Maine*. I learned later that nobody knows how the *Maine* was exploded, whether some man did it or it was an act of God. I was going along with millions of other Americans who were about ready for a war to throw the Spanish government out of Cuba and let the people of Cuba have their republic. If a war did come, I knew what I would do. Across March and early April while the country roared with excitement, I went on sandpapering and thinking but I didn't tell my blank-faced boss what I was thinking.

President McKinley declared war and on April twenty-sixth I was sworn into Company C., Sixth Infantry Regiment of Illinois Volunteers, for two years of service. The regiment had been part of the State Militia. Company C was a living part of Galesburg, had its drill hall, marched in uniform with rifles and bayonets on public occasions, and went to Springfield once a year for regimental maneuvers. The company needed a dozen recruits to fill its quota and I was among the earliest. I knew most of the privates and had worked for Corporal

Cully Rose at the Auditorium. About three-fourths of the members were from Galesburg and the rest from farms and country towns around Galesburg. They elected their own officers and you could hear fellows say, "No West Pointers in his regiment."

When I quit my job and told the family I was going to be a soldier they were sad and somewhat puzzled, but they knew they couldn't stop me. Mart spoke for the family, "We'd like the honor of having a United States soldier in the family but we don't want you to be killed." I said it might not be a real war and if it was I might not get shot because some soldiers always come back home. And besides, having seen the West I would now see the East and maybe the Atlantic Ocean and Cuba. The family were all there, with hundreds of other families, when the train carrying Company C pulled out from the Q. depot, now the "Burlington station."

On the fair grounds at Springfield we were quartered in an immense brick building used for livestock exhibits. Where prize milk cows and blue-ribbon bulls had slept on straw we likewise had straw under our blankets in late April and early May. We were not lacking the lads who could moo like a Guernsey cow or bellow like a Holstein bull. While still in civilian clothes I was handed a Springfield rifle and put through the manual of arms and company drill.

In about ten days I slid into a uniform, a heavy blue wool shirt, a coat of dark blue with brass buttons that went to the throat, pants of a light-blue wool cloth double as thick as the coat cloth. This was the same uniform the privates under Grant and Sherman had worn thirty-five years before, intended for wear in those border states of the South where snow fell and zero weather might come as at Fort Donelson the night Grant attacked. The little cap wouldn't shed rain from your ears, and above the stiff black visor it ran flat as though your head should be flat there. I felt honored to wear the uniform of famous Union armies and yet I had mistrust of it.

In a big room of the state-capitol building a hundred of us passed before an examining surgeon, a German with a pronounced accent and a high falsetto voice. He was no stickler for regulations, this surgeon. When our friend Joe Dunn came he was found to be an inch or two short of the required height. The tears began running down Joe's face. The surgeon looked toward officers near by and they gave him a nod. And he wrapped the measuring tape around a finger, measured again and found that Joe would pass.

We roamed around the capital, walked past the governor's house, out past the home of Abraham Lincoln. On the train to Washington

rumors ran thick and fast about how soon we would be shooting Spaniards. On the day coaches we each had a wicker-covered seat to sit in and to take our night's sleep in. Canned beans, canned salmon, bread and coffee, were the rations. At some stations crowds met the train with cheers and smiles. The train arrived in Washington and the night was dark when it was shunted to Falls Church, Virginia. We marched two miles to level ground with underbrush and woods around it. We put up tents and slept on the ground, two soldiers to a tent. The next morning we went to the woods, cut saplings with crotched sticks and branches and made bunks to lay our blankets on.

I was in luck to have for a tent mate Andrew Tanning, as clean, scrupulous and orderly a corporal as ever served Uncle Sam. He was born in Sweden, had a prim face, a small mouth with a neat small mustache, and at no moment in our tent bunks at arm's length from each other did he ever let out one echo of a snore. Twice a week he wrote letters to his fine Swede girl in Galesburg whom he later married. Next to her he loved his Springfield rifle, and he kept it spotless. He took for himself the number of his rifle and would enter the tent saying, "Here comes Old Thirty-eight." He had belonged to Company C for two years and was a member of the Monarch Club, so I had danced with his sweetheart, Amanda Hanson, and her sister Tillie who was slim and in a waltz light as a white feather in a blue wind. Andy had been houseman of the Union Hotel when I was its barbershop porter. So we had plenty to talk about.

Across late May and all of June we drilled. We filled our canteens from a piped water supply and washed our shirts, socks, and underclothing at a murky creek in the woods. Most of the time we ate field rations as though we were in a campaign, bean soup and pork and beans more often than any other items. Our company cook—Arthur Metcalf, with his moon face and wide smiling mouth—was a prize. He did the best he could with what the War Department, through its quartermasters, let him have. I saw him one morning patiently cut away from a flitch of pork about a quarter of it that was alive with maggots. This was seven miles from the City of Washington where the Department of War had its office.

Our captain was Thomas Leslie McGirr, a second-rank Galesburg lawyer, a tall heavy man with a distinct paunch, heavy jaws, and a large mustache slightly graying. He kept by him a large yellow-haired St. Bernard dog named Smuggler, who in sight of the men was occasionally fed juicy sirloin steaks. Our first lieutenant was Conrad Byloff, my classmate in the Seventh Ward school, who had learned the boilermaker's trade working for the Q. His father had been a captain in the Swedish army, and Con himself seemed to be a born commander. The men had depths of affection for him; he could be stern giving commands, but he never drilled us without giving us a smile that said we could get fun out of what we were doing. Our second lieutenant was Daniel K. Smyth, a scholar and a gentleman ever considerate of his men.

Of the nine sergeants and eleven corporals I couldn't think of one I hated. How can you possibly forget a first sergeant who trains his voice every day by six and eight times calling off a hundred names? After a few weeks some of the men without looking in a book could call the roll from Benjamin Anderson to Henry Clay Woodward as smoothly as F. Elmer Johnson, first sergeant, who kept records, read orders, and was the hardest-worked man in the company. Corporal Ed Peckenpaugh was up and down the company street and only the hard of hearing failed to get his baritone giving out "I Guess I'll Have to Telegraph My Baby." Corporal James Switzer was the company bugler, a handsome boy of seventeen, nicknamed "Mim."

Ten of our company were Knox students and two were from Lombard; twenty or more were farm boys. At least twenty had had fathers, uncles, or near kinsmen in the Civil War. All had mixed motives in enlisting. Love of adventure, or a curiosity about facing dangers and standing hardships was one and, I would judge, the outstanding one. A mystic love of country and the flag was there in degree among most of the men. Breaking away from a monotonous home environment to go where there was excitement could be read in the talk of some fellows. At least two of the older men had troublesome wives at home. The hope of pensions after service was sometimes definitely mentioned. Over all of us in 1898 was the shadow of the Civil War and the men who fought it to the end that had come only thirty-three years before our enlistment. Our motives were as mixed as theirs. In the lonely hours of guard duty you could study about why you had enlisted.

On leave for a day we walked two miles to Falls Church, took a trolley to Washington, saw the Capitol and walked past the White House. I had my first look at the Ford Theatre outside and inside and the outside of the Peterson House across the street.

For our State Militia caps we got felt hats with wide brims, and to replace our Springfield rifles we were issued Krag-Jörgensens. July sixth saw hustling and gabble. We began riding an Atlantic Coast Line train across Virginia and North Carolina to Charleston, South Carolina. We had our first look at tobacco and cotton growing, at the mansions, cabins, and hovels of the South, and at stations here and there men selling bottles of "cawn lickah" that had the color of rain water. We slept overnight in our coach seats and the next day quartered in big cotton warehouses on the wharf. We went swimming next to the wharf, and you could see the Illinois prairie boys taking mouthfuls of Atlantic Ocean water to taste it, then calling to each other, "It *is* salt, isn't it?" As we strolled around Charleston in our Civil War uniforms, the people were warmhearted and cordial. Restaurants and saloons refused to take our money for what they served us. Negroes stood quietly to one side and took off their hats to us. We had been issued hardtack, tough and flat biscuits that were as good as money. On a dare, a Southern Belle gave one of our boys a big resounding kiss for one hardtack.

We saw lying at anchor the *Rita,* a lumber-hauling freighter, the first ship our navy had captured from the Spanish. Six companies of the

Sixth Illinois boarded her on July eleventh, each man given a bunk made of new rough lumber. Running your bare arm or leg over it, you met splinters. The air below was heavy, warm and humid. On clear nights several hundred men brought their blankets up and covered the upper deck as they slept. The first day out one man said, "This tub rolls like a raw egg in a glass of whisky." One of the seasick said to another, "Why is your face so lemon-green?" The rations were mostly cold canned beans and canned salmon. The day or two when canned tomatoes were issued we called holidays. The band played every day and men were thankful. A waterspout was sighted one day, one shark and a few flying fish another day, and the landlubbers felt this was part of what they had come for.

The *Rita* arrived in Guantánamo Bay, Cuba, on the evening of July seventeenth, our band playing and cheers coming to us from the decks of famous battleships, the *Oregon,* the *Indiana,* the *Iowa,* and more cheers from cruisers and torpedo boats. In the morning Colonel Jack Foster and staff officers went ashore and came back soon with word that Santiago was taken and we wouldn't be put ashore to fight in Cuba. Some men were disappointed; others were satisfied. Also, it was reported, there were ashore some four hundred troop cases of yellow fever and Colonel Jack had been ordered to get back to the *Rita* at once.

We lay at anchor a few days, and when we sailed out of Guantánamo Bay, rumors ran that we were going to Porto Rico. If we had been reading United States newspapers, we would have believed we were going to land at Cape Fajardo near San Juan, the capital of Porto Rico. But about halfway to Porto Rico, General Nelson A. Miles, commander of the three thousand men in this expedition, changed his mind. Instead of landing at Cape Fajardo on the north coast we would land on the south coast of Porto Rico. The idea came to him that since the War Department had told the newspapers and the newspapers had told the world where his expedition was going to land and march and fight it might be safer and easier to land somewhere else where he wasn't expected. There were those who said afterward that to attack the fortified harbor of San Juan would have required the navy and the guns of the fleet and General Miles as an army man preferred to land on the south coast and have the army take over the island from the south so that in time San Juan wouldn't have much of an island to govern. We heard later too that the Secretary of War and many others in the United States were stupefied to learn that General Miles had changed his mind and begun operations on the south coast.

Soon after daylight on July twenty-fifth we sighted a harbor and moved into it. Ahead we saw gunfire from a ship and landing boats filled with blue-jackets moving toward shore. We were ordered to put on our cartridge belts and with rifles get into full marching outfits. We heard shooting, glanced toward shore and saw white puffs of smoke while we stood waiting our turns to climb down rope ladders into long boats called lighters. We were rowed to a shallow beach where we dropped into water above our hips. Holding rifles over our heads, we waded ashore.

We were in Guánica, a one-street town with palm and coconut trees new to us. We expected to be ordered into action against Spanish troops somewhere in the town or near-by hills. We were marched to a field near the town where we waited over noon and afternoon. We ate our supper of cold canned beans and hardtack and soon were ordered to march. When we came to a halt we waited in the dark and heard shots that seemed not far away. This was the one time on that island when most of us expected to go into battle. And it didn't happen. We waited and marched back to our field near Guánica.

In the morning we marched to Yauco and on to Ponce, finding those towns surrendered. We camped in a wooded ravine two nights. After the first two or three hours of mosquito bites, sleeping in our underwear and barefoot, we put on our pants, wool shirts, and socks, for all of the moist heat. They were large, ravenous, pitiless mosquitoes. "They came with bugles sounding mess call," said one man with a swollen face. I had one eye closed by the swellings around it. Some fellows had both eyes closed. On the second night I followed others in wrapping my rubber poncho around my head. After an hour I would wake with an aching head from foul air breathed over too many times. I would throw the poncho off, beat away the mosquitoes, wrap the poncho around my head again, then sleep till awakening with a headache—and repeat.

On roads and streets as we marched were barefooted men and women smiling and calling to us *"Puerto Rico Americano."* For four hundred years this island had been run by a Spanish government at Madrid. Now it was to be American and it was plain that the island common people liked the idea and had more hope of it. More than once we saw on the roadside a barefoot man wearing only pants, shirt, and hat, eating away at an ear of parched corn. We saw knee-high children wearing only a ragged shirt, and their little swollen bellies told of not enough food and not the right kind.

We camped at Ponce a few days and then began a march up mountain roads. The August tropic heat was on. We carried cartridge belt, rifle, bayonet, blanket roll, half a canvas pup tent, haversack with rations, a coat. We still wore the heavy blue-wool pants of the '65 Army of the Potomac and thick canvas leggings laced from ankles to knees. On one halt after another there were men tearing their blankets in two so as to lessen weight to carry. I tore a third of mine away. Some let the whole blanket go. Men fell out, worn-out, and there were sunstroke cases. It was an eight-mile march upgrade. We halted for the night on a slope above the road. We were sleeping and all was quiet about midnight. Suddenly came a shriek. Then a series of yells and shrieks and several companies of men were rushing headlong down the slope to the road. Men sleeping or just awakened were trampled and bruised. It was found that one of the bullocks hauling carts loaded with supplies and ammunition had got loose and hunting for grass had tramped on a sleeper who gave the first piercing shriek that was taken up by others. We went up the slope and back to our sleep calling it the "First Battle of Bull Run."

We camped on a slope on the edge of Adjuntas, where we saw the American flag run up. Cook Metcalf over a long afternoon had boiled a tinned beef we named "Red Horse." For all the boiling it was stringy and tasteless. We set up our pup tents, laid our ponchos and blankets on the ground, and went to sleep in a slow drizzle of rain. About three o'clock in the morning there was a heavy downpour that kept up, and the downhill water soaked our blankets. We got out of our tents, wrung our blankets as dry as we could and threw them with ponchos over our shoulders. Then a thousand men stood around waiting for daylight and hoping the rain would let up. When daylight came Metcalf managed some hot pork and beans with coffee. Midmorning the sun came out and we dried and marched on to Utuado.

There at Utuado came news, "The protocol has been signed and peace is declared and we are ordered back to Ponce." Marching down the mountain roads we had climbed came easy along with rumors that we would take transports home from Ponce. We were lighthearted and cried, "Hurrah for the protocol!" It was a new funny word we liked. We slept a night in a building used for drying coffee. Each man fitted nicely into a dry bin enclosure rich with a coffee smell.

At Ponce many of us weighed to see what we had sweated and groaned out. All but a half-dozen men had lost weight. The scales said my one hundred and fifty-two pounds in April had gone down to one hundred and thirty pounds in August. Many were gaunt and thin, with a slightly yellow tint on the skin. Uniforms were fading, here and there ragged and torn. Hats had holes in them.

Our transport with the whole Sixth Illinois sailed for New York. We were divided into messes of eight men for rations. A tin of "Red Horse" would be handed to one man who opened it. He would put it to his nose, smell of it, wrinkle up his face, and take a spit. The next man would do the same, and the next till the eight men of the mess had smelled, grimaced, and spit. Then that tin of "Red Horse" was thrown overboard for many of the fishes of the Atlantic Ocean who might like it. Somehow we got along on cold canned beans, occasional salmon, and the reliable hardtack. What we called "Red Horse" soon had all the country scandalized with its new name of "Embalmed Beef."

On the transport we went through a ceremonial we had gone through many times before. A circle of men might be sitting on deck talking and jollying when one would call out "Shirts off! Time for inspection!" Then each man would run his eyes over all parts of the shirt, especially the seams, pick off the gray backs and crush them. Underwear and pants were more of a problem. In camp we boiled them occasionally when there was time and a big kettle of water.

When Richard Harding Davis wrote that for the troops under General Miles "Porto Rico was a picnic" he was remembering he had lived with the high commanding officers. When he wrote, "In comparison to the Santiago nightmare, the Porto Rican expedition was a *fête des fleurs,*" he was writing sober and awful historical fact. But only by comparison with that nightmare of blood, fever, and blunders was our campaign a feast of flowers. Mud and mosquitoes are not roses and poinsettias. Nor is sleeping in rain and marching in a baking sun carrying fifty pounds a feast. Few are the picnics where they eat from baskets holding canned beans, hardtack, and "Red Horse" and then take off their shirts and pluck out "seam squirrels." The war, though a small one, was the first in which the United States sent troops on ocean transports to fight on foreign soil and acquire island possessions. It was a small war edging toward immense consequences.

We sailed into the port of New York at night, docked at Weehawken, and in the morning saw a small crowd waving at us. On the dock I bought a loaf of white bread for a nickel and a quart of milk for another nickel. As I ate that bread and milk I felt that I had been an animal and was now a human being—it was so clean, tasty, delicious. We were in the newspapers, and as we roamed around New York City, men and women stopped us to ask where we had been, some to ask if we had news of regiments their boys were in, others to ask what we might want in the way of food or drink. People saw we looked lean, somewhat faded and ragged, tanned by sun and sea, hard-bitten by circumstance and insects. There was hospitality that made us feel good about the country. They acted like we were heroes. We had our doubts about that but we did know we could use more fresh victuals and boiling hot water with strong soap. At moments you just had to reach in to scratch at an armpit.

Again in a train of coaches with wicker seats we rode and slept, reached Springfield, Illinois, and camped there while our muster-out papers were arranged. When our train pulled into the Burlington station at Galesburg on September twenty-first we had been gone only five months but we looked like we had been somewhere. The station platform swarmed with a crowd that overran Seminary Street for a block to the north, and from there on to Main Street the sidewalks were thick with people. I caught my mother's face and others of the family laughing and waving their hands high. We made a company formation and marched to the Company C drill hall.

I went that evening with Mary to a farmhouse near Dahinda where she was teaching a country school. They put me in a room with a four-poster feather bed, and I sank into the feathers for a sleep. I tossed around a half-hour, then got out of the bed and in thirty seconds went to sleep on the rag carpet on the floor.

The next day I went home. Mart said, "Well, you didn't get killed, did you?" "No, they didn't give me a chance." "What did you learn?" Mart went on. "I learnt more than I can use." "Well," said Mart, "last year you were a hobo and this year a soldier. What's next with you?" "Maybe I'll go to college." "College! That'll be something!"

My father gave me a rich smile and handshake that wilted me. He said he stayed on the job the day before and when shopmen asked why he didn't take the day off, he said. "I will see my boy at home and he will tell me everything." Mother said it had been a big summer for him, with the shopmen and neighbors often asking, "How's the boy, Gus?" or, "Company C is getting a long ways from home, Gus. We hope your boy comes through all right." Mart told me such talk hit our Old Man deep and it seemed that now he was sure he was an Americanized citizen. I gave him fifty dollars of my muster-out money, which came to one hundred and three dollars and seventy-three cents in all.

We were in the newspapers that week. The Army and Navy League gave us a banquet at the Universalist Church and the Ladies' Society of the First Presbyterian Church another big dinner. The biggest affair was an oyster supper in the basement of the First Methodist Church where ex-Mayor Forrest F. Cooke, Congressman George W. Prince, and the Reverend W. H. Geistweit spoke. President Finley of Knox read a poem about our exploits—a freegoing poem with nice touches of humor, and a printed copy of it in a little book with red covers was presented to each member of Company C.

In nearly every life come sudden little events not expected that change its course. Two such events came for me. Private George R. Longbrake of Company C, whose back yard on Brooks Street touched our back yard on Berrien, had spoken to me on the transport about my going to Lombard, now a university, where he had been a student for a year. He asked whether I would enter if, as he believed, they would give me free tuition for a year. I said yes. So after all the cheering and the church banquets were over, he came to me to say the arrangement had been cheerfully made at Lombard. Private Lewis W. Kay, one of the two Lombard students in Company C, had died of fever about the time of our muster-out.

Then came Wiz Brown saying there was a fire-department job vacant. The department had two "call men" who slept at the fire house at night and reported by telephone in the daytime if the fire whistle blew. If it was a big fire they bicycled to it as fast as their pedals would take them. A call man was paid ten dollars a month. "That's nice money, Cully, and I'm sure if I speak to Mayor Carney he'll appoint you," said Wiz. He appointed me. I bought a bicycle and a blue shirt with two rows of pearl buttons of silver-dollar size and a big collar that buttoned far down the chest. I began sleeping on the second floor of the Prairie Street fire house. We were sixteen men sleeping in one room. Alongside each iron frame bed was a pair of rubber boots with pants and when the alarm bell rang we stepped out of bed, pulled up the pants, ran to slide down a brass pole and hop on the chemical wagon or the hose cart. Chief Jim O'Brien gave me a glad hand and said, "Considering where you've been, Charlie, I think you'll make a good fireman."

I enrolled at Lombard for classes in Latin, English, inorganic chemistry, elocution, drama, and public speaking. They had an "elective system," and that was what I elected. In a few days I would report at eight o'clock in the morning for a class in Latin under Professor Jon W. Grubb. Years back I had seen him milk a cow and drive her to pasture. I thought it would be interesting to study Caesar's *Commentaries* with a professor who could wear overalls and milk a cow. I would have to leave class when the fire whistle blew but that wasn't often enough to bother either the class or the professor.

I was going to get an education. I remembered Lottie Goldquist saying you could never get enough of it.

❀ ABE LINCOLN
GROWS UP

❁ ❁ ❁

Chapter I

IN THE YEAR 1776, when the thirteen American colonies of England gave to the world that famous piece of paper known as the Declaration of Independence, there was a captain of Virginia militia living in Rockingham County, named Abraham Lincoln.

He was a farmer with a 210-acre farm deeded to him by his father, John Lincoln, one of the many English, Scotch, Irish, German, Dutch settlers who were taking the green hills and slopes of the Shenandoah Valley and putting their plows to ground never touched with farming tools by the red men, the Indians, who had held it for thousands of years.

The work of driving out the red men so that the white men could farm in peace was not yet finished. In the summer of that same year of 1776, Captain Abraham Lincoln's company took a hand in marches and fights against the Cherokee tribes.

It was a time of much fighting. To the south and west were the red men. To the north and east were white men, the regiments of British soldiers, and Virginia was sending young men and corn and pork to the colonial soldiers under General George Washington. Amos Lincoln, a kinsman of Abraham, up in Massachusetts, was one of the white men who, the story ran, rigged out as Indians, went on board a British ship and dumped a cargo of tea overboard to show their disobedience, contempt, and defiance of British laws and government; later Amos was a captain of artillery in the colonial army.

There was a Hananiah Lincoln who fought at Brandywine under Washington and became a captain in the Twelfth Pennsylvania regiment; and Hananiah was a first cousin of Abraham. Jacob Lincoln, a brother of Abraham, was at Yorktown, a captain under Washington at the finish of the Revolutionary War. These Lincolns in Virginia came from Berks County in Pennsylvania.

Though they were fighting men, there was a strain of Quaker blood running in them; they came in part from people who wore black clothes only, used the word "thee" instead of "you," kept silence or spoke "as the spirit of the heart moved," and held war to be a curse from hell; they were a serene, peaceable, obstinate people.

Now Abraham Lincoln had taken for a wife a woman named Bathsheba Herring. And she bore him three sons there amid the green hills and slopes of the Shenandoah Valley, and they were named Mordecai, Josiah, and Thomas. And she bore two daughters, named Mary and Nancy.

This family of a wife and five children Abraham Lincoln took on horses in the year 1782 and moved to Kentucky. For years his friend, Daniel Boone, had been coming back from trips to Kentucky, sometimes robbed of all his deerskins and bearskins and furs of fox and mink, sometimes alone and without the lusty young bucks who had started with him for Kentucky. And listening to Boone's telling of how the valleys were rich with long slopes of black land and blue grass, how there were game and fish, and tall timber and clear running waters—and seeing the road near his farm so often filled with parties of men and families headed for the wilderness beyond the mountains—he began thinking about taking up land for himself over there. It was his for forty cents an acre. He wanted to be where he could look from his cabin to the horizons on all sides—and the land all his own—was that it? He didn't know. It called to him, that country Boone was talking about.

Boone and his friends had worn a trail following an old buffalo path down the Shenandoah Valley to Lexington and around to Cumberland Gap in Tennessee, then northwest into Kentucky. It had become more than a trail, and was called the Wilderness Road. It was the safest way to Kentucky because the British and the Indians still had a hold on the Ohio River water route, the only other way to reach Kentucky.

Moving to Kentucky had been in Abraham Lincoln's thoughts for some time, but he didn't finally decide to go until the state of Virginia started a land office and made new laws to help straighten out tangled land-titles in Kentucky.

While Bathsheba was still carrying in her arms the baby, Thomas, it happened that Abraham Lincoln sold his farm, and in accordance with the laws of Virginia she signed papers giving up her rights to her husband's land, declaring in writing on the 24th day of September, 1781, that "she freely and voluntarily relinquished the same without the Force threats or compulsion of her husband." Then they packed their belongings, especially the rifle, the ax, and the plow, and joined a party which headed down the Wilderness Road through Cumberland Gap and up north and west into Kentucky.

Abraham and Bathsheba (or Batsab) Lincoln sign their names
to a deed in the courthouse of Rockingham County, Virginia

Tall mountains loomed about them with long blue shadows at
sunup and sundown as they traveled, camped, broke camp, and traveled again. And as they watched the mountains they slanted their keen-
est eyes on any moving patch of shrub or tree—the red men who
ambushed enemies might be there.

There had been papers signed, and the land by law belonged to the
white men, but the red men couldn't understand or didn't wish to un-

derstand how the land was gone from them to the white men. Besides, the red men had been fighting among themselves for favorite hunting grounds and fishing waters; there had been hundreds of years of fighting; now they were fighting white men by the same weapons, ways, and ambushes as they fought red men. And so, though the scenery was good to look at, the white men traveling the Wilderness Road kept a keen eye on the underbrush and had scouts ahead at the turn of the road and scouts behind.

Some towns and villages then were paying a dollar to two dollars a piece for Indian scalps.

Coming through safe to Kentucky, Abraham Lincoln located on the Green River, where he filed claims for more than two thousand acres. He had been there three or four years when, one day as he was working in a field, the rifle shot of an Indian killed him. His children and his children's children scattered across Kentucky, Tennessee, Indiana, and Illinois.

Tom Lincoln, the child of Abraham and Bathsheba, while growing up, lived in different places in Kentucky, sometimes with his kith and kin, sometimes hiring out to farmers, mostly in Washington County, and somehow betweenwhiles managing to learn the carpenter's trade and cabinet-making. He bought a horse—and paid taxes on it. He put in a year on the farm of his uncle, Isaac Lincoln, on the Wautauga River in East Tennessee. He moved to Hardin County in Kentucky while still a young bachelor, and bought a farm on Mill Creek, paid taxes on the farm, kept out of debt, and once bought a pair of silk suspenders for a dollar and a half at a time when most men were using homemade hickory-bark galluses.

As Tom Lincoln came to his full growth he was about five feet, nine inches tall, weighing about 185 pounds, his muscles and ribs close-knit, so that one time a boy joking with him tried to find the places between his ribs but couldn't put a finger in between any place where a rib ended and the muscle began. His dark hazel eyes looked out from a round face, from under coarse black hair. He was a slow, careless man with quiet manners, would rather have people come and ask him to work on a job than to hunt the job himself. He liked to sit around and have his own thoughts.

He wasn't exactly lazy; he was sort of independent, and liked to be where he wasn't interfered with. A little slab of bacon with hoecake or a little corn-bread and milk every day, and he was satisfied. He drank whisky but not often. The sober Baptists saw more of him than those who were steady at licking up liquor. He was a wild buck at fighting, when men didn't let him alone. A man talked about a woman once in a way Tom Lincoln didn't like. And in the fight that came, Tom bit a piece of the man's nose off. His neighbors knew him as a good man to let alone. And his neighbors knew him for a good workman, a handy man with the ax, the saw, the drawknife, and the hammer. Though he was short-spoken, he knew yarns, could crack jokes, and had a reputation as a story-teller when he got started. He never had much time for the alphabet, could read some, and could sign his name.

Church meetings interested him. He had been to cabins on Sunday mornings; the worshipers sat where it was half dark. Windows hadn't been cut in the walls; light came in through the door; words of the sermon came from a preacher in half-shadows. And he had gone to service in the evening when the cabin was lighted by the burning logs of the fireplace. Sometimes he felt stirred inside when a young woman kneeling on the floor would turn a passionate, longing face to the roof of the cabin and call, "Jesus, I give everything to thee. I give thee all. I give thee all. I am wholly thine!"

He had heard different preachers; some he liked better than others; some he was suspicious of; others he could listen to by the hour. There was a Reverend Jesse Head he had heard preach over at Springfield in Washington County, and he had a particular liking for Jesse Head, who was a good chair-maker, a good cabinet-maker, and an active exhorter in the branch of the Methodist church that stood against Negro slavery and on that account had separated from the regular church. When Tom joined the Baptists it was in that branch of the church which was taking a stand against slavery.

❀ ❀ ❀

Chapter II

DURING THOSE YEARS when Tom Lincoln was getting into his twenties, the country in Hardin County and around Elizabethtown was still wilderness, with only a few farms and settlements. Kentucky had been admitted to the Union of states; there were places in the state where civilization had dented the wilderness; but it was still a country of uncut timber, land unknown to the plow, a region where wolves and bear, wild animals and the Indians still claimed their rights and titles, with tooth and fang, claw and club and knife.

They talked in Elizabethtown about Miles Hart, who lived near by, and how he was killed by the Indians after he had used up his powder, how his wife Elizabeth and her two children were taken by the Indians, and how, on an outdoor march with the Indians, she was sent away, as Indian squaws were, by herself, to build a fire in the snow and give birth to her child. The child lived six months, but its mother was several years in the hands of the Indians before a Frenchman bought her near Detroit and sent her back to her relatives in Kentucky, where she again married and was raising a family. It was nearly twenty years since Elder John Gerrard, the Baptist preacher, had come to Hardin County. He preached nine months, and then one day, when a hunting party was surprised by Indians, all got away except Elder Gerrard, who was lame, and whether the Indians killed him, burned him at the stake, or took him along as a slave, nobody ever heard. There were many things to talk about around Elizabethtown. There was a Negro living there called General Braddock, a free man; he had been given his freedom because, when his master's cabin was attacked by Indians, he had killed nine of the red men and saved the lives of his owner's family.

There was the time when Henry Helm and Dan Vertrees were killed by the Indians; a red man wrestled a gun away from a white man and had his war-ax raised to bring down and split the head of the white man; it was then Nicholas Miller, quick as a cat, made a jump, snatched the white man away and killed the Indian. One man who saw it, John Glenn, said, "Miller snatched the white man from the Indian as he would a chicken from a hawk." There was talk about how, even though the wilderness life was full of danger, men kept coming on, the Wilderness Road and the Ohio River bringing more and more settlers year by year, some speaking in one form or another the language of Daniel Boone, calling himself "an instrument ordained by God to settle the wilderness." Also there were those who knew that Dragging Canoe, chief of the Chickamauga tribe of Indians, after a powwow when white men and red signed papers at Wautauga, had pointed his finger northwest toward Kentucky, saying words translated as "Bloody ground! . . . And dark and difficult to settle." It seemed that the ground, the soil, and the lay of the land in Kentucky had an old name among the Indians as a land for war.

As the crossroads grew into settlements in Hardin County, there was hard feeling between the crowd around Elizabethtown and the settlers in the valley over near Hodgen's mill, about where the county seat should be located and the courthouse built. On election days, when the members of the county board were chosen, the voters clashed. The hard feeling lasted nearly ten years. At least fifty combats of fist and skull took place, though it was generally understood that the only time the fighting was not strictly fair and square rough-and-tumble combat was when a young man named Bruce tried to gash his enemies by kicking them with shoes pointed with sharp iron pieces shaped like the "gaffs" which are fastened to the feet of fighting cocks, Bruce himself being a rooster-fight sport.

The first jail in Elizabethtown cost the county $42.60. The sheriff was discouraged with it, and in 1797 a new jail was built, costing $700.00, with stocks and whipping-post. Many of the prisoners were in for debt and both white and black men were lashed on their naked backs at the public whipping-post. The stocks were built so that each prisoner had to kneel with his hands and head clamped between two grooved planks. If the prisoner was dead drunk he was laid on his back with his feet in the stocks and kept there till he was sober.

The same year the jail was built, it happened that a man in for debt set fire to it when the jailer was away; the prisoner was nearly roasted to death but was saved, though the jail burned down; after which he was indicted for arson, and acquitted because he was a first-rate bricklayer and the town needed his work.

The time of the grand "raisin' " of the courthouse in 1795 in the middle of August was remembered; on that day forty strong men raised the frames and big logs into place while many women and children looked on, and at noon the men all crowded into the Haycraft double log-house to eat hearty from loaves of bread baked in a clay oven, roast shotes, chickens, ducks, potatoes, roast beef with cabbage and beans, old-fashioned baked custard and pudding, pies, pickles, and "fixin's."

Grand juries held their sessions in the woods alongside the courthouse. In 1798 their entire report was, "We present Samuel Forrester for profane swearing"; on several occasions they mention Isaac Hynes, the sheriff, for "profane swearing." The sheriff was a distiller and his stillhouse was in one year recommended for use as the county jail.

When people spoke of "the time Jacob was hung," they meant the year 1796 and the Negro slave, Jacob, who was "reproved for sloth" and killed his owner with an ax; a jury fixed the value of the slave at 80 pounds, or $400; he broke jail, was taken again, and on hanging day the sheriff hired another black man "to tie the noose and drive the cart from under," leaving the murderer hanging in midair from the scaffold. A large crowd came in Sunday clothes, with lunch baskets, to see the law take its course.

If in that country they wished to speak of lighter things, they could talk about pancakes; it was a saying that a smart woman, a cook who was clever, could toss a pancake off the skillet up through the top of the chimney and run outdoors and catch it coming down. Eggs were five cents a dozen. And one year a defendant in a case at law got a new trial on showing that in his case the jury, after retiring and before agreeing on a verdict, "did eat, drink, fiddle, and dance." Such were some of the community human cross-weaves in the neighborhood where Tom Lincoln spent the years just before he married.

❁ ❁ ❁

Chapter III

TOM LINCOLN WAS looking for a woman to travel through life with, for better or worse. He visited at the place of Christopher Bush, a hard-working farmer who came from German parents and had raised a family of sons with muscle. "There was no back-out in them; they never shunned a fight when they considered it necessary; and nobody ever heard one of them cry 'Enough.' "

Also there were two daughters with muscle and with shining faces and steady eyes. Tom Lincoln passed by Hannah and gave his best jokes to Sarah Bush. But it happened that Sarah Bush wanted Daniel Johnston for a husband and he wanted her.

Another young woman Tom's eyes fell on was a brunette sometimes called Nancy Hanks because she was a daughter of Lucy Hanks, and sometimes called Nancy Sparrow because she was an adopted daughter of Thomas and Elizabeth Sparrow and lived with the Sparrow family.

Lucy Hanks had welcomed her child Nancy into life in Virginia in 1784 and had traveled the Wilderness Road carrying what was to her a precious bundle through Cumberland Gap and on into Kentucky. The mother of Nancy was nineteen years old when she made this trip, leaving Nancy's father back in Virginia. She could croon in the moist evening twilight to the shining face in the sweet bundle, "Hush thee, hush thee, thy father's a gentleman." She could toss the bundle into the air against a far, hazy line of blue mountains, catch it in her two hands as it came down, let it snuggle to her breast and feed, while she asked, "Here we come—where from?"

And while Nancy was still learning to walk and talk, her mother Lucy was talked about in and around Harrodsburg, Kentucky, as too free and easy in her behavior, too wild in her ways.

What was clear in the years that had passed was that Lucy Hanks was strong and strange, loved love and loved babies, had married a man she wanted, Henry Sparrow, and nine children had come and they were all learning to read and write under her teaching. Since she had married the talk about her running wild had let down.

After she married Henry Sparrow her daughter Nancy went under the roof of Thomas Sparrow, a brother of Henry, and Elizabeth Hanks Sparrow, a sister of Lucy. Under the same roof was an adopted boy named Dennis Hanks, a son of a Nancy Hanks who was one of three sisters of Lucy. There were still other Nancy Hankses in Hardin County and those who spoke of any Nancy Hanks often had to mention which one they meant.

Tom Lincoln had seen this particular Nancy Hanks living with the Sparrows and noticed she was shrewd and dark and lonesome. He had heard her tremulous voice and seen her shaken with sacred desires in church camp-meetings; he had seen her at preachings in cabins when her face stood out as a sort of picture in black against the firelights of the burning logs. He knew she could read the Bible, and had read in other books. She had seen a few newspapers and picked out pieces of news and read her way through.

Her dark skin, dark brown hair, keen little gray eyes, outstanding forehead, somewhat accented chin and cheek-bones, body of slender build, weighing about 130 pounds—these formed the outward shape of a woman carrying something strange and cherished along her ways of life. She was sad with sorrows like dark stars in blue mist. The hope was burned deep in her that beyond the harsh clay paths, the everyday scrubbing, washing, patching, fixing, the babble and the gabble of today, there are pastures and purple valleys of song.

She had seen tall hills there in Kentucky. She had seen the stark backbone of Muldraugh's Hill become folded in thin evening blankets with a lavender mist sprayed by sunset lights, and for her there were the tongues of promises over it all.

She believed in God, in the Bible, in mankind, in the past and future, in babies, people, animals, flowers, fishes, in foundations and roofs, in time and the eternities outside of time; she was a believer, keeping in silence behind her gray eyes more beliefs than she spoke. She knew . . . so much of what she believed was yonder—always yonder. Every day came scrubbing, washing, patching, fixing. There was so little time to think or sing about the glory she believed in. It was always yonder. . . .

The day came when Thomas Lincoln signed a bond with his friend, Richard Berry, in the courthouse at Springfield in Washington County, over near where his brother, Mordecai, was farming, and the bond gave notice: "There is a marriage shortly intended between Thomas Lincoln and Nancy Hanks." It was June 10, 1806. Two days later, at Richard Berry's place, Beechland, a man twenty-eight years old and a woman twenty-three years old came before the Reverend Jesse Head, who later gave the county clerk the names of Thomas Lincoln and Nancy Hanks as having been "joined together in the Holy Estate of Matrimony agreeable to the rules of the Methodist Episcopal Church."

After the wedding came "the infare," the Kentucky style wedding celebration. One who was there said, "We had bear-meat, venison, wild turkey and ducks, eggs wild and tame, maple sugar lumps tied on a string to bite off for coffee or whisky, syrup in big gourds, peach-and-honey; a sheep that two families barbecued whole over coals of wood burned in a pit, and covered with green boughs to keep the juices in; and a race for the whisky bottle."

The new husband put his June bride on his horse and they rode away on the red clay road along the timber trails to Elizabethtown. Their new home was in a cabin close to the courthouse. Tom worked at the carpenter's trade, made cabinets, door-frames, window sash, and coffins. A daughter was born and they named her Sarah. Tom's reputation as a solid, reliable man, whose word could be depended on, was improved after his quarrels with Denton Geoheagan.

He took a contract to cut timbers and help put up a new sawmill for Geoheagan; and when Geoheagan wouldn't pay he went to law and won the suit for his pay. Geoheagan then started two suits against Lincoln, claiming the sawmill timbers were not cut square and true. Lincoln beat him in both suits, and noticed that afterward people looked to him as a reliable man whose word could be depended on.

It was about this time the building of the third Hardin County jail was finished in Elizabethtown, with an old-time dungeon underground. The first jailer was Reverend Benjamin Ogden, who was a Methodist preacher, also a chair-maker and worker in wood.

In May and the blossom-time of the year 1808, Tom and Nancy with little Sarah moved out from Elizabethtown to the farm of George Brownfield, where Tom did carpenter work and helped farm.

The Lincolns had a cabin of their own to live in. It stood among wild crab-apple trees.

And the smell of wild crab-apple blossoms, and the low crying of all wild things, came keen that summer to the nostrils of Nancy Hanks.

The summer stars that year shook out pain and warning, strange laughters, for Nancy Hanks.

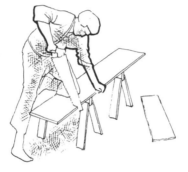

❁ ❁ ❁

Chapter IV

THE SAME YEAR saw the Lincolns moved to a place on the Big South Fork of Nolin's Creek, about two and a half miles from Hodgenville. They were trying to farm a little piece of ground and make a home. The house they lived in was a cabin of logs cut from the timber nearby.

The floor was packed-down dirt. One door, swung on leather hinges, let them in and out. One small window gave a lookout on the weather, the rain or snow, sun and trees, and the play of the rolling prairie and low hills. A stick-clay chimney carried the fire smoke up and away.

One morning in February of this year, 1809, Tom Lincoln came out of his cabin to the road, stopped a neighbor and asked him to tell "the granny woman," Aunt Peggy Walters, that Nancy would need help soon.

On the morning of February 12, a Sunday, the granny woman was there at the cabin. And she and Tom Lincoln and the moaning Nancy Hanks welcomed into a world of battle and blood, of whispering dreams and wistful dust, a new child, a boy.

A little later that morning Tom Lincoln threw some extra wood on the fire, and an extra bearskin over the mother, went out of the cabin, and walked two miles up the road to where the Sparrows, Tom and Betsy, lived. Dennis Hanks, the nine-year-old boy adopted by the Sparrows, met Tom at the door.

In his slow way of talking—he was a slow and a quiet man—Tom Lincoln told them, "Nancy's got a boy baby." ** A half-sheepish look was in his eyes, as though maybe more babies were not wanted in Kentucky just then.

The boy, Dennis Hanks, took to his feet, down the road to the Lincoln cabin. There he saw Nancy Hanks on a bed of poles cleated to a corner of the cabin, under warm bearskins.

She turned her dark head from looking at the baby to look at Dennis and threw him a tired, white smile from her mouth and gray eyes. He stood by the bed, his eyes wide open, watching the even, quiet breaths, of this fresh, soft red baby.

"What you goin' to name him, Nancy?" the boy asked.

"Abraham," was the answer, "after his grandfather."

Soon came Betsy Sparrow. She washed the baby, put a yellow petticoat and a linsey shirt on him, cooked dried berries with wild honey for Nancy, put the one-room cabin in better order, kissed Nancy and comforted her, and went home.

Little Dennis rolled up in a bearskin and slept by the fireplace that night. He listened for the crying of the newborn child once in the night and the feet of the father moving on the dirt floor to help the mother and the little one. In the morning he took a long look at the baby and said to himself, "Its skin looks just like red cherry pulp squeezed dry, in wrinkles."

He asked if he could hold the baby. Nancy, as she passed the little one into Dennis's arms, said, "Be keerful, Dennis, fur you air the fust boy he's ever seen."

** These words are from the Eleanor Atkinson interview with Dennis Hanks. Throughout this work conversational utterances are based word for word on sources deemed authentic.—The Author.

And Dennis swung the baby back and forth, keeping up a chatter about how tickled he was to have a new cousin to play with. The baby screwed up the muscles of its face and began crying with no let-up.

Dennis turned to Betsy Sparrow, handed her the baby and said to her, "Aunt, take him! He'll never come to much."

So came the birth of Abraham Lincoln that 12th of February in the year 1809—in silence and pain from a wilderness mother on a bed of corn-husks and bearskins—with an early laughing child prophecy he would never come to much.

And though he was born in a house with only one door and one window, it was written he would come to know many doors, many windows; he would read many riddles and doors and windows.

The Lincoln family lived three crop years on the farm where baby Abraham was born. It was a discouraging piece of land with yellow and red clay, stony soils, thick underbrush, land known as "barrens." It was called the Rock Spring farm because at the foot of one of its sloping hills the rocks curved in like the beginning of a cave; coats of moss spotted the rocks and rambled with quiet streaks of green over the gray; a ledge of rock formed a beckoning roof with room for people to stand under; and at the heart of it, for its center, was a never-ending flow of clear, cool water.

With the baby she called Abe in her arms, Nancy Hanks came to this Rock Spring more than once, sitting with her child and her thoughts, looking at running water and green moss. The secrets of the mingled drone and hush of the place gave her reminders of Bible language, "Be ye comforted," or "Peace, be still."

Cooking, washing, sewing, spinning, weaving, helping keep a home for a man and two babies, besides herself, in a one-room cabin, took a good deal of her time. If there were flies creeping over the face of the baby Abe, she had to drop her work and shoo the flies away. There were few hours in the year she was free to sit with her child and her thoughts, listening to the changing drone and hush of Rock Spring saying, "Be ye comforted," or "Peace, be still."

The baby grew, learning to sit up, to crawl over the dirt floor of the cabin; the gristle became bone; the father joked about the long legs getting longer; the mother joked about how quick he grew out of one shirt into another.

Sparrows and Hankses who came visiting said, "He's solemn as a papoose." An easy and a light bundle he was to carry when the family moved to a farm on Knob Creek, eight miles from Hodgenville, on the main highway from Louisville to Nashville.

❀ ❀ ❀

Chapter V

ON THE KNOB Creek farm the child Abraham Lincoln learned to talk, to form words with the tongue and the roof of the mouth and the force of the breath from lungs and throat. "Pappy" and "Mammy," the words of his people meaning father and mother, were among the first syllables. He learned what the word "name" meant; his name was Abraham, the same as Abraham in the Bible, the same as his grandfather Abraham. It was "Abe" for short; if his mother called in the dark, "Is that you, Abe?" he answered, "Yes, Mammy, it's me." The name of the family he belonged to was "Lincoln" or "Linkun," though most people called it "Linkern" and it was sometimes spelled "Linkhorn."

The family lived there on Knob Creek farm, from the time Abe was three or so till he was past seven years of age. Here he was told "Kaintucky" meant the state he was living in; Knob Creek farm, the Rock Spring farm where he was born, Hodgenville, Elizabethtown, Muldraugh's Hill, these places he knew, the land he walked on, was all part of Kentucky.

Yet it was also part of something bigger. Men had been fighting, bleeding, and dying in war, for a country, "our country"; a man couldn't have more than one country any more than he could have more than one mother; the name of the mother country was the "United States"; and there was a piece of cloth with red and white stripes having a blue square in its corner filled with white stars; and this piece of cloth they called "a flag." The flag meant the "United States." One summer morning his father started the day by stepping out of the front door and shooting a long rifle into the sky; and his father explained it was the day to make a big noise because it was the "Fourth of July," the day the United States first called itself a "free and independent" nation.

His folks talked like other folks in the neighborhood. They called themselves "pore" people. A man learned in books was "eddicated." What was certain was "sartin." The syllables came through the nose;

joints were "j'ints"; fruit "spiled" instead of spoiling; in corn-planting time they "drapped" the seeds. They went on errands and "brung" things back. Their dogs "follered" the coons. Flannel was "flannen," a bandanna a "bandanner," a chimney a "chimbly," a shadow a "shadder," and mosquitoes plain "skeeters." They "gethered" crops. A creek was a "crick," a cover a "kiver."

A man silent was a "say-nothin'." They asked, "Have ye et?" There were dialogues, "Kin ye?" "No, I cain't." And if a woman had an idea of doing something she said, "I had a idy to." They made their own words. Those who spoke otherwise didn't belong, were "puttin' on." This was their wilderness lingo; it had gnarled bones and gaunt hours of their lives in it.

Words like "independent" bothered the boy. He was hungry to understand the meanings of words. He would ask what "independent" meant and when he was told the meaning he lay awake nights thinking about the meaning of the meaning of "independent." Other words bothered him, such as "predestination." He asked the meaning of that and lay awake hours at night thinking about the meaning of the meaning.

❀ ❀ ❀

Chapter VI

SEVEN-YEAR-OLD Abe walked four miles a day going to the Knob Creek school to learn to read and write. Zachariah Riney and Caleb Hazel were the teachers who brought him along from A B C to where he would write the name "A-b-r-a-h-a-m L-i-n-c-o-l-n" and count numbers beginning with one, two, three, and so on. He heard twice two is four.

The schoolhouse was built of logs, with a dirt floor, no window, one door. The scholars learned their lessons by saying them to themselves out loud till it was time to recite; alphabets, multiplication tables, and the letters of spelled words were all in the air at once. It was a "blab school"; so they called it.

The Louisville and Nashville pike running past the Lincoln cabin had many different travelers. Covered wagons came with settlers moving south and west, or north to Ohio and Indiana; there were peddlers with knickknacks to spread out and tell the prices of; congressmen, members of the legislature meeting at Lexington, men who had visited Henry Clay at Ashland.

Coming back from a fishing trip, with one fish, Abe met a soldier who came from fighting in the Battle of New Orleans with General Jackson, and Abe, remembering his father and mother had told him to be good to soldiers, handed the soldier the one fish.

The Lincolns got well acquainted with Christopher Columbus Graham, a doctor, a scientist, who was beginning to study and write books about the rocks, flowers, plants, trees, and wild animals of Kentucky; Graham slept in the bed while the Lincolns slept on the floor of the cabin, more than once; he told in the evening talk about days camping with Daniel Boone, and running backward with Boone so as to make foot-tracks pointing forward to mislead the Indians; he talked about stones, leaves, bones, snake-skins he was carrying in a sack back to Louisville; he mentioned a young storekeeper at Elizabethtown, named John James Audubon, who had marvelous ways with birds and might some day write a great book about birds. The boy Abe heard traveling preachers and his father talk about the times when they held church meetings in cabins, and every man had his rifle by his side, and there were other men with rifles outside the cabin door, ready for Indians who might try to interrupt their Sabbath worship. And the boy never liked it when the talkers slung around words like "independent" and "predestination," because he lay awake thinking about those long words.

Abe was the chore-boy of the Knob Creek farm as soon as he grew big enough to run errands, to hold a pine-knot at night lighting his father at a job, or to carry water, fill the woodbox, clean ashes from the fireplace, hoe weeds, pick berries, grapes, persimmons for beer-making. He hunted the timbers and came back with walnuts, hickory and hazel nuts. His hands knew the stinging blisters from using a hoe-handle back and forth a summer afternoon, and in autumn the mash of walnut-stain that wouldn't wash off, with all the rinsing and scrubbing of Nancy Hanks's homemade soap. He went swimming with Austin Gollaher; they got their backs sunburnt so the skin peeled off.

Wearing only a shirt—no hat nor pants—Abe rode a horse hitched to a "bull-tongue" plow of wood shod with iron. He helped his father with seed corn, beans, onions, potatoes. He ducked out of the way of the heels of the stallion and brood mares his father kept and paid taxes on.

The father would ride away to auctions, once coming home with dishes, plates, spoons, and a wash basin, another time with a heifer, and again with a wagon that had been knocked down to the highest bidder for 8½ cents.

Abe and his sister picked pails of currants and blueberries for mother Nancy to spread in the sun to dry and put away for winter eating. There were wild grapes and pawpaws; there were bee trees with wild honey; there were wild crab-apples and red haws. If it was a good corn year, the children helped shell the corn by hand and put it between two big flag stones, grinding it into cornmeal. The creeks gave them fish to fry. Tom Lincoln took his gun and brought back prairie turkey, partridge, rabbit, sometimes a coon, a bear, or a deer; and the skins of these big animals were tanned, cut and sewed into shirts, trousers, moccasins; the coonskins made caps.

There were lean times and fat, all depending on the weather, the rains or floods, how Tom Lincoln worked and what luck he had fishing and hunting. There were times when they lived on the fat of the land and said God was good; other times when they just scraped along and said they hoped the next world would be better than this one.

It was wilderness. Life dripped with fat and ease. Or it took hold with hunger and cold. All the older settlers remembered winter in the year 1795, when "cold Friday" came; Kentucky was "cold as Canada," and cows froze to death in the open fields. The wilderness is careless.

Between the roadway over the top of Muldraugh's Hill and the swimming-hole where Abe Lincoln and Austin Gollaher ducked each other, there are tall hills more correctly called limestone bluffs. They crowd around Knob Creek and shape the valley's form. Their foundations are rocks, their measurements seem to be those of low mountains rather than hills. They seem to be aware of proportions and to suggest a quiet importance and secrets of fire, erosion, water, time, and many repeated processes that have stood them against the sky so that human settlers in the valley feel that around them are speakers of reserves and immensities.

The valley through which Knob Creek wanders there near Muldraugh's Hill, shooting its deep rushes of water when the hill rains flush the bottoms, has many keepers of the darker reticences of the crust of the earth and the changers that hold on to their lives there. That basic stream has a journal of its movement among pools inconceivably quiet in their mirrorings during days when the weather is fair and the elements of the sky at ease, and again of movement among those same pools when the rampages between the limestone banks send the water boiling and swirling. The naming of Muldraugh's Hill was a rich act in connotation, for it has whisperings of namelessly shrewd and beautiful wishes that the older and darker landscapes of Ireland breathe.

Trees crowd up its slopes with passionate footholds as though called by homes in the rocky soil; their climbings have covered sides and crests till they murmur, "You shall see no tall hills here unless you look at us." Caverns and ledges thrust their surprises of witchery and wizardry, of gnomes and passwords, or again of old-time intimations and analogues, memories of reckless rains leaving wave-prints to hint or say Muldraugh's Hill and the Knob Creek valley are old-timers in the making of the world, old-timers alongside of the two-footed little mover known as man. In the bottom lands the honeysuckle ranges with a strength nothing less than fierce; so deep are its roots that, unless torn away by the machines of man, the bees count on every year a boomer harvest of its honey-stuff; black and brown butterflies, spotted and streaked with scrolls and alphabets of unknown tongues from the world of wings—these come back every year to the honeysuckle.

Redbud, wild rose, and white daisies that look like scatterings of snow on green levels rise up with their faces yearly. Birds have made the valley a home; oncoming civilization has not shut off their hopes; homes for all are here; the martins learned a thousand years before the white man came that ten martins that fight with despair can kill and pick the eyes out of the head of a hawk that comes to slaughter and eat martins. And horses have so loved the valley, and it has so loved them in return, that some of the fastest saddle and riding nags remembered of men got their flying starts here.

Such was the exterior of the place and neighborhood where Abe Lincoln grew up from three to seven years of age, where he heard travelers talk, where he learned to write and sign his name, where, in fact, he first learned the meanings of names and how to answer, "Yes, it's me," if his mother called in the dark, "Is that you, Abe?"

Chapter VII

IN THE YEAR 1816 Tom Lincoln was appointed road surveyor. The paper naming him for that office said he was named in place of George Redman to repair the road "leading from Nolen to Pendleton, which lies between the Bigg Hill and the Rolling Fork." It further commanded "that all hands that assisted said Redman do assist Lincoln in keeping said road in repair." It was a pasty red clay road. That the county was beginning to think about good roads showed that civilization was breaking through on the wilderness. And that Tom Lincoln was named as road surveyor showed they were holding some respect for him as a citizen and taxpayer of that community. At the county courthouse the recorder of deeds noticed that Thomas Lincoln signed his name, while his wife, Nancy, made her mark.

Thomas Lincoln
Nancy X Lincoln
her
mark

Knob Creek settlers taking their corn to Hodgens Mill or riding to Elizabethtown to pay their taxes at the court or collect bounties on wolfskins at the county courthouse, talked a good deal about land-titles, landowners, landlords, land-laws, land-lawyers, land-sharks. Tom Lincoln about that time was chopping down trees and cutting brush on the Knob Creek land so as to clear more ground, raise corn on it and make a farm out of it. And he wasn't satisfied; he was suspicious that even if he did get his thirty acres cleared and paid for, the land might be taken away from him. This was happening to other settlers; they had the wrong kind of papers. Pioneers and settlers who for years had been fighting Indians, wolves, foxes, mosquitoes, and malaria had seen their land taken away; they had the wrong kind of papers. Daniel Boone, the first man to break a path from civilization through and into the Kentucky wilderness, found himself one day with all his rich, bluegrass Kentucky lands gone, not an acre of his big farms left; he had the wrong kind of papers; that was why he moved from Kentucky to Missouri.

Though Tom Lincoln was paying taxes on his thirty-acre farm, he was sued as a "tresspasser." He had to prove he wasn't a squatter—which he did. He went to court and won his suit. His little thirty-acre piece was only one of many pieces of a 10,000-acre tract surveyed in 1784 and patented to one man, Thomas Middleton, in 1786.

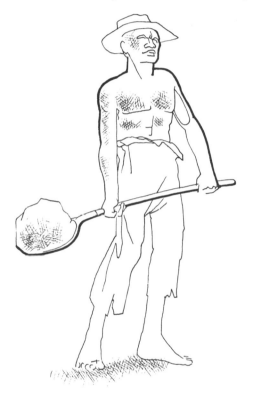

Poor white men were having a harder time to get along. Hardin County had been filling up with Negroes, slave black men, bought and sold among the rich and well-to-do. The Hodgens, La Rues, and other first families usually had one or two, or six or a dozen, Negroes. More than half the population of Hardin County were colored. And it seemed that as more slave black men were brought in, a poor white man didn't count for so much; he had a harder time to get along; he was free with the freedom of him who cannot be sold nor bought, while the black slave was free with the security of the useful horse, mule, cow, goat, or dog whose life and health is worth money to the owner.

Already, in parts of Kentucky and farther south, the poor white men, their women and children, were using the name of "nigger" for the slaves, while there were black slaves in families of quality who used the name of "po' w'ite" for the white people who owned only their clothes, furniture, a rifle, an ax, perhaps a horse and plow, and no land, no slaves, no stables, and no property to speak of.

While these changes were coming in Kentucky, the territory of Indiana came into the Union as a state whose law declared "all men are born equally free and independent" and "the holding any part of the human creation in slavery, or involuntary servitude, can only originate in usurpation and tyranny." In crossing the Ohio River's two shores, a traveler touched two soils, one where the buying and selling of black slaves went on, the other where the Negro was held to be "part of human creation" and was not property for buying and selling. But both soils were part of the Union of states.

Letters and reports reaching Hardin County about this time told of rich, black lands in Indiana, with more bushels of corn to the acre than down in Kentucky, Government land with clear title, the right kind of papers, for two dollars an acre. This helped Tom Lincoln to decide in the year 1816 to move to Indiana. He told the family he would build a flatboat, load the household goods on it, float by creeks to the Ohio River, leave the household goods somewhere along the river while he went afoot up into Indiana, located his land, and registered it. Then he would come back, and the family, afoot and on horseback, would move to the new farm and home.

❀ ❀ ❀

Chapter VIII

THE BOY, ABE, had his thoughts, some running ahead wondering how Indiana would look, some going back to his seven little years in Kentucky. Here he had curled around his mother's apron, watched her face, and listened to her reading the Bible at the cabin log-fire, her fingers rambling through his hair, the hands patting him on the cheek and under the chin. God was real to his mother; he tried to make pictures in his head of the face of God far off and away in the sky, watching Kentucky, Hodgenville, Knob Creek, and all the rest of the world He had made. His thoughts could go back to the first time on a winter night around the fire when he lay flat on his stomach listening to his father as he told about his brothers, Mordecai and Josiah, and their father, Abraham Lincoln, who had staked out claims for more than 2,000 acres of land on the Green River. One day Abraham Lincoln and his three boys were working in a field; all of a sudden the father doubled up with a groan of pain and crumpled to the ground, just after the boys had heard a rifle-shot and the whining of a bullet. "Indians," the boys yelled to each other.

And Mordecai ran to a cabin; Josiah started across the fields and woods to a fort to bring help, while Tom Lincoln—little knee-high Tom—stooped over his father's bleeding body and wondered what he could do. He looked up to see an Indian standing over him, and a shining bangle hanging down over the Indian's shoulder close to the heart.

The Indian clutched upward with his hands, doubled with a groan and crumpled to the ground; Mordecai with a rifle at a peephole in the cabin had aimed his rifle at the shining bangle hanging down close to the Indian's heart, and Tom was so near he heard the bullet plug its hole into the red man.

And for years after that Mordecai Lincoln hated Indians with a deadly hate; if he heard that Indians were loose anywhere in a half-day's riding, he took his best rifles, pistols, and knives, and went Indian-killing.

There was Dr. Christopher Columbus Graham from Louisville, telling how the Indians were chasing Daniel Boone, and Boone saw a grapevine climbing high up a big oak; and he cut the grapevine near the root, took a run and a swing and made a jump of forty feet, so the Indians had to lose time finding sight and smell of his foot-tracks again.

And there were caves, worth remembering about in that part of Kentucky, and especially the biggest one of all, Mammoth Cave, fifty miles south; they said a thousand wagons could drive in and there would be room for another thousand.

And there was the foxy Austin Gollaher, his playmate. Up a tree he climbed one time, Abe dropped a pawpaw down into a coonskin cap; he guessed it was Austin's cap he was putting a smear of pawpaw mash in, but Austin had seen the trick coming and changed caps. So he had to wipe the smear out of his own cap.

Once he was walking on a log across Knob Creek when the rains had raised the creek. Just under the log, and under his feet, was the rush of the yellow muddy water. The log was slippery; his feet slippery. His feet went up in the air; he tumbled to the bottom of the creek; he came up, slipped again, came up with his nose and eyes full of water, and then saw Austin Gollaher on the bank holding out a long pole. He took hold of the pole and Austin pulled him to the bank.

Maybe he would grow up; his feet would be farther away from his head and his chin if he grew up; he could pick apples without climbing a tree or throwing clubs—if he grew up. Maybe then, after growing up, he would know more about those words he heard men saying, "in-de-pend-ent," "pre-des-ti-na-tion." Daniel Boone—yes, he could understand about Daniel Boone—wearing moccasins and a buckskin shirt. But George Washington and Thomas Jefferson, and the President in Washington, James Madison—they were far off; they were sort of like God; it was hard to make pictures of their faces.

How many times he had gone to the family Bible, opened the big front cover, and peeped in at the page which tells what the book is! There were the words: "The Holy Bible, containing the Old and New Testaments, with Arguments prefixed to the Different Books and Moral and Theological Observations illustrating each Chapter, composed by the Reverend Mr. Osterwald, Professor of Divinity." And then pages and pages filled with words spelled out like the words in the spelling-book he had in school. So many words: heavy words—mysterious words!

About wolf heads, he could understand. He saw a man in Elizabethtown one time carrying two big wolf heads. The man had shot the wolves and was going to the courthouse, where they paid money for wolf heads. Yes, this he could understand. Wolves kill sheep and cattle in the fields; they come to the barns for pigs and chickens; he had heard them howling and sniffing on winter nights around the Knob Creek cabin and up the hills and gorges.

And there was his mother, his "mammy," the woman other people called Nancy or Nancy Hanks. . . . It was so dark and strange about her. There was such sweetness. Yet there used to be more sweetness and a fresher sweetness. There had been one baby they buried. Then there was Sally—and him, little Abe. Did the children cost her something? Did they pull her down? . . . The baby that came and was laid away so soon, only three days after it came, in so little a grave: that hurt his mother; she was sick and tired more often after that. . . . There were such lights and shadows back in her eyes. She wanted—

what did she want? There were more and more days he had to take care of her, when he loved to bring cool drinking water to her—or anything she asked for.

Well—a boy seven years old isn't supposed to know much; he goes along and tries to do what the big people tell him to do. . . . They have been young and seen trouble: maybe they know. . . . He would get up in the morning when they called him; he would run to the spring for water. . . . He was only seven years old—and there were lots of frisky tricks he wanted to know more about.

He was a "shirt-tail boy." . . . Three boys teased him one day when he took corn to Hodgen's Mill; they wouldn't be satisfied till he had punched their noses. . . . A clerk in the store at Elizabethtown gave him maple sugar to sit on a syrup keg and suck while his mother bought salt and flour. And the clerk was the only man he knew who was wearing store clothes, Sunday clothes, every day in the week. . . . The two pear trees his father planted on the Rock Spring farm . . . the faces of two goats a man kept down in Hodgenville . . . Dennis Hanks saying, "Abe, your face is solemn as a papoose."

It wouldn't be easy to forget that Saturday afternoon in corn-planting time when other boys dropped the seed-corn into all the rows in the big seven-acre field—and Abe dropped the pumpkin seed. He dropped two seeds at every other hill and every other row. The next Sunday morning there came a big rain in the hills; it didn't rain a drop in the valley, but the water came down the gorges and slides, and washed ground, corn, pumpkin seeds, and all clear off the field.

A dark blur of thoughts, pictures, memories and hopes moved through the head of little seven-year-old Abe. The family was going to move again. There was hope of better luck up north in Indiana. Tom's older brother, Josiah, was farming along the Big Blue River. Rich black corn-land was over there in "Indianny," more bushels to the acre than anywhere in Kentucky.

❀ ❀ ❀

Chapter IX

IN THE FALL of the year 1816, Abe watched his father cut down trees, cut out logs, and fasten those logs into a flatboat on Knob Creek. Abe ran after tools his father called for, sometimes held a hammer, a saw and a knife in his hands ready to give his father the next one called for. If his father said, "Fetch me a drink of water," the boy fetched; his legs belonged to his father. He helped carry chairs, tables, household goods, and carpenter's tools, loading them onto the flatboat. These, with four hundred gallons of whisky, "ten bar'ls," Tom had loaded onto the boat, made quite a cargo. Tom Lincoln, who was not

much of a drinking man, had traded his farm for whisky, which was a kind of money in that day, and $20.00 cash.

Nancy Hanks and Sarah and Abe stayed on the farm while the husband and father floated down Knob Creek to Salt River and into the Ohio River. Tom was out of luck when the flatboat turned over so that the tool chest, household goods and four barrels of whisky slid out of the boat. Most of the whisky and some of the other goods he managed to fish up from the river bottom. Then he crossed the Ohio River, landed on the Indiana side at Thompson's Ferry and left his whisky and household goods at the house of a man called Posey.

He started off on foot into the big timbers of what was then Perry County, later divided into Spencer County. He decided to live and to farm on a quarter-section of land on Little Pigeon Creek; he notched the trees with his ax, cleared away brush and piled it, as the Government land-laws required. This was his "claim," later filed at the Land Office in Vincennes, Indiana, as the Southwest Quarter of Section Thirty-two, Town Four South, Range Five West, to be paid for at $2.00 an acre. His Indiana homestead was now ready for a cabin and a family; he walked back to the Knob Creek home in Kentucky and told the family he reckoned they'd all put in the winter up in "Indianny."

They had fifty miles to go, in a straight line "as the crow flies," but about one hundred miles with all the zigzags and curves around hills, timbers, creeks and rivers.

Pots, pans, kettles, blankets, the family Bible, and other things were put into bags and loaded on two horses. Nancy and Sarah climbed on one horse, Tom and Abe on the other. When it was hard going for the horses, the father and mother walked. Part of the way on that hundred-mile ride made little Abe's eyes open. They were going deeper into the wilderness. In Kentucky there were ten people to the square mile and in Indiana only three. As Abe sat on the horse plodding along, he saw miles and miles of beeches, oaks, elms, hard and soft maples, hung and run over with the scarlet streamers and the shifting gray hazes of autumn.

Then they came to the Ohio River. The Frenchmen years before named it "La Belle Rivière," meaning it was a sheen of water as good to look at as a beautiful woman. There she lay—the biggest stretch of shining water his eyes had ever seen. And Abe thought how different it was from Knob Creek, which he could walk across on a log—if he didn't let his feet slip from under. They crossed the river, and at the house of the man called Posey they got a wagon, loaded the barrels of whisky and the household goods, and drove sixteen miles to their "claim." The trail was so narrow that a few times Tom Lincoln got off the wagon with an ax and cut brush and trees so the wagon could pass through. It was a hired wagon and horses they came with, and the wagon and horse-team were taken back to Posey.

Tom Lincoln, his wife, boy, and girl, had arrived on a claim at Little Pigeon Creek, without a horse or a cow, without a house, with a little piece of land under their feet and the wintry sky high over. Naked they had come into the world; almost naked they came to Little Pigeon Creek, Indiana.

The whole family pitched in and built a pole-shed or "half-faced camp." On a slope of ground stood two trees about fourteen feet apart, east and west. These formed the two strong corner-posts of a sort of cabin with three sides, the fourth side open, facing south. The sides and the roof were covered with poles, branches, brush, dried grass, mud; chinks were stuffed where the wind or the rain was trying to come through. At the open side a log-fire was kept burning night and day. In the two far corners inside the camp were beds of dry leaves on the ground. To these beds the sleepers brought their blankets and bearskins.

Here they lived a year. In the summer time and fair weather, the pole-shed was snug enough. When the rainstorms or wind and snow broke through and drenched the place, or when the south or southwest wind blew the firesmoke into the camp so those inside had to clear out, it was a rough life.

The mother sang. Nancy Hanks knew songs her mother, Lucy, had heard in Virginia. The ballad of Fair Ellender told of the hero coming home with the Brown Girl who had lands and gold. Fair Ellender taunted: "Is this your bride? She seemeth me plagued brown." And for that, the Brown Girl leaped over a table corner and put a slim little knife through Fair Ellender's heart. Then out came the hero's sword and he cut off the Brown Girl's head and "slung it agin the wall." Then he put the sword through his own heart.

And there was the ballad of Wicked Polly, who danced and ran wild and told the old folks, "I'll turn to God when I get old, and He will then receive my soul." But when death struck her down while she was young and running wild, she called for her mother, and with rolling eyeballs, cried, "When I am dead, remember well, your wicked Polly screams in hell."

Tom chopped logs for a cabin forty yards away while Abe did the best he could helping Nancy and Sarah trim the branches off the logs, cut brush, clear ground for planting, hoe weeds, tend the log-fire. The heaviest regular chore of the children was walking a mile away to a spring and carrying a bucket of water back home. Their food was mostly game shot in the woods near by; they went barefoot most of the year; in the winter their shoes were homemade moccasins; they were up with the sun and the early birds in the morning; their lighting at night was fire-logs and pine-knots. In summer and early fall the flies and mosquitoes swarmed.

In the new cabin Tom Lincoln was building, and on this Little Pigeon Creek farm, the Lincoln family was going to live fourteen years.

❀ ❀ ❀

Chapter X

AS ABE LINCOLN, seven years old, going on eight, went to sleep on his bed of dry leaves in a corner of the pole-shed there on Little Pigeon Creek, in Indiana, in the winter of 1816, he had his thoughts, his feelings, his impressions. He shut his eyes, and looking-glasses began to work inside his head; he could see Kentucky and the Knob Creek farm again; he could see the Ohio River shining so far across that he couldn't begin to throw a stone from one side to the other.

And while his eyes were shut he could see the inside of the pole-shed, the floor of earth and grass, the frying-pan, the cooking-pot, the water-pail he and his sister carried full of water from the spring a mile away, and the log-fire always kept burning. And sometimes his imagination, his shut eyes and their quick-changing looking-glasses would bring the whole outdoor sky and land indoors, into the pole-shed, into the big shifting looking-glasses inside of his head. The mystery of imagination, of the faculty of reconstruction and piecing together today the things his eyes had seen yesterday, this took hold of him and he brooded over it.

One night he tried to sleep while his head was working on the meaning of the heavy and mysterious words standing dark on the pages of the family Bible; the stories his mother told him from those pages; all the people in the world drowned, the world covered with water, even Indiana and Kentucky, all people drowned except Noah and his family; the man Jonah swallowed by a whale and after days coming out of the belly of the whale; the Last Day to come, the stars dropping out of the sky, the world swallowed up in fire.

And one night this boy felt the southwest wind blowing the log-fire smoke into his nostrils. And there was a hoot-owl crying, and a shaking of branches in the beeches and walnuts outside, so that he went to the south opening of the shed and looked out on a winter sky with a high quarter-moon and a white shine of thin frost on the long open spaces of the sky.

And an old wonder took a deeper hold on him, a wonder about the loneliness of life down there in the Indiana wilderness, and a wonder about what was happening in other places over the world, places he had heard people mention, cities, rivers, flags, wars, Jerusalem, Washington, Baltimore.

He might have asked the moon, "What do you see?" And the moon might have told him many things.

That year of 1816 the moon had seen sixteen thousand wagons come along one turnpike in Pennsylvania, heading west, with people hungry for new land, a new home, just like Tom Lincoln. Up the Mississippi River that year had come the first steamboat to curve into the Ohio River and land passengers at Louisville. The moon had seen the first steamboat leave Pittsburgh and tie up at New Orleans. New wheels, wagons, were coming, an iron horse snorting fire and smoke. Rolling-mills, ingots, iron, steel, were the talk of Pennsylvania; a sheet copper mill was starting in Massachusetts.

The moon could see eight million people in the United States, white men who had pushed the Indians over the eastern mountains, fighting to clear the Great Plains and the southern valleys of the red men. At Fallen Timbers and at Tippecanoe in Indiana, and down at the Great Bend of the Tallapoosa, the pale faces and copper faces had yelled and grappled and Weatherford had said, "I have done the white people all the harm I could; if I had an army I would fight to the last; my warriors can no longer hear my voice; their bones are at Talladega, Tallushatches, Emuckfaw, and Tohopeka; I can do no more than weep." The red men had been warned by Jefferson to settle down and be farmers, to double their numbers every twenty years as the white people did, the whites in "new swarms continually advancing upon the country like flocks of pigeons."

The moon had seen two men, sunburned, wind-bitten and scarred, arrive at the White House just four years before Abe Lincoln was born. The two men had been on a three-year trip, leaving Washington in 1802, riding and walking across the Great Plains, the Rockies and Sierras, to the Pacific Coast country, and then back to Washington. What those two, Lewis and Clark, had to tell, opened the eyes of white people to what a rich, big country they lived in. Out along that trail Jefferson could see "new swarms advancing like flocks of pigeons."

And how had these eight million people come to America, for the moon to look down on and watch their westward swarming? Many were children of men who had quarreled in the old countries of Europe, and fought wars about the words and ways of worshiping God and obeying His commandments. They were Puritans from England, French Huguenots, German Pietists, Hanoverians, Moravians, Saxons, Austrians, Swiss, Quakers, all carrying their Bibles. Also there were Ulster Presbyterians from North Ireland, and Scotch Presbyterians. They came by their own wish. Others who came not by their own wish were fifty thousand thieves and murderers sent from British prisons and courts. Dr. Samuel Johnson, the same man who said, "Patriotism is the last refuge of a scoundrel," had called Americans "a race of convicts." Convicted men in England, offered the choice of hanging or being shipped to America, had given the answer, "Hang me."

The moon had seen boys and girls by thousands kidnaped off the streets of English cities and smuggled across to America. And each year for fifty years there had come a thousand to fifteen hundred "indentured servants," men and women who had signed papers to work for a certain master, the law holding them to work till their time was up.

The moon had seen sailing-ships start from ports in Europe and take from six weeks to six months crossing the Atlantic. Aboard those ships often were "stench, fumes, vomiting, many kinds of sicknesses, fever, dysentery, scurvy, the mouth-rot, and the like, all of which come from old and sharply salted food and meat, also from bad and foul water."

Such were a few of the things known to the fathers and grandfathers of part of the eight million people in America that the moon was looking down on in the winter nights of 1816. And in the years to come the moon would see more and more people coming from Europe.

Seldom had the moon in its thousands of years of looking down on the earth and the human family seen such a man as the Napoleon Bonaparte whose bayonets had been going in Europe for fifteen years, shoving kings off thrones, changing laws, maps, books, raising armies, using them up, and raising new armies, until people in some regions were saying, "The red roses of this year grow from the blood-wet ground of the wars we fought last year." And at last the terrible Napoleon was caged, jailed, on the lonely island of St. Helena. Crying for the "liberty and equality" of France to be spread over the world, he had led armies to believe and dream of beating down all other armies in Europe that tried to stand against him. Then he was a lean shadow; he had become fat; the paunch stuck out farther than is allowed to conquerors. He had hugged armfuls of battle-flags to his breast while telling an army of soldiers, "I cannot embrace you all, but I do so in the person of your general." It hurt his ears when, captured and being driven in an open carriage, he heard sarcastic people along the streets mock at him with the call, "Long live the Emperor!" He would die far from home, with regrets, the first man to be Napoleonic.

When Napoleon sold to Jefferson the Great Plains between the Mississippi River and the Rocky Mountains, the moon saw only a few Indians, buffalo hunters and drifters, living there. The price for the land was fifteen million dollars; Jefferson had to argue with people who said the price was too high. Such things the moon had seen. Also, out of war-taxed and war-crippled Europe the moon could see steady lines of ships taking people from that part of the Round World across the water to America. Also, lines of ships sailing to Africa with whisky, calico, and silk, and coming back loaded with Negroes.

And as the wagons, by thousands a year, were slipping through the passes of the Allegheny Mountains, heading west for the two-dollar-an-acre Government land, many steered clear of the South; they couldn't buy slaves; and they were suspicious of slavery; it was safer to go farming where white men did all the work. At first the stream of wagons and settlers moving west had kept close to the Ohio River. Then it began spreading in a fan-shape up north and west.

The moon could see along the pikes, roads, and trails heading west, broken wagon-wheels with prairie grass growing up over the spokes and hubs. And near by, sometimes, a rusty skillet, empty moccasins, and the bones of horses and men.

In the hot dog-days, in the long rains, in the casual blizzards, they had stuck it out—and lost. There came a saying, a pithy, perhaps brutal folk proverb, "The cowards never started and the weak ones died by the way."

Such were a few of the many, many things the moon might have told little Abe Lincoln, nearly eight years old, on a winter night in 1816 on Little Pigeon Creek, in the Buckhorn Valley, in southern Indiana—a high quarter-moon with a white shine of thin frost on the long open spaces of the sky.

He was of the blood and breath of many of these things, and would know them better in the years to come.

❁ ❁ ❁

Chapter XI

DURING THE YEAR 1817, little Abe Lincoln, eight years old, going on nine, had an ax put in his hands and helped his father cut down trees and notch logs for the corners of their new cabin, forty yards from the pole-shed where the family was cooking, eating, and sleeping.

Wild turkey, ruffed grouse, partridge, coon, rabbit, were to be had for the shooting of them. Before each shot Tom Lincoln took a rifle-ball out of a bag and held the ball in his left hand; then with his right hand holding the gunpowder horn he pulled the stopper with his teeth, slipped the powder into the barrel, followed with the ball; then he rammed the charge down the barrel with a hickory ramrod held in both hands, looked to his trigger, flint, and feather in the touch-hole —and he was ready to shoot—to kill for the home skillet.

Having loaded his rifle just that way several thousand times in his life, he could do it in the dark or with his eyes shut. Once Abe took the gun as a flock of wild turkeys came toward the new log cabin, and, standing inside, shot through a crack and killed one of the big birds; and after that somehow, he never felt like pulling the trigger on game-birds. A mile from the cabin was a salt lick where deer came; there the boy could have easily shot the animals, as they stood rubbing their tongues along the salty slabs or tasting of a saltish ooze. His father did the shooting; the deer killed gave them meat for Nancy's skillet; and the skins were tanned, cut, and stitched into shirts, trousers, mitts, moccasins. They wore buckskin; their valley was called the Buckhorn Valley.

After months the cabin stood up, four walls fitted together with a roof, a one-room house eighteen feet square, for a family to live in. A stick chimney plastered with clay ran up outside. The floor was packed and smoothed dirt. A log-fire lighted the inside; no windows were cut in the walls. For a door there was a hole cut to stoop through. Bedsteads were cleated to the corners of the cabin; pegs stuck in the side of a wall made a ladder for young Abe to climb up in a loft to sleep on a hump of dry leaves; rain and snow came through chinks of the roof onto his bearskin cover. A table and three-legged stools had the top sides smoothed with an ax, and the bark-side under, in the style called "puncheon."

A few days of this year in which the cabin was building, Nancy told Abe to wash his face and hands extra clean; she combed his hair, held his face between her two hands, smacked him a kiss on the mouth, and sent him to school—nine miles and back—Abe and Sally hand in hand hiking eighteen miles a day. Tom Lincoln used to say Abe was going to have "a real eddication," explaining, "You air a-goin' to larn readin', writin', and cipherin'."

He learned to spell words he didn't know the meaning of, spelling the words before he used them in sentences. In a list of "words of eight syllables accented upon the sixth," was the word "incomprehensibility." He learned that first, and then such sentences as "Is he to go in?" and "Ann can spin flax."

Some neighbors said, "It's a pore make-out of a school," and Tom complained it was a waste of time to send the children nine miles just to sit with a lot of other children and read out loud all day in a "blab" school. But Nancy, as she cleaned Abe's ears in corners where he forgot to clean them, and as she combed out the tangles in his coarse, sandy black hair, used to say, "Abe, you go to school now, and larn all you kin." And he kissed her and said, "Yes, Mammy," and started with his sister on the nine-mile walk through timberland where bear, deer, coon, and wildcats ran wild.

Fall time came with its early frost, and they were moved into the new cabin, when horses and a wagon came breaking into the clearing one day. It was Tom and Betsy Sparrow and their seventeen-year-old boy, Dennis Hanks, who had come from Hodgenville, Kentucky, to cook and sleep in the pole-shed of the Lincoln family till they could locate land and settle. Hardly a year had passed, however, when both Tom and Betsy Sparrow were taken down with the "milk sick," beginning with a whitish coat on the tongue. Both died and were buried in October on a little hill in a clearing in the timbers near by.

Soon after, there came to Nancy Hanks Lincoln that white coating of the tongue; her vitals burned; the tongue turned brownish; her feet and hands grew cold and colder, her pulse slow and slower. She knew she was dying, called for her children, and spoke to them her last choking words. Sarah and Abe leaned over the bed. A bony hand of the struggling mother went out, putting its fingers into the boy's sandy black hair; her fluttering guttural words seemed to say he must grow up and be good to his sister and father.

So, on a bed of poles cleated to the corner of the cabin, the body of Nancy Hanks Lincoln lay, looking tired . . . tired . . . with a peace settling in the pinched corners of the sweet, weary mouth, silence slowly etching away the lines of pain and hunger drawn around the gray eyes where now the eyelids closed down in the fine pathos of unbroken rest, a sleep without interruption settling about the form of the stooped and wasted shoulder-bones, looking to the children who tiptoed in, stood still, cried their tears of want and longing, whispered "Mammy, Mammy," and heard only their own whispers answering, looking to these little ones of her brood as though new secrets had come to her in place of the old secrets given up with the breath of life.

And Tom Lincoln took a log left over from the building of the cabin, and he and Dennis Hanks whipsawed the log into planks, planed the planks smooth, and made them of a measure for a box to bury the dead wife and mother in. Little Abe, with a jackknife, whittled pinewood pegs. And then, while Dennis and Abe held the planks, Tom bored holes and stuck the whittled pegs through the bored holes. This was the coffin, and they carried it the next day to the same little timber clearing near by, where a few weeks before they had buried Tom and Betsy Sparrow. It was in the way of the deer-run leading to the saltish water; light feet and shy hoofs ran over those early winter graves.

So the woman, Nancy Hanks, died, thirty-six years old, a pioneer sacrifice, with memories of monotonous, endless everyday chores, of mystic Bible verses read over and over for their promises, and with memories of blue wistful hills and a summer when the crab-apple blossoms flamed white and she carried a boy-child into the world.

She had looked out on fields of blue-blossoming flax and hummed "Hey, Betty Martin, tiptoe, tiptoe"; she had sung of bright kingdoms by and by and seen the early frost leaf its crystals on the stalks of buttonweed and redbud; she had sung:

> You may bury me in the east,
> You may bury me in the west,
> And we'll all rise together in that morning.

❁ ❁ ❁

Chapter XII

SOME WEEKS LATER, when David Elkin, elder of the Methodist church, was in that neighborhood, he was called on to speak over the grave of Nancy Hanks. He had been acquainted with her in Kentucky, and to the Lincoln family and a few neighbors he spoke of good things she had done, sweet ways she had of living her life in this Vale of Tears, and her faith in another life yonder past the River Jordan.

The "milk sick" took more people in that neighborhood the same year, and Tom Lincoln whipsawed planks for more coffins. One settler lost four milch cows and eleven calves. The nearest doctor for people or cattle was thirty-five miles away. The wilderness is careless.

Lonesome and dark months came for Abe and Sarah. Worst of all were the weeks after their father went away, promising to come back.

Elizabethtown, Kentucky, was the place Tom Lincoln headed for. As he footed it through the woods and across the Ohio River, he was saying over to himself a speech—the words he would say to Sarah

Bush Johnston, down in Elizabethtown. Her husband had died a few years before, and she was now in Tom's thoughts.

He went straight to the house where she was living in Elizabethtown, and, speaking to her as "Miss Johnston," he argued: "I have no wife and you no husband. I came a-purpose to marry you. I knowed you from a gal and you knowed me from a boy. I've no time to lose; and if you're willin' let it be done straight off."

Her answer was, "I got debts." She gave him a list of the debts; he paid them; a license was issued; and they were married on December 2, 1819.

He could write his name; she couldn't write hers. Trying to explain why the two of them took up with each other so quickly, Dennis Hanks at a later time said, "Tom had a kind o' way with women, an' maybe it was somethin' she took comfort in to have a man that didn't drink an' cuss none."

Little Abe and Sarah, living in the lonesome cabin on Little Pigeon Creek, Indiana, got a nice surprise one morning when four horses and a wagon came into their clearing, and their father jumped off, then Sarah Bush Lincoln, the new wife and mother, then John, Sarah, and Matilda Johnston, Sarah Bush's three children by her first husband. Next off the wagon came a feather mattress, feather pillows, a black walnut bureau, a large clothes-chest, a table, chairs, pots and skillets, knives, forks, spoons.

Abe ran his fingers over the slick wood of the bureau, pushed his fist into the feather pillows, sat in the new chairs, and wondered to himself, because this was the first time he had touched such fine things, such soft slick things.

"Here's your new mammy," his father told Abe as the boy looked up at a strong, large-boned, rosy woman, with a kindly face and eyes, with a steady voice, steady ways. The cheek-bones of her face stood out and she had a strong jaw-bone; she was warm and friendly for Abe's little hands to touch, right from the beginning. As one of her big hands held his head against her skirt he felt like a cold chick warming under the soft feathers of a big wing. She took the corn-husks Abe had been sleeping on, piled them in the yard and said they would be good for a pig-pen later on; and Abe sunk his head and bones that night in a feather pillow and a feather mattress.

Ten years pass with that cabin on Little Pigeon Creek for a home, and that farm and neighborhood the soil for growth. There the boy Abe grows to be the young man, Abraham Lincoln.

Ten years pass and the roots of a tree spread out finding water to carry up to branches and leaves that are in the sun; the trunk thickens, the forked limbs shine wider in the sun, they pray with their leaves in the rain and the whining wind; the tree arrives, the mystery of its coming, spreading, growing, a secret not even known to the tree itself; it stands with its arms stretched to the corners the four winds come from, with its murmured testimony, "We are here, we arrived, our roots are in the earth of these years," and beyond that short declaration, it speaks nothing of the decrees, fates, accidents, destinies, that made it an apparition of its particular moment.

Abe Lincoln grows up. His father talks about the waste of time in "eddication"; it is enough to "larn readin', writin', cipherin' "; but the stanch, yearning stepmother, Sarah Bush Lincoln, comes between the boy and the father. And the father listens to the stepmother and lets her have her way.

❀ ❀ ❀

Chapter XIII

WHEN HE WAS eleven years old, Abe Lincoln's young body began to change. The juices and glands began to make a long, tall boy out of him. As the months and years went by, he noticed his lean wrists getting longer, his legs too, and he was now looking over the heads of other boys. Men said, "Land o' Goshen, that boy air a-growin'!"

As he took on more length, they said he was shooting up into the air like green corn in the summer of a good corn-year. So he grew. When he reached seventeen years of age, and they measured him, he was six feet, nearly four inches, high, from the bottoms of his moccasins to the top of his skull.

These were years he was handling the ax. Except in spring plowing-time and the fall fodder-pulling, he was handling the ax nearly all the time. The insides of his hands took on callus thick as leather. He cleared openings in the timber, cut logs and puncheons, split firewood, built pig-pens.

He learned how to measure with his eye the half-circle swing of the ax so as to nick out the deepest possible chip from off a tree-trunk. The trick of swaying his body easily on the hips so as to throw the

heaviest possible weight into the blow of the ax—he learned that.

On winter mornings he wiped the frost from the ax-handle, sniffed sparkles of air into his lungs, and beat a steady cleaving of blows into a big tree—till it fell—and he sat on the main log and ate his noon dinner of corn bread and fried salt pork—and joked with the gray squirrels that frisked and peeped at him from high forks of near-by walnut trees.

He learned how to make his ax flash and bite into a sugar-maple or a sycamore. The outside and the inside look of black walnut and black oak, hickory and jack oak, elm and white oak, sassafras, dogwood, grapevines, sumac—he came on their secrets. He could guess close to the time of the year, to the week of the month, by the way the leaves and branches of trees looked. He sniffed the seasons.

Often he worked alone in the timbers, all day long with only the sound of his own ax, or his own voice speaking to himself, or the crackling and swaying of branches in the wind, and the cries and whirs of animals, of brown and silver-gray squirrels, of partridges, hawks, crows, turkeys, sparrows, and the occasional wildcats.

The tricks and whimsies of the sky, how to read clear skies and cloudy weather, the creeping vines of ivy and wild grape, the recurrence of dogwood blossoms in spring, the ways of snow, rain, drizzle, sleet, the visitors of sky and weather coming and going hour by hour —he tried to read their secrets, he tried to be friendly with their mystery.

So he grew, to become hard, tough, wiry. The muscle on his bones and the cords, tendons, cross-weaves of fiber, and nerve centers, these became instruments to obey his wishes. He found with other men he could lift his own end of a log—and more too. One of the neighbors said he was strong as three men. Another said, "He can sink an ax deeper into wood than any man I ever saw." And another, "If you heard him fellin' trees in a clearin', you would say there was three men at work by the way the trees fell."

He was more than a tough, long, rawboned boy. He amazed men with his man's lifting power. He put his shoulders under a new-built corncrib one day and walked away with it to where the farmer wanted it. Four men, ready with poles to put under it and carry it, didn't need their poles. He played the same trick with a chicken house; at the new, growing town of Gentryville near by, they said the chicken house weighed six hundred pounds, and only a big boy with a hard backbone could get under it and walk away with it.

A blacksmith shop, a grocery, and a store had started up on the crossroads of the Gentry farm. And one night after Abe had been helping thresh wheat on Dave Turnham's place, he went with Dennis Hanks, John Johnston, and some other boys to Gentryville where the farm-hands sat around with John Baldwin, the blacksmith, and Jones, the storekeeper, passed the whisky jug, told stories, and talked politics and religion and gossip. Going home late that night, they saw something in a mud puddle alongside the road. They stepped over to see whether it was a man or a hog. It was a man—drunk—snoring—sleeping off his drunk—on a frosty night outdoors in a cold wind.

They shook him by the shoulders, doubled his knees to his stomach, but he went on sleeping, snoring. The cold wind was getting colder. The other boys said they were going home, and they went away leaving Abe alone with the snoring sleeper in the mud puddle. Abe stepped into the mud, reached arms around the man, slung him over his shoulders, carried him to Dennis Hanks's cabin, built a fire, rubbed him warm and left him sleeping off the whisky.

And the man afterward said Abe saved his life. He told John Hanks, "It was mighty clever of Abe to tote me to a warm fire that night."

So he grew, living in that Pigeon Creek cabin for a home, sleeping in the loft, climbing up at night to a bed just under the roof, where sometimes the snow and the rain drove through the cracks, eating sometimes at a table where the family had only one thing to eat— potatoes. Once at the table, when there were only potatoes, his father spoke a blessing to the Lord for potatoes; the boy murmured, "Those are mighty poor blessings." And Abe made jokes once when company came and Sally Bush Lincoln brought out raw potatoes, gave the visitors a knife apiece, and they all peeled raw potatoes, and talked about the crops, politics, religion, gossip.

Days when they had only potatoes to eat didn't come often. Other days in the year they had "yaller-legged chicken" with gravy, and corn dodgers with shortening, and berries and honey. They tasted of bear meat, deer, coon, quail, grouse, prairie turkey, catfish, bass, perch.

Abe knew the sleep that comes after long hours of work outdoors, the feeling of simple food changing into blood and muscle as he worked in those young years clearing timberland for pasture and corn crops, cutting loose the brush, piling it and burning it, splitting rails, pulling the crosscut saw and the whipsaw, driving the shovel-plow, harrowing, planting, hoeing, pulling fodder, milking cows, churning butter, helping neighbors at house-raisings, log-rollings, corn-huskings.

He found he was fast, strong, and keen when he went against other boys in sports. On farms where he worked, he held his own at scuffling, knocking off hats, wrestling. The time came when around Gentryville and Spencer County he was known as the best "rassler" of all, the champion. In jumping, foot-racing, throwing the maul, pitching the crowbar, he carried away the decisions against the lads of his own age always, and usually won against those older than himself.

He earned his board, clothes, and lodgings, sometimes working for a neighbor farmer. He watched his father, while helping make cabinets, coffins, cupboards, window frames, doors. Hammers, saws, pegs, cleats, he understood first-hand, also the scythe and the cradle for cutting hay and grain, the corn-cutter's knife, the leather piece to protect the hand while shucking corn, and the horse, the dog, the cow, the ox, the hog. He could skin and cure the hides of coon and deer. He lifted the slippery two-hundred-pound hog carcass, head down, holding the hind hocks up for others of the gang to hook, and swung the animal clear of the ground. He learned where to stick a hog in the under side of the neck so as to bleed it to death, how to split it in two, and carve out the chops, the parts for sausage grinding, for hams, for "cracklings."

Farmers called him to butcher for them at thirty-one cents a day, this when he was sixteen and seventeen years old. He could "knock a beef in the head," swing a maul and hit a cow between the eyes, skin the hide, halve and quarter it, carve out the tallow, the steaks, kidneys, liver.

And the hiding-places of fresh spring water under the earth crust had to be in his thoughts; he helped at well-digging; the wells Tom Lincoln dug went dry one year after another; neighbors said Tom was always digging a well and had his land "honeycombed"; and the boy, Abe, ran the errands and held the tools for the well-digging.

When he was eighteen years old, he could take an ax at the end of the handle and hold it out in a straight horizontal line, easy and steady—he had strong shoulder muscles and steady wrists early in life. He walked thirty-four miles in one day, just on an errand, to please himself, to hear a lawyer make a speech. He could tell his body to do almost impossible things, and the body obeyed.

Growing from boy to man, he was alone a good deal of the time. Days came often when he was by himself all the time except at breakfast and supper hours in the cabin home. In some years more of his time was spent in loneliness than in the company of other people. It happened, too, that this loneliness he knew was not like that of people in cities who can look from a window on streets where faces pass and repass. It was the wilderness loneliness he became acquainted with, solved, filtered through body, eye, and brain, held communion with in his ears, in the temples of his forehead, in the works of his beating heart.

He lived with trees, with the bush wet with shining raindrops, with the burning bush of autumn, with the lone wild duck riding a north wind and crying down on a line north to south, the faces of open sky and weather, the ax which is an individual one-man instrument, these he had for companions, books, friends, talkers, chums of his endless changing soliloquies.

His moccasin feet in the winter-time knew the white spaces of snowdrifts piled in whimsical shapes against timber slopes or blown in levels across the fields of last year's cut corn stalks; in the summertime his bare feet toughened in the gravel of green streams while he laughed back to the chatter of bluejays in the red-haw trees or while he kept his eyes ready in the slough quack-grass for the cow-snake, the rattler, the copperhead.

He rested between spells of work in the springtime when the upward push of the coming out of the new grass can be heard, and in autumn weeks when the rustle of a single falling leaf lets go a whisper that a listening ear can catch.

He found his life thrown in ways where there was a certain chance for a certain growth. And so he grew. Silence found him; he met silence. In the making of him as he was, the element of silence was immense.

❀ ❀ ❀

Chapter XIV

IT WAS A little country of families living in one-room cabins. Dennis Hanks said at a later time, "We lived the same as the Indians, 'ceptin' we took an interest in politics and religion."

Cash was scarce; venison hams, bacon slabs, and barrels of whisky served as money; there were seasons when storekeepers asked customers, "What kind of money have you today?" because so many sorts of wildcat dollar bills were passing around. In sections of timberland, wild hogs were nosing out a fat living on hickory nuts, walnuts, acorns; it was said the country would be full of wild hogs if the wolves didn't find the litters of young pigs a few weeks old and kill them.

Farmers lost thirty and forty sheep in a single wolf raid. Toward the end of June came "fly time," when cows lost weight and gave less milk because they had to fight flies. For two or three months at the end of summer, horses weakened, unless covered with blankets, under the attacks of horse-flies; where one lighted on a horse, a drop of blood oozed; horses were hitched to branches of trees that gave loose rein to the animals, room to move and fight flies.

Men and women went barefoot except in the colder weather;

women carried their shoes in their hands and put them on just before arrival at church meetings or at social parties.

Rains came, loosening the top soil of the land where it was not held by grass roots; it was a yellow clay that softened to slush; in this yellow slush many a time Abe Lincoln walked ankle-deep; his bare feet were intimate with the clay dust of the hot dog-days, with the clay mud of spring and fall rains; he was at home in clay. In the timbers with his ax, on the way to chop, his toes, heels, soles, the balls of his feet, climbed and slid in banks and sluices of clay. In the corn-fields, plowing, hoeing, cutting, and shucking, again his bare feet spoke with the clay of the earth; it was in his toenails and stuck on the skin of his toe-knuckles. The color of clay was one of his own colors.

In the short and simple annals of the poor, it seems there are people who breathe with the earth and take into their lungs and blood some of the hard and dark strength of its mystery. During six and seven months each year in the twelve fiercest formative years of his life, Abraham Lincoln had the pads of his foot-soles bare against clay of the earth. It may be the earth told him in her own tough gypsy slang one or two knacks of living worth keeping. To be organic with running wildfire and quiet rain, both of the same moment, is to be the carrier of wave-lines the earth gives up only on hard usage.

❁ ❁ ❁

Chapter XV

HE TOOK SHAPE in a tall, long-armed cornhusker. When rain came in at the chinks of the cabin loft where he slept, soaking through the book Josiah Crawford loaned him, he pulled fodder two days to pay for the book, made a clean sweep, till there wasn't a blade left on a cornstalk in the field of Josiah Crawford.

His father was saying the big boy looked as if he had been rough-hewn with an ax and needed smoothing with a jack-plane. "He was the ganglin'est, awkwardest feller that ever stepped over a ten-rail snake fence; he had t' duck to git through a door; he 'peared to be all j'ints."

His stepmother told him she didn't mind his bringing dirt into the house on his feet; she could scour the floor; but she asked him to keep his head washed or he'd be rubbing the dirt on her nice whitewashed rafters. He put barefoot boys to wading in a mud-puddle near the horse-trough, picked them up one by one, carried them to the house upside down, and walked their muddy feet across the ceiling. The mother came in, laughed an hour at the foot-tracks, told Abe he ought to be spanked—and he cleaned the ceiling so it looked new.

The mother said, "Abe never spoke a cross word to me in his life since we lived together." And she said Abe was truthful; when Tilda Johnston leaped onto Abe's back to give him a scare on a lonely timber path, she brought the big axman to the ground by pulling her hands against his shoulders and pressing her knee into his backbone. The ax-blade cut her ankle, and strips from Abe's shirt and Tilda's dress had to be used to stop the blood. By then she was sobbing over what to tell her mother. On Abe's advice she told her mother the whole truth.

As time went by, the stepmother of Abe became one of the rich, silent forces in his life. Besides keeping the floors, pots, pans, kettles, and milk-crocks spick and span, weaving, sewing, mending, and managing with sagacity and gumption, she had a massive, bony, human strength backed with an elemental faith that the foundations of the world were mortised by God with unspeakable goodness of heart toward the human family. Hard as life was, she was thankful to be alive.

Once she told Abe how her brother Isaac, back in Hardin County, had hot words with a cowardly young man who shot Isaac without warning. The doctors asked Isaac if they could tie him down while they cut his flesh and took out the bullet. He told them he didn't need to be tied down; he put two lead musket-balls in between his teeth and ground his teeth on them while the doctors cut a slash nine inches long and one inch deep till they found the bullet and brought it out. Isaac never let out a moan or a whimper; he set his teeth into the musket-balls, ground them into flat sheets, and spat them from his mouth when he thanked the doctors.

Sally Bush, the stepmother, was all of a good mother to Abe. If he broke out laughing when others saw nothing to laugh at, she let it pass as a sign of his thoughts working their own way. So far as she was concerned he had a right to do unaccountable things; since he never lied to her, why not? So she justified him. When Abe's sister, Sarah, married Aaron Grigsby and a year after died with her newborn child, it was Sally Bush who spoke comfort to the eighteen-year-old boy of Nancy Hanks burying his sister and the wraith of a child.

A neighbor woman sized him up by saying, "He could work when he wanted to, but he was no hand to pitch in like killing snakes." John Romine made the remarks: "Abe Lincoln worked for me, but was always reading and thinking. I used to get mad at him for it. I say he was awful lazy. He would laugh and talk—crack his jokes and tell stories all the time; didn't love work half as much as his pay. He said to me one day that his father taught him to work, but he never taught him to love it."

A misunderstanding came up one time between Abe Lincoln and William Grigsby. It ended with Grigsby so mad he challenged Abe to a fight. Abe looked down at Grigsby, smiled, and said the fight ought to be with John Johnston, Abe's stepbrother. The day was set for the fight; each man was there with his seconds; the mauling began, with the two fighters stripped to the waist, beating and bruising each other with bare knuckles.

A crowd stood around, forming a ring, cheering, yelling, hissing, till after a while they saw Johnston getting the worst of it. Then the

ring of people forming the crowd was broken as Abe Lincoln shouldered his way through, stepped out, took hold of Grigsby and threw that fighter out of the center of the fight-ring.

Then Abe Lincoln called out, "I'm the big buck of this lick." And looking around so his eyes swept the circle of the crowd he let loose the challenge, "If any of you want to try it, come on and whet your horns." A riot of wild fist-fighting came then between the two gangs and for months around the Jones grocery store there was talk about which gang whipped the other.

After a fox-chase with horses, Uncle Jimmy Larkin was telling how his horse won the race, was the best horse in the world, and never drew a long breath; Abe didn't listen; Uncle Jimmy told it again, and Abe said, "Why don't you tell us how many short breaths he drew?" It raised a laugh on Jimmy, who jumped around threatening to fight, till Abc said quictly, "Now, Larkin, if you don't shut up I'll throw you in that water."

Asked by Farmer James Taylor if he could kill a hog, he answered, "If you will risk the hog I'll risk myself."

He had the pride of youth that resents the slur, the snub, besides the riotous blood that has always led youth in reckless exploits. When he was cutting up didos one day at the Crawford farm-house, Mrs. Crawford asked, "What's going to become of you, Abe?" And with mockery of swagger, he answered, "Me? I'm going to be president of the United States."

Driving a horse at the mill, he was sending the whiplash over the nag and calling, "Git up, you old hussy; git up, you old hussy." The horse let fly a hind foot that knocked down the big boy just as he yelled, "Git up." He lay bleeding, was taken home, washed, put to bed, and lay all night unconscious. As his eye winkers opened the next day and he came to, his tongue struggled and blurted, "You old hussy," thus finishing what he started to say before the knockdown.

❁ ❁ ❁

Chapter XVI

A MILE ACROSS the fields from the Lincoln home was the Pigeon church, a log-built meeting-house put up in 1822 after many discussions among members about where to locate. On June 7, 1823, William Barker, who kept the minutes and records, wrote that the church "received Brother Thomas Lincoln by letter." He was elected the next year with two neighbors to serve as a committee of visitors to the Gilead church, and served three years as church trustee. Strict watch was kept on the conduct of members and Tom served on committees to look into reported misconduct between husbands and wives, brothers and sisters, of neighbor against neighbor.

William Barker once entered the subscriptions for the support of the church as follows: "We the undersined do asign our names to pay the sevrial somes annexed to our names in produce this fall to be delivered betwixt the first and 20th of December the produce is as follows corn wheat whiskey pork Linnen wool or any other article or material to do the work with. the produce will be Dilevered at the meting hoas in good marchanable produce." Among the subscribers was recorded, "undersined"—"Thomas Lincoln in corn manufactured pounds 24."

Along with the earliest settlers in Indiana had come Catholic priests, and Baptist and Presbyterian preachers, and Methodist circuit riders. Churches had been organized, and the members, with prayer and songs, hewed the logs and raised the frames of their meeting-house for worship. Time had been when the circuit-rider traveled with Bible in one hand and rifle in the other, preaching to members, sinners, and "scorners" in settlers' cabins or in timber groves. To the members, the Bible, and the lands, names, stories, texts, and teachings of the Bible, were overshadowing realities, to be read, thought over, interpreted, and used in daily life. To "grow in grace" and to arrive at "grace abounding," to be "strong in sperrit," to "cast out delusion," were matters connected definitely with the daily life of arising, building a fire, breaking the ice sheets on water, and starting a kettle to boil, and then going forth to the chores of the barn and the horse-trough, the corncrib, the pigpen. Such biblical words as "malice," "mercy," and "charity" were topics of long explanations.

Most of the church people could read only the shortest words in the Bible, or none at all. They sat in the log meeting-house on the split-log benches their own axes had shaped, listening to the preacher reading from the Bible by the light of fire-logs. The pronunciation of the words Egypt, Mesopotamia, Babylon, Damascus, set minds to work imagining places less real to them than Rockport, Boonville, Vincennes, Cincinnati. Epithets and texts enunciated often by preachers became tissues of their spiritual lives; the words meant something beyond the actual words in "weeping and wailing and gnashing of teeth," "an eye for an eye, and a tooth for a tooth," "by the waters of Babylon." They could see the direct inference to be drawn from, "The fathers have eaten sour grapes and the children's teeth are set on edge," or the suggestions in "Let not your heart be troubled," or "Let him who is without sin cast the first stone," or "As ye would that others should do unto you, do ye even so unto them."

Their own morning-glories, honeysuckle, and blooming perennials came to leafage out of the rhythmic text, "Consider the lilies of the field, how they grow; they toil not, neither do they spin; and yet I say unto you, that even Solomon in all his glory was not arrayed like one of these." They felt enough portents in the two words, "Jesus wept," for the arrangement of that as a verse by itself.

At the Pigeon church one of the favorite hymns was "How Tedious and Tasteless the Hours," and another, "Oh, to Grace How Great a Debtor!" and another began with the lines:

> When I can read my title clear
> To mansions in the skies.

To confess, to work hard, to be saving, to be decent, were the actions most praised and pleaded for in the sermons of the preachers. Next to denying Christ, the worst sins were drinking, gambling, fighting, loafing, among the men, and gossiping, back-biting, sloth, and slack habits, among the women. A place named Hell where men, women, and children burned everlastingly in fires was the place where sinners would go.

In a timber grove one summer Sunday afternoon, a preacher yelled, shrieked, wrung his hands in sobs of hysterics, until a row of women were laid out to rest and recover in the shade of an oak-tree, after they had moaned, shaken, danced up and down, worn themselves out with "the jerks" and fainted. And young Abe Lincoln, looking on, with sober face and quiet heart, was thoughtful about what he saw before his eyes.

The Sabbath was not only a day for religious meetings. After the sermon, the members, who rode horses many miles to the meeting-house, talked about crops, weather, births and deaths, the growing settlements, letters just come, politics, Indians, and land-titles.

Families had prayers in the morning on arising, grace at breakfast, noon prayers and grace at dinner, grace at supper, and evening prayers at bedtime. In those households, the manger at Bethlehem was a white miracle, the Black Friday at Golgotha and the rocks rolled away for the Resurrection were near-by realities of terror and comfort, dark power and sustenance. The Sabbath day, Christmas, Easter, were days for sober thoughts and sober faces, resignation, contemplation, rest, silence. Verses in the Gospel of St. John had rhythm and portent. "I am the way, the truth, and the life. . . . He that believeth in me shall not perish but shall have everlasting life."

Besides a wisdom of short syllables covering all the wants of life in the Lord's Prayer, they found a melodious movement of musical intention in the arrangement of its simple words. It was like a walk from a green valley to a great mountain to pronounce with thoughtful cadence: "Give us this day our daily bread. And forgive us our trespasses as we forgive those who trespass against us. And lead us not into temptation but deliver us from evil."

The glisten of dewdrops on wheat straws, in the gray chill of daybreak on harvest fields, shone in the solemn assurance of, "Yea, though I walk through the valley of the shadow of death, I will fear no evil: . . . thy rod and thy staff they comfort me."

There was occupation of the imaginative gift, a challenge even to the sleeping or crying senses of color and form, hidden in the picture of Jacob's ladder stretching from the man in earth-slumber up beyond the limits of sky; in the drama of Jonah entering the belly of the whale and later issuing forth from that darkness; in the swift stride of the four horsemen of the apocalypse; in the coat of many colors worn by Joseph and the dream of seven years of famine to come upon Egypt; in the flawless and clear-eyed sheep-boy David, walking with sling and stone to win battle against the stiff-necked giant Goliath by reason of one fierce stone pounded home to the forehead of the swaggerer; in the massive prefigurements of preparation for calamity or destruction of mortal pride to be found in the episodes of Noah's ark and the upthrust and comedown of the Tower of Babel.

After a day of plowing corn, watching crop pests, whittling beanpoles, capturing strayed cattle, and fixing up a hole in a snake-rail fence, while the housewife made a kettle of soap, hoed the radishes and cabbages, milked the cows, and washed the baby, there was a consolation leading to easy slumber in the beatitudes: "Blessed are the meek: for they shall inherit the earth. . . . Blessed are the pure in heart, for they shall see God. Blessed are the peacemakers: for they shall be called the children of God." It was not their business to be sure of the arguments and the invincible logic that might underlie the Bible promises of heaven and threats of hell; it was for this the preacher was hired and paid by the corn, wheat, whisky, pork, linen, wool, and other produce brought by the members of the church.

The exquisite foretokening, "In my Father's house are many mansions: if it were not so I would have told you," was but a carrying farther of the implications of that cry from the ramparts of the unconquerable, "O death, where is thy sting? O grave, where is thy victory?"

Beyond Indiana was something else; beyond the timber and underbrush, the malaria, milk-sick, blood, sweat, tears, hands hard and crooked as the roots of walnut trees, there must be something else.

Young Abraham Lincoln saw certain of these Christians with a clean burning fire, with inner reckonings that prompted them to silence or action or speech, and they could justify themselves with a simple and final explanation that all things should be done decently and in order. Their door-strings were out to sinners deep in mire, to scorners seemingly past all redemption; the Jesus who lived with lawbreakers, thieves, lepers crying "Unclean!" was an instrument and a light vivifying into everyday use the abstractions behind the words "malice," "mercy," "charity."

They met understanding from the solemn young Lincoln who had refused to join his schoolmates in torturing a live mud-turtle, and had written a paper arguing against cruelty to animals; who when eleven years old took his father's rifle and shot a prairie turkey and had never since shot any game at all; who could butcher a beef or hog for food but didn't like to see rabbit blood; who wanted to be a river steamboat pilot but gave up in simple obedience when his father told him he was needed at home; who as a nine-year-old boy helped get a traveling preacher to speak some sort of final ceremonial words over the winter grave of Nancy Hanks Lincoln; who would bother to lug on his shoulders and save from freezing the body of a man overloaded with whisky; who had seen one of his companions go insane and who used to get up before daylight and cross the fields to listen to the crooning, falsetto cackling, and disconnected babbling of one whose brain had suddenly lost control of things done decently and in order.

The footsteps of death, silent as the moving sundial of a tall sycamore, were a presence. Time and death, the partners who operate leaving no more track than mist, had to be reckoned in the scheme of life. A day is a shooting-star. The young Lincoln tried to rhyme this sentiment:

> Time! what an empty vapor 'tis!
> And days how swift they are:
> Swift as an Indian arrow—
> Fly on like a shooting star,

The present moment just is here,
Then slides away in haste,
That we can never say they're ours,
But only say they're past.

His mother Nancy Hanks and her baby that didn't live, his sister Sarah and her baby that didn't live—time and the empty vapor had taken them; the rain and the snow beat on their graves. The young man who was in his right mind and then began babbling week in and week out the droolings of a disordered brain—time had done it without warning. On both man and the animals, time and death had their way. In a single week, the milk-sick had taken four milch-cows and eleven calves of Dennis Hanks, while Dennis too had nearly gone under with a hard week of it.

At the Pigeon Creek settlement, while the structure of his bones, the build and hang of his torso and limbs, took shape, other elements, invisible, yet permanent, traced their lines in the tissues of his head and heart.

❁ ❁ ❁

Chapter XVII

PIONEERS ARE HALF gypsy. The lookout is on horizons from which at any time another and stranger wandersong may come calling and take the heart, to love or to kill, with gold or with ashes, with bluebirds burbling in ripe cornfields or with rheumatism or hog cholera or mortgages, rust and bugs eating crops and farms into ruin.

They are luck-hunters. And luck—is it *yonder?* Over the horizon, over yonder—is there a calling and a calling? The pioneers, so often, are believers in luck . . . out yonder.

And always the worker on land, who puts in crops and bets on the weather and gambles in seed corn and hazards his toil against so many whimsical, fateful conditions, has a pull on his heart to believe he can read luck signs, and tell good luck or bad luck to come, in dreams of his sleep at night, in changes of the moon, in the manners of chickens and dogs, in little seeming accidents that reveal the intentions and operations of forces beyond sight and smell.

They have noticed certain coincidences operating to produce certain results in the past. And when again those coincidences arise they say frankly, "I'm superstitious—what happened before is liable to happen again." The simple saying among simple people, "If a bird lights in a window there will be a death in that house," goes back to the fact that there have been deaths, and many of them, in houses to which a bird came and sat on a window-sill and picked his wings and put on dark assumptions.

Down in Indiana, as Abe Lincoln grew up, he cherished his sweet dreams, and let the bitter ones haunt him, and tried to search out from the muddled hugger-mugger of still other dreams whether the meaning was to be sweet or bitter. His father had had portentous dreams; his father told how in a night's sleep once he saw a wayside path to a strange house; he saw the inside walls, the chairs, the table, the fireplace in that house; at the fireside a woman was sitting, and her face, eyes, and lips came clear; she was paring an apple; she was the woman to be his wife. This was the dream, and in his night's sleep it came again and again; he could not shake it off. It haunted him till he went to the path, followed the path to the house, went inside and there saw the woman, sitting at the fireside paring an apple; her face, eyes, and lips were those he had seen so often in his night sleep; and the rest of his dream came to pass. Tom Lincoln had told this to his son, Abe, and the boy searched his dreams for meanings. He learned to say of certain coincidences, "I'm superstitious," feeling that what had happened before under certain combinations of events would probably happen again.

Even the water underground, the streams and springs, were whimsical, unreliable, ran by luck, it seemed, in southern Indiana. Not far from the Lincolns was a region where rivers dipped down into limestone and faded out of sight. "Lost rivers," they were called. In Wyandotte Cave a walker could go fifteen miles around the inside. In some counties there was no telling when a good well would give out and say, "No more water here."

Abe's father hired a man to come with a witch-hazel and tell by the way the magic stick pointed where to dig a well that wouldn't go dry. The well was dug where the witch-hazel said it should be dug. And that well went dry just as others before had on the Lincoln farm.

Besides superstitions there were sayings, to be spoken and guessed about, old pieces of whim and wisdom out of bygone generations of Kentuckians, of English, Scotch, and Irish souls. Potatoes, growing underground, must be planted in the dark of the moon, while beans,

growing above-ground, must be planted in the light of the moon. The posts of a rail fence would sink in the ground if not set in the dark of the moon. Trees for rails must be cut in the early part of the day and in the light of the moon. If in planting corn you skipped a row there would be a death in the family. If you killed the first snake you saw in the spring, you would win against all your enemies that year. If rheumatism came, skunk-grease or red worm-oil rubbed where the ache was would cure it.

Steal a dishrag, people said, and hide it in a tree-stump and your wart will go away. If you have many warts, tie as many knots in a string as there are warts, and bury the string under a stone. A dog crossing a hunter's path means bad luck unless he hooks his two little fingers together and pulls till the dog is out of sight. Feed gunpowder to dogs and it will make them fierce. To start on a journey and see a white mule is bad luck. If a horse breathes on a child, the child will have the whooping-cough. Buckeyes carried in the pocket keep off the rheumatism.

When a man is putting up a crop of hay or shucking a field of corn or driving a load of wood, the weather has a particular interest for him. Out of the lives of farmers, timber-workers, ox-drivers, in Kentucky and Indiana, have come sayings:

If the sun shines while it is raining, it will rain again the next day; birds and hens singing during the rain indicate fair weather; if roosters crow when they go to roost it is a sign of rain; the first thunder in the spring wakes up the snakes from their winter sleep; when chickens get on a fence during a rain and pick themselves, it is a sign of clear weather; when the rain gets thick and heavy, almost like mist, it will turn cold; if a bobwhite says bob only once there will be rain; rain from the east rains three days at least; if it rains before seven it will clear before eleven; if there is lightning in the north it will rain in twenty-four hours; lightning in the south means dry weather.

"If a man can't skin he must hold a leg while some one else does," was a saying among the butcher gangs Abe Lincoln worked with. Men in those gangs would indicate a short distance by saying it was "far as you can throw a bull by the tail." A strong whisky "would make a rabbit spit in a dog's face." There were admonitions: "Spit against the wind and you spit in your own face," or "Don't see all you see, and don't hear all you hear."

Then, too, there were sayings spoken among the men only, out of barn-life and handling cattle and hogs; the daily chores required understanding of the necessary habits of men and animals.

And naturally in field and kitchen, among young and old, there were the phrases and epithets, "as plain as the nose on your face; as easy as licking a dish; as welcome as the flowers in May; as bare as the back of my hand; before the cat can lick her ear; as red as a spanked baby."

And there were eloquent Irish with blessings, maledictions, and proverbs. "Better be red-headed than be without a head." "No man can live longer at peace than his neighbors like." "I think his face is made of a fiddle; every one that looks on him loves him." "She's as dirty as a slut that's too lazy to lick herself." "A liar must have a good memory." "It's an ill fight where he that wins has the worst of it." "Hills look green that are far away." "It will be all the same after you're dead a hundred years."

Among the young people were whimsies often spoken and seldom believed. Fancy was on a loose leash in some of these. "If you can make your first and little finger meet over the back of your hand, you will marry." "If you spit on a chunk of firewood and speak your sweetheart's name, he will come before it burns out." "The new moon must never be seen through the trees when making a wish." "If a butterfly comes into the house a lady will call wearing a dress the color of the butterfly." "If you sing before breakfast you will cry before night." "If the fire roars there will be a quarrel in the family."

"If two hens fight in the barnyard there will be two ladies calling." "If your ears burn somebody is gossiping about you." "If your hand itches you will get a present or shake hands with a stranger; if your right foot itches you are going on a journey; if the left foot itches you are going where you are not wanted; if your nose itches away from home you are wanted at home, but if your nose itches at home some one is coming to see you; if your right eye itches you will cry and if it is the left eye you will laugh." "If you break a looking-glass you will have seven years of bad luck." "If you let a baby under a year old look in the mirror it will die." "It is bad luck to step over a broom."

Among the games played at parties by the young people in Indiana was the farm classic "Skip to My Lou" which tells of a little red wagon painted blue, a mule in the cellar kicking up through, chickens in the haystack shoo shoo shoo, flies in the cream jar shoo shoo shoo, rabbits in the bean patch two by two.

> Hurry up slow poke, do oh do,
> Hurry up slow poke, do oh do,
> Hurry up slow poke, do oh do,
> Skip to my Lou, my darling.
>
> I'll get her back in spite of you,
> I'll get her back in spite of you,
> I'll get her back in spite of you,
> Skip to my Lou, my darling.
>
> Gone again, what shall I do?
> Gone again, what shall I do?
> Gone again, what shall I do?
> Skip to my Lou, my darling.
>
> I'll get another one sweeter than you,
> I'll get another one sweeter than you,
> I'll get another one sweeter than you,
> Skip to my Lou, my darling.

And there were other classics such as "Way Down in the Pawpaw Patch," "All Chaw Hay on the Corner," "Pig in the Parlor," "Old Bald Eagle, Sail Around," and "Pop Goes the Weasel." The game of "Old Sister Phoebe," with a quaint British strain, had song couplets:

Old Sister Phoebe, how merry were we,
The night we sat under the juniper tree,
The juniper tree, high-o, high-o,
The juniper tree, high-o.

Take this hat on your head, keep your head warm,
And take a sweet kiss, it will do you no harm.

It will do you no harm, but a great deal of good,
And so take another while kissing goes good.

In "Thus the Farmer Sows His Seed," an ancient human dialogue is rehearsed:

> Come, my love, and go with me,
> And I will take good care of thee.
>
> I am too young, I am not fit.
> I cannot leave my mamma yet.
>
> You're old enough, you are just right,
> I asked your mamma last Saturday night.

Among a people who spun their own wool and wove their own cloth, as their forefathers had done, there was the inheritance of the game of "Weevily Wheat," danced somewhat like the Virginia Reel, with singing passages:

> O Charley, he's a fine young man,
> O Charley, he's a dandy,
> He loves to hug and kiss the girls,
> And feed 'em on good candy.
>
> The higher up the cherry tree,
> The riper grow the cherries,
> The more you hug and kiss the girls,
> The sooner they will marry.
>
> My pretty little pink, I suppose you think
> I care but little about you.
> But I'll let you know before you go,
> I cannot do without you.

It's left hand round your weevily wheat.
It's both hands round your weevily wheat.
Come down this way with your weevily wheat.
It's swing, oh, swing, your weevily wheat.

Among the best-remembered favorites in the neighborhood around the Lincoln farm in Indiana were "Skip to My Lou," "Old Sister Phoebe," "Thus the Farmer Sows His Seed," and "Weevily Wheat."

They had patriotic songs for the Fourth of July, chief of which was "Hail Columbia," printed as follows:

Hail! Columbia, happy land!
Hail! ye heroes, heav'n-born band,
Who faught and bled in freedom's cause,
Who faught, &c.

And when the storm of war is gone,
Enjoy the peace your valor won;
Let independence be your boast,
Ever mindful what it cost,
Ever grateful for the prize,
May its altar reach the skies.

✿ ✿ ✿

Chapter XVIII

THE FARM BOYS in their evenings at Jones's store in Gentryville talked about how Abe Lincoln was always reading, digging into books, stretching out flat on his stomach in front of the fireplace, studying till midnight and past midnight, picking a piece of charcoal to write on the fire shovel, shaving off what he wrote, and then writing more—till midnight and past midnight. The next thing Abe would be reading books between the plow handles, it seemed to them. And once trying to speak a last word, Dennis Hanks said, "There's suthin' peculiar-some about Abe."

He wanted to learn, to know, to live, to reach out; he wanted to satisfy hungers and thirsts he couldn't tell about, this big boy of the backwoods. And some of what he wanted so much, so deep down, seemed to be in the books. Maybe in books he would find the answers to dark questions pushing around in the pools of his thoughts and the drifts of his mind. He told Dennis and other people, "The things I want to know are in books; my best friend is the man who'll git me a book I ain't read." And sometimes friends answered, "Well, books ain't as plenty as wildcats in these parts o' Indianny."

This was one thing meant by Dennis when he said there was "suthin' peculiarsome" about Abe. It seemed that Abe made the books tell him more than they told other people. All the other farm boys had gone to school and read "The Kentucky Preceptor," but Abe picked out questions from it, such as "Who has the most right to complain, the Indian or the Negro?" and Abe would talk about it, up one way and down the other, while they were in the cornfield pulling fodder for the winter. When Abe got hold of a storybook and read about a boat that came near a magnetic rock, and how the magnets in the rock pulled all the nails out of the boat so it went to pieces and the people in the boat found themselves floundering in water, Abe thought it was funny and told it to other people. After Abe read poetry, especially Bobby Burns's poems, Abe began writing rhymes himself. When Abe sat with a girl, with their bare feet in the creek water, and she spoke of the moon rising, he explained to her it was the earth moving and not the moon—the moon only seemed to rise.

John Hanks, who worked in the fields barefooted with Abe, grubbing stumps, plowing, mowing, said: "When Abe and I came back to the house from work, he used to go to the cupboard, snatch a piece of corn bread, sit down, take a book, cock his legs up high as his head, and read. Whenever Abe had a chance in the field while at work, or at the house, he would stop and read." He liked to explain to other people what he was getting from books; explaining an idea to someone else made it clearer to him. The habit was growing on him of reading out loud; words came more real if picked from the silent page of the book and pronounced on the tongue; new balances and values of words stood out if spoken aloud. When writing letters for his father or the neighbors, he read the words out loud as they got written. Before writing a letter he asked questions such as: "What do you want to say in the letter? How do you want to say it? Are you sure that's the best way to say it? Or do you think we can fix up a better way to say it?"

As he studied his books his lower lip stuck out; Josiah Crawford noticed it was a habit and joked Abe about the "stuck-out lip." This habit too stayed with him.

He wrote in his Sum Book or arithmetic that Compound Division was "When several numbers of Divers Denominations are given to be divided by 1 common divisor," and worked on the exercise in multiplication; "If 1 foot contain 12 inches I demand how many there are in 126 feet." Thus the schoolboy.

What he got in the schools didn't satisfy him. He went to three different schools in Indiana, besides two in Kentucky—altogether about four months of school. He learned his A B C, how to spell, read, write. And he had been with the other barefoot boys in butternut jeans learning "manners" under the school teacher, Andrew Crawford, who had them open a door, walk in, and say, "Howdy do?" Yet what he tasted of books in school was only a beginning, only made him hungry and thirsty, shook him with a wanting and a wanting of more and more of what was hidden between the covers of books.

He kept on saying, "The things I want to know are in books; my best friend is the man who'll git me a book I ain't read." He said that to Pitcher, the lawyer over at Rockport, nearly twenty miles away, one fall afternoon, when he walked from Pigeon Creek to Rockport and borrowed a book from Pitcher. Then when fodder-pulling time came a few days later, he shucked corn from early daylight till sundown along with his father and Dennis Hanks and John Hanks, but after supper he read the book till midnight, and at noon he hardly knew the taste of his cornbread because he had the book in front of him. It was a hundred little things like these which made Dennis Hanks say there was "suthin' peculiarsome" about Abe.

Besides reading the family Bible and figuring his way all through the old arithmetic they had at home, he got hold of "Æsop's Fables," "Pilgrim's Progress," "Robinson Crusoe," and Weems's "The Life of Francis Marion." The book of fables, written or collected thousands of years ago by the Greek slave, known as Æsop, sank deep in his mind. As he read through the book a second and third time, he had a feeling there were fables all around him, that everything he touched and handled, everything he saw and learned had a fable wrapped in it somewhere. One fable was about a bundle of sticks and a farmer whose sons were quarreling and fighting.

There was a fable in two sentences which read, "A coachman, hearing one of the wheels of his coach make a great noise, and perceiving that it was the worst one of the four, asked how it came to take such a liberty. The wheel answered that from the beginning of time, creaking had always been the privilege of the weak." And there were shrewd, brief incidents of foolery such as this: "A waggish, idle

fellow in a country town, being desirous of playing a trick on the sim-
plicity of his neighbors and at the same time putting a little money in
his pocket at their cost, advertised that he would on a certain day
show a wheel carriage that should be so contrived as to go without
horses. By silly curiosity the rustics were taken in, and each succeeding group who came out from the show were ashamed to confess to
their neighbors that they had seen nothing but a wheelbarrow."

The style of the Bible, of Æsop's fables, the hearts and minds back
of those books, were much in his thoughts. His favorite pages in them
he read over and over. Behind such proverbs as, "Muzzle not the ox
that treadeth out the corn," and "He that ruleth his own spirit is
greater than he that taketh a city," there was a music of simple wisdom and a mystery of common everyday life that touched deep spots
in him, while out of the fables of the ancient Greek slave he came to
see that cats, rats, dogs, horses, plows, hammers, fingers, toes, people,
all had fables connected with their lives, characters, places. There

was, perhaps, an outside for each thing as it stood alone, while inside of it was its fable.

One book came, titled, "The Life of George Washington, with Curious Anecdotes, Equally Honorable to Himself and Exemplary to His Young Countrymen. Embellished with Six Steel Engravings, by M. L. Weems, formerly Rector of Mt. Vernon Parish." It pictured men of passion and proud ignorance in the government of England driving their country into war on the American colonies. It quoted the far-visioned warning of Chatham to the British parliament, "For God's sake, then, my lords, let the way be instantly opened for reconciliation. I say instantly; or it will be too late forever."

The book told of war, as at Saratoga. "Hoarse as a mastiff of true British breed, Lord Balcarras was heard from rank to rank, loud-animating his troops; while on the other hand, fierce as a hungry Bengal tiger, the impetuous Arnold precipitated heroes on the stubborn foe. Shrill and terrible, from rank to rank, resounds the clash of bayonets —frequent and sad the groans of the dying. Pairs on pairs, Britons and Americans, with each his bayonet at his brother's breast, fall forward together faint-shrieking in death, and mingle their smoking blood." Washington, the man, stood out, as when he wrote, "These things so harassed my heart with grief, that I solemnly declared to God, if I know myself, I would gladly offer myself a sacrifice to the butchering enemy, if I could thereby insure the safety of these my poor distressed countrymen."

The Weems book reached some deep spots in the boy. He asked himself what it meant that men should march, fight, bleed, go cold and hungry for the sake of what they called "freedom."

"Few great men are great in everything," said the book. And there was a cool sap in the passage: "His delight was in that of the manliest sort, which, by stringing the limbs and swelling the muscles, promotes the kindliest flow of blood and spirits. At jumping with a long pole, or heaving heavy weights, for his years he hardly had an equal."

Such book talk was a comfort against the same thing over again, day after day, so many mornings the same kind of water from the same spring, the same fried pork and corn-meal to eat, the same drizzles of rain, spring plowing, summer weeds, fall fodder-pulling, each coming every year, with the same tired feeling at the end of the day, so many days alone in the woods or the fields or else the same people to talk with, people from whom he had learned all they could teach him. Yet there ran through his head the stories and sayings of other people, the stories and sayings of books, the learning his eyes had caught from books; they were a comfort; they were good to have because they were good by themselves; and they were still better to have because they broke the chill of the lonesome feeling.

He was thankful to the writer of Æsop's fables because that writer stood by him and walked with him, an invisible companion, when he pulled fodder or chopped wood. Books lighted lamps in the dark rooms of his gloomy hours. . . . Well—he would live on; maybe the time would come when he would be free from work for a few weeks, or a few months, with books, and then he would read. . . . God, then he would read. . . . Then he would go and get at the proud secrets of his books.

His father—would he be like his father when he grew up? He hoped not. Why should his father knock him off a fence rail when he was asking a neighbor, passing by, a question? Even if it was a smart question, too pert and too quick, it was no way to handle a boy in front of a neighbor. No, he was going to be a man different from his father. The books—his father hated the books. His father talked about "too much eddication"; after readin', writin', 'rithmetic, that was enough, his father said. He, Abe Lincoln, the boy, wanted to know more than the father, Tom Lincoln, wanted to know. Already Abe knew more than his father; he was writing letters for the neighbors; they hunted out the Lincoln farm to get young Abe to find his bottle of ink with blackberry brier root and copperas in it, and his pen made from a turkey buzzard feather, and write letters. Abe had a suspicion sometimes his father was a little proud to have a boy that could write letters, and tell about things in books, and outrun and outwrestle and rough-and-tumble any boy or man in Spencer County. Yes, he would be different from his father; he was already so; it couldn't be helped.

In growing up from boyhood to young manhood, he had survived against lonesome, gnawing monotony and against floods, forest and prairie fires, snake-bites, horse-kicks, ague, chills, fever, malaria, "milk-sick."

A comic outline against the sky he was, hiking along the roads of Spencer and other counties in southern Indiana in those years when he read all the books within a fifty-mile circuit of his home. Stretching up on the long legs that ran from his moccasins to the body frame with its long, gangling arms, covered with linsey-woolsey, then the lean neck that carried the head with its surmounting coonskin cap or straw hat—it was, again, a comic outline—yet with a portent in its shadow. His laughing "Howdy," his yarns and drollery, opened the doors of men's hearts.

Starting along in his eleventh year came spells of abstraction. When he was spoken to, no answer came from him. "He might be a thousand miles away." The roaming, fathoming, searching, questioning operations of the minds and hearts of poets, inventors, beginners who take facts stark, these were at work in him. This was one sort of abstraction he knew; there was another: the blues took him; coils of multiplied melancholies wrapped their blue frustrations inside him, all that Hamlet, Koheleth, Schopenhauer have uttered, in a mesh of foiled hopes. "There was absolutely nothing to excite ambition for education," he wrote later of that Indiana region. Against these "blues," he found the best warfare was to find people and trade with them his yarns and drolleries. John Baldwin, the blacksmith, with many stories and odd talk and eye-slants, was a help and a light.

Days came when he sank deep in the stream of human life and felt himself kin of all that swam in it, whether the waters were crystal or mud.

He learned how suddenly life can spring a surprise. One day in the woods, as he was sharpening a wedge on a log, the ax glanced, nearly took his thumb off, and left a white scar after healing.

"You never cuss a good ax," was a saying in those timbers.

❁ ❁ ❁

Chapter XIX

SIXTEEN-YEAR-OLD Abe had worked on the farm of James Taylor, at the mouth of Anderson Creek, on that great highway of traffic, the Ohio River. Besides plowing and doing barn and field work, he ran the ferryboat across the Ohio. Two travelers wanted to get on a steamboat one day, and after Abe sculled them to it and lifted their trunks on board they threw him a half-dollar apiece; it gave him a new feeling; the most he had ever earned before that was at butchering for thirty-one cents a day. And when one of the half-dollars slipped from him and sank in the river, that too gave him a new feeling.

At Anderson Creek ferry, he saw and talked with settlers, land buyers and sellers, traders, hunters, peddlers, preachers, gamblers, politicians, teachers, and men shut-mouthed about their business. Occasionally came a customer who looked as if he might be one of the "half horse, half alligator men" haunting the Ohio watercourse those years. There was river talk about Mike Fink, known on the Ohio as the "Snapping Turtle" and on the Mississippi as "The Snag," the toughest of the "half horse, half alligator" crowd; he was a famous marksman and aiming his rifle from his keel-boat floating the Ohio had shot off the tails of pigs running loose in the bottom lands.

Along the water-front of Louisville, Mike Fink had backed up his claim, "I can outrun, outhop, outjump, throw down, drag out, and lick any man in the country; I'm a Salt River roarer; I love the wimming and I'm chockfull of fight." They tried him for crimes in Louisville and acquitted him for lack of sufficient evidence; he waved a red bandanna for a good-by and told them he would come back to face their other indictments.

One of Mike's nicknames was "The Valley King." In a dispute with a man who claimed to have royal blood of France in his veins, Mike closed the argument by kicking the representative of royalty from the

inside of a tavern to the middle of a street, with the words, "What if you are a king? Ain't we all kings over here?" His keel-boat was named "The Lightfoot." Mike's rival among the "half horse, half alligator" men was Little Billy, whose challenge ran, "I'm Little Billy, all the way from North Fork of Muddy Run and I can whip any man in this section of the country. Maybe you never heard of the time the horse kicked me an' put both his hips out o' j'int—if it ain't true, cut me up for catfish bait. I'm one o' the toughest—live forever and then turn to a white-oak post. I can outrun, outjump, outswim, chaw more tobacco and spit less, drink more whisky and keep soberer, than any man in these parts."

"Fights was fights in them days." Travelers had a proverb that a tavern was hardly safe if the proprietor had a nose or an ear off. It was a sign the landlord couldn't take care of himself.

Many travelers carried jugs of whisky, with corncob stoppers. Their common names for the raw article were such as "Red Eye," "Fire Water," "Cider Royal," "Blue Ruin," "Fool Water," "Bug Juice," though there were special brands indicative of lore and lingo with their names, "Clay and Huysen," "Race Horse," "Ching Ching," "Tog," "Rappee," "Fiscal Agent," "T. O. U.," "Tippena Pecco," "Moral Suasion," "Vox Populi," "Ne Plus Ultra," "Shambro," "Pig and Whistle," "Silver Top," "Poor Man's Punco," "Split Ticket," "Deacon," "Exchange," "Stone Wall," "Virginia Fence," "Floater," and "Shifter."

In Louisville, men played billiards all night, and there were no closing hours for the saloons and poker-rooms; a legend ran of one gambler dealing the cards when alarm was sounded that a steamboat at the river landing was on fire, and he went on asking the players, "How many?" as though steamboats caught fire every day. The Hope Distillery Company, capitalized at $100,000, was operating with grain from the near-by Kentucky and Scioto River valleys, while one Dr. McMurtrie called the Hope concern "a gigantic reservoir of damning drink; they manufacture poison for the human race; of what avail are the reasonings of philanthropists?"

So risky was travel that the Indiana legislature specifically permitted travelers to carry concealed weapons of any kind. There were traders from Cincinnati to New Orleans who were familiar with a regular dialogue, which they rehearsed to each other when they had the same room or bed in a tavern. "Stranger," one would say, "it's been a mighty long time since you and me slep' together." "Yep," came the regulation answer. "Got the same old smell you used to have?" "You *bet."* "Air you as lousy as ever?" "That's me." "Put 'er thar!" Then with a handshake and a swig from the jug they went to their sleep. There were tales of mosquitoes of a certain breed along the Ohio River; two could kill a dog, ten a man.

Men who had made trips up and down the river more than once had a song with a chorus:

> Hard upon the beach oar!
> She moves too slow.
> All the way to Shawneetown,
> Long time ago.

A song, "The Hunters of Kentucky," written by Samuel Woodworth, the author of "The Old Oaken Bucket," was heard occasionally amid the Ohio River traffic. It was about the Kentuckians at the Battle of New Orleans; a force of 2,250 of them had marched overland, arriving half-naked; women of New Orleans cut and sewed 1,127 "pairs of pantaloons" for them from wool blankets, in less than five days. Part of the song ran:

> And if a daring foe annoys,
> No matter what his force is,
> We'll show him that Kentucky boys
> Are alligator-horses.

After telling about the breastworks erected for the battle, the song had this to say:

> Behind it stood our little force,
> None wished it to be greater,
> For every man was half a horse
> And half an alligator.

Lawyers with books in their saddlebags took the ferryboat across the Ohio; law and order was coming to that wild young country, they believed; they could remember only ten years back how the law of the Territory of Indiana provided that a horse-thief should have two hundred lashes with a whip on his bare back and stay in jail till the horse was paid for, and the second time he was caught horse-stealing he was shot or hanged; for stealing cattle or hogs the thief had his shirt taken off and was given thirty-nine lashes.

Hunters crossed Anderson Creek ferry who could tell how George

Doty in 1821 up in Johnson County killed 300 deer. They said Noah Major, one of the first settlers in Morgan County, estimated there were 20,000 deer in that country when he came in 1820, six years before. Circuit riders could tell about Peter Cartwright, who twenty years before was riding the Salt River district in Kentucky, occasionally getting over into Indiana; once Cartwright labored with a community of Shakers till eighty-seven of that sect were "rescued from the delusion." Those circuit riders could tell about Samuel Thornton Scott, the Presbyterian wilderness preacher, who swam the White River, losing his hat and one boot, arriving at Vincennes, as one friend said, "neither naked nor clad, barefoot nor shod."

Old-timers came along who could tell how the Indians in 1809 were stealing horses, burning barns and fences, killing settlers, running off with cattle and chickens, and how General Hopkins with 1,200 soldiers burned the Indian villages along the Wabash, their log cabins, gardens, orchards, stationed rangers to hunt down every Indian they found, till the time came when there was not a red man on the Wabash or south of that river in the state of Indiana.

Others could tell of Daniel Ketcham, who was taken by Indians, kept over winter near Madison, loaded like a mule and marched to one of the Miami rivers, where his skin was blacked and he was handed a looking-glass and told to have a last look at himself before burning at the stake. A daughter of the chief, wearing five hundred silver brooches, made a thirty-minute speech, words flying fast and with defiance. Then she let Ketcham loose, two Indian women washed the black off him "and the white blood out"; he was taken to the tent of their mother, who offered him her hand but, being drunk, fell off her seat before he could take the hand. He carried wood, pounded corn, escaped and returned home to his wife, who had pledged neighbors that Ketcham, who was a famous wheat-stacker, would be home in time for stacking that year.

The ferry boy at Anderson Creek watched and listened to this human drift across the Ohio River, the bushwhackers and bad men who called themselves bad, and the others who called themselves good. Civilization went by, boats and tools breaking ways. Steamboats came past in a slow and proud pageantry making their fourteen- to twenty-day passage from New Orleans to Pittsburgh; geography became fact to the boy looking on; the flags on the steamboats were a sign of that long stretch of country the steamboats were crossing. Strings of flatboats passed, loaded with produce, pork, turkeys, chicken, cornmeal, flour, whisky, venison hams, hazel-nuts, skins, furs, ginseng; this was farm produce for trading at river ports to merchants or to plantation owners for feeding slaves. Other trading boats carried furniture, groceries, clothes, kitchenware, plows, wagons, harness; this was from manufacturing centers, consignments to storekeepers and traders. Houseboats, arks, sleds, flatboats with small cabins in which families lived and kept house, floated toward their new homesteads; on these the women were washing, the children playing. The life-flow of a main artery of American civilization, at a vivid line of growth, was a piece of pageantry there at Anderson Creek.

❀ ❀ ❀
Chapter XX

YOUNG ABE WAS out with ax, saw, and draw-knife building himself a light flatboat at Bates's Landing, a mile and a half down the river from Anderson's Creek. He was eighteen years old, a designer, builder, navigator; he cut down trees, hewed out planks pegged and cleated together the bottoms and sides of his own boat, wood from end to end.

Pieces of money jingled in his pockets. Passengers paid him for sculling them from Bates's Landing out to steamboats in the middle of the Ohio River.

He studied words and figurations on pieces of money. Thirteen stars stood for the first Thirteen States of the Union. The silver print of an eagle spreading its wings and lifting a fighting head was on the half-dollar. As though the eagle were crying high, important words, above its beak was inscribed "E Pluribus Unum"; this meant the many states should be One, young Abe learned.

Circled with the thirteen stars were the head and bust of a motherly-looking woman. On her forehead was the word "Liberty." Just what did *She* mean?

Waiting for passengers and looking out on the wide Ohio to the drooping trees that dipped their leaves in the water on the farther shore, he could think about money and women and eagles.

A signal came from the opposite shore one day and Lincoln rowed across the river. As he stepped out of his boat two men jumped out of the brush. They took hold of him and said they were going to "duck" him in the river. They were John and Lin Dill, brothers who operated a ferry and claimed Abe had been transporting passengers for hire contrary to the law of Kentucky.

As they sized up Abe's lean husky arms they decided not to throw him in the river. He might be too tough a customer. Then all three went to Squire Samuel Pate, justice of the peace, near Lewisport.

A warrant for the arrest of Abraham Lincoln was sworn out by John T. Dill. And the trial began of the case of "The Commonwealth of Kentucky versus Abraham Lincoln," charged with violation of "An Act Respecting the Establishment of Ferries."

Lincoln testified he had carried passengers from the Indiana shore out to the middle of the river, never taking them to the Kentucky shore. And the Dill brothers, though sore and claiming the defendant Lincoln had wronged them, did not go so far as to testify he had "for reward set any person over a river," in the words of the Kentucky statute.

Squire Pate dismissed the warrant against Lincoln. The disappointed Dills put on their hats and left. Lincoln sat with Squire Pate for a long talk. If a man knows the law about a business he is in, it is a help to him, the Squire told young Abe.

They shook hands and parted friends. Afterwards on days when no passengers were in sight and it was "law day" at Squire Pate's down the river, Abe would scull over and watch the witnesses, the constables, the Squire, the machinery of law, government, justice.

The State of Indiana, he learned, was one thing, and the State of Kentucky, something else. A water line in the middle of a big river ran between them. He could ask: "Who makes state lines? What *are* state lines?"

❀ ❀ ❀

Chapter XXI

IN THE YEAR 1825, ox teams and pack horses came through Gentryville carrying people on their way to a place on the Wabash River they called New Harmony. A rich English business man named Robert

Owen had paid $132,000.00 for land and $50,000.00 for live stock, tools, and merchandise, and had made a speech before the Congress at Washington telling how he and his companions were going to try to find a new way for people to live their lives together, without fighting, cheating, or exploiting each other, where work would be honorable yet there would be time for play and learning; they would share and share alike, each for all and all for each. In January, 1826, Owen himself, with a party of 30 people came down the Ohio River in what was called the "boatload of knowledge."

More ox wagons and pack horses kept coming past the Gentryville crossroads; about a thousand people were joined in Owen's scheme at New Harmony on the Wabash. The scheme lighted up Abe Lincoln's heart. His eyes were big and hungry as a hoot-owl's as he told Dennis Hanks, "There's a school and thousands of books there and fellers that know everything in creation." The schooling would have cost him about $100 a year and he could have worked for his board. But Tom Lincoln had other plans for his son Abe.

Across the next three years the boy grew longer of leg and arm, tougher of bone and sinew, with harder knuckles and joints. James Gentry, with the largest farms in the Pigeon Creek clearings, and a landing on the Ohio River, was looking the big boy over. He believed Abe could take his pork, flour, meal, bacon, potatoes, and produce to trade down the Mississippi River, for cotton, tobacco, and sugar. Young Abe was set to work on a flatboat; he cut the oaks for a double bottom of stout planks, and a deck shelter, two pairs of long oars at bow and stern, a check-post, and a setting pole for steering.

As the snow and ice began to melt, a little before the first frogs started shrilling, in that year of 1828, they loaded the boat and pushed off.

In charge of the boat Mr. Gentry had placed his son Allen, and in charge of Allen he had placed Abe Lincoln, to hold his own against any half horse, half alligator bush-whackers who might try to take the boat or loot it, and leave the bones of those they took it from, at Cave-in-Rock on the Illinois shore, or other spots where the skeletons of flatboatmen had been found years after the looters sold the cargo down the river. The honesty of Abe, of course, had been the first point Mr. Gentry considered; and the next point had been whether he could handle the boat in the snags and sand-bars. The two young men pushed off on their trip of a thousand miles to New Orleans, on a wide, winding waterway, where the flatboats were tied up at night to the river-bank, and floated and poled by day amid changing currents,

strings of other flatboats, and in the paths of the proud white steamboats.

Whitecaps rose and broke with their foam feathers, a mile, two miles, beyond the limit of eyesight, as fresh winds blew along the Ohio River. Cave-in-Rock was passed on the Illinois shore, with its sign, "Wilson's Liquor Vault and House of Entertainment," with a doorway 25 feet high, 80 feet wide, and back of that entrance a cavern 200 feet deep, a 14-foot chimney leading to an upper room, where one time later were found 60 human skeletons, most of them rivermen lured and trapped by the Wilson gang that camped at Hurricane Island near by.

Timber-covered river bluffs stood up overlooking the river like plowmen resting big shoulders between the plow-handles; twisted dumps and runs of clay banks were like squatters who had lost hope and found rheumatism and malaria; lone pine trees had silhouetted their dry arms of branches on reefs where they dissolved and reappeared in river-mist lights as if they struggled to tell some secret of water and sky before going under.

The nineteen-year-old husky from Indiana found the Mississippi River as tricky with comic twists as Æsop's fables, as mystical, boding, and promising as the family Bible. Sand-bars, shoals, and islands were scattered along with the look of arithmetic numbers. Sudden rains, shifting winds, meant new handling of oars. A rising roar and rumble of noise might be rough water ahead or some whimsical current tearing through fallen tree-branches at the river side. A black form seems to be floating up-river through a gray drizzle; the coming out of the sun shows it is an island point, standing still; the light and air play tricks with it.

The bends of the river ahead must be watched with ready oars and sweeps or the flatboat naturally heads in to shore. Strong winds crook the course of the boat, sometimes blowing it ashore; one of the crew must hustle off in a rowboat, tie a hawser to a tree or stump, while another man on the big boat has a rope at the check-post; and they slow her down. Warning signals must be given at night, by waving lantern or firewood, to other craft.

So the flatboat, "the broadhorn," went down the Father of Waters, four to six miles an hour, the crew frying their own pork and corn-meal cakes, washing their own shirts, sewing on their own buttons.

Below Baton Rouge, among the sugar plantations known as the "Sugar Coast," they tied up at the plantation of Madame Duquesne one evening, put their boat in order, spoke their good nights to any sweet stars in the sky, and dropped off to sleep. They woke to find seven Negroes on board trying to steal the cargo and kill the crew; the long-armed Indiana husky swung a crab-tree club, knocked them galley-west, chased them into the woods, and came back to the boat and laid a bandanna on a gash over the right eye that left a scar for life as it healed. Then they cut loose the boat and moved down the river.

At New Orleans they traded, sold the rest of their cargo of potatoes, bacon, hams, flour, apples, jeans, in exchange for cotton, tobacco, and sugar, and sold the flatboat for what it would bring as lumber. And they lingered and loitered a few days, seeing New Orleans, before taking steamer north.

On the streets and by-streets of that town, which had floated the flags of French, British, and American dominion, young Abraham Lincoln felt the pulses of a living humanity with far heartbeats in wide, alien circles over the earth: English sailors who sang "Ranzo" and "Boney," "Hangin' Johnny," and "O Fare-you-well, My Bonny Young Girls"; Dutchmen and French in jabber and exclamative; Swedes, Norwegians, and Russians with blond and reddish mustaches

and whiskers; Spaniards and Italians with knives and red silk handkerchiefs; New York, Philadelphia, Boston, Rome, Amsterdam, become human facts; it was London those men came from, ejaculating,
" 'Ow can ye blime me?"

Women in summer weather wearing slippers and boots; creoles with
dusks of eyes; quadroons and octoroons with elusive soft voices;
streets lined with saloons where men drank with men or chose from
the women sipping their French wine or Jamaica rum at tables, sending quiet signals with their eyes or openly slanging the sailors, teamsters, roustabouts, rivermen, timber cruisers, crap-shooters, poker
sharps, squatters, horse thieves, poor whites; bets were laid on steamboat races; talk ran fast about the construction, then going on, of the
New Orleans & Pontchartrain Railroad, to be one of the first steam
railroads in America and the world; slaves passed handcuffed into
gangs headed for cotton fields of one, two, six thousand acres in size;
and everywhere was talk about niggers, good and bad niggers, how to
rawhide the bad ones with mule whips or bring 'em to N' Orleans and
sell 'em; and how you could trust your own children with a good
nigger.

As young Abe Lincoln and Allen Gentry made their way back
home to the clearings of Pigeon Creek, Indiana, the tall boy had his
thoughts. He had crossed half the United States, it seemed, and was
back home after three months' vacation with eight dollars a month
pay in his pocket and a scar over the right eye.

That year Indiana University was to print its first catalogue, but
Abe Lincoln didn't show up among the students who registered. He
was between the plow handles or pulling fodder or sinking the ax in
trees and brush, and reading between times "Pilgrim's Progress," a
history of the United States, the life of Francis Marion, the life of Ben
Franklin, and the book he borrowed from Dave Turnham, the con-
stable. The title-page of the book said it contained, "The Revised
Laws of Indiana, adopted and enacted by the general assembly at
their eighth session. To which are prefixed the Declaration of Independence, the Constitution of the United States, the Constitution of
the State of Indiana, and sundry other documents connected with the
Political History of the Territory and State of Indiana. Arranged and
published by the authority of the General Assembly."

The science of government, theories of law, and schemes of administration spread themselves before the young man's mind as he crept
along from page to page, wrestling with those statutes of Indiana and
other documents. It was tough plowing through that book, with the

satisfaction, however, that he could keep what he earned. Crimes and punishments were listed there, in black and white, fine distinctions between murder and manslaughter, between burglary, robbery, larceny, forgery, trespass, nuisance, fraud; varied circumstances of assault and battery, affray, unlawful assembly, rout and riot.

❀ ❀ ❀

Chapter XXII

READING THE *Louisville Gazette* which came weekly to Gentryville, working out as chore-boy, field-hand and ferryman, walking a fifty-mile circuit around the home cabin, flatboating down the Ohio and Mississippi, the young man Abraham Lincoln took in many things with his eyes that saw and his ears that heard and remembered. A Virginia planter named Edward Coles had quit Virginia and come down the Ohio River with his slaves, ending his journey in Illinois, where he had deeded a farm to each of his slaves with papers of freedom. The Erie Canal in New York, a big ditch for big boats to run on, was finished; it cost seven and a half million dollars but it connected the Great Lakes and the Atlantic Ocean and it meant that the north ends of Indiana and Illinois, besides other prairie stretches, were going to fill up faster with settlers. The first railroad in the United States, a stub line three miles long, was running iron-wheeled wagons on iron rails at Quincy, Massachusetts. A settlement called Indianapolis had been cleared away. Glass and nails were arriving in southern Indiana now; there used to be none at all ten years back. The famous Frenchman, General LaFayette, came up the Mississippi from New Orleans and visited Kaskaskia, where a reception was held in a mansion with the windows kept open for the benefit of people outside who wanted to have a look in. Sam Patch, who slid down Niagara Falls once, and lived, had slid down the Genesee Falls at Rochester, New York, and was killed.

It was interesting that Henry Clay, the famous congressman and orator from Kentucky, was nicknamed "The Mill Boy of the Slashes," and came from a family of poor farmers and used to ride to mill with a sack of corn. It was interesting to hear a story that Henry Clay's wife was asked by a Boston woman in Washington, "Doesn't it distress you to have Mr. Clay gambling with cards?" and that she answered, "Oh, dear, no! He most always wins."

Fragments of talk and newspaper items came about Daniel Webster, and his Bunker Hill speech at the cornerstone of the Bunker Hill monument, or John Marshall, Chief Justice of the Supreme Court, and a decision in law, but they were far off. There was a sharp-tongued senator from Virginia, John Randolph of Roanoke, who was bitter against John Calhoun, vice president of the United States; and John Randolph one day pointed his finger at Calhoun and said: "Mr. Speaker! I mean Mr. President of the Senate and would-be President of the United States, which God in His infinite mercy avert." And Randolph during a hot speech would call to a doorkeeper, "Tims, more porter," taking every ten or fifteen minutes a foaming tumbler of malt liquor, drinking two or three quarts during a long speech.

And neither Calhoun nor anybody else interfered with John Randolph when, on the floor of the Senate, he called John Quincy Adams, the President of the United States, "a traitor," or Daniel Webster "a vile slanderer," or Edward Livingston "the most contemptible and degraded of beings, whom no man ought to touch, unless with a pair of tongs." In some stories about famous men there seemed to be a touch of the comic; John Randolph on the Senate floor called Henry Clay a "blackleg"; they fought a duel with pistols; Clay shot Randolph twice in the pantaloons; Randolph shot off his pistol once "accidentally" and once in the air; both sides came through alive and satisfied.

Southern and western congressmen kept dueling pistols in their Washington outfits; some had special pistols inlaid with gold. A Philadelphia gunsmith named Derringer was winning popularity with a short pistol to be carried in the hip pocket and used in street fights. At the "exclusive" assembly balls in Washington, the women's skirts came down to slightly above the ankles; their silk stockings were embroidered with figures called "clocks" and their thin slippers had silk rosettes and tiny silver buckles. The fashionable men of "exclusive" society affairs wore frock coats of blue, green, or claret cloth, with gilt buttons; shirts were of ruffled linen; they had baggy "Cossack" pantaloons tucked into "Hessian" boots with gold top tassels.

Everybody in the capital knew that the justices of the Supreme Court took snuff from their snuffboxes while hearing causes argued; that Henry Clay was moderate about drinking whisky, while Daniel Webster went too far; that Andrew Jackson smoked a corn-cob pipe, and his enemies were free to say Mrs. Jackson too enjoyed her daily pipe. Protests were made to the Government against the transportation of the mails on Sunday; in Philadelphia church people stretched chains fastened with padlocks across the streets to stop the passage of mail-coaches.

The stories drifted west about white men in New York City who held political processions in which they marched dressed like Indians; they had organized the Tammany Society back in 1789; the members died but Tammany lived on. The big excitement of New York politics had been the struggle of De Witt Clinton, the governor, to put through the digging of the Erie Canal, against Tammany opposition.

> Oh, a ditch he would dig from the lakes to the sea.
> The Eighth of the world's matchless Wonders to be.
> Good land! How absurd! But why should you grin?
> It will do to bury its mad author in.

So Tammany sang at the start. But De Witt Clinton stuck with the tenacity of his forefathers who had fought against the Indians and against the British king. When he won out, the rhymes ran:

> Witt Clinton is dead, St. Tammany said,
> And all the papooses with laughter were weeping;
> But Clinton arose and confounded his foes—
> The cunning old fox had only been sleeping.

There had been the four years John Quincy Adams was President. He had been elected in a three-cornered fight that ended on election day with Andrew Jackson having the most votes cast for him but not a majority. This had put the contest into Congress, where Henry Clay had thrown his forces to Adams; and Adams's first move was to appoint Clay Secretary of State. The Jackson men said it was a crooked deal. Jackson had handed in his resignation as Senator from Tennessee and started work on his political fences for 1828, while his New York Tammany friend, Martin Van Buren, was booming him up North. All the four years Adams was President, the moves in Congress were aimed at bagging the Presidency in 1828. Investigating committees worked overtime; each side dug for the other's scandals: Adams's past personal record; Jackson's handling of six deserters at Mobile in 1815, when 1,500 soldiers were drawn up at parade rest to watch thirty-six riflemen fire at six blindfolded men, each man kneel-

ing on his own coffin; Adams's bills for wall paper and paint in reno-
vating the White House; Jackson's alleged marriage to his wife before
she was properly divorced.

In the background of all the bitter personal feelings, the slander
and the slack talk of politics, a deep, significant drift and shift was
going on. Part of it was the feeling of the West and Southwest, the raw
and new country, against the East and New England, the settled and
established country. Added to this was a feeling that Jackson stood
for the rough, plain people who work, as against the people who
don't. That was the issue, as the Jackson crowd presented it, so that
even Abe Lincoln in Spencer County, Indiana, was caught in the
drive of its enthusiasm, and wrote:

> Let auld acquaintance be forgot
> And never brought to mind;
> May Jackson be our President,
> And Adams left behind.

Jackson rode to election on a tumultuous landslide of ballots. His
wife, Rachel, said, "Well, for Mr. Jackson's sake, I am glad, but for my
own part I never wished it." And the home women of Nashville se-
cretly got ready dresses of satin and silk for her to wear in Washington
as the first lady of the land; then death took her suddenly; her husband for hours refused to believe she had breathed her last; he had
killed one man and silenced others who had spoken against her. One
woman wrote, "General Jackson was never quite the same man afterward; her death subdued his spirit and corrected his speech."

Then the new President-elect sailed down the Cumberland River to
the Ohio, stopped at Cincinnati and Pittsburgh, and went on to Washington for an inauguration before a crowd of ten thousand people,
whose wild cheering of their hero showed they believed something
new and different had arrived in the government of the American republic. Daniel Webster, writing a letter to a friend, hit off the event by
saying: "I never saw such a crowd. People have come five hundred
miles to see General Jackson, and they really seem to think the country is rescued from some dreadful danger." The buckskin shirts of
Kentucky settlers and the moccasins of Indian fighters from Tennessee
were seen in the crowd, and along with politicians, preachers, merchants, gamblers, and lookers-on, swarmed in to the White House reception, took their turns at barrels of whisky, broke punch-bowls of
glass and chinaware, emptied pails of punch, stood on the satin-cov-
ered chairs and had their look at "Andy Jackson, Our President,"

who was shoved into a corner where a line of friends formed a barrier to protect the sixty-two-year-old man from his young buck henchmen.

Thus began an eight-year period in which Andrew Jackson was President of the United States. He came to the White House with the mud of all America's great rivers and swamps on his boots, with records of victories in battles against savage Indian tribes and trained Continental European generals who had fought Napoleon, with shattered ribs and the bullets of Tennessee duelists and gun-fighters of the Southwest in his body; he knew little grammar and many scars, few classics and many fast horses.

Jackson came taking the place of John Quincy Adams, who was asking large funds for a national university and a colossal astronomical observatory, "a lighthouse of the skies," a lovable, decent man who knew all the capes, peninsulas, and inlets of New England, who had been across the Atlantic and stood by the Thames and the Seine rivers, and had never laid eyes on the Mississippi nor the Wabash River. Harvard went under as against the Smoky Mountains and Horseshoe Bend. Jackson came in with 178 electoral votes as against 83 for Adams, after national circulation by his enemies of a thick pamphlet entitled, "Reminiscences; or an Extract from the Catalogue of General Jackson's Youthful Indiscretions, between the Age of Twenty-Three and Sixty," reciting fourteen fights, duels, brawls, shooting and cutting affairs, in which it was alleged he had killed, slashed, and clawed various American citizens. It was told of him that he asked a friend the day after the inaugural what the people were saying of his first message. "They say it is first-rate, but nobody believes you wrote it," was the answer. To which Jackson rejoined, "Well, don't I deserve just as much credit for picking out the man who could write it?"

One nickname for him was "Old Hickory"; he had lived on acorns and slept in the rain; now he sat in a second-story room of the White House smoking a cob pipe, running the United States Government as he had run his armies, his political campaigns, his Tennessee plantation, his stable of racing horses, with a warm heart, a cool head, a sharp tongue, recklessly, cunningly; he was simple as an ax-handle, shrewd as an Indian ambush, mingling in his breast the paradoxes of the good and evil proverbs of the people.

Jackson was the son of a north-of-Irelander who came to America with only a pair of hands. "No man will ever be quite able to comprehend Andrew Jackson who has not personally known a Scotch-Irishman." His breed broke with their bare hands into the wilderness beyond the Allegheny Mountains, and more than any other one stock of

blood is credited with putting the western and southwestern stretches of territory under the dominion of the central federal government at Washington. The mellowed and practiced philosopher, Thomas Jefferson, once wrote a letter with the passage, "When I was president of the Senate, he (Jackson) was a senator, and he could never speak on account of the rashness of his feelings. I have seen him attempt it repeatedly and as often choke with rage." And yet, unless the Jackson breed of men, even their extreme type, "the half horse, half alligator men," had pushed with their covered wagons, their axes and rifles, out into the territory of the Louisiana Purchase, Jefferson would have had no basis nor data for his negotiations in that mammoth land deal. Though in the presence of the ruffled linen of the Senate Jackson did "choke with rage," he faced Creek Indians, or seasoned troops from Napoleonic campaigns, or mutineers of his own army, with a cool and controlled behavior that was beyond the range of comprehension of models of etiquette in Washington.

With Jackson in the White House came a new politics, better and worse. The ax of dismissal fell on two thousand postmasters, department heads and clerks. An Administration daily newspaper, the *Washington Globe,* began publication; all office-holders earning more than one thousand dollars a year had to subscribe or lose their jobs. The editor was asked to soften an attack on an Administration enemy, and replied, "No, let it tear his heart out." Wives of Cabinet members refused to mix socially with Peggy O'Neill; talk ran that she was "fast" and of too shady a past even though now married to the Secretary of War. As the scandal dragged on, Jackson wrote hundreds of letters in her defense, sometimes using the phrase that she was "chaste as snow"; the husbands of the offended Cabinet members' wives resigned from the Cabinet; Jackson knocked the ashes from his cob pipe, appointed fresh and willing Cabinet members, and life went on as before.

When his postmaster-general, a tried and loyal friend, rebelled at making the wholesale dismissals required by the politicians, Jackson pushed him to a seat on the Supreme Court bench, and appointed a more willing post-office chief. One friend said he was an actor, that after storming at a caller, and closing the door, he would chuckle over his pipe and say, "He thought I was mad." A mail-coach robber, condemned to be hanged, reminded the President that once at a horse-race near Nashville he had told General Jackson to change his bets from a horse whose jockey had been "fixed" to lose the race; the death sentence was commuted to ten years in prison. "Ask nothing but what is right, submit to nothing wrong," was his advice on policies with European countries. He was well thought of by millions who believed there was truth lurking behind his sentiment, "True virtue cannot exist where pomp and parade are the governing passions; it can only dwell with the people—the great laboring and producing classes that form the bone and sinew of our confederacy." He was alluded to as "the Tennessee Barbarian" or "King Andrew the First" in certain circles, yet the doormats of the White House got acquainted with the shoes, boots, and moccasins of a wider range of humanity as he ran the Federal Government during those first years of the eight in which he was to be President.

❀ ❀ ❀

Chapter XXIII

ALL THE WAY down the Mississippi to the Gulf and back, Abe Lincoln had heard about Andrew Jackson in that year of 1828 when Jackson swept that country with a big landslide. In the newspapers that came to the post office at Gentryville, in the talk around Jones's store, in the fields harvesting, and at meetings, Andrew Jackson was the man talked about. With Andrew Jackson for President, the plainest kind of people could go into the White House and feel at home; with that kind of man, who smoked a cob pipe, talked horse sense, and rode reckless horses, and who had whipped the British at New Orleans, the Government would be more like what was meant in the Declaration of Independence and the Fourth of July speeches. Thus the talk ran.

Young Abe Lincoln heard it. The personality and the ways of Andrew Jackson filled his thoughts. He asked himself many questions and puzzled his head about the magic of this one strong, stormy man filling the history of that year, commanding a wild love from many people, and calling out curses and disgust from others, but those others were very few in Indiana. The riddles that attach to a towering and magnetic personality staged before a great public, with no very definite issues or policies in question, but with some important theory of government and art of life apparently involved behind the personality—these met young Abe's eyes and ears.

It was the year he wrote in the front cover of "The Columbian Class Book" the inscription, "Abe Lincoln 1828." The preface of the book said it contained "pieces calculated to interest the attention of the scholar and impress the mind with a knowledge of useful facts." And he borrowed from Josiah Crawford "The Kentucky Preceptor," the preface of that book saying, "Tales of love, or romantic fiction, or anything which might tend to instil false notions into the minds of children have not gained admission." There were essays on Magnanimity, Remorse of Conscience, Columbus, Demosthenes, On the

Scriptures as a Rule of Life, the speech of Robert Emmet on why the English government should not hang an Irish patriot, stories of Indians, and the inaugural address of President Jefferson twenty-four years previous to that year. Jefferson spoke of "the agonizing spasms of infuriated man, seeking through blood and slaughter his long-lost liberty" in the French Revolution. Let America remember that free speech, and respect for the opinions of others, are measures of safety, was the advice of Jefferson.

Then Abe Lincoln read the passage from the pen of Jefferson: "If there be any among us who would wish to dissolve this Union, or to change its republican form, let them stand as monuments of the safety with which error of opinion may be tolerated where reason is left free to combat it. I know, indeed, that some honest men fear a republican government cannot be strong, that this government is not strong enough. . . . I believe this, on the contrary, the strongest government on earth."

Young nineteen-year-old Abe Lincoln had plenty to think about in that year of 1828, what with his long trip to New Orleans and back, what with the strong, stormy Andrew Jackson sweeping into control of the Government at Washington, and the gentle, teasing, thoughtful words of Thomas Jefferson: "Sometimes it is said that man cannot be trusted with the government of himself. Can he then be trusted with the government of others?"

❁ ❁ ❁

Chapter XXIV

FOR MORE THAN twenty years Johnny Appleseed had been making his name one to laugh at and love in the log cabins between the Ohio River and the northern lakes. In 1806, he loaded two canoes with apple seeds at cider mills in western Pennsylvania and floated down the Ohio River to the Muskingum, along which he curved to White Woman Creek, the Mohican, the Black Fork, making a long stay on the borders of Licking Creek and in Licking County, where many farmers were already thanking him for their orchards. As he ran out of seeds he rode a bony horse or walked back to western Pennsylvania to fill two leather bags with apple seeds at cider mills; then in the

Ohio territory where he tramped, he would pick out loamy land, plant the seeds, pile brush around, and tell the farmers to help themselves from the young shoots. He went barefoot till winter came, and was often seen in late November walking in mud and snow. Neither snakes, Indians nor foreign enemies had harmed him. Children had seen him stick pins and needles into his tough flesh; when he sat at a table with a farmer family he wouldn't eat till he was sure there was plenty for the children. Asked if he wasn't afraid of snakes as he walked barefoot in the brush, he pulled a New Testament from his pocket and said, "This book is protection against all danger here and hereafter." When taken in overnight by a farmer, he would ask if they wanted to hear "some news right fresh from heaven," and then stretch out on the floor and read, "Blessed are the meek, for they shall inherit the earth" and other Beatitudes. A woman said of his voice that it was "loud as the roar of winds and waves, then soft and soothing as the balmy airs that quivered the morning-glory leaves about his gray beard."

Once the camp-fire of Johnny Appleseed drew many mosquitoes which were burning; he quenched the fire, explaining to friends, "God forbid that I should build a fire for my comfort which should be the means of destroying any of His creatures!" During most of the year he wore no clothes except for a coffee sack with armholes cut in it; and a stump preacher once near the village of Mansfield was crying, "Where now is there a man who, like the primitive Christians, is traveling to Heaven barefooted and clad in coarse raiment?" when Johnny Appleseed came forward to put a bare foot on the pulpit stump and declare, "Here's your primitive Christian." A hornet stung him and he plucked out the hornet from a wrinkle of the coffee sack and let it go free. He claimed that his religion brought him into conversations with angels; two of the angels with whom he talked were to be his wives in heaven provided he never married on earth. What little money he needed came from farmers willing to pay for young apple trees. As settlements and villages came thicker, he moved west with the frontier, planting apple seeds, leaving trails of orchards in his paths over a territory of a hundred thousand square miles in Ohio and Indiana.

These were the years John James Audubon, who had kept a store in Elizabethtown, Kentucky, was traveling the Ohio and Mississippi River regions, with knapsack, dog, and gun, hunting birds, to paint them in oil on canvas "with their own lively animated ways when seeking their natural food and pleasure." He was among pioneers who moved from Kentucky and settled at Princeton, Indiana, a walker who walked on thousand-mile trips, leaving his wife to stay with friends while he lived with wild birds and shot them and sketched their forms.

Audubon's notebook told of canoeing in flood-swollen Mississippi river-bottom lands. "All is silent and melancholy, unless when the mournful bleating of the hemmed-in deer reaches your ear, or the dismal scream of an eagle or a heron is heard, or the foul bird rises, disturbed by your approach, from the carcass on which it was allaying its craving appetite. Bears, cougars, lynxes, and all other quadrupeds that can ascend the trees, are observed crouched among their top branches; hungry in the midst of abundance, although they see floating around them the animals on which they usually prey. They dare not venture to swim to them. Fatigued by the exertions which they have made in reaching dry land, they will there stand near the hunter's fire, as if to die by a ball were better than to perish amid the waste of waters. On occasions like this, all these animals are shot by hundreds."

Audubon went East to Philadelphia in 1824, gave an exhibition of his paintings, sold less than enough to pay for the show, and was told not to publish his work. In 1827 he began his issues of a work titled "The Birds of America," which when finished was in eighty-seven parts. That same year he reached London, where a barber cut off the ringlets of hair falling to his shoulders, and he wrote, under date of March 19, 1827, "This day my hair was sacrificed, and the will of God usurped by the wishes of Man. My heart sank low." He became an international authority, and sat up till half-past three one morning writing a paper to be read the next day before the Natural History Society of London on the habits of the wild pigeon. "So absorbed was my whole soul and spirit in the work, that I felt as if I were in the woods of America among the pigeons, and my ears filled with the sound of their rustling wings."

After reading his paper before the society, Audubon wrote the commentary: "Captain Hall expressed some doubts as to my views respecting the affection and love of pigeons, as if I made it human, and raised the possessors quite above the brutes. I presume the love of the (pigeon) mothers for their young is much the same as the love of woman for her offspring. There is but one kind of love: God is love, and all his creatures derive theirs from his; only it is modified by the different degrees of intelligence in different beings and creatures."

Thus Audubon, who had sold Sunday clothes to his customers in Elizabethtown, Kentucky. He and Abe Lincoln had footed the same red clay highways of Hardin County, floated the same Ohio and Mississippi rivers, fought in the night against other forms of life that came to kill. Both loved birds and people. Each was a child of hope.

❀ ❀ ❀

Chapter XXV

IN THE FALL of 1829, Abraham Lincoln was putting his ax to big trees and whipsawing logs into planks for lumber to build a house on his father's farm. But his father made new plans; the lumber was sold to Josiah Crawford; and the obedient young axman was put to work cutting and sawing trees big enough around to make wagon-wheels, and hickories tough enough for axles and poles on an ox-wagon.

The new plans were that the Lincoln family and the families of Dennis Hanks and Levi Hall, married to Abe's step-sisters, thirteen people in all, were going to move to Macon County over in Illinois, into a country with a river the Indians named Sangamo, meaning "the land of plenty to eat." The Lincoln farm wasn't paying well; after buying eighty acres for $2.00 an acre and improving it for fourteen years, Tom Lincoln sold it to Charles Grigsby for $125.00 cash before signing the papers.

The milk-sick was taking farm animals; since Dennis Hanks lost four milk-cows and eleven calves in one week, besides having a spell of the sickness himself, Dennis was saying, "I'm goin' t' git out o' here and hunt a country where the milk-sick is not; it's like to ruined me."

In September Tom Lincoln and his wife had made a trip down to Elizabethtown, Kentucky, where they sold for $123.00 the lot which Mrs. Lincoln had fallen heir to when her first husband died; the clerk, Samuel Haycraft, filled out the deed of sale, declaring that she "was examined by me privately and apart from her said husband" and did "freely and willingly subscribe to the sale." And Tom, with the cash from this sale and the money from the sale of his own farm, was buying oxen, or young steers, and trading and selling off household goods.

Moving was natural to his blood; he came from a long line of movers; he could tell about the family that had moved so often that their chickens knew the signs of another moving; and the chickens would walk up to the mover, stretch flat on the ground, and put up their feet to be tied for the next wagon trip.

The men-folks that winter, using their broadaxes and draw-knives on solid blocks of wood, shaping wagon wheels, had a church scandal to talk about. Tom Lincoln and his wife had been granted by the Pigeon church a "letter of Dismission," to show they had kept up their obligations and were regular members. Sister Nancy Grigsby had then come in with a "protest" that she was "not satisfied with Brother and Sister Lincoln." The trustees took back the letter, investigated, gave the letter again to Brother and Sister Lincoln, and to show how they felt about it, they appointed Brother Lincoln on a committee to straighten out a squabble between Sister Nancy Grigsby and Sister Betsy Crawford. And it was jotted down in the Pigeon church records and approved by the trustees.

The ox wagon they made that winter was wood all through, pegs, cleats, hickory withes, and knots of bark, holding it together, except the wheel rims, which were iron. Bundles of bed-clothes, skillets, ovens, and a few pieces of furniture were loaded, stuck, filled and tied onto the wagon; early one morning the last of the packing was done. It was February 15, 1830; Abraham Lincoln had been four days a full-grown man, a citizen who "had reached his majority"; he could vote at elections from now on; he was lawfully free from his father's commands; he could come and go now; he was footloose.

At Jones's store he had laid in a little stock of pins, needles, buttons, tinware, suspenders, and knickknacks, to peddle on the way to Illinois.

And he had gone for a final look at the winter dry grass, the ruins of last year's wild vine and dogwood over the grave of Nancy Hanks. He and his father were leaving their Indiana home that day; almost naked they had come, stayed fourteen years, toiled, buried their dead, built a church, toiled on; and now they were leaving, almost naked. Now, with the women and children lifted on top of the wagon-load, the men walked alongside, curling and cracking their whip-lashes over the horns or into the hides of the half-broken young steers.

And so the seven-yoke team of young steers, each with his head in a massive collar of hardwood, lashed and bawled at with "Gee," "Haw," "G' lang" and "Hi thar, you! Git up!" hauled the lumbering pioneer load from the yellow and red clay of Spencer County, in southern Indiana, to the black loam of the prairie lands in Macon County, Illinois.

They had crossed the Wabash River, the state line of Illinois, and the Sangamo River, on a two-week trip with the ground freezing at night and thawing during the day, the steers slipping and tugging, the wagon axles groaning, the pegs and cleats squeaking. A dog was left behind one morning as the wagon crossed a stream; it whined, ran back and forth, but wouldn't jump in and swim across; young Lincoln took off boots and socks, waded into the icy water, gathered the hound in his arms and carried it over.

Near the Indiana-Illinois state line, Lincoln took his pack of needles and notions and walked up to a small farmhouse that seemed to him to be "full of nothing but children." They were of assorted sizes, seventeen months to seventeen years in age, and all in tears. The mother, red-headed and red-faced, clutched a whip in her fingers. The father, meek, mild, cow-headed, stood in the front doorway as if waiting for his turn to feel the thongs. Lincoln thought there wouldn't be much use in asking the woman if she wanted any needles and notions; she was busy, with a keen eye on the children and an occasional glance at her man in the doorway.

She saw Lincoln come up the path, stepped toward the door, pushed her husband out of the way, and asked Lincoln what was his business. "Nothing, madam," he answered gently, "I merely dropped in as I came along to see how things were going." He waited a moment.

"Well, you needn't wait," the woman snapped out. "There's trouble here, and lots of it, too, but I kin manage my own affairs without the help of outsiders. This is jest a family row, but I'll teach these brats their places ef I have to lick the hide off every one of 'em. I don't do much talkin' but I run this house, so I don't want no one sneakin' round tryin' to find out how I do it, either."

Around them as they crossed the first stretch of the Grand Prairie was a land and soil different from Indiana or Kentucky. There were long levels, running without slopes up or hollows down, straight to the horizon; arches and domes of sky covered it; the sky counted for more, seemed to have another language and way of talk, farther silences, too, than east and south where the new settlers had come from. Grass stood up six and eight feet; men and horses and cattle were lost to sight in it; so tough were the grass-roots that timber could not get rootholds in it; the grass seemed to be saying to the trees, "You shall not cross"; turf and sky had a new way of saying, "We are here—who are you?" to the ox-wagon gang hunting a new home.

Buffalo paths, deer tracks, were seen; coon, possum, and wolf signs were seen or heard. And they met settlers telling how the sod was so tough it had broken many a plow; but after the first year of sod-corn, the yield would run 50 bushels to the acre; wheat would average 25 to 30 bushels, rye the same, oats 40 to 60 bushels; Irish potatoes, timothy hay, and all the garden vegetables tried so far would grow. Horses and cattle, lean from short fodder through the winter, would fatten and shine with a gloss on their hair when turned loose in the wild grass in spring. Beds of wild strawberries came ripe in June and stained horses and cattle crimson to the knees. Wild horses and wild hogs were still to be found.

The outfit from Indiana raised a laugh as they drove their steers and wagon into the main street of Decatur, a county-seat settlement where court would hold its first session the coming May. To the question, "Kin ye tell us where John Hanks' place is?" the Decatur citizens told them how to drive four miles, where they found John, talked over old Indiana and Kentucky times, but more about Illinois. After the night stay, John took the Lincoln family six miles down the Sangamo River, where he had cut the logs for their cabin. There young Lincoln helped raise the cabin, put in the crops, split rails for fences. He hired out to Major Warnick near by, read the few books in the house, and passed such pleasant talk and smiles with the major's daughter, Mary, and with another girl, Jemima Hill, that at a later time neighbors said he carried on courtships, even though both girls married inside of a year after young Lincoln kept company in those parts. He was asking himself when he would get married, if ever.

He wrote back to Jones at Gentryville that he doubled his money on the peddler's stock he sold; he earned a pair of brown jean trousers by splitting four hundred rails for each yard of the cloth. With new outlooks came new thoughts; at Vincennes, on the way to Illinois, he had seen a printing-press for the first time, and a juggler who did sleight-of-hand tricks. John Hanks put him on a box to answer the speech of a man who was against improvements of the Sangamo River; and John told neighbors, "Abe beat him to death." More and more he was delivering speeches, to trees, stumps, potato rows, just practicing, by himself.

Fall came, with miasma rising from the prairie, and chills, fever, ague, for Tom Lincoln and Sally Bush, and many doses of "Barks," a Peruvian bark and whisky tonic mixture, bought at Renshaw's general store in Decatur. Then came Indian summer, and soft weather, till Christmas week. And then a snowstorm.

For forty-eight hours, with no let-up, the battalions of a blizzard filled the sky, and piled a cover two and a half feet deep on the ground. No sooner was this packed down and frozen than another drive of snow came till there was a four-foot depth of it on the level. It was easy picking for the light-footed wolves who could run on the top crust and take their way with cattle. Wheat crops went to ruin; cows, hogs, horses died in the fields. Connections between houses, settlements, grain mills, broke down; for days families were cut off, living on parched corn; some died of cold, lacking wood to burn; some died of hunger lacking corn.

Those who came through alive, in the years after, called themselves "Snowbirds." The Lincoln family had hard days. It was hard on new settlers with no reserve stocks of meat, corn, and wood; young Lincoln made a try at wading through to the Warnick house four miles off, nearly froze his feet, and was laid up at home.

As the winter eased off, the Lincoln family moved southeast a hundred miles to Goose Nest Prairie, in the southern part of Coles County.

❁ ❁ ❁

Chapter XXVI

EIGHT MILES FROM the new farm was the town of Charleston. Young Lincoln drove there with an ox team and sold loads of cordwood split with his own ax. One afternoon he was late in selling his wood and decided with dark coming on he wouldn't try to drive his ox team to the farm. Tarlton Miles, the horse doctor, living just outside of Charleston, took him in overnight, and they sat up till midnight talking.

In the morning, Lincoln goaded his steers on out to the farm, drove wedges with a maul, split more cordwood. In the evening, as he lay on a board reading, a stranger came to the house and asked to stay overnight. Tom Lincoln said there were only two beds, one belonged to his son, and it depended on whether his son wanted to sleep with a stranger. The two shared the bed that night. . . . It was a country where the veterinary surgeon took in the ox-driver and the ox-driver took in the stranger.

Over in Cumberland County, which joined Coles, the champion

wrestler was Dan Needham. It came to his ears several times that the new tall boy over at Goose Nest could throw him. "I can fling him three best out of four any day," was Needham's answer. At a house-raising at Wabash Point the two faced each other, each one standing six feet, four inches, each a prairie panther. "Abe, rassle 'im," said Tom Lincoln.

Abe held off; the crowd egged both of them on. They grappled four times and each time Needham went under. Then Needham lost his head, threatened a fist fight, calmed down with hearing Lincoln's drawling banter, and at last put out his hand with a grin and said, "Well, I'll be damned." And they shook hands.

In February, 1831, there came to the neighborhood of John Hanks, when Abe Lincoln was lingering there, a man named Denton Offut, a hard drinker, a hustler, and a talker shrewd with his tongue, easy with promises, a believer in pots of gold at the rainbow end. He would have a flatboat and cargo to go to New Orleans, all ready for Abe Lincoln, John Hanks, and John Johnston, "as soon as the snow should go off," if they would meet him on a Sangamo River branch near the village of Springfield. They were there at the time set but Denton Offut wasn't; they walked to Springfield, asked for Offut, found him drunk at the Buckhorn Tavern, and helped sober him.

Offut hired them at twelve dollars a month, gave them permission to go onto Government timber-land and get out gunwales for the flat-boat, while the rest of the needed lumber could come from Kirkpat-rick's sawmill, charged to Offut. They slung together a camp outfit and started building, with Lincoln calling himself "chief cook and bottle-washer." A sleight-of-hand performer came along and giving his show asked for an empty hat to take eggs out of. Lincoln offered his hat in a hesitating way, saying he hesitated not so much out of respect for the hat as for the eggs.

Two men whose canoe turned over and got away from them were shivering in a tree on a raw April day with the freshet-flooded San-gamo River under them. Lincoln got out across the rampaging waters to the tree, on a log with a rope tied to it; the men in the tree strad-dled the log and were pulled on shore. People began talking about Lincoln's cool wit.

Thirty days saw the flatboat finished, loaded, and on her way, with Lincoln on deck in blue homespun jeans, jacket, vest, rawhide boots with pantaloons stuffed in, and a felt hat once black but now, as the owner said, "sunburned till it was a combine of colors." On April 19, rounding the curve of the Sangamo at the village of New Salem, the boat stuck on the Cameron mill-dam, and hung with one third of her slanted downward over the edge of the dam and filling slowly with water, while the cargo of pork-barrels was sliding slowly so as to over-weight one end.

She hung there a day while all the people of New Salem came down to look at the river disaster, which Lincoln fixed by unloading the pork barrels into another boat, boring a hole in the end of the flat-boat as it hung over the dam, letting the water out, dropping the boat over the dam and reloading. As she headed toward the Mississippi watercourse, New Salem talked about the cool head and ready wit of the long-shanked young man with his pantaloons stuffed in his raw-hide boots.

Again Lincoln floated down the Mississippi River, four to six miles an hour, meeting strings of other flatboats, keel-boats, arks, sleds, proud white steamboats flying flags. Stepping off their flatboat at New Orleans, Lincoln and Hanks went nearly a mile, walking on flatboats, to reach shore. Stacks of pork and flour from the West, and piles of cotton bales from the South, stood on the wharves. Some shippers, about one in six, were cursing their luck; on the long haul from north of the Ohio River their pork and flour had spoiled; all they got for their trip was the view of the Mississippi River scenery. In New Orleans, Lincoln saw advertisements of traders offering to "pay the highest prices in cash for good and likely Negroes" or to "attend to the sale and purchase of Negroes on commission." A firm advertised: "We have now on hand, and intend to keep throughout the entire year, a large and well-selected stock of Negroes, consisting of field hands, house servants, mechanics, cooks, seamstresses, washers, ironers, etc., which we can sell and will sell as low or lower than any other house here or in New Orleans; persons wishing to purchase would do well to call on us before making purchases elsewhere, as our fresh and regular arrivals will keep us supplied with a good and general assortment; our terms are liberal; give us a call."

One trader gave notice: "I will at all times pay the highest cash prices for Negroes of every description, and will also attend to the sale of Negroes on commission, having a jail and yard fitted up expressly for boarding them." Another announced: "The undersigned would respectfully state to the public that he has forty-five Negroes now on hand, having this day received a lot of twenty-five direct from Virginia, two or three good cooks, a carriage driver, a good house boy, a fiddler, a fine seamstress, and a likely lot of field men and women; all of whom he will sell at a small profit; he wishes to close out and go on to Virginia after a lot for the fall trade." There were sellers advertising, "For sale—several likely girls from 10 to 18 years old, a woman 24, a very valuable woman 25, with three very likely children," while buyers indicated wants after the manner of one advertising, "Wanted—I want to purchase twenty-five likely Negroes, between the ages of 18 and 25 years, male and female, for which I will pay the highest prices in cash."

An Alabama planter advertised, "Runaway—Alfred, a bright mulatto boy, working on plantation; about 18 years old, pretty well grown, has blue eyes, light flaxen hair, skin disposed to freckles; he will try to pass as free-born." Another Alabama planter gave notice: "One hundred dollars reward for return of a bright mulatto man slave, named Sam; light sandy hair, blue eyes, ruddy complexion, is so white as very easily to pass for a free white man."

Lincoln saw one auction in New Orleans where an octoroon girl was sold, after being pinched, trotted up and down, and handled so the buyer could be satisfied she was sound of wind and limb. After a month's stay he worked his passage, firing a steamboat furnace, up the Mississippi River, stayed a few weeks on his father's farm in Coles County, Illinois, and then spoke the long good-by to home and the family roof.

Saying good-by to his father was easy, but it was not so easy to hug the mother, Sally Bush, and put his long arms around her, and lay his cheeks next to hers and say he was going out into the big world to make a place for himself.

The father laughed his good-by, and not so long after told a visitor: "I s'pose Abe is still fooling hisself with eddication. I tried to stop it, but he has got that fool idea in his head, and it can't be got out. Now I hain't got no eddication, but I get along far better'n ef I had. Take bookkeepin'—why, I'm the best bookkeeper in the world! Look up at that rafter thar. Thar's three straight lines made with a firebrand: ef I sell a peck of meal I draw a black line across, and when they pay, I take a dishcloth and jest rub it out; and that thar's a heap better'n yer eddication." And the visitor who heard this told friends that Thomas Lincoln was "one of the shrewdest ignorant men" he had ever seen.

With his few belongings wrapped in a handkerchief bundle tied to a stick over his shoulder, Abraham was on his way to New Salem.

Index of Titles for Stories and Poems